# STUDIES IN
## COMPARATIVE ECONOMICS 7

Studies in Comparative Economics

# MODERN

# ECONOMIC

# GROWTH

RATE, STRUCTURE, AND SPREAD

by Simon Kuznets

NEW HAVEN AND LONDON
YALE UNIVERSITY PRESS

# FOREWORD

Modern economics has been bred chiefly in Western Europe and the United States, and despite its aspiration toward generality it bears the stamp of institutions and issues characteristic of these areas.

But the economic world no longer revolves about London and New York. Dozens of new nations are struggling toward economic independence and industrial growth under institutional arrangements quite unlike those of the West. Economies of a novel type also extend eastward from central Europe to the Bering Strait and have been busily developing their own principles as a by-product of administrative experience. It is asserted that "Western economics" has only limited analytical value in these other countries.

The problem of the content and relevance of economics thus arises inescapably. Are the economic principles taught in the West really susceptible of general application? Or are they culture-bound and relevant mainly to industrial capitalist countries? Is it possible to create a general economics which would be as useful in Poland or India as in Canada or France? Or must we be content with several species of economics which will remain distinct in intellectual content and applicability?

"Comparative economics" has been regarded as a separate area of the economics curriculum, consisting of a botanical classification of national economies into a few loosely labeled boxes. But surely any course in economics is potentially comparative. A concern with comparative experience can profitably be infused into any of the standard branches of economic study. This series is inspired by the hope that a rethinking of particular branches of economics in world perspective, combined with a bibliography of available material from many countries, may help teachers to give their courses a broader and more comparative orientation.

In pursuing this objective, we deliberately chose autonomy over standardization. Each author was left free to determine his own approach and method of treatment. The essays thus differ considerably in length, analytical as against descriptive emphasis, geographical coverage, and other respects. How far the original intent of the series has been accomplished is for the profession to judge.

We are grateful to the authors who have struggled with possibly insoluble problems, to the Ford Foundation for its support of the enterprise, and to the staff of the Yale University Press for their helpful cooperation.

> *The Inter-University Committee on Comparative Economics:* Abram Bergson, Arthur R. Burns, Kermit Gordon, Richard Musgrave, William Nicholls, Lloyd Reynolds (Chairman)

# ACKNOWLEDGMENTS

Much of the discussion presented here is based on data and analysis contained in studies initiated or assisted by the Committee on Economic Growth of the Social Science Research Council.

Lillian E. Weksler assisted, patiently and skillfully, in the preparation, checking, and editing of this manuscript—as she has done with many of my research papers and monographs in the past.

The manuscript was reviewed critically by Professor Moses Abramovitz of Stanford University; and I profited greatly from his detailed criticisms and questions. I am also indebted to my colleague, Professor Abram Bergson, for numerous helpful comments on substance and style; and to Professor Lloyd G. Reynolds of Yale University for his general comments on several of the chapters.

Simon Kuznets

December 1965

# CONTENTS

Contents

# TABLES

Tables

Tables

# 1 THE GENERAL FRAMEWORK

We identify the economic growth of nations as a sustained increase in per capita or per worker product, most often accompanied by an increase in population and usually by sweeping structural changes. In modern times these were changes in the industrial structure within which product was turned out and resources employed—away from agriculture toward nonagricultural activities, the process of industrialization; in the distribution of population between the countryside and the cities, the process of urbanization; in the relative economic position of groups within the nation distinguished by employment status, attachment to various industries, level of per capita income, and the like; in the distribution of product by use—among household consumption, capital formation, and government consumption, and within each of these major categories by further subdivisions; in the allocation of product by its origin within the nation's boundaries and elsewhere; and so on. And, of course, nations do not live alone but in association with others, so that the growth of one affects others and is in turn affected by them. Hence, in addition to the aggregative and structural, there are the international aspects of economic growth. Much of the work in the field is concerned with the quantitative characteristics of aggregate changes and structural shifts in, and relations among, nations undergoing the process of growth. Much of the model building,

1

whether in mathematical symbols or in words, attempts to reproduce in a highly simplified form some of the relations prevailing between additions to population and to labor force, investment in capital (whether material or embodied in human beings), and technological changes as the independent variables, and the growth of total and per capita and per worker product as the dependent variables—for a country or for the various sectors; or the relations among nations with different endowments of resources and different rates of economic growth.

Since we are concerned with the comparative study of the economic growth of nations and are particularly interested in growth within the span of the last two centuries, it is helpful to consider this span a distinctive economic epoch. By an economic epoch we mean a relatively long period (extending well over a century) possessing distinctive characteristics that give it unity and differentiate it from the epochs that precede or follow it. An epochal innovation may be described as a major addition to the stock of human knowledge which provides a potential for sustained economic growth—an addition so major that its exploitation and utilization absorb the energies of human societies and dominate their growth for a period long enough to constitute an epoch in economic history.

Consider as an illustration the epoch of merchant capitalism in Western Europe. It extends from the end of the fifteenth to the second half of the eighteenth century, covering well over two and a half centuries, and is characterized by the innovation of a breakthrough by Western Europe to the New World. This breakthrough, leading to an enormous increase in the stock of useful knowledge and to its exploitation, was itself a consequence of improvements in science and technology, bearing upon navigation, ships, and weapons, and of advances in domestic production and political organization. But one may conveniently focus on the geographical revolution and argue that with the technology of the period it took 250 years for the small and backward societies of Europe to develop the potential of growth af-

2

forded them by this revolution—which was to provide a flow of precious metals, of new agricultural and other products, and the possibility of settlement outside the circumscribed area of Western Europe. The epoch has been characterized as "merchant capitalism" presumably to stress the strategic role of overseas trade in the economic growth of the time—in the countries that could take advantage of the opportunities provided by the epochal innovation. The medieval city-economy epoch of the eleventh to fifteenth centuries and the antecedent epoch of feudal organization provide additional illustrations. And if we were more familiar with the broad sweep of history in other long-settled areas outside of the European orbit, we might be able to delimit other epochs—of the agricultural irrigation empires, of nomadic states, and so on. In each case the economic epoch would bear the stamp of a unique major innovation.

Many problems would arise in the application of this concept of an economic epoch to the broad sweep of human history. But it is neither possible nor necessary to discuss them here. Instead, we shall attempt to specify the concept further since it has close bearing on discussion below of the distinctive characteristics of economic growth in the modern epoch.[1]

First, the distinction and definition of epochs in the long stretch of human life on this planet is partly a matter of judgment, dependent upon the scholar's interest. He may wish to distinguish the 500,000 years of Paleolithic food-gathering, hunting, and fishing from the following five to

1. The brief comments that follow deal with a theme that has been discussed extensively in the literature on periodization in, and generalization from, history. The purpose here is to suggest a framework within which to organize a variety of partly interconnected quantitative comparisons relating to the modern economic growth of nations.

For references to the literature and summary discussion of many of the issues see Louis Gottschalk, ed., *Generalization in the Writing of History* (Chicago, 1963); Social Science Research Council, *Bulletin No. 54* (New York, 1946) and *Bulletin No. 64* (New York, 1954). The first and second of these three reports contain extensive bibliographies.

seven thousand years of food production and concentrate on the slow but significant changes in the techniques of making stone implements. Or he may choose to begin with recorded human history and distinguish the early irrigation empires from the aggressive tributary states, antiquity from the Middle Ages, and so on. The particular innovation selected and the length and scope of the epoch will be determined by the scholar's emphasis.

But, second, the element of choice is limited by the sweep of events as the scholar sees them, particularly by the requirement that the epoch define a stretch of human history throughout which some specified set of forces is operating and dominant. The pattern of life during the epoch must be seen as the realization of the potentialities involved in the single complex identified as the epochal innovation, not as the result of a new set of major forces that overshadows the innovation. To put it in technical terms, the epoch must be so defined that a single trend line can be effectively fitted to it. The line must remain unbroken; any major changes would require the investigator to terminate the old trend line and begin a new one. Because it is difficult to distinguish long-lasting, dominating complexes of epochal innovations among the variety of forces that determine human history and because such epochs can be distinguished at various levels of social life (political, economic, cultural, etc., all of which are interrelated), the long stretch of human history cannot be definitively partitioned into a sequence of epochal innovations.

Third, at least within the more recent stretches of possibly seven thousand years of recorded history, the epochal innovations are not just artifacts of the scholarly imagination. They are attested to by a variety of evidence showing awareness of such innovations by their contemporaries. To be sure, the full sweep of an epochal innovation and its full range are to be seen only after it has run its course—in retrospect and with hindsight. But the major features of the epoch are already apparent long before its end; and after the revolutionary breakthroughs that initiate it have occurred, even the less prescient of contemporary observers often realize what is taking place. For example, the contemporaries of the merchant-capitalism epoch realized, even as we do now, that overseas expansion and the exploitation of contacts with the New World was *the* major source of quickening economic growth for many countries in Western Europe. It is particularly important to note that an epochal innovation operates throughout the course of an epoch and that this continuity, even if subject to the dynamics of unfolding, is what imparts unity to the epoch. This does not mean that the innovation is so dominant that we—or the epoch's contemporaries—can ignore everything else that is going on. But it can be argued that the epochal innovation is the source of widely ramifying growth impulses, in fact, and so perceived by contemporaries.

Fourth, while some epochal innovations may be largely technological, the exploitation of the potential of growth provided by them usually requires much social invention—changes in arrangements by which people are induced to cooperate and participate in economic activity. Thus, to revert to our illustration of merchant capitalism, the geographic discovery that constituted the epochal innovation could not have been exploited adequately without a variety of new institutional devices, e.g. the chartered monopolistic corporation, the "international" commodity exchanges, and for that matter the mercantilist policy that was evolved by the competing nations in their attempt to wrest from the pioneers a share in the gains from the innovation. Conversely, when an epochal innovation is largely a social invention—and we can view the creation of the independent city within the feudal network as such—its significance for economic growth is fully realized only after the differentiation and specialization thus made possible are associated with a variety of technological changes to yield a marked secular increase in economic productivity. The interplay of technological and institutional changes is thus of the essence of the economic growth that takes place within the framework constituted by some epochal innovation.

5

Fifth, it follows that any orderly cumulative pattern of growth within an epoch is associated with this interplay between technological and social change. In addition to the major epochal innovation, other technological and social developments gradually evolve. The sources of the economic growth that occurred in a Western European state during merchant capitalism are multiple: the quickening expansion of overseas trade, the social inventions produced in response to the potentials of such trade, and the investment of profits from overseas trade in growth industries of domestic origin. The dynamics of growth within the epoch thus constitute not only the cumulative effects of new knowledge opened up by the epochal innovation, but also the effects of the new institutions created by it.

One implication of this interplay of technological and social change must be stressed: growth during any epoch is a matter not only of aggregative change but also of structural shifts. Even if the impulse to growth is provided by a major technological innovation, the societies that adopt it must modify their preexisting institutional structure. This means substantial changes in the organization of society— an emergence of new institutions and a diminishing importance of the old. Changes will occur in the relative position of various economic and social groups. The length of the period involved in the full exploitation of an epochal innovation may in fact result from the difficulties that societies encounter in responding to the changing potentialities of the epochal innovation with the institutional adjustments required if the new potentialities are to be realized.

Sixth, insofar as an epoch is marked by a substantial addition to the stock of human knowledge and those societies that take advantage of it necessarily undergo a prolonged process of learning, changes must ensue in the systems of views that dominate and govern the behavior of men. These views—on the relation of man to man and of man to the universe—cannot but be affected by the epochal

6

innovation as its potentialities are applied in the process of technological and institutional change. Thus, the discovery of the New World, the basis for the epoch of merchant capitalism, was bound not only to have direct technological and economic consequences and to call forth institutional changes, but also to affect the views of the societies participating in the discovery—views on social organization, on natural conditions, on established religion, in fact on the validity of many long-held beliefs. Indeed, it might be argued that the effect of an epochal innovation on the beliefs of men is a major feature of an epoch; that some changes in the older beliefs, shaped largely by the earlier and more limited experience, are prerequisites for the institutional modifications. Hence, an economic epoch implies an interplay of technological and economic changes not only with institutional modifications but also with shifts in beliefs entertained by the societies that participate in it; and the time and effort required to overcome the resistance of old beliefs and to evolve the new and more appropriate spiritual framework may partially account for the length of epochs.

Finally, given the division of mankind into separate social units—tribes, temple cities, empires, city-states, national states, and so on—the epochal innovations afford opportunities to more than one such social unit, even though the number of units affected by the several epochs and hence the degree of universality of their significant impacts have differed in the course of human history. Here again one would have to know much more of the course of world history than we do to speak authoritatively. But since, as is obvious, each epoch with which we are familiar affected a number of social units, the comparative study of economic growth has a double task. First, it must consider the internal patterns of economic growth—the sequence of sustained changes in magnitude and structure of economic activity within each unit as it experiences the growth associated with a given epoch. Second, it must consider the spread of

7

a given epochal innovation from the societies that pioneer the utilization of its growth potentials to the first series of followers, and then to succeeding ones.

The formulation of the second task presupposes a specific notion of how an epochal innovation originates and spreads: that an innovation does not emerge at one and the same time in the different societies that will eventually participate in its exploitation and exhibit growth based on it. The innovation is pioneered by the one or two units that, for a variety of reasons, can best assume this role. The geographical revolution was not made initially and equally by all the states of Western Europe that subsequently grew by drawing upon the economic potential of the New World. The pioneers in this case were Spain and Portugal, just as Great Britain was the pioneer in the industrial revolution that ushered in the modern epoch of economic growth. And it was only at a later date that other states found it possible to participate. It is this sequence and the diverse types of adaptation required that should be studied if the mechanism and the pattern of the spread—as well as its ultimate limits —are to be understood.[2]

EPOCHAL INNOVATION OF THE MODERN PERIOD

The preceding comments, sketchy as they are, must suffice as an introduction to the main question here. If economic growth of nations within the last two hundred years represents a process within the framework of a new economic epoch, what is the epochal innovation that is being exploited?

We may begin the answer to this question by a digression into semantics. Before the recent emergence of industrialized nations like the U.S.S.R. under the aegis of an authoritarian state organization controlled by a single political party, it

2. This aspect of the spread of modern economic growth is touched upon again in connection with international relations in Chap. 6. It is discussed in some detail when we consider the extent of spread of modern economic growth to date in Chap. 9.

was customary to refer to the modern economic epoch as "industrial capitalism." "Industrial" was intended to mean that the sources of growth lay largely in the nonagricultural sectors of the economy—in industry proper; "capitalism" was intended to suggest that the institutional framework was largely private business—private ownership of means of production and legal freedom of labor. The term was not only inadequate but to a large extent misleading. It was inadequate because it was based, especially in the Marxian literature, on the experience of too small a sample of states over too short a period. It was misleading because it suggested that technological and institutional changes in agriculture were less important and less autonomous than those in nonagricultural industries. In fact, they were of cardinal importance, and they clearly stemmed from the same source as the technological and institutional changes in the "new" industries. The term was also misleading in that industrialization is possible under nonbusiness auspices—unless one treats the authoritarian states as completely sui generis. Even then, we have the experience of the non-Communist nations of the nineteenth and early twentieth centuries that substantially limited the free operation of business enterprise and private ownership of means of production.

The epochal innovation that distinguishes the modern economic epoch is the extended application of science to problems of economic production. We may call this long period "the scientific epoch"—although this may be too broad a term if the cumulative application of science results in some further revolutionary breakthroughs. Permitting our imagination to soar, we might say that when further progress of science and technology results in mass communication with and use of other planets, we may well enter a new economic epoch—even though the additions to useful knowledge will still be largely the result of contributions of science and science-based technology. But this particular semantic problem can be left to future generations.

By science we mean the study of observable and testable

9

characteristics of the physical world in accordance with the canons of validity accepted by the groups of practitioners called scientists. By science-based technology we mean applied knowledge which rests, in the reliability of its predictions and practices, upon the verified general knowledge in the sciences and upon specific observations on materials, and so on. Ignoring the weighty problems hidden behind these definitions, we may say that certainly since the second half of the nineteenth century, the major source of economic growth in the developed countries has been science-based technology—in the electrical, internal combustion, electronic, nuclear, and biological fields, among others. But even if we go further back, one could argue that of the three major technological inventions associated with the Industrial Revolution—in the fields of cotton textiles, iron, and the steam engine—the last was by far the most important and fundamental to subsequent growth; and it was its success that assured, even before the scientific basis was provided for it, the efficiency of the purely empirical discoveries of new methods of smelting pig iron or producing bar iron. Yet Watt's revolutionary changes in the steam engine represent essentially the application of scientific work and a scientific approach—ranging from the tables of steam expansion prepared much earlier in the scientific laboratories of the time to a typically scientific analysis of energy exchange. In that sense the steam engine was the earliest major science-based invention—and it dominated much of the first century of modern economic growth.

Lest the statements above are misunderstood as a definitive interpretation, we hasten to add that there may well be a case for arguing that the first century of modern economic growth—from the mid-eighteenth to the mid-nineteenth century—was dominated by empirical inventions; and that it was only in the second half of the nineteenth century that the rapid growth of science and recognition of its usefulness brought about a conscious and systematic application of basic scientific discoveries to problems of economic production and human welfare. This lack of assurance or clarity concerning the date of the beginning of the modern scientific epoch is typical. And yet, at the present juncture, it seems better to extend the period to the mid-eighteenth century because the intellectual and cultural milieu within which the basic steam inventions were made also produced the burgeoning of modern science and brought about its more extended applications.[3]

This leads directly to the implications behind the phrase "application of science." It was the *application* that was crucial, not merely for the economic growth that ensued but almost equally for its feedback effects upon the growth of science itself—a kind of self-stimulation of further economic growth. Even a casual reading of the history of science

3. The typical difficulty alluded to in the text lies in the distinction between the influences that provide a given epoch with its *initial* impulse and the central role that the epochal innovation eventually assumes. In the epoch of merchant capitalism, the geographical expansion was itself given an initial impulse by changes in European technology, economics, and politics; and in the modern epoch, the Industrial Revolution of the late eighteenth century in Great Britain was associated with gradual improvements in trade, finance, and agriculture that provided the base for the initial technological developments. It was only later that scientific progress itself became dominant; and we clearly oversimplify by identifying an epoch completely with an innovation that may not, and usually would not, be dominant in the earlier phases.

Nor should the discussion be taken to mean that all modern technological inventions were induced by new scientific discoveries; many could better be viewed as responses to demand rather than to change in supply (i.e. of new knowledge). See Jacob Schmookler, *Invention and Economic Growth* (Cambridge, Mass., 1966), particularly Chap. 3 and 4, for a demonstration of demand-responsiveness of inventions. It may well be that the distinctive characteristic of the modern economic epoch is not the science orientation of its technology, but rather the basic change in views that harnessed human ingenuity to the material satisfaction of wants—a point suggested in the text below, emphasizing conditions of *application* of science. Yet modern science is the obvious instrument of the change in views that made possible the vast increase in productive power, and even if the growth of science was a permissive rather than a compelling factor, the reference to the science base of much of modern technology as a definitive feature of the modern epochal innovation may be justified.

in the last two centuries reveals the powerful stimulus to further growth of science provided by its extensive application in production practices and for the benefit of human beings—in supplying further resources for science and, in particular, providing new information about previously unknown aspects of nature. In short, application of science was equivalent in a sense to the establishment of many experimental laboratories which provided new data to stimulate scientific progress further.

The application of science meant a proper climate of human opinion in which both the pursuit and use of science could be fostered; and thus when we say that the modern epoch is distinguished by application of science to problems of economic production and human welfare we imply that it is distinguished by a climate of human opinion, by some dominant views on the relation of man to the universe that foster science and its application. In this connection it is particularly important to stress the interrelations of technological, social, and spiritual change, mentioned above in commenting on the concept of an economic epoch. Application of science via technology would not have taken place without changes in social institutions. New attitudes were needed to accommodate and foster adjustment of social institutions and practices to the exploitation of the potential provided by science-based technology.

It is not amiss here to try to formulate this set of views, this *Weltanschauung,* which permits and fosters the application of science to economic technology, both physical and social. Vague as the theme is and difficult as a precise formulation may be, an attempt should be made; for the dominant views of an economic epoch are as distinctive and as important as the technological and social epochal innovation that characterizes it.

The broad views associated with the modern economic epoch can be suggested by three terms: secularism, egalitarianism, and nationalism.[4] By secularism we mean concen-

---

4. These again are brief comments on a wide theme. Different terms, emphasizing somewhat different aspects of values reflected in patterns

tration on life on earth, with a scale of priorities that assigns a high rank to economic attainment within an acceptable framework of social institutions, as contrasted with a view of life on earth as a brief transitional phase that deserves relatively little attention. To be sure, this definition would make Max Weber's interpretation of Protestantism, with its implied recognition of one's work as fulfilling a vocation chosen by a deity, a secular rather than a religious belief. But it may be argued that insofar as such a belief *impedes* the free choice of occupation and the freedom of the individual to follow economic criteria within the socially accepted limits, it is nonsecular and therefore not the view that we claim is associated with the modern economic epoch. For it must be recognized that the secular outlook in this sense (regardless of its causes or of the conditions that help sustain it) has been a distinctive characteristic of the *Weltanschauung* in those societies that have participated in modern economic growth, and it can be considered an indispensable accompaniment of modern economic growth.

Egalitarianism means a denial of any inborn differences among human beings, unless and except as they manifest themselves in human activity. The connection is obvious between science (which demands testable evidence), secularism (which makes man paramount and life on this earth his main concern), and egalitarianism (which makes every man a full-fledged participant in the community of men). Of course, this notion is subject to limits imposed by nationalism, but within such limits no allowance is made for innate distinction hallowed by untestable myth or by some association with powers beyond this earth. Indeed, one could go

---

of behavior and judgments, could be used, e.g. those advanced in sociological theory (see a discussion of the Talcott Parsons scheme in Bert F. Hoselitz, *Sociological Aspects of Economic Growth*, Glencoe, 1960, pp. 23–52). But a thorough discussion of these topics is beyond my competence; all that is intended here is to suggest the more obvious aspects of views that appear to be associated with modern economic growth and to stress that the current economic epoch, like the earlier, implies certain sets of views and is incompatible with others.

further and, at the danger of oversimplifying sociology, argue that it is the increased power of man over resources provided by science that constituted the basis for the view of man as captain of his destiny in this world (secularism) and erased the need for mythological bases to justify the otherwise necessary higher economic returns to an upper-class minority (egalitarianism), since the general rise in per capita economic product made the remaining inequality tolerable on purely rational grounds. A typical illustration of this egalitarian philosophy even in a conservative outlook is the American nineteenth-century doctrine of stewardship of wealth, with its echoes in Andrew Mellon in the 1920s. Large incomes were justified because they were received by the economically efficient and were used by them as capable stewards for society as a whole. In premodern days the large incomes of the church were felt to be justified because the church dignitaries were assumed to be free from the sins of avarice, etc.; those in the hands of the anointed nobility were justified on the theory of the nobles' superiority on religious or mythological grounds. The shift in bases of social prestige and political power was a reflection of egalitarianism that contributed greatly to economic growth by inducing a much larger flow of talent and energy into economic rather than other pursuits.

As already indicated, egalitarianism is severely limited by nationalism, as in the older days it was limited by the extended family unit, or by hereditary class distinctions, or by discrimination between the lay masses and the religious professionals. Nationalism is the claim of community of feeling, grounded in a common historical past and its cultural heritage—in its extreme form, an overriding claim of allegiance of the members to the larger community and sovereignty vis-à-vis all groups beyond the national unit. It is hardly an accident that the three slogans of the French Revolution—the political corollary of the Industrial Revolution and an important element in the modern economic epoch—have nationalist connotations: liberty—internally from traditional oppressions that run counter to equality, externally from tyranny from abroad; equality—for members of a nation-state; fraternity—for these same members of a community to which their allegiance must be strong. It does not require a close reading of modern history to recognize these nationalist connotations of the French Revolution slogans; and indeed our own Constitution reveals them clearly. One need hardly expatiate on the sustained development of nationalistic tendencies in the organization of the world during the modern economic epoch.

This summary discussion of the epochal innovation that underlies modern economic growth should be concluded by two cautionary remarks. First, the sharp breaks suggested by the distinctions between economic epochs do not occur in reality. Some of the economic growth in modern times was not grounded on science-based technology, but was due to a slow, trial-and-error process of learning; the partition of Africa late in the nineteenth century was, so to speak, a postscript to merchant capitalism within the new epoch, made possible by the steam railroads. Conversely, science-based technological changes took place in earlier epochs. Furthermore, neither secularism nor egalitarianism is all-pervasive, even in the economically most developed countries; and nationalism varies greatly in intensity, showing no close positive correlation with economic development. In the light of these comments, it should be clear that all we suggest is that science-based technology and the broad views needed for its successful exploitation by human societies were so dominant in the countries that sustained modern economic growth as to constitute a distinctive feature of the modern economic epoch.

Second, we are still in the midst of this epoch; and while sufficient time has elapsed and sufficiently varied experience has accumulated to permit us to distinguish its basic features, it is in no sense a closed chapter. Hence, while we can deal with the characteristics of the modern economic epoch as we see them now, the final shapes of these characteristics are presently hidden from us. This limitation, however, should affect primarily questions of degree rather than kind, of intensity rather than being. It will be most important to bear this limitation in mind in evaluating the specific empirical coefficients—their stability and variability over time and space.

### PROBLEMS OF DEFINITION AND MEASUREMENT

The definition given at the beginning of this chapter, like all definitions, is intended to delimit the field of inquiry and to do so by specifying the features that characterize economic growth—thus providing guides to study. When considered as a guide to measurement, the definition gives rise to several questions that should be stated explicitly and answered at least tentatively. These questions relate to: (1) the unit for which economic growth is studied; (2) the inclusion in the definition of increase in population (and in per capita product); (3) the meaning of product; (4) the specifications of sustained increase.

*Unit To Be Studied*—That we deal with the economic growth of nations, those large human societies with sufficient political independence and often overriding sovereignty to make their own decisions on basic economic and related issues, rather than of families, firms, industries, regions, races, and the like, may be a scholar's personal preference. But for the choice to be justified objectively, as it should be, three different but related arguments can be adduced.[5] First, a nation-state can operate as a sovereign entity largely because its common historical and cultural heritage results in a community of feeling, in a sense of belonging together and apart from others; and this in turn gives rise to an interest in, and concern about, the past, present, and prospective progress of the nation-state, including economic progress. It is this interest and concern that makes reports about population, national product, agri-

5. For a more detailed discussion see Simon Kuznets, "The State as a Unit in Study of Economic Growth," *Journal of Economic History*, *11* (Winter 1951).

cultural crops, and industrial production, headline items in the daily press of so many countries. Second, the nation-state has governmental agencies capable of making many long-term decisions that either promote or impede economic growth—through a host of executive, legislative, and judicial acts, ranging from administrative rules on taxation, licensing, and utility regulation to such basic matters as legislation concerning freedom of markets, of association, or of property. Hence, if the study of economic growth is oriented to policy problems, the study should be centered on units that possess the major policy-making power. Third, insofar as the sovereign state (or any reasonable approximation to it) makes many of the decisions that set the conditions for and affect the course of economic growth of the large societies under its aegis—and it may be the only agency capable of resolving major conflicts arising in the course of economic growth—even a study that aims only at understanding how growth occurred would do best to begin with the nation-state as unit. For a complex and widespread process can best be studied if its manifestations are grouped around units that affect its course, rather than around units that bear little perceptible relation to the process. Thus, it would obviously make little sense to study economic growth for groups of families classified by the initial letter of their family names, for this particular classification has no obvious bearing upon the process of economic growth.[6]

Even if we agree to use nation-states as units in the study of economic growth—because the common historical and cultural heritage of each, different from that of others, provides the basis for a strong interest in its economic progress and for secular decisions in the way of policy actions setting and affecting the course of economic growth

6. The easy availability of data, quantitative and other, for nation-states rather than for other units, should be mentioned. But it is only a reflection of the more basic arguments made in the text as to the importance of nation-states in making secular decisions directly bearing upon the course of economic growth.

—difficult problems still remain in any substantive research. Thus questions arise about the propriety of treating, as relatively independent units, the very small states that function largely as satellites of a large state or of a group of them; or about the unity of the very large states, which, at some earlier stages of economic development, were congeries of regions with greatly differing economic performance. And above all the problem must be faced whether modern economic growth, whose basic source is the application of a *transnational* resource like science and science-based technology, can be effectively studied in terms of *national* units.

Our choice of nation-states as units of study is but a first step and will necessarily be supplemented, and its limitations reduced, by others. The effect of differences in size of states on economic growth, for example, can be examined in comparative analysis; and in fact there will be some discussion of the question in Chapter 6. The analysis of structural differences and changes within countries should bear upon regional differences and the extent of unity, within large states, at different stages of development. And nation-states can be grouped into larger units if this seems desirable for better analysis. It should be remembered that in defining economic growth we stressed not only the increase in population and in per capita income of the country, but also structural changes and international aspects: the latter two clearly complement the observation of the unit as a whole, the first by distinguishing significant parts within it and observing their interrelated changes in the process of growth, the second by observing a number of units, comparing their interrelations, and establishing their sequence in the spread of modern economic growth from the pioneers to the followers. There is thus an explicit provision for testing the assumption of relative independence and unity of nation-states in the course of modern growth, and for further breakdowns or aggregations if more effective analysis requires them, even if in this preliminary and

18

broad study we may not be able to advance far in such testing.

In short, choice of any basic unit for initial grouping of evidence and analysis is a first step, necessarily subject to limitations, since no single criterion of distinction can fully exhaust the determinants of a complex process. The advantage of beginning with the nation-state is that, of all feasible units, it is the one most closely related to modern economic growth, and hence most promising in its capacity to reveal many significant similarities and differences without hopelessly obscuring others.

*Increase of Population*—It may seem surprising to include in the definition of economic growth of a nation the increase in both population and per capita product. Would we not classify as a nation enjoying economic growth one in which population was stable but per capita product increased in a sustained and substantial fashion? Or conversely, one in which population grew markedly but per capita product remained the same? And should an increase in population be included when it is inimical to an increase in per capita product, so that the effort of the presently underdeveloped countries to accelerate economic growth would mean an irrational effort to increase already large population numbers?

The puzzle is resolved if we distinguish between the definition of economic growth as a *desirable* process or goal—for various types of countries with different relations of population to resources—and the definition of economic growth as it has been observed for various economic epochs in the past. Obviously it would be desirable for many underdeveloped countries today to minimize the increase in population and to strive for a marked rise in per capita product. It may, in the long run, prove desirable for many presently developed countries to minimize the increase in both population and per capita income and try to confine economic growth to an increase in product per man-hour or,

19

even more, to changes in the structure of output and use of resources that would better satisfy certain needs without necessarily raising the level of per capita income. But what may seem desirable today is different from what has occurred in the past, and may well change the path of economic growth in the future.

Our definition is intended to formulate the constituent characteristics of economic growth as actually observed in the past. More specifically, it relates to the economic growth observed over the last two hundred years. It is a fact that, by and large, the nations that have exhibited economic growth of the dimensions associated with modern times have shown a sustained and marked rise not only in per capita product but also in population. As we shall see, such a combination of rises in population and per capita product does not appear to have characterized the premodern past; and the definition of economic growth for that period would perhaps stress only increase in population or only increase in per capita product, and probably the former. To be applicable to a number of economic epochs, economic growth might perhaps be defined as a sustained increase in population attained without a perceptible lowering of per capita product, i.e. in combination with either stability or rise in per capita product. But for modern economic growth, the center of our interest, the inclusion of the increase in both population and per capita product is indispensable, for it stresses an important aspect of modern economic growth: the interplay between sustained rises in population and rises in economic performance substantial enough to assure an upward trend in per capita product.

*Meaning of Product*—Specifying the meaning of "product," the magnitude of which is fundamental in the definition and measurement of economic growth, involves the full range of problems discussed at length and for many decades in the literature on national income and social accounts. In distinguishing the economic from other aspects of social life, one must consider questions of scope or of inclusion and exclusion; in drawing the line between costs (or intermediate products) and final output, one encounters questions of grossness and netness; and in reducing the diverse economic activities and resulting products to a common denominator, one must consider questions of valuation or weighting. All these problems are accentuated when product is used to gauge economic growth, because such growth is necessarily accompanied by many institutional and structural changes—which shift the line between economic and noneconomic, modify the cost–output relations, and change, often drastically, the relations of prices, the only feasible basis of valuation.

It is impossible to discuss here all the questions arising in defining national product.[7] Yet it must be stressed that the prevailing practices, upon the results of which we must rely for much of our knowledge of the rate and structure of economic growth, rest on agreed-upon notions of the ends of economic activity and the means by which gains in product can be attained. This can be clearly seen from a few illustrations. First, assume that a society places a high valuation upon religious pursuits so that half of the able-bodied, working-age population are in monasteries, leading an ascetic life and devoting their time to prayer. Would we consider the results of such activity economic product, assign some value to it, and include that in the national income? This is not the practice in accepted national income accounting, although the incomes of the clergy, a tiny part of the labor force, are included in most countries. If this illustration seems unrealistic, consider India's large, and in our terms, unproductive cattle stock: its preservation presumably provides some psychic income to a substantial part of India's population; yet the current measures of

7. Some of these will be noted in connection with specific measures in the substantive chapters that follow. For discussion of the basic assumptions in the definition of national product see Simon Kuznets, *National Income and Its Composition, 1919–1938* (New York, 1941), Chap. 1, and the first part of Simon Kuznets, "National Income: A New Version," *Review of Economics and Statistics*, 30 (August 1948).

national product omit such income because the agreed-upon ends of economic activity make no allowance for this type of product and this use of economic resources. Second, assume that a society enslaves part of its population, keeping it at the lowest level of subsistence and extracting a surplus for the benefit of the free groups. Would we measure the social product in accordance with this practice, i.e. limit it to the product accruing to the slaveowners, after deducting an allowance for the consumption of slaves, and in calculating per capita income relate the total to the number of slaveowners alone? Or, again to illustrate the problem of means, assume that a society expends its surplus above the subsistence of its people to attack and exploit other nations. Would we include the gains from such aggression in the national product and use the latter as a measure of the economic growth of the aggressor society? The practices of national income accounting would answer both these questions in the negative.

The accepted definition and measures of national product reflect the broad features of modern societies dominated by the ideas of secularism, egalitarianism, and nationalism, noted in our early discussion. These rule out, in terms of ultimate ends, a high valuation of asceticism and religious professionalism, the admissibility of slavery, and the pursuit of gain through aggression at the expense of other nations. Indeed, in line with our discussion above it may be argued that in *any* epoch the accepted notions of ends and means of economic activity reflect the prevalent features of the societies that are among the leaders in the epoch's economic growth; and that the emergence of these prevalent notions is itself an important constituent feature of an economic epoch.

It is hardly surprising that the definition of national product used for measuring modern economic growth embodies the accepted notions of means and ends of economic activity, reflecting the main features of modern economic society: it is the most direct way of understanding modern economic growth. To be sure, only problems of data supply and expediency prevent us from defining, measuring, and valuing national product for modern times in terms of the notions prevailing in Egypt in the third century B.C., or in the feudal society of Europe in the early Middle Ages. We might have some difficulty in finding the modern counterpart of the funerary investments of the ancient Egyptians and in deciding whether to count the dead, at least those within the immediately past generation, in the denominator of the fraction, product/population; or in deriving the baron-equivalent of a serf in accordance with the notions of feudal society. But statistical ingenuity could overcome these problems, as well perhaps as those involved in assigning values to modern products that had not even been dreamed of by our Egyptian and medieval forebears. Yet the results, intriguing as they might be, would hardly reveal how modern economic growth comes about, its similar and divergent characteristics for different countries, and the mechanism of its structural change. (Structural measures also depend upon a common denominator in terms significant for the impact upon the human beings who are the active agents in modern society.) If we are to understand modern economic growth, we must measure its magnitudes in terms of the modern system of ends, means, and values. Further, if we want to contrast modern economic growth with earlier periods and patterns of growth, we must evaluate and appraise the earlier periods also in modern terms in full knowledge that part of the difference would be due to the fact that the societies of the earlier times did not share many of the notions of means, ends, and values that constitute impulses to growth in modern times. This is not to argue against using different systems of notions for different economic epochs, if it is desirable. The argument here is only that if our interest is in modern economic growth, the basic notions of modern economic society as to ends, means, and values must be used even for comparison with earlier times.

Of course, there are many arbitrary elements in specifying means, ends, and values for the modern period. These are clearly evident in the treatment of many controversial aspects of national income accounting, e.g. nonmarketed commodities and services, services not embodied in commodities, outlay on military material, and the base year for which prices are to be used as weights. Even within the modern period and among countries that have sustained modern economic growth, the structure of society differs sufficiently to give rise to serious problems of comparability. Thus there is a genuine question whether the social structure and price system of the U.S.S.R. (and even more, of Communist China) are sufficiently similar to those in the free countries to give meaning to quantitative comparisons of economic growth—except for such inadequate indexes as steel production, etc. There is also an element of artificiality in the national product estimates for many underdeveloped countries, which are based on notions of means, ends, and values appropriate to developed countries. A similar artificiality exists in the national product estimates even of developed countries a hundred years ago, which are based on the system of price weights prevailing today. And, as will be discussed in Chapter 6, the very inequality among nations in economic performance in modern times produces aggressive elements in international relations, with effects on national product that may be difficult to adjust for. But these are all specific problems to which some useful answers can be provided by modifications of definition and measurement that adjust the comparisons or provide alternatives. These problems of comparability, either in space or in time, should not overwhelm us to the point of our despairing of the possibility of meaningful and objectively testable measures of national product in relation to the population. There is, after all, a strong element of community of human wants and needs, translatable in the modern economic epoch into a set of widely prevalent notions of means, ends, and values of economic activity.

With all these problems in defining and measuring comprehensive aggregates like national product, it may be thought that more circumscribed measures, whose meaning can be more easily specified, might be taken as indexes of economic growth. For example, if certain production sectors are typically modern, in the sense that they are using the science-based technology of modern times, the increase in *their* output—either total or per capita—might seem a less equivocal measure of economic growth than an increase in the more diverse congeries of goods entering total national product. One might then try to measure the economic growth of a country by the increase in per capita output of one or several modern sectors, setting aside for the moment any difficulties that might arise in identifying these for a given country and for a long period.

It can hardly be denied that the growth of modern sectors is of primary interest in the study of the mechanism of economic growth, particularly if one adheres to the view that at any given time in the history of a country's economy some dynamic "leading" sectors are the loci of rapid growth which, through various linkages, induce growth elsewhere in the economy. But unless the relation between changes in these modern, "leading" sectors and the rest of the economy is significant, stable, and general, a marked rise in these modern sectors may have little effect on the persistently stagnating remainder of the economy of some countries and thus on their overall growth; whereas in other countries a smaller rise in the output of the modern sectors may have a far greater effect on the growth of the economy. Presumably a variety of factors determine and affect this relation between the modern or "leading" sectors and the rest of the economy, but insofar as one of these factors is the relative magnitudes of the individual sectors, we must again face the problem of defining and measuring the aggregate of which a leading sector is a part.

In defining and measuring the economic growth of a country, there is at present no escape from the obligation to be comprehensive. Our knowledge of the structure is still not firm enough to permit us to use a part as representative of the whole. Indeed, there is danger in making premature claims that we can do so; in assuming, for example, that a few blast furnaces and electric power stations in and of themselves—not for what they represent (under certain conditions *but not always*), and not for what they may induce elsewhere (under certain conditions *but not always*)—are reliable evidence of significant growth of a country's economy. And this comment applies even to an index of manufacturing production or of mechanical energy consumption.

This does not mean that a whole battery of such partial indexes could not be constructed—one that would provide a sound basis for diagnosing growth of a country's economy. But it would be a sizable research task to identify an adequate number of such partial indexes; and even then, they would remain nonadditive unless we could assign the proper weights to them, which we cannot do now. Particularly, they would not now yield an easily additive aggregate like national product, of which so many significant subdivisions can be measured as components.

*Sustained Increase*—By a sustained increase we mean a rise of such magnitude that it is not overshadowed by short-term fluctuations. And by a sustained trend in structure, e.g. a shift toward nonagricultural sectors, we mean one in which the rise in the share of nonagricultural activities in output (or in labor force) is not overshadowed by short-term fluctuations in the shares.

But what is meant by short-term fluctuations and by an adequate magnitude of long-term trends relative to these up-and-down movements? The answer must be in terms of social experience, since all these statistical concepts assume meaning only in such terms. Given the economic cycles of modern times, which range in duration from less than four to nine years and may involve a decline as great as a fifth of the secular level, a cumulative increase in total or per capita product of a few percentage points even over a long period, say thirty years, can hardly be considered sustained and taken safely as a measure of secular rise—unless there is substantive evidence that a cyclical decline in the foreseeable future will not reduce it to insignificant dimensions. By contrast, a substantial rise over a shorter period, say fifteen to twenty years, which even a marked cyclical contraction is not likely to reduce more than a fifth or a quarter, may be treated as evidence of a rising secular trend, i.e. of economic growth. A similar comment can be made regarding changes in shares of industrial sectors, or other structural aspects of economic growth.

Therefore, in order to establish the sustained character of a rise or of a structural change, we must know the duration and magnitude of short-term fluctuations that may affect the level and structure of a country's economic performance.[8] More important than the length of the period is the magnitude of the change that transcends the short-term fluctuations relative to the amplitude of the fluctuations. The periods required to observe the sustained change that we identify as economic growth are long—a minimum of thirty to forty years—because no less a stretch of historical experience can reveal the variety of short-term fluctuations to which the economy is subject. If we have evidence of a sizable movement, relative to the fluctuations, over this long period, we can presume that the forces making for economic growth are marked and persistent, and we can concern ourselves with the growth mechanism. To be sure, further analysis may demonstrate that the growth forces are transitory, or that the short-term fluctuations can be far wider than those observed at first. But unless such additional evidence appears, a substantial movement over a period long enough to have revealed a variety of short-term disturbances can be taken as an indication of the existence of economic growth.

In Chapter 2 we shall deal more directly with the sus-

8. Thus, if we distinguish long swings (on the average, about twenty years) in the rate of growth, even a longer period must be covered in order to establish the underlying long-term rate of increase or of structural shift. For a more detailed discussion of the concept of secular trends as sustained, long-term movements, see Simon Kuznets, *Capital in the American Economy* (Princeton, 1961), pp. 36–54.

tained character of modern economic growth. Here we only wish to emphasize the observation that the long-term movements, the secular trends thus defined, are not a kind of artificial order imposed retrospectively upon a social life that is in reality irregular and fluctuating, without definite direction as to level and structure. On the contrary, individuals, families, and other human institutions have been aware of the distinction between the long-term trend and the short-term changes in considering their lifetimes and the lifetimes of their children or successors, in laying plans, and in interpreting currently changing situations. The long-term trends are a reality because people plan for them, because societies have designed institutions to deal with them, and because useful knowledge is sufficient to limit short-term declines. The time horizons involved may differ from individuals to families and from families to larger organized groups of people, but they are all long enough to transcend the short-term fluctuations and to permit economic growth in our sense of the term—both in aspiration and, given the power, in fulfillment.

### PLAN FOR FURTHER DISCUSSION

Having touched upon the basic features of the modern economic epoch and the major questions that arise in defining economic growth of nations, we are ready for the main task of this monograph: a review of the aggregative, structural, and international characteristics of the economic growth of nations in modern times. Additional questions of definition and measurement will arise in connection with structural changes and international comparisons, and more should be said about the modern economic epoch as contrasted with others, but such discussion is best presented in connection with the substantive findings on various aspects of growth.

In Chapter 2 we deal with the aggregative characteristics—the modern rates of increase in population, per capita product, and total product—and compare them with what little we know of premodern rates. Since population, particularly the labor force, and capital are the two major productive factors, we also consider the rates of increase per unit of input and the extent to which modern economic growth may be associated with a rise in efficiency rather than an increase in input of labor and material capital.

The discussion in Chapter 3 deals with trends in industrial structure, i.e. the changing proportional contributions of the major sectors—agriculture, industry, and services—to aggregate product, and their changing shares in labor force and other productive factors. Three shifts in productive structure, associated with modern economic growth, are considered in some detail: first, the movement away from agriculture, usually referred to as industrialization; second, the change in structure within industry proper, and particularly in manufacturing; and, finally, shifts in structure of the services sector. Here and in the chapters that follow only the main trends can be observed and discussed, but an attempt is made to suggest some ad hoc explanations of these shifts and indicate the factors causing them.

Chapter 4 is devoted to a discussion of the distribution of product and income. Following a quantitative summary of the transition from output of product to the distribution of income claims, the discussion deals with trends in factor shares—the share of income from assets, the shares of capital and labor, the underlying problem of allocation of entrepreneurial income, and the share of compensation of employees. The chapter concludes with a discussion of the distribution of personal income by size, dealing first with the vexing problems of the definition of units and income, and then with the long-term trends in the distributions for the developed countries discernible in the available data.

The pattern of product use is the topic of Chapter 5. After the broad classes of use—household consumption, government consumption, capital formation—are distinguished and statistically illustrated, the trends in this three-class pattern of use are summarized and evaluated. A detailed discussion of the long-term trends in the financing and structure of capital formation and in the capital–output ratios follows. The chapter concludes with a summary of trends in the structure of household consumption and notes the relation between these trends and the cross-section income (or expenditure) elasticities of demand for various categories of consumer goods.

While Chapter 2 deals with *aggregative* aspects of modern economic growth, and Chapters 3–5 examine the trends in the *internal* structure of the developed economies in the course of their growth, Chapters 6–9 are devoted to *international* aspects. Chapter 6 concentrates on trends in international relations, emphasizing the growing interdependence among developed countries and between them and the rest of the world. The discussion centers on the international relations that reflect such interdependence: the availability to all nations of a growing transnational stock of useful knowledge—of additions to both material and social technology whose source is largely in the growth of basic and applied science; and the international flows of resources and goods, including movements of people, already noted in Chapter 2, foreign trade, and international capital flows. A third level of international relations, at which political power is exercised, is briefly noted, since it seems to be connected with the differential impact of modern economic growth on different nations, adding to the power of some more than to that of others. The chapter concludes with reflections on the implications of these international relations and flows for the use of the nation-state as the unit of study, and for the definition of the universe of developed countries for which an attempt to establish similar and variant characteristics of modern economic growth is warranted.

Chapters 2–6 concentrate on what we now identify as economically developed countries, largely non-Communist, since it is from their long-term records that we can learn the basic patterns of modern economic growth. Chapter 7 deals with as much of the world as is covered by aggregative and structural data for recent (post-World War II) years; and the emphasis is on international diversity in economic performance, particularly on the underdeveloped and generally less developed countries. First, current differences in per capita product are considered and an attempt is made to evaluate, if only tentatively, the significance of the wide contrasts shown by the aggregate data. Consideration is then given to the question whether the wide diversity is of recent origin or has existed over a long perod.

In Chapter 8 we provide a summary of the economic structure of underdeveloped countries in comparison with that of developed countries—in a sense paralleling the discussion of structural changes associated with economic growth in the developed countries in Chapters 3–5. The distinctive demographic, political, and other noneconomic structures of the less developed countries are touched upon.

Chapter 9, the last substantive chapter, is devoted to the question of the spread of modern economic growth. Some comments are offered on the possible reasons for what may seem to be a limited spread in the world to date.

Three aspects of the discussion to follow warrant mention here. First, it is largely a summary of empirical, primarily quantitative, work on modern economic growth; its limitations reflect those of the author and also those of work done so far in the field. This means that if such work proceeds at a vigorous pace, as it has in recent years, parts of the summary will, it is hoped, become obsolete in the not too distant future, although the broader conclusions may not be affected. Second, while comparisons with the premodern past are attempted, the scarcity of firm quantitative work relating to that past forces our discussion to be casual in the sense that extensive documentation is impossible, and limits the diagnosis of differences to those that are so prominent as to be beyond wide margins of error. Yet reference to the more distant past is indispensable for understanding much of the present, both in the developed countries and particularly in many of the underdeveloped countries that retain so much of their historical heritage. Third, limited as the empirical and quantitative work in the field of economic growth has been, the accumulation of findings has far outrun the formulation of adequate theoretical analysis to account for them. To put it differently, the contribution of theories of the type that employs a sufficient number of variables with tested empirical coefficients has lagged far behind the accumulation of empirical findings. Nor are the findings so complete as to permit the formulation of adequately tested analytical hypotheses. As a result, the explanations adduced in the course of discussion are ad hoc, and necessarily casual.

The tentative nature of many of the empirical findings is due primarily to the ambitiously wide scope of our survey: the reliability of the underlying data and validity of findings would have been strengthened if we had limited the view to the long-term records of the one or two developed countries with the best data. But if we had limited the scope we would have failed in our purpose: to search for common characteristics of modern economic growth, recognizing that each country has its peculiarities and that the development records of one or two countries are insufficient for the distinction between the general and the specific. In that sense, an intensive study of one or a few countries provides only partial, if extremely valuable, raw materials; and the field must be extended even if this involves difficult judgments concerning the acceptability of some of the records and reliance on a variety of estimates with different and sometimes wide margins of error.

The ad hoc nature of many of the hypotheses and analytical conjectures scattered through the discussion was, in a way, forced upon us. If we had used simple, consistent, and closed models, we might have avoided much of the casual discussion; but we would not have been able to establish any determinate relation to observable economic growth. On the other hand, we were reluctant to leave the empirical findings as simple statements of fact, ignoring the associations among them that appear to be statistically and analytically significant. By advancing some conjectures, raising some questions as to the factors behind them, we hoped to indicate possible connections with a wider realm of knowledge. The warning concerning the casual character of many of the hypotheses is not intended as an apology —either here or with reference to the ambitiously wide scope of coverage. Both such scope and the presentation of relevant if partial explanations are perilous but indispensable steps toward an increasingly realistic view of modern economic growth and a better appreciation of the important questions to be asked—with the hope that they may eventually be answered.

# 2 GROWTH OF POPULATION AND PRODUCT

We begin with growth of population, for it is people who produce economic growth and consume its yield; and the increase in population is a distinctive characteristic and condition of modern economic growth. The subject is vast, and our aim is to note only the main features of modern demographic processes most relevant to our central topic.

### HIGH RATE OF POPULATION GROWTH

The first finding to be emphasized is the high rate of increase in population since 1750, the period within which modern economic growth is observed. Table 2.1 suggests the orders of magnitude. Although the data on population prior to 1750 are rough estimates, they are sufficiently acceptable to confirm the finding of marked acceleration in the rate of growth in recent centuries.

Several observations, extending and specifying the findings suggested in Table 2.1, can be made. First, given the age of mankind, estimated to range well over 500,000 years, and a world population in the year zero of 210 million, the rate of population growth over the millennia before the Christian era must have been much lower even than that for the first millennium A.D., 0.3 per cent per decade.[1] If we

1. The world population estimate about years 0 to 30 is put between 210 and 250 million in W. S. and E. S. Woytinsky, *World Population and Production* (New York, 1953), pp. 33–34. We use the lower figure here to maximize the rate of growth from 0 to 1000.

TABLE 2.1

World Population, 1000 to 1960

| | About 1000 (1) | 1750 (2) | 1750 (3) | 1960 (4) |
|---|---|---|---|---|
| *Total (millions)* | | | | |
| 1. World | 275 | 749 | 728 | 3,010 |
| 2. Europe (including Asiatic Russia) | 47 | 156 | 144 | 640 |
| 3. Asia (excluding Asiatic Russia) | 165* | 492* | 475 | 1,684 |
| 4. Other | 63 | 101 | 109 | 686 |
| a. Africa | 50 | 90 | 95 | 257 |
| b. Americas and Oceania | 13* | 11* | 14 | 429 |
| 5. Area of European settlement (2 + 4b) | 60* | 167* | 158 | 1,069 |
| *Percentage distribution* | | | | |
| 6. Europe | 17 | 21 | 20 | 21 |
| 7. Asia | 60* | 66* | 65 | 56 |
| 8. Other | 23 | 13 | 15 | 23 |
| a. Africa | 18 | 12 | 13 | 9 |
| b. Americas and Oceania | 5* | 1* | 2 | 14 |
| 9. Area of European settlement | 22* | 22* | 22 | 35 |
| *Rate of growth per decade, periods marked by successive dates (%)* | | | | |
| 10. World | | 1.3 | | 7.0 |
| 11. Area of European settlement | | 1.4 | | 9.5 |
| 12. All other | | 1.3 | | 6.0 |

* Oceania included with Asia.

*Sources: Cols. 1 and 2:* From M. K. Bennett, *The World's Food* (New York, 1954), p. 9.

*Col. 3:* The Carr-Saunders estimates in United Nations, *The Determinants and Consequences of Population Trends* (New York, 1963), Table 2, p. 11.

*Col. 4:* From U.N., *Demographic Yearbook, 1963* (New York, 1963), Table 2, p. 142.

start with an Adam and Eve as late as 500,000 B.C., the implicit rate of growth is about 0.004 per cent per decade. This does not preclude a rate of population growth in some earlier periods comparable with those since 1750, but it is highly unlikely except for large percentage changes from a tiny absolute base. By means of the estimates of world population since 1000 (given in the source cited for columns 1 and 2 of Table 2.1), we can compare the growth from 1750 to 1950—well over 200 per cent—with that for spans of two centuries going back to the year 1000. From 1000 to 1650 the average rise over a two-century period was slightly over 20 per cent, or less than a tenth of that for 1750–1950; and even in the last span before 1750 (i.e. from 1550 to 1750) the total rise was only about 60 per cent. In short, it is only relatively recently that mankind attained both the large numbers *and* the high rates of growth that are characteristic of the modern era. In this respect, as in many others, the modern era is unique; and much of what we learn from the premodern past must be qualified because of the smaller magnitudes involved.

Second, the acceleration in the rate of population growth appears to have been almost universal, characterizing the underdeveloped countries of Asia as well as Europe and the area of European settlement, where most developed countries are found. But the rate of population growth in recent centuries has been higher in the area of European settlement than in the rest of the world (see Table 2.1, lines 11 and 12, column 4), indicating that, subject to qualifications to be noted below, population has grown more rapidly in the countries that evinced modern economic growth. Other comparisons support this finding: people of European stock increased from about 150 million in 1750 to about 800 million in 1950, a rise of 433 per cent; whereas the rest of the world's population grew from about 580 to about 1,600 million, or less than 200 per cent.[2] An alternative calculation shows that the population of the European countries that are now fully developed (Germany, France, the United Kingdom excluding Ireland, the Scandinavian countries, Belgium, and the Netherlands), combined with North America and Oceania, rose from 59 million in 1750 to 372 million in 1950, or over 500 per cent; whereas population in the rest of the world rose from 669 to 2,137 million, respectively, or slightly over 200 per cent.[3]

2. See ibid., p. 36.

3. The figures for the European countries in 1750 are from B. Ts. Urlanis, *Growth of Population in Europe* (in Russian, Moscow, 1941), pp. 414–15; for world population in 1750, from U.N., *Population Trends*, Table 2, p. 11; all others are from U.N., *Demographic Yearbook, 1963*, Tables 2 and 4.

Third, modern economic growth originated in the smaller European countries and spread largely in Europe and to the overseas descendants of Europe, whereas the large populous countries of Asia and Africa are still underdeveloped. Consequently, even though the spread of the modern industrial system has meant successive additions of new units to the group of developed countries, and even though population growth in the countries that did develop was much higher than in others, successful development of the potentials of modern economic growth is limited, even today, to a minority of the world's population. If, by a most generous interpretation, we classify all areas of European settlement as developed, and add Japan, the total in 1950 would be about 1 billion, or four-tenths of the world population of 2.5 billion. But if we omit from the developed countries much of Eastern Europe, some of Southern Europe, and most of Latin America, the fraction drops appreciably. Application of the per capita income criterion only strengthens the impression. If lack of development is taken to mean a per capita income in 1958 of less than $200, over 60 per cent of the world population were in undeveloped countries. And if $575 per capita is viewed as an acceptable minimum level of economic development, only slightly over a fifth of the 1958 world population was at or above that level.[4] We shall return to this finding, and some of its implications, in Chapter 7.

While world population grew about 7 per cent per decade from 1750 to 1960 (Table 2.1, line 10, column 4), there was a marked acceleration *within* that period (Table 2.2). The rate of increase in world population was less than 5 per cent per decade between 1750 and 1800, and then rose to over 14 per cent in the last long period, from 1930 to 1960. But since this acceleration in the rate of population growth is a reflection of the spread of new demographic patterns to rising proportions of the world population, it is the levels and patterns of movement by continents that are of main interest here.

4. See Table 7.2, p. 368.

## TABLE 2.2
### World Population, by Continents, 1750–1960

| | Europe and Asiatic Russia (1) | North America[a] (2) | Latin America (3) | Oceania (4) | Area of European settlement[b] (5) | Asia (6) | Africa (7) | World (8) |
|---|---|---|---|---|---|---|---|---|
| **Totals (millions)** | | | | | | | | |
| 1. 1750 | 144 | 1 | 11 | 2 | 158 | 475 | 95 | 728 |
| 2. 1800 | 192 | 6 | 19 | 2 | 219 | 597 | 90 | 906 |
| 3. 1850 | 274 | 26 | 33 | 2 | 335 | 741 | 95 | 1,171 |
| 4. 1900 | 423 | 81 | 63 | 6 | 573 | 915 | 120 | 1,608 |
| 5. 1930 | 532 | 135 | 109 | 10.4 | 786 | 1,072 | 157 | 2,015 |
| 6. 1950 | 576 | 167 | 162 | 13.0 | 918 | 1,384 | 207 | 2,509 |
| 7. 1960 | 640 | 200 | 212 | 16.5 | 1,069 | 1,684 | 257 | 3,010 |
| **Rate of growth per decade (%)** | | | | | | | | |
| 8. 1750–1800 | 5.9 | 43.1 | 11.6 | 0 | 6.7 | 4.7 | −1.1 | 4.5 |
| 9. 1800–1850 | 7.4 | 34.1 | 11.7 | 0 | 8.9 | 4.4 | 1.1 | 5.3 |
| 10. 1850–1900 | 9.1 | 25.5 | 13.8 | 24.6 | 11.3 | 4.3 | 4.8 | 6.5 |
| 11. 1900–1930 | 7.9 | 18.6 | 20.0 | 20.1 | 11.1 | 5.4 | 9.4 | 7.8 |
| 12. 1930–1960 | 6.4 | 14.0 | 24.8 | 16.6 | 10.8 | 16.2 | 17.9 | 14.3 |
| 13. 1950–1960 | 11.1 | 19.8 | 30.9 | 26.9 | 16.4 | 21.7 | 24.2 | 20.0 |

a. Includes the United States, Canada, Alaska, St. Pierre, and Miquelon.
b. Includes North America, Latin America, Europe (including Asiatic U.S.S.R.), and Oceania.
Sources: *Lines 1–4:* Carr-Saunders' estimates for 1750–1900 in U.N., *Population Trends*, Table 2, p. 11.
*Lines 5–7:* From U.N., *Demographic Yearbook, 1963*, Table 2.

The acceleration of the rate of population growth appeared earliest in Europe, where the influence of modern economic growth was first felt; reinforced by the much higher rates of increase on the continents to which European population spread (particularly North America), the rate of growth of total population in the area of European settlement accelerated even more (see columns 1, 2, and 5, lines 8–10). But this process came to an end in the twentieth century; in Europe, in particular, the rates of population growth in the twentieth century (with the exception of the recent decade) are significantly below the peak in the second half of the nineteenth century.

The patterns of growth in Latin America, Asia, and Africa are distinctly different. The marked acceleration in population growth begins much later than in Europe— largely in the twentieth century, and there is no sign of decline from peak levels. The variety of growth patterns would naturally be multiplied if we were to distinguish countries rather than continents. But the important findings here are that the modern type of population growth, with its high rates, is initiated at different dates in the old parts of the world (i.e. excluding the relatively empty areas in North America and Oceania); that the identity of the areas in the acceleration phase of population growth is shifting; and that the acceleration in the rate of growth of world population, *within* the modern period, will have run its course once the modern patterns have spread to all parts of the world. The shifts in relative rates of growth between Europe and Asia, between North and Latin America, stand out quite clearly.

One consequence of the shift in locus, revealed in Table 2.2, should be noted. In the earlier phases of the modern period, until the twentieth century, the high rates of population growth characterized the area of European settlement—older areas within which modern economic growth was taking place, or relatively "empty" areas to which Europeans were migrating and in which European descendants could adopt high birth rate patterns without encountering major economic obstacles. Thus from 1750 to 1900 the rate of population growth in the area of European settlement was appreciably higher than in Asia and Africa (see columns 5–7, lines 8–10). This was still true from 1900 to 1930 (line 11). But from 1930 to 1960, population growth in the area of European settlement, while not much lower than in 1900–30, was distinctly below the greatly augmented rates for Asia and Africa (line 12); and if we characterize Latin America as an area of European settlement in which economic growth has been most halting, the recent inverse association between the rates of population growth and degree of success in attaining modern economic levels becomes more striking. Thus, at least judging by the large area units distinguished in Table 2.2, one may conclude that while in the earlier periods population grew most rapidly in those countries and areas in which economic performance, on a per capita basis, was high and rising, in the recent decades population growth was most rapid in the countries and areas in which economic performance was relatively low.

BIRTHS, DEATHS, AND MIGRATION

On a world scale, population increase is the excess of births over deaths. Until men learn how to travel and migrate to other planets, withdrawal from world population can only be by death. And until other practices of reproduction are devised and adopted (e.g. artificial incubation), addition to world population can only be by birth. An accelerating high rate of world population growth can therefore be attained only by an increase in the birth rate, reduction in the death rate, or both. The contribution of these trends in births and deaths to the high rate of population increase in modern times is important to economic growth.

Data on births and deaths are far scantier than those on population. They are summarized in Table 2.3, the selection of countries emphasizing those with the longest records. The rates are all crude, i.e. ratios of total annual births and deaths to total population, regardless of age and sex structure. But they are the immediate determinants of rates of population growth on a world scale, where the rates of natural and total increase are identical. For any smaller area the net balance of immigration over emigration must also be taken into account.

Records for only a few countries reach back to the first half of the eighteenth century, but it is clear even from this small sample that the decline in the death rates has been the more conspicuous trend and the major cause of the acceleration and high level of population increase in modern times. In the early eighteenth century, death rates, even in the European countries, were 30 per thousand or more; and scattered evidence for these countries suggests that in the earlier centuries the rates were significantly higher, perhaps 40 per thousand or over. By the 1950s, crude death rates were in the neighborhood of 10 per thousand in the developed countries. Undoubtedly, over the period from the first half of the eighteenth century to the 1950s, the death rates in almost all parts of the world dropped 20 points per thousand, or more; and even in the presently underdeveloped areas these rates, which are still over 20 per thousand, must have been above 40 per thousand in earlier times.

This reduction in death rates alone could account for the acceleration and high rates of population growth in modern times. If we assume that in the premodern centuries the rate of natural increase was, at most, 1 per thousand (i.e. 0.1 per cent per year, which agrees with the rate of 1.3 or 1.4 per cent per decade in Table 2.1, column 2, lines 10–12, for 1000–1750), a decline in the death rate of 20 points would, provided the birth rate remains unchanged, raise the rate of natural increase from 1 to 21 per thousand. Or if we assume, to simplify the argument, that the death rates declined along a straight line from 1750 to 1950, the decline in the average for the two centuries would be 10 points; and the rise in the rate of natural increase would be from 1 per thousand before 1750 to 11 per thousand on the average for the two recent centuries. This

## TABLE 2.3

Birth Rates, Death Rates, and Rates of Natural Increase, Selected Countries, Long Periods (crude rates per 1,000)

| | Mid-1700s (1) | End of 1700s (2) | Mid-1800s (3) | 1891–1900 (4) | 1920–29 (5) | 1950–59 (6) |
|---|---|---|---|---|---|---|
| *England and Wales* | (1731–70) | (1781–1820) | (1841–60) | | | |
| 1. B.R. | 37 | 37 | 33 | 30 | 19 | 16 |
| 2. D.R. | 32 | 25 | 22 | 18 | 12 | 12 |
| 3. R.N.I. | 5 | 12 | 11 | 12 | 7* | 4 |
| *Denmark* | (1736–70) | (1771–1830) | (1841–60) | | | |
| 4. B.R. | 31 | 31 | 31 | 30 | 21 | 17 |
| 5. D.R. | 29 | 25 | 20 | 18 | 11 | 9 |
| 6. R.N.I. | 2 | 6 | 11 | 12 | 10 | 8 |
| *Finland* | (1731–70) | (1771–1830) | (1841–60) | | | |
| 7. B.R. | 42 | 38 | 36 | 32 | 24 | 21 |
| 8. D.R. | 29 | 27 | 26 | 20 | 15 | 9 |
| 9. R.N.I. | 13 | 11 | 10 | 12 | 9 | 12 |
| *Norway* | (1736–70) | (1771–1830) | (1841–60) | | | |
| 10. B.R. | 34 | 31 | 32 | 30 | 21 | 18 |
| 11. D.R. | 28 | 23 | 18 | 16 | 11 | 9 |
| 12. R.N.I. | 6 | 8 | 14 | 14 | 10 | 9 |
| *Sweden* | (1736–70) | (1771–1830) | (1841–60) | | | |
| 13. B.R. | 34 | 33 | 32 | 27 | 18 | 17 |
| 14. D.R. | 29 | 26 | 21 | 16 | 12 | 10 |
| 15. R.N.I. | 5 | 7 | 11 | 11 | 6 | 7 |
| *Belgium* | | | (1841–60) | | | |
| 16. B.R. | | | 30 | 29 | 20 | 17 |
| 17. D.R. | | | 23 | 19 | 14 | 12 |
| 18. R.N.I. | | | 7 | 10 | 6 | 5 |

| | | | | | | |
|---|---|---|---|---|---|---|
| *France* | (1771–75) | (1801–05) | (1841–60) | | | |
| 19. B.R. | 40 | 33 | 27 | 22 | 19 | 19 |
| 20. D.R. | | | 24 | 21 | 17 | 12 |
| 21. R.N.I. | | | 3 | 1 | 2 | 7 |
| *Germany* | | | (1841–60) | | | |
| 22. B.R. | | | 36 | 36 | 21 | 17 |
| 23. D.R. | | | 27 | 22 | 13 | 11 |
| **24. R.N.I.** | | | 9 | 14 | 8 | 6 |
| *Netherlands* | | (1813–24) | (1841–60) | | | |
| 25. B.R. | | 38 | 33 | 33 | 25 | 22 |
| 26. D.R. | | | 26 | 18 | 11 | 8 |
| 27. R.N.I. | | | 7 | 15 | 14 | 14 |
| *Switzerland* | | | (1828) | | | |
| 28. B.R. | | | 37 | 28 | 19 | 17 |
| 29. D.R. | | | | 19 | 13 | 10 |
| 30. R.N.I. | | | | 9 | 6 | 7 |
| *Italy* | | | (1862–70) | | | |
| 31. B.R. | | | 38 | 35 | 29 | 18 |
| 32. D.R. | | | 30 | 24 | 17 | 10 |
| 33. R.N.I. | | | 8 | 11 | 12 | 8 |
| *United States* | | (1790–1800) | (1870–80) | | | |
| 34. B.R. | | 55 | 40 | 33 | 21 | 25 |
| 35. D.R. | | 25 | 23 | 19 | 12 | 9 |
| 36. R.N.I. | | 30 | 17 | 14 | 9 | 16 |
| *Canada* | | | (1867–75) | | | |
| 37. B.R. | | | 34 | 28 | 26 | 28 |
| 38. D.R. | | | 18 | 16 | 12 | 8 |
| 39. R.N.I. | | | 16 | 12 | 14 | 20 |

TABLE 2.3—Continued

| | Mid-1700s (1) | End of 1700s (2) | Mid-1800s (3) | 1891–1900 (4) | 1920–29 (5) | 1950–59 (6) |
|---|---|---|---|---|---|---|
| *Australia* | | | (1871–75) | | | |
| 40. B.R. | | | 37 | 42 | 23 | 23 |
| 41. D.R. | | | 16 | 13 | 10 | 9 |
| 42. R.N.I. | | | 21 | 29 | 13 | 14 |
| *New Zealand* | | | (1871–75) | | | |
| 43. B.R. | | | 40 | 27 | | 26 |
| 44. D.R. | | | 13 | 10 | | 9 |
| 45. R.N.I. | | | 27 | 17 | | 17 |

44

*Sources: Cols. 1 and 2:* England and Wales from John Brownlee, "The History of the Birth and Death Rates in England and Wales Taken as a Whole, From 1570 to the Present Time," *Public Health,* 29 (July 1916), 232; Denmark, Finland, Norway, and Sweden through 1800 from H. Gille, "The Demographic History of the Northern European Countries in the Eighteenth Century," *Population Studies,* 3 (June 1949), 63–65, 1801–30 from Corrado Gini and Stefano Somagyi, *Proceedings of the International Congress for the Study of Population,* 7 (Rome, 1934), Tables XXII and XXIX; France and the Netherlands from ibid.; the United States based on W. H. Grabill, C. V. Kiser, and P. K. Whelpton, *The Fertility of American Women* (New York, 1958), pp. 5–8.

*Cols. 3 and 4:* England and Wales from B. R. Mitchell and Phyllis Deane, *Abstract of British Historical Statistics* (Cambridge, 1962), Table 10, pp. 29–30 and Table 12, pp. 36–37; Finland (col. 3) and Switzerland (col. 3) from Gini and Somagyi, *Proceedings,* 7, Tables XXII and XXIX; Italy from Istituto Centrale di Statistica, *Sommario di Statistiche Storiche Italiane, 1861–1955* (Rome, 1958), Table 6, p. 44; the United States based on Simon Kuznets, "Long Swings in the Growth of Population and in Related Economic Variables," *Proceedings of the American Philosophical Society,* 102 (February 1958), Table 1, p. 37, Table 3, p. 39, and Table 5, p. 41; Canada from O. J. Firestone, *Canada's Economic Development, 1867–1953* (London, 1958), Table 84, pp. 242–43; all other countries from Robert R. Kuczynski, *The Measurement of Population Growth* (London, 1935), Table 29, pp. 104–05 and Table 47, pp. 162–63.

*Col. 5:* from U.N., *Demographic Yearbook, 1959,* Table 9 and *Demographic Yearbook, 1955,* Table 25.

*Col. 6:* from U.N., *Demographic Yearbook, 1963,* Tables 19 and 23.

is more than sufficient to account for the acceleration in the rate of growth of population shown in Table 2.1, in comparisons of 1750–1960 with the preceding seven and a half centuries; or for the acceleration in the rate of population growth shown for the world and for settled continents in Table 2.2. Although for shorter periods within the last two centuries, and for some areas, higher birth rates and the rates of migration were also important factors contributing to the rate of population growth—a point to which we shall return below—for the whole modern period and the world, for most of the subperiods and areas within it, the decline in the death rates was the major and perhaps the only source of the acceleration and high rates of growth of population.

Several aspects of this decline are relevant to economic growth. First, the curve of death rates by age, in earlier times and even today, is U-shaped: the rates are high in infancy (0 to 1 year of age)—from 200 to over 300 per thousand in the earlier days, drop sharply to a trough in the late teens, and remain low until the second rise which begins at about age 50. The modern decline in death rates, which has benefited all groups, has been most conspicuous in the younger groups and least in the advanced age groups.[5] Since in earlier times the young groups were large proportions of the population and their death rates were high, most of the lives saved were in these younger groups. This much greater reduction in mortality of the young groups was associated with the greater relative advance in the prevention and control of infectious, respiratory, and digestive diseases, which are most prevalent among the young, than in the prevention and control of circulatory diseases and cancer, which are most prevalent among the older groups.[6]

5. See U.N., *Population Trends*, p. 55. Chapter 4 summarizes a wide literature dealing with factors affecting mortality trends.

6. See for example the data in W. P. D. Logan, "Mortality in England and Wales from 1848 to 1947," *Population Studies, 4* (September 1950), 132–78.

Second, in premodern and even during early modern times death rates were much higher in the cities than in the rural areas. Two examples will indicate the orders of magnitude. In the London area, the crude death rate during the period 1701–50 was 49 per thousand, compared with a rate of 33 per thousand for England and Wales.[7] In the United States, as late as 1830, death rates by age groups, from 5 to 15 and 19 to 79, were over twice as high in Boston, New York, and Philadelphia as in 44 rural townships of New England.[8] Indeed the death rates in premodern cities were so high that despite high birth rates, the cities constituted deficit areas: in 1701–50, London, with a birth rate of 38 per thousand (compared with 34 for England and Wales) suffered a rate of natural *decrease* of 11 per thousand. In more recent times no developed country has experienced a differential unfavorable to urban population. Obviously, the reduction in mortality of the urban population has been far greater than that of the rural population.

Third, even the scanty evidence in Table 2.3 indicates that the decline in the death rate, like the acceleration in the rate of population growth, began at different dates in different parts of the world. Until the last two to three decades, the decline in the death rate was associated with economic conditions; and low death rates were attained only when economic performance was adequate enough to assure not only the satisfaction of needs for living but also the resources for public health and other services relevant to saving and prolonging life. Even in 1958–62 death rates for Latin America, Asia, and Africa were estimated to be 14, 20, and 23 per thousand, respectively, compared with 10, 9, or 8 per thousand for Europe, North America, and Oceania.[9] By and large, the differences in timing of the decline in the death rates accounted for the differences

7. See Phyllis Deane and W. A. Cole, *British Economic Growth, 1688–1959* (Cambridge, 1962), Table 28, p. 127.

8. See Yasukichi Yasuba, *Birth Rates of the White Population in the United States, 1800–1860* (Baltimore, 1961), Table III-1, p. 75.

9. U.N., *Demographic Yearbook, 1963*, Table 2.

in timing of the acceleration of rates of population growth.

Fourth, until quite recently, the decline in the death rate, impressive and rapid as it is compared with the long pre-modern past, has been a slow process. In England, Denmark, and Sweden, a decline of 10 points, from about 30 in the mid-eighteenth century, took roughly a century; and it was almost as long a period again before the rates dropped to the recent levels of about 10 per thousand. A major factor may have been the rapid growth in the proportion of the urban population and the slower buildup of the medical and public health resources needed to cope with the augmented morbidity problems of mushrooming cities. Whatever the reason, in the countries in which the death rates began to decline long before the recent decades, the rates of decline, while far greater than they must have been in the pre-eighteenth century past, were fairly moderate. But in recent decades, in countries with relatively high death rates, the decline, once begun, has proceeded at impressively rapid rates. Clearly the striking advances in public health and medicine during the last two to three decades have permitted far more rapid reductions in death rates, unrelated to the much slower process of economic growth, than ever before possible.[10]

Turning now to the birth rates, we observe from Table 2.3 that even in the eighteenth and early nineteenth centuries, in the early phases of the modern period, there was a wide spread among countries—even those populated by European stock. Comparison of the rate for the United States in the early nineteenth century, 55 per thousand (and probably no lower in the eighteenth century), with the rate of about 30 per thousand for Denmark and Sweden, and almost 40 for Finland (see lines 34, 4, 7, and 13) indicates that some older countries in Europe made significant adjustments to reduce the birth rate, when the supply of land

10. For a discussion of this recent trend and of other aspects of death rates over the last century see George J. Stolnitz, "A Century of International Mortality Trends," *Population Studies, 9* (July 1955) and *10* (July 1956).

and other resources was not as favorable as in the United States or Finland. Delays in marriage caused by restrictions imposed by institutional arrangements in agriculture and in the town guilds may have been effective; and even voluntary controls after marriage are not out of the question. The point is relevant for it suggests that changes in premodern institutional practices, many of which accompany the beginning of modern economic growth, may have eased the restrictions on the birth rates, permitting them to rise for a while above the previous levels, and may have contributed to the acceleration in the rate of population growth. There may therefore be much validity in recent writings that stress the role of rising birth rates in the early acceleration of population growth in some older European countries.[11] This finding bears upon underdeveloped countries today, for they also may have retained a number of institutional practices (e.g. prohibition of remarriage of widows) that keep the birth rates below their high potential level. Abandonment of such practices under the pressure of modernization, as well as the possible reduction of diseases that cause involuntary sterility, may produce a significant rise in the birth rate that could continue for a

11. See H. J. Habbakuk, "English Population in the Eighteenth Century," *Economic History Review, 6* (December 1953); John T. Krause, "Changes in English Fertility and Mortality, 1781–1850," *Economic History Review, 11* (August 1958); and P. G. Ohlin, "The Positive and Preventive Check: A Study of the Rate of Growth of Pre-industrial Population," (Ph.D. dissertation, Harvard University, 1956).

Furthermore, the aggregate birth rate for large population complexes, e.g. total population of European stock, may rise because of a shift of population toward areas with generally higher birth rates. Unquestionably, the migration of Europeans to North America and Oceania in and of itself raised the birth rate for the aggregate; and continued to do so as long as the birth rate overseas was higher than in Europe. This is another form of easing the restrictions on birth rates imposed by the premodern institutions in the older countries of Europe. Of course, the migrants might have been among the most prolific in Europe, and might have shown the same high birth rates if they had remained at home; but this conjecture is unlikely.

long period before other effects of modernization and economic growth combine to bring it down.

While it is tempting to pursue this topic further, evidence on rises in birth rates during the early phases of modern economic growth is not easily available; and in the broad picture to be painted here it must be regarded as but a detail, albeit an important one. Over the long sweep of modern times our concern is not so much with the effects of a *rise* as with the effects of a *decline* in birth rates. For whatever happened in the eighteenth and early nineteenth centuries in the European countries in which quickening economic growth might have raised the birth rates, from the second half of the nineteenth century for the older European countries and even earlier for their offshoots overseas, the dominant trend was a long-term decline.

This decline was evident in three countries of overseas European settlement early in the nineteenth century. In the United States, by the mid-nineteenth century the crude birth rate was already a quarter below the high levels of the late eighteenth century; and the decline proceeded apace (Table 2.3, line 34). In New Zealand the rate declined a third from the 1870s to the 1890s (line 43). In Canada the rate dropped from 34 per thousand in 1867–75 to 28 per thousand in 1891–1900 (line 37). In Australia, however, the rate rose from the 1870s to the end of the nineteenth century, but by the 1920s it had dropped to less than two-thirds of the level in the 1870s (line 40). In Western European countries the decline began in the last quarter of the nineteenth century; and by the 1950s the rates were about half of those of the mid-nineteenth century. Thus beginning with the mid-nineteenth century for the older developed countries of Europe and early in the nineteenth century for the European offshoots overseas, high rates of population growth were attained *despite* declining birth rates and were due either to a decline in death rates or to immigration.

In the less developed European countries the declines

49

in the birth rates began much later; and in many of the less developed areas of the world, particularly Latin America, Asia, and Africa, the downward trend is still to come. Yet in almost all these countries the decline in the death rates has already begun and, as noted above, is proceeding rapidly. The rise in the rate of natural increase, produced by the widening gap between the declining death rate and the stationary birth rate, has thus been striking; and it reproduces, in an exaggerated fashion, the gap observed in the earlier decades of the nineteenth century in the older countries of Western Europe.

Of the many aspects of the modern decline in birth rates, only two can be noted here.[12] First, the decline was due to decisions by the people concerned, not to a rise in involuntary sterility; and the decisions were within the framework of marriage, i.e. the decline was in marital fertility, owing to the spread of family planning, rather than to delay in age of marriage or decline in the marriage rate. Second, fertility and birth rates are much affected by economic and related factors: cross-section data for several developed countries until the very recent periods reveal a negative association between level of income and economic status and the birth or fertility rate (evident also in the lower birth rates for urban groups compared with the rural, and for well educated groups compared with the poorly educated). These differences shown in cross-section analysis may reflect the gradual spread of birth control and family limitation practices from the upper income and social groups downward. Whatever the case, the negative association between birth rates, and possibly rates of natural increase, and income position is an important factor in recent economic growth.

12. For a discussion summarizing a vast literature see U.N., *Population Trends,* Chap. 5; and for an interesting analysis of the relation between fertility and social structure see Kingsley Davis and Judith Blake, "Social Structure and Fertility: An Analytic Framework," *Economic Development and Cultural Change, 4* (April 1956).

One result of the combination of long-term trends in birth and death rates should be noted. In the earlier phases of the modern period, and even more so in premodern times, both birth and death rates were high—running from 30 to over 50 per thousand—and the rate of natural increase was small. Death rates declined before birth rates and, as a result, the rate of natural increase rose appreciably. In developed countries and in many underdeveloped, death rates are down to 10 per thousand, and there is an obvious limit to further reduction. Barring catastrophes, the future course of death rates will be either stationary or slightly downward, and the effects of such trends on future rates of population growth are bound to be minor—certainly compared with the declines of 20 or more points witnessed since the mid-eighteenth century. Hence, except in the rapidly diminishing number of countries with death rates still well above 10 per thousand, the future course of population growth is primarily a matter of birth rates.

For individual countries, the units with which we shall deal in most of the discussion of economic growth, population change is a combination of natural increase with the balance of international migration. The migration of interest here is the movement across the country's boundaries of people intending a change in long-term residence, and excludes tourism, commuting, and other movements involving temporary stays. Ideally, the data would be based on this distinction of intentions and would cover a long period and the full flow across all national boundaries, but long-term series with complete coverage of international migration are not available. We do have fairly comprehensive long-term estimates of *intercontinental* emigration and immigration and long-term records of emigration and immigration for selected individual countries. Fortunately, data are available for Europe, the continent with the largest intercontinental emigration in the modern period; and since such emigration far outran the intra-European, inter-

TABLE 2.4

Intercontinental Migration, 1801 to 1946–55
(absolute figures in millions)

| | 1801–20 (1) | 1821–50 (2) | 1851–80 (3) | 1881–1910 (4) | 1911–40 (5) | 1946–55 (6) |
|---|---|---|---|---|---|---|
| *Emigration from Europe* | | | | | | |
| 1. *Total flow, per decade* | | | | | | |
| a. Gross | 0.12 | 0.98 | 2.89 | 8.49 | 5.39 | na |
| b. Net | 0.12 | 0.90 | 2.37 | 5.89 | 3.32 | 4.36 |
| 2. *As % of average population* | | | | | | |
| a. Gross | 0.1 | 0.4 | 1.0 | 2.2 | 1.1 | na |
| b. Net | 0.1 | 0.4 | 0.8 | 1.5 | 0.7 | 0.8 |
| 3. *Share in net decennial change in population plus emigration (%)* | | | | | | |
| a. Gross | 0.9 | 5.2 | 11.7 | 19.5 | 14.4 | na |
| b. Net | 0.9 | 4.8 | 9.8 | 14.4 | 9.4 | 6.8 |
| *Immigration into the United States* | | | | | | |
| 4. *Total flow, per decade* | | | | | | |
| a. Gross | 0.12 | 0.82 | 2.57 | 5.91 | 3.46 | 1.95 |
| b. Net | 0.12 | 0.75 | 2.11 | 4.10 | 2.13 | 1.70 |
| 5. *As % of average population* | | | | | | |
| a. Gross | 1.7 | 5.5 | 7.2 | 8.5 | 3.0 | 1.3 |
| b. Net | 1.7 | 5.0 | 5.9 | 5.9 | 1.9 | 1.1 |
| 6. *Share in net decennial change in population (%)* | | | | | | |
| a. Gross | 5.6 | 18.0 | 28.7 | 42.4 | 26.2 | 7.7 |
| b. Net | 5.6 | 16.5 | 23.5 | 29.4 | 16.1 | 6.7 |

*Sources: Lines 1a and 1b:* Gross emigration from Europe beginning in 1846 is from Kirk, *Europe's Population in the Interwar Years,* Table 1, p. 279. Extrapolation to the beginning of the nineteenth century was by data in Gustav Sundbärg, *Aperçus Statistiques Internationaux, 11* (Stockholm, 1908), Table 57, p. 107. We shifted from gross to net in cols. 1–5 by the ratios of gross to net immigration into the United States, lines 4a and 4b below. Line 1b, col. 6 is from Dudley Kirk, "Major Migrations since World War II," in Milbank Memorial Fund, *Selected Studies of Migration since World War II* (New York, 1958), Table 1, pp. 18–19.

*Lines 2a and 2b:* Decadal flow expressed as percentages of population at midperiod (1810 for col. 1; average of 1830 and 1840 for col. 2; average of 1860 and 1870 for col. 3; average of 1890 and 1900 for col. 4; average of 1920 and 1930 for col. 5; 1950 for col. 6). Underlying population estimates for cols. 1–4 are from Sundbärg, *Aperçus Statistiques, 11,* Table 11, pp. 34–35; for cols. 5 and 6 from U.N., *Demographic Yearbook, 1963,* Table 2, the average for 1920 and 1930 reduced 35 million to exclude Asiatic Russia.

# Growth of Population and Product

*Lines 3a and 3b:* Percentage shares of lines 1a and 1b in the sum of net change in total population and either gross or net emigration. The underlying population figures are from the sources cited for lines 2a and 2b, except that for col. 5 the 1910 figure was extrapolated from the 1900 estimate by European population, given in W. S. Woytinsky, *Die Welt in Zahlen, 1* (Berlin, 1925), 24; the U.N. population figure for 1940 was reduced 40 million to exclude Asiatic Russia; and the change in col. 6 was roughly estimated to be 60 million, the difference between the 1945 and the 1955 estimates.

*Lines 4a and 4b:* The gross immigration data beginning with 1820 are from United States, Bureau of the Census, *Historical Statistics of the United States, Colonial Times to 1957* (Washington, 1961), Series C 88, pp. 56–57. Col. 1 is based on the figure of 250,000 for the period between the close of the Revolutionary War and 1819, cited in ibid., p. 48. Net immigration for 1821–1940 is from Simon Kuznets and Ernest Rubin, "Immigration and the Foreign Born," National Bureau of Economic Research, *Occasional Paper 46* (New York, 1954), table on p. 94, using the Willcox estimates for 1820–70; for col. 1 we assumed that gross and net were identical; for col. 6 to derive net we used departures of immigrants given in *Historical Statistics*, Series C 156, p. 64.

*Lines 5a–6b:* The underlying population figures (for continental U.S.) are from ibid., Series A 20, p. 8 and A 1, p. 7 for cols. 1–5; from U.N., *Demographic Yearbook, 1960*, Table 4 for col 6. For procedure and selection of years see source notes for lines 2 and 3.

national migration,[13] we can gain some notion of the most important flows in international migration from the intercontinental movements (Table 2.4).

The bulk of total intercontinental emigration, for which we have estimates since the 1800s, was from Europe—over 95 per cent of the total for 1846–1932; and the bulk of intercontinental immigration was to the United States until the very recent years—almost 58 per cent of the total for 1821–1932.[14] It is highly significant that the populations of Asia and Africa barely participated in this flow during the nineteenth and twentieth centuries and that the preponderant bulk of emigrants, almost all from Europe, went to North America (67 per cent for 1821–1932), Australia and New Zealand (6 per cent), and two countries in Latin America (Argentina and Brazil, with 11 and 7 per cent, respectively). The movement was thus largely limited to Europe and the

13. Dudley Kirk, *Europe's Population in the Interwar Years* (Princeton, 1946), pp. 97–104.

14. For these and other data in this paragraph see W. S. and E. S. Woytinsky, *World Population and Production,* Table 33, p. 72.

few European offshoots overseas, in North America and Oceania.

With this introductory observation, we may comment on the major findings suggested by Table 2.4, keeping in mind that the difference between gross and net migration is the movement in the opposite direction.

Even if we allow for understatement, the ratios of emigration to average population and even to population change seem small, but two aspects must be emphasized for proper interpretation. First, through most of the nineteenth and in the early twentieth century emigration from Europe was essentially voluntary, unrestricted, and in response to greater economic opportunities in the country of destination. Emigration was thus dominated by persons in prime working ages; comparisons with labor force and changes in it would be more significant. If we assume realistically that the labor force was between 35 and 45 per cent of total population and assume somewhat unrealistically that *all* migrants were members of the labor force, the relevant percentages would be more than twice as large as in Table 2.4. The second consideration bearing on European emigration (see lines 1–3) is that the base is too wide and the time periods may be too long. During the nineteenth and early twentieth centuries, when intercontinental emigration was high and unimpeded by legal restrictions either at origin or at destination, the identity of the countries in Europe with high emigration proportions changed continuously—moving from the northwestern to northern to central to southern and eastern areas, as different countries entered the phase of transition to modern economic growth that displaced people in agriculture and in some urban occupations (with the conspicuous exception of Ireland where the emigration peak was due to an early breakdown of the rural economy rather than to the beginning of its technological and organizational transformation). Data for these crucial periods for individual countries would yield emigration proportions much larger than those in Table 2.4. To illustrate, the data on immigrants to the United States by country of origin for the single decade of largest immigration, show (to use just two cases) that Scandinavian immigrants in 1880–89, 672 thousand, constituted over 7 per cent of the total population of the countries of origin; Italian immigrants in 1905–14, 2.2 million, amounted to over 6 per cent of Italy's population.[15]

With such rates of inflow into the United States alone, and the corresponding proportions to the labor force over twice as high, the quantitative importance of the outflow, which siphoned off during a decade perhaps more than the decade's total increase in the labor force, becomes apparent. Undoubtedly, intercontinental (and presumably other international) emigration served as a safety valve for successive European countries as they entered the initial phases of modern economic growth with their dislocating effects on population and an accelerated natural increase. Likewise, the importance of this immigration for the major countries of destination, exemplified by the United States, is obvious. With the share of net immigration in additions to total population ranging from 16 to 29 per cent (line 6b) and thus perhaps from a quarter to a half of the total increase in the labor force, the quantitative contribution of immigration to the growth of population and labor force in the United States is impressive.[16]

15. The immigration data are from *Historical Statistics of the United States*, Series C 92 and C 99, p. 56. Population for Sweden is from Erik Lindahl, Einar Dahlgren, and Karin Kock, *National Income of Sweden, 1861–1930* (London, 1937), Part Two, Table 64, pp. 4–5; for Norway from Juul Bjerke, "Some Aspects of Long-Term Economic Growth of Norway," a paper presented at the 1959 Conference of the International Association for Research in Income and Wealth held at Portoroz (mimeo.), Table II.3; for Denmark from Kjeld Bjerke and Niels Ussing, *Danmarks Nationalprodukt, 1870–1950* (Copenhagen, 1958), Table 1, p. 142; and for Italy from Istituto Centrale di Statistica, *Indagine Statistica sullo Sviluppo del Reddito Nazionale dell' Italia dal 1861 al 1956* (Rome, 1957), Table 37, pp. 251–52.

16. The comparison of net immigration with net changes in population should properly allow for deaths of the former within the average decade. But the resulting downward adjustment of the ratios would be minor. Decadal deaths of immigrants in 1870–1900 in the United States were not much more than 5 per cent (see Kuznets and Rubin, "Immigration and the Foreign Born," Table B-4, p. 100).

The significance of intercontinental, and presumably international, migration in the growth of countries of origin and of destination in the nineteenth and early twentieth centuries lends importance to the failure of Asia, Africa, and much of Latin America to participate—even before World War I—and to the sharp decline in these flows after World War I. Not only did migration decline because of wars and legal restrictions, but its character changed—particularly between the late 1920s and early 1930s and until the very recent decade—away from economically oriented movement of people largely in the prime working ages toward refugee-type movement of people with a much wider spread by age and sex (and in some years with emphasis on the dependent young and old). Perhaps it merits specific notice that Japan, which entered the phase of modern economic growth well before the twentieth century, could not fully participate in the emigration toward the more developed areas. Nor were those European and other countries that began industrializing in the 1920s in a position to participate in the free and large flow that prevailed before World War I— and not only because of restriction in countries of destination. In some of the latecomers to industrialization, e.g. the U.S.S.R. and other Communist countries, exit was barred by the authoritarian structure of society, which served to isolate the population and prevent exposure to the temptations of the demonstration effect of the more developed countries. Thus restrictions at points of origin and destination both tended to reduce the migration adjustments to economic growth to levels far below those prevailing in the nineteenth and early twentieth centuries.

### SOME ECONOMIC IMPLICATIONS OF POPULATION GROWTH

The modern population trends sketched briefly in the preceding two sections—the acceleration and high rates of increase in numbers, the decline in death rates, the trends in birth rates, and the great volume (for most of the period) of international economically oriented migration—have

56

been, in good part, a result of economic growth, if we regard such growth as the capacity to sustain increasing numbers at the same or higher material levels of living. Underlying both processes was an increase in the stock of useful knowledge, relating to the problems not only of health and prolongation of life but also of economic production. In turn, the modern demographic patterns, once established, also set conditions for modern economic growth and may have contributed significantly to the rise in economic performance per capita. It is with these consequences of the population trends for modern economic growth that we are concerned here. In the present state of our knowledge, these specific effects of population growth are not easy to discern, let alone to measure; and the discussion must perforce be speculative and illustrative rather than complete and definitive.

Let us assume that those countries that did develop during the last two centuries could, given the same accumulation of reproducible capital, increase their population without reducing per capita product—either because of access to an increasing stock of natural resources due to migration overseas and to revolutionary changes in the transportation and trade network, or because technological progress allowed substitution for and economy in the use of available natural resources. Given this crucial assumption, it can be argued that the modern increase in population has contributed to a rise in product per capita in several direct ways. First, the composition of population by age has shifted in favor of the most productive years. This point can be illustrated by comparing the age structures of population today, for countries grouped by per capita income and hence economic performance. If we consider ages 15–59 as the most productive, we find that the average ratio of that group to total population is about 58 per cent for the 19 countries with per capita income of $575 or more and only about 51.3 per cent for the 34 countries with per capita income of less than $200.[17] Second, the decline in birth

17. See Table 8.2, p. 438.

rates, offset fully or partly by the decline in mortality, has eliminated the enormous waste involved in rearing a large number of infants only to have them die before they could contribute to society's product and welfare; and it also released a large proportion of the potential female labor force to gainful occupations.[18] Third, the decline in the death rates has meant a decline in the rates of morbidity, i.e. of the incidence of disease with its temporarily or permanently disabling effects on the productivity of the population. Fourth, increasing population with undiminished per capita product has meant an increasing total product and greater opportunities for economies of scale—either for individual countries or, through international trade, for large population complexes and markets. Fifth, a high rate of expansion of production and markets—and a steadier rate resulting from control over epidemics and other disasters that make for violent changes in death rates and in population growth—has provided more favorable conditions for venturesome entrepreneurial undertakings; for under such conditions the penalties of errors of overexpansion are far milder than under conditions of slow and fluctuating growth. Insofar as entrepreneurial proclivity to expand and take risks is an important factor in economic growth, it contributes to a higher rate of growth per capita. Finally, given sustained levels of living and hence of training and skill per capita, a larger population means more potential contributors to the stock of useful knowledge; and there may well be advantages of scale in the production of useful knowledge equally as important as in the production of simpler economic goods.[19]

The above list—far from complete—of the possible direct contributions of population growth to rise in product per

18. For an interesting discussion see W. Lee Hansen, "A Note on the Cost of Children's Mortality," *Journal of Political Economy, 65* (June 1957).

19. For a discussion of this point and some related ones see Simon Kuznets, "Population Change and Aggregate Output," in Universities-National Bureau of Economic Research Committee, *Demographic and Economic Change in Developed Countries* (Princeton, 1960).

capita, under conditions of effective supply of natural resources, is not presented as a claim that all the effects are favorable. Adverse effects include: the reduction of savings and capital accumulation rates resulting from too high a population growth; the limit on economies of scale beyond which expansion of population and markets would have no positive effects on productivity. There is the possibility that in some countries and periods a lower rate of population growth might have resulted in a higher rate of growth of product per capita (e.g. in the early transition phases in many older European countries). The purpose of the remarks above is merely to stress the often overlooked expansive effects of population growth and the role that they may play in explaining the high rate of growth in per capita product.

But some specific aspects of the modern population trends set conditions within which economic growth takes place and so constitute constraints to which the economic growth processes must adjust. While there may be some ultimate effects on growth in per capita product, our interest lies in the chain of consequences by which these are brought about.

Consider, for example, the greater decline in the death rates of younger groups and of urban populations and the possible effects of an alternative set of differentials in the reduction of mortality. If we were to assume that the death rates for infants and the young groups had declined slightly, but that there had been a much larger decline in the death rates of adult and more advanced age groups, accompanied, as would be natural, by the preservation of vigor and health many years longer, a number of important consequences would follow. To begin with, the higher rate of natural increase could not be attained unless the fertility rate *rose,* since the increased proportion of females beyond the childbearing ages would have to be offset by increased fertility within the childbearing ages. The continuation of high death rates at infant and young ages would mean at least continuation of, or more likely a rise in, already high fertility rates, with all the effects on family size, continued heavy domestic engagement of women until they have passed the childbearing ages, and everything else that follows. Then, the survival of people to more advanced ages, combined with retention of productive power, would necessitate considerable adjustment—extension of working life, room for a more prolonged accumulation of skill and experience, shifting proportions between working life and retirement, and changes in the structure of family units, consumers' demand, and general patterns of life which we may have difficulty in visualizing. Given the dependence of the life cycle of generations, the structure of the family, and the proportions of various age groups in the population on the differential impact of declining death rates, and given the variety of ways in which these characteristics of the population shape the structure and pace of economic life, obviously the latter would have been quite different if the reduction in the age-specific mortality rates had been different.

The differential impact of reduction of mortality on urban and rural populations has been equally important. If, to emphasize the argument, we were to assume that the death rates declined only in rural areas and remained as high in the cities as they were in premodern times—i.e. higher than the high birth rates—the drains on the population of the cities would have limited urbanization, since it would have threatened an absolute population decline (and would in any case have been a major obstacle to cityward migration). Since urbanization is a necessary condition for industrialization and modern economic growth and essential to the economies of scale of modern industry, the obstacles to modern economic growth would have been formidable indeed. Obviously the ability to reduce the mortality of dense population aggregates has been an indispensable requirement of the modern economic process.

Similarly far-reaching social and economic consequences may be ascribed to the decline in the birth rate and the more extensive international migration toward the areas of greater economic opportunity. The combination of low birth and death rates that permitted the transition from the large, extended, multiple-generation family to the smaller, nuclear two- or one-generation family, and the differential spread of lower birth rates, reflected in the inverse association in cross-section data between birth and natural increase rates and income per capita, have both been of major importance in shaping economic growth. They have influenced the adjustment of human beings to economic opportunities, the structure of ultimate demand, and the allocation of resources to rearing and training of the young—to name a few effects. In particular, the continuous disparity within countries between differential rates of natural increase of several groups in the population, on the one hand, and the locus of differential economic opportunities, on the other, have necessitated vast internal migration—to be discussed in a later chapter in connection with changes in industrial structure accompanying modern economic growth. This internal migration has meant a removal of the younger generations from the family origins to the locus of their active participation in the economic system. It has meant a detachment of the individual from his place of origin, a break between blood and economic ties, and has facilitated the adjustment to and selection of economic opportunities by means of objective tests of performance rather than on the basis of family and status. The possible impact on the efficiency of the modern economy as a productive system is profound; and the possible contribution to the rise in product per capita is of major dimensions. In this respect the effects of international migration have been even more marked. The uprooting of the migrant—his separation not only from his family but also from the institutions and surroundings of his native country—has meant not only an orientation toward economic opportunities and a drive to exploit them that were far less restrained by traditions and ties than they would have been at home, but also a far greater concentration on economic success. These shifts in orientation may well have been more important than the mere transfer of human resources to areas of greater economic opportunity; and they continued beyond the first generation immigrant to at least the second, if not further.[20]

Modern demographic patterns have affected the structure of the family, the relations of successive generations and the mechanisms by which people adjusted to changing and differing economic opportunities; and have thus shaped much of the structure of modern economic growth, while indirectly contributing to the high rate of increase in product per capita. Finally, population trends have affected the general views and attitudes of people; and these views and attitudes, though elusive and difficult to formulate unequivocally, are important in shaping behavior in the creation of and response to economic opportunities. The growing control over death, particularly over its catastrophic and less predictable aspects represented by epidemics and infectious diseases, and the increasing use of deliberate human decisions in birth control and family planning must both have reflected and strengthened a belief in man's power to command his destiny, or at least to be relatively free from unknown and uncontrollable terrors. Just as increasing knowledge and power over the rest of nature—the growth in basic science and applied technology—must have contributed to the beliefs and views of modern man on natural order and on the possibility of employing it for useful ends, so must the increasing control over death and disposition over birth have contributed greatly to modern attitudes, which in turn must have played a large role in facilitating modern economic growth, through their emphasis on progress, the value of systematic knowledge and plan, and receptivity to new ideas with respect to nature and society. Despite the continuing existence of attitudes unfavorable to many problems of social adjustment, modern man's general outlook is surely far more favorable to eco-

20. For a more detailed discussion of effects of migration, particularly internal migration, on economic growth, see Simon Kuznets, "Introduction," in Hope T. Eldridge and Dorothy Swaine Thomas, *Demographic Analyses and Interrelations*, vol. III of *Population Redistribution and Economic Growth, United States, 1870–1950*, American Philosophical Society Memoirs, *61* (Philadelphia, 1964).

nomic growth than that of his forebears in premodern times or, for that matter, than that of his contemporaries in the less developed, more tradition-bound countries. And to this change in views the greater control over deaths and births, reflected in modern population trends, must have contributed. While modern man, like his ancestors, still is born in travail and dies in pain, there is more power of human decision and far less unpredictable terror over both birth and death; and insofar as this power strengthens the belief that man's fate is in man's hands, it contributes to material advancement in this world.

### GROWTH OF PRODUCT, TOTAL AND PER CAPITA

Provided that per capita product remained the same or declined only slightly, the much higher rates of population growth in modern times necessarily meant higher rates of growth in total product. The capacity to sustain rapidly increasing numbers at the same or only slightly lower levels of living, in and of itself, can be viewed as economic growth. But the distinctive characteristic of modern economic growth is the combination of high rates of increase in population with high rates of increase in per capita product—with the obvious implication of enormous increases in total product. It is to the growth in per capita and total product that we now turn.

A selective view is provided in Table 2.5. The choice of countries is necessarily limited by the availability of long-term estimates with fairly continuous coverage. But we limited the selection further to countries for which the records revealed a sufficiently long period—no shorter than five decades—of the high rates of increase of population and per capita product that are characteristic of modern economic growth. For all fourteen countries in Table 2.5 the record covers at least half a century, and for over half of them the coverage is close to a century. Most of the developed countries are included; and the choice is wide enough to convey an adequate notion of the overall rates of

TABLE 2.5

Growth of National Product, Population, and per Capita Product, Selected Countries, Long Periods (product in constant prices)

| | Duration of period (years) (1) | Rate of growth per decade (%) | | | Coefficient of multiplication in a century | | |
|---|---|---|---|---|---|---|---|
| | | Total product (2) | Population (3) | Product per capita (4) | Total product (5) | Population (6) | Product per capita (7) |
| *England and Wales–United Kingdom* | | | | | | | |
| 1. 1700 to 1780 | 80 | 5.3 | 3.2 | 2.0 | 1.7 | 1.4 | 1.2 |
| 2. 1780 to 1881 | 101 | 28.2 | 13.1 | 13.4 | 12.0 | 3.4 | 3.5 |
| 3. 1855–59 to 1957–59 | 101 | 21.1 | 6.1 | 14.1 | 6.8 | 1.8 | 3.7 |
| *France* | | | | | | | |
| 4. 1841–50 to 1960–62 | 105.5 | 20.8 | 2.5 | 17.9 | 6.6 | 1.3 | 5.2 |
| *Germany–West Germany* | | | | | | | |
| 5. 1851–55 to 1871–75 | 20 | 17.6 | 7.7 | 9.2 | | | |
| 6. 1871–75 to 1960–62 | 88 | 31.1 | 11.2 | 17.9 | 15.0 | 2.9 | 5.2 |
| *Netherlands* | | | | | | | |
| 7. 1900–04 to 1960–62 | 59 | 29.7 | 14.3 | 13.5 | 13.5 | 3.8 | 3.5 |
| *Switzerland* | | | | | | | |
| 8. 1890–99 to 1957–59 | 63.5 | 25.7 | 8.3 | 16.1 | 9.8 | 2.2 | 4.4 |
| *Denmark* | | | | | | | |
| 9. 1870–74 to 1960–62 | 89 | 31.8 | 10.4 | 19.4 | 15.8 | 2.7 | 5.9 |
| *Norway* | | | | | | | |
| 10. 1865–74 to 1960–62 | 91.5 | 29.0 | 8.4 | 19.0 | 12.7 | 2.2 | 5.7 |
| *Sweden* | | | | | | | |
| 11. 1861–65 to 1960–62 | 98 | 36.9 | 6.7 | 28.3 | 23.2 | 1.9 | 12.1 |

| | | | | | | | |
|---|---|---|---|---|---|---|---|
| *Italy* | | | | | | | |
| 12. 1861–65 to 1898–1902 | 37 | 9.7 | 6.8 | 2.7 | 10.7 | 1.9 | 5.6 |
| 13. 1898–1902 to 1960–62 | 61 | 26.8 | 6.8 | 18.7 | | | |
| *United States* | | | | | | | |
| 14. 1839 to 1960–62 | 122 | 42.5 | 21.6 | 17.2 | 34.5 | 7.1 | 4.9 |
| *Canada* | | | | | | | |
| 15. 1870–74 to 1960–62 | 89 | 40.7 | 19.1 | 18.1 | 30.3 | 5.7 | 5.3 |
| *Australia* | | | | | | | |
| 16. 1861–65 to 1959/60–1961/62 | 97.5 | 34.1 | 24.2 | 8.0 | 18.6 | 8.7 | 2.2 |
| *Japan* | | | | | | | |
| 17. 1879–81 to 1959–61 | 80 | 42.0 | 12.3 | 26.4 | 33.4 | 3.2 | 10.4 |
| *European Russia–U.S.S.R.* | | | | | | | |
| 18. 1860 to 1913 | 53 | 30.2 | 13.8 | 14.4 | 14.0 | 3.6 | 3.8 |
| 19. 1913 to 1958 | 45 | 35.7 | 6.4 | 27.4 | | | |
| 20. 1928 to 1958 | 30 | 53.8 | 6.9 | 43.9 | 74.1 | 1.9 | 38.0 |

*Sources:* For all countries except Australia, data are from Simon Kuznets, *Postwar Economic Growth: Four Lectures* (Cambridge, Mass., 1964), Table 4, pp. 63–66. For Australia, total product is from N. G. Butlin, *Australian Domestic Product, Investment and Foreign Borrowing, 1861–1938/39* (Cambridge, 1962), Table 269, pp. 460–61, carried forward to 1948/49 by real product in constant prices, obtained by correspondence from B. D. Haig, Australia National University; to 1953/54 by gross national product in Colin Clark, *Conditions of Economic Progress* (3d ed., London, 1957), Table IX, pp. 90 ff.; to 1961/62 by data supplied by the U.N. Statistical Office. Population in 1863 is based on the 1860 figure in Australia, Bureau of Census and Statistics' *Year Book of the Commonwealth of Australia, 1951* (Canberra, 1951), p. 521 carried forward by the annual series on population increase in N. G. Butlin, "Colonial Socialism in Australia, 1860–1900," in Hugh G. J. Aitken, ed., *The State and Economic Growth* (New York, 1959), Table 2, p. 33. Population in 1960 is from the U.N, *Demographic Yearbook, 1963*, Table 4.

modern growth of total and per capita product as well as of the range of differences in the latter.[21]

For some countries in Table 2.5, e.g. England, Germany, Italy, and Russia, the records cover a period (of at least twenty years) before the acceleration of the rate of product associated with the initial phases of modern economic growth; and the rates for these early years are shown but are excluded from the averages for the long spans. The latter cover the period since modern economic growth began and are adjusted for changes in territory (when these involve significant breaks in the population totals) but include periods of war and similar disturbances. To exclude such periods would require the resolution of the difficult question whether only the years of actual conflict or the immediate prewar and postwar years should also be omitted. The exclusion would imply a debatable assumption that proneness to war is not a characteristic of modern economic growth, and that such growth should therefore be limited to conditions of peace. Hence, these averages record the performance of the economies in the process of modern economic growth, including whatever expansive or depressive effects wars and their aftermaths have had.

Naturally, the underlying measures of total product are synthetic and, while generally conforming to accepted national accounting definitions, are subject to a variety of errors. No firm magnitudes can be attached to these errors; yet it is fair to say that those arising out of difficulties of estimation (as distinct from the biases inherent in the definitions and choices of price weights) are not large enough to

21. Data for other countries can be found in Clark, *Conditions of Economic Progress* (3d ed.) and Simon Kuznets, "Quantitative Aspects of the Economic Growth of Nations: I. Levels and Variability of Rates of Growth," *Economic Development and Cultural Change, 5* (October 1956). The Kuznets paper is one of a series, of which nine have been published and the tenth is in press, with the general title, "Quantitative Aspects of the Economic Growth of Nations," which will be referred to hereafter by the short title, "Quantitative Aspects," followed by the Roman numeral indicating the specific paper in the series; details appear in the List of References.

invalidate the major conclusions that follow. The conceptually imposed biases discussed in Chapter 1 may be more serious, particularly if one rejects the underlying definitions of economic product or is concerned with the effects of inadequate price bases. But if the definitions are considered workable, and an allowance is made for any distortion introduced by inadequate price weights, the rough magnitudes may serve to reveal at least the major aggregative features of modern economic growth; and we turn now to a listing of those suggested by Table 2.5.

1. While for all countries the rates of population growth are high compared with those that must have prevailed in premodern times, they differ considerably over the long periods covered. Even if we omit France with a population increase of only 2.5 per cent per decade, the range from 6 or 7 per cent for the United Kingdom, Italy, Sweden, and the U.S.S.R. (1928–58) to 20 per cent or more for the United States, Canada, and Australia is wide indeed. The difference is between some of the older countries of Europe and the younger countries overseas.

2. Except for Australia,[22] the decade rates of growth in per capita product are well above 10 per cent. For some countries, e.g. Sweden, Japan, and the U.S.S.R. (1928–58), they are more than 20 per cent per decade, implying enormous multiplication of per capita product if the rates are maintained for a century (as they were in fact in Sweden, and for 80 years in Japan). In general, in subsequent discussion we assume a rate of growth in per capita product of 15 per cent per decade as a typically low limit.

3. No clear association appears to exist in the present sample of countries, or is likely in the other developed coun-

22. The series up to the late 1930s was most elaborately and thoroughly prepared. Division into subperiods indicates that while the rates of growth of per capita product have declined, they were not high even in the early periods. The rate for 1861–1910/11 was 10.1 per cent per decade, compared with 5.0 per cent for 1910/11 to 1959/60–1961/62. Australia may genuinely be at the low range of increase in per capita product; it would require special analysis to ascertain the reasons. A supposition is offered in note 30 below.

tries, between rates of growth of population and of product per capita. Among countries with low rates of population increase—the United Kingdom (for 1855–1959), France, Italy (1898–1962), Sweden, and the U.S.S.R. (1928–58)—the rates of increase in per capita income for the last two are among the highest and those for the first three are rather moderate, if not among the lowest. Among countries with high rates of population increase, the rate of growth in per capita income for Australia is the lowest but those for the United States and Canada are quite high. Apparently other factors—relative availability of natural resources, timing of the inception of the modern growth process, or institutional conditions—complicate the effects of population growth and prevent a simple association between it and growth in per capita product: and population growth itself may have both expansive and depressive effects on the increase in per capita product that differ in their weight in conjunction with other factors.

4. Fairly high rates of growth in per capita product and in population mean, of course, high rates of increase in total product. For periods associated with modern economic growth, these range from a minimum of about 21 per cent per decade for France and the United Kingdom to over 40 per cent for the United States, Canada, and Japan, to over 50 per cent for the U.S.S.R. (1928–58). Continued over periods as long as most in Table 2.5, these rates result in enormous multiplication of the total magnitude of performance: a decadal rate of growth of 20 per cent means a multiplication in a century to over 6 times the initial level; a rate of 50 per cent means a rise to about 58 times the initial level.

Three aspects of the growth rates in product summarized in Table 2.5 deserve emphasis. First, the rates are substantially higher than they must have been in premodern times. This is patently clear for the rates of growth of *total* product since, as already indicated, rates of population increase have been much higher and since, certainly for the countries in Table 2.5 and all now developed countries, per capita product did not decline. But most significant are the high rates of increase in *per capita* product. That they are much higher than those prevailing over similarly long periods before the inception of modern growth can be inferred from a variety of evidence. The most direct are measures of growth in per capita product in immediately preceding periods; and those shown in Table 2.5 (for England and Wales, Germany, Italy, and Russia) are much lower than for the later, modern growth periods. Furthermore, these periods are themselves probably characterized by higher rates of increase in per capita product than the longer stretches of still earlier experience. Data on per capita product over long periods in premodern times are lacking, but we can support the preceding statement by projecting the modern rates of growth backward. A rate of 15 per cent per decade—a moderately low rate for most countries in Table 2.5—means that in a century per capita product rises to over 4 times its initial level; in two centuries the rise is to 16.4 times the early level; in three centuries to 66.2 times. For a decadal rate of growth of 20 per cent, the coefficients of multiplication are 6.2 in a century; 38.3 in two centuries; 237.4 in three centuries. Thus if per capita product had grown 15 per cent per decade for three centuries before the 1960s, per capita product in the 1660s would have been 1/66th of the present level. But a per capita income at even a twentieth of the present levels could not have sustained the population of even the most developed countries; and the assumed rates of growth in per capita product could not have been maintained, in most countries, for over two centuries.[23] It follows that the rates of increase in per capita product in the premodern past could have been as high as the modern rates only if we assumed that per capita product in some more distant past was as high as in the 1960s and had then declined to the

23. For some discussion of the implications of backward projection of modern growth rates for a number of countries see Simon Kuznets, *Six Lectures on Economic Growth* (Glencoe, 1959), Table 3, p. 27 and discussion on pp. 25–26.

low levels immediately preceding modern times—an assumption denied by a variety of historical evidence.[24]

The second feature of modern aggregative growth, not presented in Table 2.5 since it would require a great amount of detail, is the relative steadiness of its rate over time—compared with the variability of such rates in premodern times. This conclusion is highly probable, particularly for rates of growth of total product: viewed in, say, decadal units, the very steadiness of modern population growth, freed from the catastrophic impacts of epidemics and the fluctuations in birth rates associated with them, would make for a greater stability in the rates of growth of total product. Other contributing factors are: technological progress in agriculture, which reduces the chance of crop failures; improvements in transportation, which permit the widening of sources of supply; the decline in the share in total product of agriculture, and the increase in the shares of other industries, technologically more controllable—all basic features of modern growth. Apparently, short of breakdowns of the social system, modern conditions permit a steady growth, even in per capita product, that was not possible in premodern times. And except during periods of violent revolutionary change in institutions and of major wars—both necessarily limited—modern growth rates are steady; successive subperiods (say of one or two decades)

24. It is tempting to offer as support for our suggestion that the rates of growth in per capita income in premodern times were low, the general views of contemporary writers on economic and social progress. The arguments of writers in the seventeenth and eighteenth centuries that population tends to grow faster than resources and that a rise in per capita income is only a matter of a temporary lag of population growth, and the retention even by John Stuart Mill in the middle of the nineteenth century of the prevalent conviction of the imminence of the stationary state because of the pressure of limited natural resources seem to indicate that the growth of per capita product in the past was too low and its cumulative impact too slight to modify such views. But argument from writings of theorists whose conclusions have not been established by testable empirical evidence is treacherous; and its pursuit, to be effective, would take us far afield.

rarely show a drop in the rate of growth below a fairly high positive minimum.[25]

The third aspect that merits stressing is the differences among countries in rates of growth, and particularly the effects of such differences on rapid shifts in economic magnitude. Even if we exclude the countries not fully developed and the most recent entrants into the process of modern economic growth, and confine our attention to the European countries other than Italy, we find wide differences in rates of growth—with implied effects on shifts of weight among countries. Consider as an illustration France and Germany: if, using the entries in Table 2.5, we assumed for these two countries rates of growth in total product from the mid-nineteenth century of about 21 and 31 per cent per decade, respectively, and assumed that both countries start with the same total product, within half a century that of Germany would be 1.4 times that of France; within less than a century it would be double.

The three aspects of growth of product just noted are interrelated. The capacity for *steady* growth makes *high* average rates of growth possible and likely; for if too many calamitous breaks should occur, obvious difficulties would arise in fully compensating for the catastrophes and achieving a high average level. The high average rates of growth make relatively moderate *proportional* differences in rates productive of large contrasts in coefficients of multiplication over longer periods: over a century the difference between the coefficients would be between 13.8 and 6.2 or over 2 to 1, when the decadal rates are 30 and 20, respectively (as they are in modern times, judging by Table 2.5); and between 2.4 and 1.8, or only 1.3 to 1, when the decadal rates are 9 and 6 per cent, respectively.[26] Such interrelations,

25. For a discussion of this aspect of growth of annual gross national product in the United States since the 1870s see Kuznets, *Capital in the American Economy,* Table 1, p. 43, and the text on pp. 40–45 on continuity of trend.

26. For a brief discussion of this point see Kuznets, "Quantitative Aspects: I," pp. 25–27.

and others to be noted, mean that the high rates of modern economic growth carry a variety of implications with them —important both in explaining how such growth comes about and in evaluating its consequences.

### GROWTH OF EFFICIENCY

The growth of national product in modern times may have been due either to an increase in input of resources, i.e. labor and capital, or to an increase in efficiency, i.e. greater output per unit of input, or to both. That a substantial proportion is attributable to a rise in inputs seems obvious: the enormous addition to population must have meant a large increase in the labor force, and the rise in total product must have led to an appreciable rise in the volume of capital accumulation and hence at least of reproducible capital. A significant share of the rise in total product must therefore be statistically allocable to an increase in inputs of labor and capital. The interesting question relates to the growth of product *per capita*. Has there been an increase in resource input per capita to which a substantial proportion of the rise in per capita product should be allocated? It is to this question that the discussion is directed.

Table 2.6 deals with the input of labor, in the simple form of man-hours per head of population derived from shares of labor force in total population and the number of hours per man-year. The table is based largely on Colin Clark's estimates of the labor force, excluding women in agriculture,[27] and of hours of work per man-year. The labor force is the total engaged, regardless of actual employment, and the hours are assumed to be those prevailing under full employment. Labor force and hours should be

27. The exclusion of women in agriculture means a higher measured rate of growth of the labor force—labor input—and therefore a correspondingly lower rate of growth of the residual reflecting efficiency. Since we conclude that the rise in per capita product in modern economic growth has been due largely to the rise in efficiency, the use of labor force including women in agriculture would have only reinforced this conclusion.

72

**TABLE 2.6**

**Man-hours of Labor per Capita, Selected Countries, Long Periods**

| | Years in period (1) | Rise in % share of labor force in population | | % Decline in length of work-year (4) | % Decline in man-hours per capita | |
|---|---|---|---|---|---|---|
| | | Absolute (2) | As % of share in initial year (3) | | Full period (5) | Per decade (6) |
| 1. Great Britain, 1870–1952 | 82 | 5.5 | 13.1 | 19.9 | 9.4 | 1.1 |
| 2. France, 1840–1952 | 112 | 2.1 | 5.4 | 38.8 | 35.5 | 3.2 |
| 3. Belgium, 1846–1951 | 105 | 5.5 | 15.8 | 30.4 | 19.5 | 1.9 |
| 4. Germany, 1877–1950 | 73 | 6.3 | 15.8 | 24.4 | 12.5 | 1.7 |
| 5. Netherlands, 1900–52 | 52 | 1.3 | 3.6 | 26.1 | 23.4 | 4.5 |
| 6. Switzerland, 1890–1951 | 61 | −0.3 | −0.7 | 24.4 | 24.9 | 4.1 |
| 7. Denmark, 1870–1951 | 81 | 10.2 | 29.4 | 35.5 | 16.5 | 2.0 |
| 8. Norway, 1865–1955 | 90 | 2.8 | 7.2 | 25.7 | 20.3 | 2.3 |
| 9. Sweden, 1861–1952 | 91 | 5.3 | 14.6 | 28.5 | 18.1 | 2.0 |
| 10. Italy, 1901–53 | 52 | −1.4 | −3.6 | 36.5 | 38.8 | 7.5 |
| 11. United States, 1850–1952 | 102 | 8.1 | 25.2 | 39.5 | 24.2 | 2.4 |
| 12. Canada, 1870–1952 | 82 | 5.8 | 18.3 | 35.0 | 23.1 | 2.8 |
| 13. Australia, 1901–03 to 1952/53 | 50.5 | −0.1 | −0.2 | 17.6 | 17.8 | 3.5 |

*Sources:* Except for Germany and Norway, based on Clark, *Conditions of Economic Progress*, 3d ed., Tables IX ff., pp. 90 ff. For each country population was derived by dividing total real income by real income per head; labor force and hours per year were given. For Germany, hours and labor force are from Paul Jostock, "The Long-Term Growth of National Income in Germany," in Simon Kuznets, ed., *Income and Wealth, Series V* (London, 1955), Table V, p. 99 and Table VI, p. 102. For Norway, population and labor force are from Juul Bjerke, "Some Aspects of Long-Term Economic Growth of Norway," Table II.6; and we assumed that the hours per year given in Clark, *Conditions*, Table XXXI, pp. 174–75 for 1891 and 1950 could be used for 1865 and 1955, respectively (the data for Sweden in ibid, Table XXXVII, pp. 181–86 show only a slight change in hours between 1865 and 1891).

measured in this fashion, since underutilization (unemployment and partial employment) reflects inefficiency of the system, and any reduction in the rate of growth of available man-hours due to this factor should not reduce the denominator of the efficiency ratio (ratio of output to resources available for input) since it should not raise the efficiency ratio.

Granted the difficulties of reliable measurement of labor force and hours, the consistency of the finding for the sample of countries and the long periods in Table 2.6 is impressive. For all the countries, except Switzerland, Italy, and Australia, the proportions of labor force to total population show an upward trend. The proportions, 30 per cent or higher in the early years, rise to 40 per cent or more. This rise may have been due to a shift in the age structure of the population in favor of working ages, associated with declines in the birth rates and in the proportions of population *below* working age; or to increasing participation of women in gainful occupations, particularly when women in agriculture are excluded; or to both trends—offsetting the effects of a rise in the age of entry into the labor force and of a lowering of the age of retirement. Whatever the reason, the proportions of gainfully occupied to total population increased; and if customary hours per man-year had remained the same, man-hours per capita would have risen in most countries.

But modern economic growth has been accompanied by a long-term decline in customary working hours per year—by fractions ranging, for the period since the mid-nineteenth century, from less than a fifth to almost two-fifths. By combining the decline in hours per year with the rise in the proportion of the labor force to total population, we can derive the net percentage change in man-hours *per capita* for the full period, i.e. on the basis of Table 2.6: $100 - [(100 - \text{col. } 4) \times (100 + \text{col. } 3) \div 100]$. For all countries in Table 2.6, without exception, the long-term decline in number of man-hours per capita is significant—ranging from about 10 to about 40 per cent for the full period and from over 1 to 7.5 per cent per decade.

If we disregard the rather exceptional results for Italy, the general conclusion is that man-hours per capita declined in most countries between 1.1 and 4.5 per cent per decade. Two inferences immediately follow. First, the increase in national product per capita, observed in Table 2.5, could not have been due to greater input of man-hours per capita, at least as a direct cause—whatever the effects of reduction in hours on the efficiency per man-hour. Second, the rate of rise in product per man-hour was distinctly higher than in product per capita. (The former can be approximated by reference to column 6 of Table 2.6 and column 4 of Table 2.5.) If, in general, the decadal rates of growth in per capita product range from 15 to 30 per cent, those in product per man-hour would range from about 18 to almost 35 per cent.

The measurement of capital input is beset with much greater difficulties than that of input of man-hours. The underlying estimate of capital should include natural resources since their relative supply presumably affects product per capita and per man-hour; and even if we had continuous and comprehensive measures of aggregate capital for the long periods, we would need some basis for deriving *annual input*. Unlike labor, most capital is not perceptibly consumed in the process of production; and we need a riskless return rate that, when applied to capital stock, would yield the current contribution of capital in the process of production.

There are few continuous and comprehensive capital stock series in current prices and even fewer in constant prices. We assembled those available in the attempt to derive some notion of the trends in the ratio of capital to product. Having these trends, we can infer the general order of magnitude of the contribution of capital input to rise in product per capita.

Table 2.7 summarizes the data on trends in capital-

TABLE 2.7

Ratio of Capital to Product, Selected Countries, Long Periods

| | Period (1) | Capital–product ratio | | |
|---|---|---|---|---|
| | | Initial date (2) | Terminal date (3) | % Change (4) |
| *Great Britain, current prices, national income* | | | | |
| 1. Total capital | 1885–1927 | 8.2 | 4.8 | −41 |
| 2. Reproducible | 1865–1933 | 4.6 | 5.0 | 9 |
| *Belgium, current prices, national income* | | | | |
| 3. Total capital | 1846–1950 | 9.3 | 5.4 | −42 |
| *Norway, 1938 prices, ndp* | | | | |
| 4. Net fixed assets | 1865–74 to 1947–56 | 4.0 | 3.2 | −20 |
| *West Germany, 1950 prices, gnp* | | | | |
| 5. Gross fixed assets | 1913 to 1950–55 | 5.4 | 4.0 | −26 |
| *United States, 1929 prices, gnp* | | | | |
| 6. Total capital | 1850–1950 | 3.5 | 2.7 | −23 |
| 7. Reproducible | 1850–1950 | 1.9 | 2.1 | 11 |
| *Australia, current prices, gnp* | | | | |
| 8. Total capital | 1903–1956 | 6.4 | 4.0 | −37 |
| *Japan, 1928–32 prices, national income* | | | | |
| 9. Total capital | 1905–1935 | 7.2 | 5.3 | −26 |
| 10. Reproducible | 1905–1935 | 2.8 | 3.0 | 7 |

*Sources: Lines 1 and 2:* From Deane and Cole, *British Economic Growth,* Table 70, p. 271 and Table 71, p. 275.

*Lines 3, 5, and 8:* From Goldsmith and Saunders, eds., *Income and Wealth, Series VIII,* Table VI, pp. 30–31.

*Line 4:* From Bjerke, "Economic Growth of Norway," Table IV.3.

*Lines 6 and 7:* Capital is from Raymond W. Goldsmith, "The Growth of Reproducible Wealth of the United States of America from 1805 to 1950," in Simon Kuznets, ed., *Income and Wealth, Series II* (Cambridge, 1952), Table II, p. 310, and excludes consumers' durables and military. Product is from unpublished annual series for 1948–52 and 1877–81 underlying estimates in Kuznets, *Capital in the American Economy,* extrapolated back to 1850 by estimates of commodity product in Robert E. Gallman, "Commodity Output, 1839–1899," in William N. Parker, ed., *Trends in the American Economy in the Nineteenth Century,* Studies in Income and Wealth, *24* (National Bureau of Economic Research, 1960), Table 1 p. 16.

*Lines 9 and 10:* From Kazushi Ohkawa and others, *The Growth Rate of the Japanese Economy since 1878* (Tokyo, 1957), Table 5, p. 166, for the ratios of reproducible capital to national income in constant prices (series $K_1/Y$)—those for 1905–24 being extended by the change from 1924 to 1935 in the new estimates. The ratios in line 9 were derived by multiplying those in line 10 by the ratios of total wealth, including land and mines (from ibid., Table 1, p. 160) to reproducible wealth (from ibid., Table 2, p. 164), both in current prices.

product ratios. Total capital refers largely to material stocks, and it includes land and subsoil resources, construction, and equipment (with allowance for depreciation to avoid duplication), inventories, and net foreign assets. The table is limited to seven countries: for some the periods are much shorter than those for product in Table 2.5, and for some, capital is short of the total required. But, by combining these estimates with relevant long-term data on incremental capital–output ratios and on the post-World War II ratios of capital to product for the same countries, we can reach several plausible conclusions concerning trends in the capital–product ratios.[28]

Table 2.7 suggests that the ratio of *reproducible* capital to national product has risen in Great Britain, the United States, and Japan; and the inference for the last is strengthened by the rise in the incremental capital–product ratio (NDCF/NDP) from 1.6 in the late nineteenth and early twentieth centuries to 3.1 in the twentieth century. There was also a rise between periods covering roughly the second half of the nineteenth century and the first half of the twentieth century in the net domestic incremental capital–output ratios for Sweden (from 2.6 to 3.6), for Norway (from 4.0 to 5.1, the decline shown in Table 2.7 being limited to the twentieth century), for Denmark (from 2.4 to 2.8), and for Australia (from 2.9 to 5.0). While for many countries such comparisons conceal a rise in the incremental capital–product ratio in the early phases of the long periods and a decline in the later phases, and while incremental ratios are not a safe guide to the average ratios, the evidence does suggest that, by and large, the trends in the ratios of reproducible capital to product have been upward, though tempered by recent declines, often to particularly low levels in the post-World War II years.[29]

28. For the long-term ratios, see Kuznets, "Quantitative Aspects: VI"; for the post-World War II ratios, see Raymond W. Goldsmith and Christopher Saunders, eds., *Income and Wealth, Series VIII* (London, 1959).

29. The incremental capital–output ratios are from Kuznets, "Quantitative Aspects: VI," Table 5, pp. 17–18.

But the picture changes when we deal with *total* capital, including land and subsoil resources. In five countries for which we have data (Great Britain, Belgium, the United States, Australia, and Japan), the ratio of total capital to product declines—despite the rise in the ratio of reproducible capital to product (available for Great Britain, the United States, and Japan) and in the incremental capital–product ratio for Australia. Obviously, with the marked decline in the proportion of land and other natural resources in total material capital which accompanies modern economic growth and industrialization, such total capital–product ratios should decline over the long period for all developed countries. At any rate, for purposes of further discussion, we can assume, most conservatively, that the total capital–product ratios remained constant in the long run and, more realistically, that they declined, from a fifth to as much as four tenths.

Constancy of the total capital–product ratios implies that total capital per head increased at the same rate as per capita product. A decline in the total capital–product ratio of, say, a quarter, means that total capital per head changed by a percentage rate equal to $\{[(100 + 0.75\ R_1) : (100 + R_2)] - 1\} \times 100$—where $R_1$ is the percentage rate of growth for product and $R_2$ the percentage rate of growth for population. This can be compared with $\{[(100 + R_1) : (100 + R_2)] - 1\} \times 100$, the percentage rate of growth of per capita product. If we divide the first expression by the second, to derive the ratio of the rate of growth of capital per head to the rate of growth of product per head, we get $(0.75\ R_1 - R_2)/(R_1 - R_2)$. This ratio is the smaller, and hence the reduction in shifting from the rate of increase in per capita product to the rate of increase in capital per head is the greater, the greater the ratio of $R_2$ to $R_1$. If the rate of population growth is about a third of the rate of growth of product, as it is for the United Kingdom (1855–59 to 1957–59), Germany, Switzerland, Denmark, and Norway in Table 2.5, the ratio in question becomes $(0.75 - 0.33)/(0.67)$, or $0.63$, indicating that the rate

78

of growth in capital per head is over a third lower than
the rate of growth in product per capita. If the rate of
population growth is about half the rate of growth of
product, as it is for the United States and Canada, the
ratio becomes (0.75 − 0.50)/0.50, or 0.5, and the rate of
growth in capital per head is only half the rate of growth
of product per capita. If the rate of population growth is
as high as seven tenths of the rate of growth of product, as
it is for Australia, the ratio becomes (0.75 − 0.70)/0.30, or
0.17, and the rate of growth in capital per head is less than
a fifth of the rate of growth of product per head.[30] The important point to observe is that if population is constant,
a decline in the total capital–product ratio means as great
a proportional reduction in the rate of increase of capital
per head, and an appreciably greater reduction in the rate
of growth of capital per head even if the rate of growth
of population is as low as one tenth of the rate of growth
of total product.

Let us return now to the assumption of a constant total
capital–product ratio and a rate of growth of capital per
head as high as that of product per capita. What was the
input represented by the former in the process that produced the latter? By relating property income or income
from assets to the total capital that yields it, we can ascertain the relevant rate of input. Income from assets, excluding the part implicitly contained in the incomes of individual entrepreneurs (i.e. return on capital excluding
entrepreneurial equity) averages about 20 per cent of total
income in developed countries and only slightly less in the
underdeveloped countries.[31] Returns on entrepreneurial

30. Incidentally, this may provide a clue for the low rate of growth
in the per capita product of Australia. If the total capital–product
ratio did decline significantly, the implication is a rather low rate of
growth of material capital per head. Table 2.7 does show a decline in
the total capital–product ratio for Australia from 6.4 in 1903 to 4.0
in 1956.

31. This and other estimates in the paragraph are from Kuznets,
"Quantitative Aspects: IV," Table 1, pp. 10–11 and discussion on pp.
15–28. For further discussion see Chap. 4 below.

equity differ widely depending upon the assumptions made in the allocation of entrepreneurial income between labor and capital, but it is realistic to assume that in the developed countries the rate is somewhat lower than for non-entrepreneurial capital (it would be very much lower relatively in the underdeveloped countries). Since entrepreneurial equity capital is at most 25 per cent of total capital in developed countries, a fair estimate of total income from assets—the contribution of capital input to total product—is about a quarter of the latter.

If we apply this ratio and assume a constant total capital–product ratio, the implied increase in total capital per head directly accounts for no more than a quarter of the total rise in product per head—and this is probably an overestimate. If we assume a decline in the total capital–product ratio of a quarter, the implied contribution of the growth in capital per head to the growth in product per head, would vary from as low as a twentieth (when the rate of population growth is 0.7 of the rate of growth of total product) to as high as a seventh (when the rate of population growth is one third of the rate of growth of total product).

The combined inputs of man-hours and capital would account for an even smaller fraction of the growth in product per capita. Since man-hours per capita are found to decline 2 to 3 per cent per decade and their weight in total product is 0.75 (since income from assets is assumed to account for 0.25), the direct contribution would be a *reduction* in the rate of growth of per capita product of 1.5 to 2.25 percentage points. If the rate of growth of per capita product is, say, 15 per cent per decade, the reduction amounts to a tenth of the rate or more. Since the increase in capital per head contributes from a twentieth to a seventh, the combined contributions of man-hours and capital must be proportionately small indeed. While various modifications can be introduced into this statistical allocation, and while the results would clearly vary among individual countries, the inescapable conclusion is that the direct contribution of man-hours and capital accumulation would hardly account for more than a tenth of the rate of growth in per capita product—and probably less. The large remainder must be assigned to an increase in efficiency in the productive resources—a rise in output per unit of input, due either to the improved quality of the resources, or to the effects of changing arrangements, or to the impact of technological change, or to all three.

This conclusion agrees with the findings of studies for the United States and Norway which attempt to allocate growth of total product between inputs of labor and capital, on the one hand, and a residual ascribable to technical change and rise in efficiency on the other;[32] for the limited share attributed to the former would be appreciably lower when resource inputs are reduced to a per capita basis. In this connection a brief reference to the analysis for the United States by Denison is in order. Setting aside the depressing effects of reduction in hours almost completely offset in Denison's analysis by resulting improvement in productivity per hour, we find that of the total growth in real national income per person employed, 1.44 per cent per year for 1909–57 (or 15.4 per cent per decade), capital and land contributed only 0.18, or about 12 per cent; while the increased education of the labor force and the increased output per unit of input, due largely to economies of scale and spread of technical knowledge, contributed together

32. For the United States see Moses Abramovitz, "Resource and Output Trends in the United States since 1870," National Bureau of Economic Research, *Occasional Paper 52* (New York, 1956); Robert M. Solow, "Technical Change and the Aggregate Production Function," *Review of Economics and Statistics, 39* (August 1957); and particularly John W. Kendrick, *Productivity Trends in the United States* (Princeton, 1961) and Edward F. Denison, "The Sources of Economic Growth in the United States and the Alternatives Before Us," Committee for Economic Development, *Supplementary Paper No. 13* (New York, 1962). For Norway see Odd Aukrust and Juul Bjerke, "Real Capital and Economic Growth in Norway, 1900–56," in Goldsmith and Saunders, eds., *Income and Wealth, Series VIII.*

1.25 (0.58 and 0.67, respectively), or over 85 per cent.[33] Since education and economies of scale are results of additions to and spread of the stock of useful knowledge, the dominant role of the latter—compared with the increase in input of resources—in the rise in product per capita is apparent.

The conclusion that increased input of man-hours and capital, as such, plays a minor role in the rise in product per capita reflects some key features of modern economic growth. Such growth clearly was not attained by greater exertion, in the way of more working hours per capita, let alone per worker. It was associated with capital accumulation, but the ratio of capital to output was kept down by capital–saving innovations, investment in human training, and other arrangements that permitted greater output with a diminished relative supply of natural resources and even of reproducible capital; and these enormous economies in the use of capital also limited the return that had to be paid for it and hence the rate of its direct contribution to current production.[34]

Indeed, it is unlikely that much of the high rate of rise in per capita product associated with modern economic growth could have been secured by an increase in quantity of inputs per capita—if only because of the constraints on supplies of labor and material capital. If the rate of growth in per capita product was 15 per cent per decade, which meant quadrupling in a century (see Table 2.5), neither

33. The figures are from Denison, "Sources of Economic Growth," Table 20, p. 149 and Table 32, p. 266. Since population growth from 1909 to 1957 was 1.33 per cent per year compared with 1.43 per cent for growth in persons employed, the increase per person employed would not be much different from the increase per capita.

34. In reaching this conclusion we disregarded quality changes in labor and capital as well as possible indirect effects of increase in size (briefly noted below). Quantity of resource inputs must not be confused with quality, since quality is largely a reflection of the additional knowledge. We wanted to stress the point that one distinctive feature of modern economic growth is the association of rise of per capita product with changes in the *quality* of resource inputs and of the arrangements for their use.

the share of labor force in total population—limited by age and sex constraints—nor hours per worker—limited by considerations of efficiency and preference for increased leisure as per capita real income rises—could have risen enough to contribute much in the *long run,* disregarding short periods of extra effort in emergency or revolutionary situations. With the ratio of labor force to population rising in the long run less than 2 per cent per decade (see Table 2.6), the maximum contribution of increased man-hours per capita could be reasonably set at about 2 per cent per decade (implying a rise in labor supply per capita of close to 3 per cent, weighted by 0.75, the share of labor's contribution in total product). The growth of reproducible capital could have been more rapid than that suggested in Table 2.7, but this would have required a much greater rise in the national capital formation or savings proportion and a corresponding decline in the proportion of product left for consumption; and such a decline is not compatible with increased efficiency of labor and the higher consumption requirements of modern life. But even if the proportional contribution of material capital noted in the illustrations above (between a twentieth and a seventh) were doubled (which would mean more than doubling the rate of growth of capital stock per head) and added to the maximum contribution of labor supply suggested above, labor and capital input would still account for less than half of the growth rate of 15 per cent per decade in per capita product, leaving more than half to be accounted for by rise in efficiency—improvements of quality of labor and capital associated with increased knowledge and better utilization. The main point here is that increasing inputs of labor and material capital per head of total population are subject to constraints arising from other aspects of life (e.g. family, in the case of labor supply) and from considerations of incentives and efficiency of the human factor; that increases in inputs per head at all approximating the high rates of growth of per capita product are extremely unlikely; and that, consequently, a major share of the growth rate *must* be due to increases in output per unit of input—at least when inputs are measured as simple man-hours and material capital.[35]

Yet a major qualification of the conclusion must be noted, and some unguarded inferences warned against. Although the absolute growth of the labor force, man-hours, and capital did not make a large *direct* contribution to the growth of product per capita, the changes in the volume of resource input may well have had indirect effects on efficiency and hence on the growth in per capita product. The earlier discussion of the economic implications of modern patterns of population growth clearly suggested that in the process of accelerated increase of population, the changes in the factors determining demographic trends and the structural changes in population may have had marked effects on the adjustment of human resources to economic opportunities and hence on per capita product. The absolute expansion of the labor force and of the capital stock could have had similar effects. Economies of scale, requiring as they do additions to technical knowledge, were also contingent upon increases in the absolute volumes of the resource inputs— and this effect is not measured in the statistical allocation presented above. Reduction in hours, which tended to keep

35. Under some conditions, particularly a forced draft of resources, the contribution of inputs to rise in per capita product can be substantial; and the residual fraction ascribable to efficiency correspondingly lower. Thus, for the U.S.S.R. for 1928-58, of the total rise in net national product per capita (in 1937 factor prices), the rise in *inputs* per capita contributed as much as 55 per cent; the residual share of the rise in efficiency is thus 45 per cent. But even here, the result is greatly affected by the unusual initial period 1928-37; and the share of the rise in efficiency was much greater for 1950-58. For the United States, by a similar computation, for 1869/78 to 1899/1908 the share of the higher inputs per capita in the rise in product per capita is only 29 per cent, leaving 71 per cent ascribable to the rise in efficiency; and for 1929-57, inputs per capita in fact declined (over 9 per cent), so that all of the rise in product per capita can be attributed to the rise in efficiency. The income and input data are from Abram Bergson, "National Income," in Abram Bergson and Simon Kuznets, eds., *Economic Trends in The Soviet Union* (Cambridge, Mass., 1963), Table I-1, pp. 4–5; population data are from the standard sources.

down the number of man-hours per capita, most likely affected the efficiency of labor per hour for the shorter working day and year. In general, the direct statistical allocation above measures only the first stage of obvious effects and disregards what may be more important secondary effects and others further removed. We therefore emphasize that the low proportions of the growth in per capita product allocated to increased input of man-hours and capital *do not* mean that the absence of such an increase in input would have resulted in only a small proportionate loss in the secular rise in per capita product. The lines of relationship between the absolute increases in population, labor force, and capital, on the one hand, and growth in per capita product, on the other, are numerous and far-reaching; and they are interwoven with the secular trends in other necessary conditions of economic growth—technological changes, changes in institutional arrangements, changes in the patterns of human responses to economic incentives and difficulties— in ways that make it difficult, if not impossible, to establish the correct partial effects of increases in inputs of man-hours and capital on growth of per capita product.

The aim of the discussion in this last section is not to show the relative unimportance of greater input of resources, but rather to emphasize that the effects of such inputs may have been more of quality than of quantity, indirect rather than direct. Analysis must therefore concentrate on the sources of the rise in efficiency—of the rise in the ratio of output to input of man-hours and capital.

One way to observe the mechanism by which such a rise in efficiency in modern economic growth was effected is to study the structural changes. While economic analysis may never reach down to the basic levels of production and spread of new knowledge and innovations, we may be able, through examining structural changes, to infer some of the ways by which efficiency was improved; and it is to the changes that occurred in industrial structure that we turn in the next chapter.

# 3 TRENDS IN INDUSTRIAL STRUCTURE

## DISTRIBUTION AMONG THREE MAJOR SECTORS

In the course of modern economic growth, the high rates of increase in population and product have been associated with marked shifts in the shares of various industries—in total output and in total productive resources used. This is hardly surprising: if population grows, its ratio to land and other natural resources changes, with different consequences for different industries; if total and per capita product grow as a result of technological change, capital investment, and improvements in the quality of productive resources, the impact on different industries is not likely to be the same. The distinctive feature of modern economic growth is not the shifts in the long-term proportions of industries in product and resources—proportions referred to here as industrial structure—but rather the rapidity of these shifts and their striking magnitude when cumulated over the decades.

The magnitude of the changes can be seen in Table 3.1. Here we distinguish three major sectors: agriculture, together with such related industries as fisheries, forestry, and trapping; industry proper—mining, manufacturing, construction, power and light utilities, transportation and communication; and services—trade, finance, real estate, personal, business, domestic, professional, and government. This grouping of many narrower divisions is, like all broad classifications, subject to criticism, for each of the three main

86

groups covers industries that differ with respect to the raw materials employed, the productive operation performed, and the final product delivered, as well as other aspects that distinguish one industry from another. In some other broad classifications mining is combined with agriculture on the ground that it too is an extractive, "primary," industry; but we have preferred to put it under industry because of the large scale of its productive unit, its close connection with manufacturing, and the distinctive trend in its share in product and resources. It would have been helpful to deal separately with the components of services, which differ so much in character of product, skills required, and type of market in which they operate. But while some of these components, and those of the industry sector, will be discussed in later sections of the chapter—on the basis of data for fewer countries—a comprehensive review of the trends in industrial structure for the complete aggregate is possible only with the broad groupings. And the three major sectors do differ significantly from each other—in the use of natural resources, in the scale of operation of the productive units common to each, in the production process in which they engage, in the final products that they contribute, and in the trends in their shares in total output and resources used.

Table 3.1 summarizes data for thirteen countries, all covered in Table 2.5, showing the rate of increase in population and product.[1] For almost all the countries the shares are based on totals in current prices. The contribution of each sector is measured by relating either net product originating or product gross of current consumption of fixed capital to the appropriate countrywide product total. Product originating, in turn, is derived either by subtracting from the current gross product of each industry the costs represented by payments to other industries (e.g. in agriculture the payments for fertilizers, pesticides, etc. purchased

1. Additional countries are covered in Kuznets, "Quantitative Aspects: II," in which transport and communication are included in the services sector. See also Clark, *Conditions of Economic Progress,* 3d ed., Chaps. 9 and 10.

TABLE 3.1

Distribution of National Product among Three Major Sectors, Selected Countries, Long Periods (underlying totals in current prices unless otherwise indicated)[a]

Shares in national product (%)

| | Agriculture | | | Industry | | | Services | | |
|---|---|---|---|---|---|---|---|---|---|
| | Initial date (1) | Terminal date (2) | Change (3) | Initial date (4) | Terminal date (5) | Change (6) | Initial date (7) | Terminal date (8) | Change (9) |
| *United Kingdom* | | | | | | | | | |
| 1. England and Wales, national income, circa 1688 to circa 1770 | 40 | 45 | +5 | 21[b] | 24[b] | +3[b] | 39[b] | 31[b] | −8[b] |
| 2. Great Britain, national income, 1801 to 1841 | 32 | 22 | −10 | 23[b] | 34[b] | +11[b] | 45[b] | 44[b] | −1[b] |
| 3. Great Britain, national income, 1841 to 1901 | 22 | 6 | −16 | 34[b] | 40[b] | +6[b] | 44[b] | 54[b] | +10[b] |
| 4. Great Britain, national income, gross of depreciation, excluding errors and omissions, 1907 to 1924 | 6 | 4 | −2 | 46(36[b]) | 51 | +5 | 48(58[b]) | 45 | −3 |
| 5. United Kingdom, gross national product, 1924 to 1955 | 4 | 5 | +1 | 52 | 56 | +4 | 44 | 39 | −5 |
| *France* | | | | | | | | | |
| 6. National income, 1789/1815 to 1825/35 | 50 | 50 | 0 | 20[b] | 25[b] | +5[b] | 30[b] | 25[b] | −5[b] |
| 7. National income, 1825/35 to 1872/82 | 50 | 42 | −8 | 25[b] | 30[b] | +5[b] | 25[b] | 28[b] | +3[b] |

| | | | | | | | | | |
|---|---|---|---|---|---|---|---|---|---|
| 8. National income, 1872/82 to 1908/10 | 42 | 35 | −7 | 30[b] | 37[b] | +7[b] | 28[b] | 28[b] | 0[b] |
| 9. Gross domestic product, 1954 to 1962 | 12 | 9 | −3 | 52 | 52 | 0 | 36 | 39 | +3 |
| *Germany* | | | | | | | | | |
| 10. 1913 Reich, national income, 1860/69 to 1905/14 | 32 | 18 | −14 | 24[b] | 39[b] | +15[b] | 44[b] | 43[b] | −1[b] |
| 11. Federal Republic, gross domestic product, 1936 to 1959 | 11 | 7 | −4 | 42[b] | 52[b] | +10[b] | 47[b] | 41[b] | −6[b] |
| *Netherlands* | | | | | | | | | |
| 12. National income, 1913 to 1938 | 16 | 7 | −9 | 33 | 40 | +7 | 51 | 53 | +2 |
| 13. Gross domestic product, 1950 to 1962 | 13 | 9 | −4 | 47 | 51 | +4 | 40 | 40 | 0 |
| *Denmark, net domestic product* | | | | | | | | | |
| 14. Current prices, 1870/74 to 1905/09 | 47 | 29 | −18 | | | | | | |
| 15. Current prices, 1905/09 to 1948/52 | 29 | 19 | −10 | | | | | | |
| 16. 1929 prices, 1870/74 to 1905/09 | 43 | 24 | −19 | | | | | | |
| 17. 1929 prices, 1905/09 to 1948/52 | 24 | 18 | −6 | | | | | | |
| *Norway* | | | | | | | | | |
| 18. Gross domestic product, 1865 to 1910 | 34 | 24 | −10 | 21[b] | 26[b] | +5[b] | 45[b] | 50[b] | +5[b] |

TABLE 3.1—*Continued*

Shares in national product (%)

| | Agriculture | | | Industry | | | Services | | |
|---|---|---|---|---|---|---|---|---|---|
| | Initial date (1) | Terminal date (2) | Change (3) | Initial date (4) | Terminal date (5) | Change (6) | Initial date (7) | Terminal date (8) | Change (9) |
| 19. Gross domestic product, 1910 to 1956 | 24 | 13 | −11 | 37(26[b]) | 53 | +16 | 39(50[b]) | 34 | −5 |
| *Sweden* | | | | | | | | | |
| 20. Gross domestic product, 1861/65 to 1901/05 | 39 | 35 | −4 | 17 | 38 | +21 | 44 | 27 | −17 |
| 21. Gross domestic product, 1901/05 to 1949/53 | 35 | 10 | −25 | 38 | 55 | +17 | 27 | 35 | +8 |
| *Italy* | | | | | | | | | |
| 22. National income, 1861/65 to 1896/00 | 55 | 47 | −8 | 20 | 22 | +2 | 25 | 31 | +6 |
| 23. National income, 1896/00 to 1951/55 | 47 | 25 | −22 | 22 | 48 | +26 | 31 | 27 | −4 |
| *United States* | | | | | | | | | |
| *Commodity product, 1839–79* | | | | | | | | | |
| 24. Current prices | 69 | 49 | −20 | 31[b] | 51[b] | +20[b] | | | |
| 25. 1879 prices | 72 | 49 | −23 | 28[b] | 51[b] | +23[b] | | | |
| *National income and aggregate payments* | | | | | | | | | |
| 26. Current prices, 1869/79 to 1919/28 | 20 | 12 | −8 | 33 | 40 | +7 | 47 | 48 | +1 |

| | | | | | | | | |
|---|---|---|---|---|---|---|---|---|
| 27. Current prices, 1919/28 to 1939/48 | 11 | 9 | −2 | 39 | 39 | 0 | 50 | 52 | +2 |
| 28. 1929 prices, 1869/78 to 1939/48 | 27 | 8 | −19 | 29 | 42 | +13 | 44 | 50 | +6 |
| 29. Current prices, 1929 to 1961/63 | 9 | 4 | −5 | 42 | 43 | +1 | 49 | 53 | +4 |
| *Canada* | | | | | | | | | |
| 30. Gross national product, 1870 to 1920 | 50 | 26 | −24 | 26[b] | 35[b] | +9[b] | 24[b] | 39[b] | +15[b] |
| 31. Gross domestic product, 1926/28 to 1961/63 | 19 | 7 | −12 | 47 | 48 | +1 | 34 | 45 | +11 |
| 32. Gross domestic product, 1949 prices, 1926/28 to 1953/55 | 28 | 15 | −13 | 37 | 48 | +11 | 35 | 37 | +2 |
| *Australia* | | | | | | | | | |
| *Gross domestic product, 1861/65 to 1934/35–1938/39* | | | | | | | | | |
| 33. Current prices | 22 | 23 | +1 | 31 | 33 | +2 | 47 | 44 | −3 |
| 34. 1910/11 prices | 18 | 24 | +6 | 31 | 30 | −1 | 51 | 46 | −5 |
| *Japan* | | | | | | | | | |
| 35. Net domestic product, 1878/82 to 1923/27 | 63 | 26 | −37 | 16 | 38 | +22 | 21 | 36 | +15 |
| 36. Net domestic product, 1950 to 1962 | 26 | 14 | −12 | 39 | 49 | +10 | 35 | 37 | +2 |
| *U.S.S.R.* | | | | | | | | | |
| 37. Net national product, 1937 factor prices, 1928 to 1958 | 49[e] | 22[e] | −27[c] | 28[c] | 58[c] | +30[c] | 23 | 20 | −3 |

TABLE 3.1—*Continued*

a. Unless otherwise indicated, in this and the other tables in this chapter agriculture includes farming, fisheries, forestry, and trapping; industry includes mining, manufacturing, construction, light and power, gas, and water, transport and communication; services include trade, finance, personal, domestic, business, professional, and government services.

b. Transport and communication are included in cols. 4–6.

c. Fisheries and forestry are included in cols. 7–9.

*Sources:* Lines 1–5: From Deane and Cole, *British Economic Growth*, Table 35, p. 156; Table 37, p. 166; Table 40, p. 175; and Table 41, p. 178.

Lines 6–8: From François Perroux, "Prise de Vues sur la Croissance de l'Economie Française, 1780–1950," in Simon Kuznets, ed., *Income and Wealth, Series V* (London, 1955), Table II, p. 61.

Line 9: From U.N., *Yearbook of National Accounts Statistics, 1961* and *1963*.

Line 10: From Paul Jostock, "The Long-Term Growth of National Income in Germany," in Kuznets, ed., *Income and Wealth, Series V*, Table VIII, p. 106.

Line 11: From U.N., *Yearbook of National Accounts Statistics, 1963* for 1956–59, extrapolated to 1952 by estimates in the *Yearbook, 1959* and to 1936 by estimates in Jostock, "Long-Term Growth," Table VIII, p. 106.

Line 12: From Kuznets, "Quantitative Aspects: II," App. Table 2, p. 69.

Line 13: From U.N., *Yearbook of National Accounts Statistics, 1957* and *1963*.

Lines 14–17: From Bjerke and Ussing, *Danmarks Nationalprodukt, 1870–1950*, Table II, pp. 144–45.

Lines 18–19: From Bjerke, "Economic Growth of Norway," Tables IV.10 and IV.14.

Lines 20–27: From Osten Johansson, "Economic Growth and Structure in Sweden, 1861–1953," a paper presented at the 1959 Conference of the International Association for Research in Income and Wealth held at Portoroz, Table 17.

Lines 22–23: From Istituto Centrale di Statistica, *Indagine Statistica*, Tables 35 and 36, pp. 245–50. Estimates for present territory for private sectors before adjustment for overlapping and depreciation were combined with those for the public sector.

Lines 24–25: From Gallman, "Commodity Output, 1839–1899," App. Table A-1, p. 43.

Lines 26–28: From Kuznets, *National Income and Its Composition, 1919–1938*, Table 14, p. 89 and Table 17, p. 102. For line 28 we assumed that the share of transportation and public utilities was 4 per cent in 1869–78 (it was 5 per cent in 1889–98).

Line 29: From Department of Commerce, *U.S. Income and Output* (Washington, 1958), Table I-10 and Department of Commerce, *Survey of Current Business* (July 1964), Table 7.

*Line 30:* From Firestone, *Canada's Economic Development, 1867–1953*, Table 68, p. 189. The total excludes rent, indirect taxes less subsidies, and net foreign investment income.

*Line 31:* From Dominion Bureau of Statistics, *National Accounts, Income and Expenditures, 1926–56 and 1963*, Table 21.

*Line 32:* From William C. Hood and Anthony Scott, *Output, Labor and Capital in the Canadian Economy* (Royal Commission on Canada's Economic Prospects, 1957), Chap. 5, App. F.

*Lines 33–34:* From Butlin, *Australian Domestic Product, Investment and Foreign Borrowing, 1861–1938/39*, Table 2, pp. 10–11 and Table 269, pp. 460–61. Agriculture includes pastoral, agriculture, and dairy, forestry, and fisheries. Industry includes mining, manufacturing, construction, private water transport, and public business undertakings (primarily railroads and other transport facilities).

*Line 35:* From unpublished revisions by Henry Rosovsky and Kazushi Ohkawa of estimates in Ohkawa and others, *The Growth Rate of the Japanese Economy*. Construction, transport and communication, and government factories were shifted from the "tertiary" sector on the basis of their share in the latter derived from ibid., Table 2, p. 104 and Table 4, p. 105. In 1923–27 that share was 27.5 per cent and we assumed 20 per cent for 1878–82.

*Line 36:* From U.N., *Yearbook of National Accounts Statistics, 1957* and *1963*.

*Line 37:* From Simon Kuznets, "A Comparative Appraisal," in Bergson and Kuznets, eds., *Economic Trends in the Soviet Union*, Table VIII-6, p. 344.

from manufacturing) or by adding the returns to factors engaged in the industry (wages and salaries, entrepreneurial income, returns on assets invested, etc.). The calculations are made separately for the many detailed industries, and the net totals are aggregated by the three major sectors; consequently, the net product originating in a sector is net of purchases by one industry from another within the same sector. In short the only duplication conceptually permitted is in gross product in which current consumption of fixed capital is not deducted.

Since aggregate growth was measured in terms of country-wide product in constant prices, it would have been useful also to measure the contribution of each industry, and hence of the three sectors, in constant prices. But this procedure raises many statistical and conceptual problems. Sectoral contributions can be adjusted for price changes in several ways. First, we can express both the value product and the purchases from other industries in constant prices—before subtracting the latter from the former. This procedure shows the contribution of the given industry after adjustment for changes not only in general price levels but also in the cost–product price relations. Second, we can adjust the net (or gross of capital consumption) product of an industry, derived from value of product and purchases in current prices (or from sums of factor returns), for changes in the prices of the product—implicitly neglecting the possible differentials in trends between prices of goods purchased from other industries and prices of the given industry's product. Third, we can adjust the net or gross income originating in an industry for the prices of goods bought by the people whose services and capital are engaged in the given industry—on the premise that although this measures their *claims* upon countrywide product in constant prices, it also reflects the society's appraisal of their *contribution*. Finally, we can adjust the compensation of productive factors engaged in a given industry for changes in prices of these factors—but we need prices for factors of

94

the same quality, both in the given industry and elsewhere in the economy.[2]

Of these various procedures the first and the fourth are most thorough in that they adjust fully for both overall and differential effects of price movements. But the first assumes relevance of a fixed cost-price structure, and the fourth requires a difficult adjustment for price changes of the "enterprise" factor; and neither is practicable: each requires far more data than are easily available and depends on price records that inadequately reflect quality changes and differentials—for goods and for resources—and may therefore lead to errors far more bizarre than those involved in the crude procedures. The procedure most commonly employed is the second, in which prices (or approximations to prices) of an industry's product are used to adjust net income originating for price changes (or value added in the base year is multiplied by volume indexes); and it has been followed for the few countries in Table 3.1 in which shares are based on totals in constant prices. Even so, the price data are rarely complete and, as already indicated, reflect quality changes poorly. In view of these limitations, the error implicit in the neglect of possible differences in trends between prices of goods purchased from other industries and prices of the industry's product does not loom too large—particularly if we consider that the proportion of such purchases to value of product is not above a fifth in most industries (e.g. agriculture, public utilities, services) and rises to a half in only a few. At any rate, with the crude price data available (and those used to derive product in constant prices in Table 2.5 are equally crude), the adjustments shown in Table 3.1 are all that are feasible. For the few countries for which we have shares in totals in both current and constant prices (Denmark, the United States, Canada, and Australia), the trends for the

2. For an interesting discussion of some of the problems involved see Paul H. David, "The Deflation of Value Added," *Review of Economics and Statistics, 44* (May 1962).

long periods covered in the two sets do not differ sufficiently to affect our broad conclusions. We may therefore summarize these trends on the assumption that they are broadly valid for shares not only in current but also in constant price totals of the type shown in Table 2.5.

1. The share of the agriculture sector in total product declined in twelve of the thirteen countries. In general, the premodern share of the sector was close to a half—and in some cases as high as two thirds—of total product (in Great Britain before 1800, line 1; France in 1825/35, line 6; Denmark in 1870/74, line 14; Italy in 1861/65, line 22; Canada in 1870, line 30; Japan in 1878/82, line 35; U.S.S.R. in 1928, line 37). By the end of the long periods covered in the table, the share of the sector was 20 per cent or less in most countries and in several less than 10 per cent. The share declined at least about 20 percentage points, often over 30. The only significant, and interesting, exception is Australia (lines 33 and 34): the share of the agriculture sector in the total in current prices remained practically constant for some eight decades, and the share in the total in constant prices rose. Apparently, the highly developed, capital-intensive agriculture of Australia was able to maintain its share because of the network of close relations with the more industrialized mother country.

2. In twelve countries the share of the industry sector in countrywide product rose. In the early phases of development, this share ranged from 20 to 30 per cent of total product. By the end of the period, in most countries it had risen 20 or more percentage points, with the shares at the terminal dates ranging from 40 to more than 50 per cent. Australia again is an exception: the share of the industry sector based on current price estimates rose and that based on constant price estimates declined, both by only one percentage point.

3. While the downward trend in the share of the agriculture sector and the upward trend in that of the industry sector are prominent and affect all countries except Australia, the movements in the share of the services sector are

neither marked nor consistent among countries or among long subperiods. In Sweden and Australia the share of the services sector declined; in Canada and Japan it rose; in most countries, the trend on balance was too small to be significant. One may, therefore, conclude that by and large the downward trend in the share of the agriculture sector was offset by the upward trend in the share of the industry sector—leaving no marked trend in the share of the residual services sector in total product.

The significance of these movements is clear if we think of them as trends in the shares of the three sectors in total product in constant prices. So viewed, a decline in the proportion of the agriculture sector means that the rate of growth of its net output was lower than the rate of growth of total output for the country; a rise in the proportion of the industry sector means that the rate of growth of its output was higher than that for total product; and constancy of the proportion of the services sector means that the rate of growth in its output was the same as that of the economy's total product. Indeed there is a simple algebraic relation between the rate at which a sector's proportion in total output changes and the ratio of its rate of growth to that of total product. Let us designate:

> the ratio of the share of a sector in total product at a given date to its share a decade earlier—$a_i$,
> the rate of growth of the sector's output per decade—$r_i$,
> the rate of growth of the country's total output per decade—$r_t$.

Then the following relation may be shown to exist:

$$r_i = a_i(1 + r_t) - 1 \qquad (1)$$

Thus, if the share of the agriculture sector declines over a century from, say, 50 to 15 per cent of total product, $a_i$ per decade is 0.887. If $r_t$, the decadal rate of growth in total product is, say, 30 per cent (judging by Table 2.5), $r_i$ for the agriculture sector is 15 per cent. If the share of the industry

97

sector rises over the century from 15 to 50 per cent of total product, $a_i$ for that sector is 1.130, and $r_i$ is 47 per cent.

One implication of equation (1), interesting in the present connection, is for the rate of growth of sectoral output *per head* of total population. Since at any given time the proportion of total sectoral output to total countrywide output equals the proportion of sectoral product per capita to total output per capita, $a_i$ for a given sector and a given period will be the same whether we deal with the share of *total* sectoral output in total countrywide output or divide both by total population. Then, if we designate the rates of growth in the per capita magnitudes $R_i$ and $R_t$, respectively, the relation can be written:

$$R_i = a_i(1 + R_t) - 1 \qquad (2)$$

If, as observed from Table 2.5, a fairly common rate of growth of per capita product is 15 per cent per decade ($R_t = 0.15$), a decline over a century in the share of the agriculture sector from 50 to 15 per cent of total product implies a rate of growth of the sector's output per head of total population of 2 per cent per decade; while the rise in the share of the industry sector over the same period from 15 to 50 per cent implies a rate of growth in the sector's output per capita of 30 per cent per decade.

We may then ask why in the course of modern economic growth output per capita in the agriculture sector rises at much lower rates than output per capita in the industry and services sectors. By putting the question in this form we can relate the findings in Table 3.1 to the usual explanation in terms of long-term income elasticities of demand—the explanation that stresses the low elasticity of demand for food and other products of agriculture and the high elasticity of demand for durable consumer goods and some services—products of the industry and services sectors. Assume that the price structure, i.e. the relations among prices of different goods (sectors), is constant over time—as it would be if the share of each sector in total product were derived by a specific price adjustment. In this case, the share of agriculture would tend to decline even more, and that of the industry sector would rise even more, than is suggested by the trends in Table 3.1. With the price structure constant, income elasticity of demand may be defined as the ratio of the percentage change in the per capita demand for a given group of products to the percentage change in real income per capita, and if we substitute "output" for "demand" and total product per capita for total income received by households per capita, income elasticity of demand for the products of a given sector, $E_i$, is $R_i/R_t$, and substituting for $R_i$ in equation (2):

$$E_i = a_i + [(a_i - 1)/R_t] \qquad (3)$$

Then, when $a_i$ is 0.887 and $R_t$ is 0.15, $E_i$ is 0.12; when $a_i$ is 1.130 and $R_t$ is 0.15, $E_i$ is 2.00.

Insofar as $E_i$ is a function of $a_i$, the reference to income elasticity of demand may seem tautological and of no importance in an explanation of the value of $a_i$. But there is more to the argument than that. We do find that at a single point in time families with different per capita incomes spend different proportions on food, clothing, durable goods, etc.; and Engel's Law reflects the wide variety of evidence on the low income elasticity of the demand for food—not derived from time series of the type used here.[3] There is thus a suggestion of a structure of human wants, invariant to social and institutional changes, which, beyond a certain minimum supply, limits the consumption of foods more narrowly than the consumption of clothing, housing, or durable goods; and *if* such an invariant structure affects final demand in the course of modern economic growth, the changing structure of product revealed in Table 3.1 could be explained in large part by this reference to human wants.

The possible relevance of income elasticities of demand for various categories of products, and hence of sectors, is particularly intriguing because their application may help

3. See in this connection H. S. Houthakker, "An International Comparison of Household Expenditure Patterns, Commemorating the Centenary of Engel's Law," *Econometrica*, 25 (October 1957).

to explain a positive association between the rate of growth of per capita product and the rapidity (magnitude per unit of time) of shifts in the industrial structure of aggregate product. Thus, if we translate, for simplicity's sake, the invariance of wants into constancy over time of income elasticities of demand (or output, with income in terms of product per capita, in constant prices), $E_i$ will be constant over time. From the preceding equations it can be shown that:

$$a_i = (1 + E_i R_t)/(1 + R_t) \qquad (4)$$

For a given value of $E_i$, deviations of $a_i$ from 1.00 (from constancy of shares, and hence stability of industrial structure) will be absolutely the larger, the larger $R_t$ is, i.e. the higher the rate of growth in per capita product in constant prices. With $E_i$ held constant at 0.5, $a_i$ would be about 0.95 if $R_t$ is 0.10, but about 0.86 if $R_t$ is 0.40; with $E_i$ held constant at 1.50, $a_i$ would be about 1.05 if $R_t$ is 0.10, and 1.14 if $R_t$ is 0.40. Thus elasticities differing from 1 and assumed to be constant over time (regardless of rises in per capita product) would in themselves produce the more marked shifts in the shares of various sectors, the higher the rates of growth in per capita product. And, of course, the very rise in per capita income may depress even further the low elasticities of demand and raise correspondingly the higher elasticities—thus again making for wider sectoral shifts.[4]

4. We shall note this association between rate of growth of per capita or per worker product and rapidity of sectoral shifts again toward the end of this chapter. In the present connection, it may be observed that if we assume constant demand elasticities for the output of one sector, say agriculture, with $E_i$ below 1.0, and also assume a constant $R_t$—which would then, according to equation (4), yield a constant $a_i$—the demand elasticity for the products of the remaining sectors combined, say $E_z$, and hence $a_z$ would have to decline. This necessarily follows, since the weighted mean of income elasticities of output for the two sectors must equal 1; and the continuous shrinkage of the weight of the lower elasticity sector would, with $E_i$ and $E_z$ both constant, raise the weighted mean above 1.0, implying an acceleration in the rate of growth of per capita product and would thus vio-

But before we can accept income elasticities of demand as reflections of invariant structure of human wants, several questions must be raised and complexities faced. Even if for the time being we proceed on the premise of a closed economy, implicitly used in the discussion so far; even if we disregard the significant part of total product not flowing to households for ultimate consumption; even if we ignore the conflicting results of cross-section analysis and long-term trend comparisons with respect to the income elasticity of demand for some products (e.g. clothing),[5] there may still be a serious question whether the observable differences in the response of consumer demand for different products to a rise in income per capita are entirely, or even largely, a matter of an invariant structure of human wants. The question relates to the role of relative prices and of the social and institutional arrangements and hence of the changes on the supply or production side that affect these price structures and arrangements, to which human wants are assumed to be invariant.

The point can be made clearer if we assume that technological changes associated with modern economic growth have been confined to agriculture and public health. In that case we would hardly have had the kind of industrialization and urbanization that has occurred; and while productivity rises in agriculture would have permitted more resources to flow into handicrafts and construction of public works (there were pyramids, temples, and cathedrals

---

late the assumption of a constant $R_t$. This impossibility of keeping income elasticities of demand for output constant for *all* sectors that differ in elasticities, when per capita product growth rates are constant, is parallel to the inconsistency between a constant rate of product per worker and constant rates of growth of sectoral product per worker combined with shifts from low to high per worker product sectors (see discussion in Simon Kuznets, "Economic Growth and the Contribution of Agriculture: Notes on Measurement," in *Proceedings of the Eleventh International Conference of Agricultural Economists,* London, 1963, pp. 42–43).

5. See note 18 below and discussion in Chaps. 5 and 8 on the application of cross-section relations to trends over time.

under conditions of agricultural surplus in premodern times), the share of agriculture in total product would probably not have declined as drastically as indicated in Table 3.1. After all, income elasticity for food and other agricultural products is above zero, some positive price elasticity might come into play, and there are ways of markedly increasing food consumption, despite the presumptive invariance of human wants—as evidenced by the Lucullan feasts of the Romans and the eating bouts of medieval Europe. The argument here is that although changes on the supply or production side do not necessarily affect the basic structure of human wants—assuming such wants could be precisely defined—they do affect the relative costs and varieties of specific goods that are comprised in those human wants; and these changes must be given their proper weight in any explanation of trends in the industrial structure of modern economic growth.

These effects of changes on the supply or production side may be either compulsory or inducive. Thus the technological changes that have accounted for the rise of modern industry and for the concomitant industrialization and urbanization have meant that consumers, who as producers had to live in the cities, have required goods and services that were not essential in the countryside. As will be seen in Chapter 5, in the urban demand even for food there was greater need for fabrication, transportation, and distribution, all outside of the agriculture sector, than in the demand of the rural population living close to the sources of food supply. Insofar as the growing need for these additional services, as well as for others (e.g. housing, personal transportation, and the like), has been *imposed* upon ultimate consumers by the shift in their patterns of life associated with the new technology, the demand for the products of the industry and services sectors may have been greater than for the products of the agriculture sector. And such differential impacts of changes in supply and demand for the products of the several sectors have not been limited to components of household consumption. More government services have been demanded not only because of the peculiar needs of urban life but also because of the greater complexities of economic organization requiring government regulation and administration. The greater specialization and territorial concentration of production in those branches in which new technology has permitted large scale plants and associated economies has meant a greater need for transportation and distribution than would have been required by more smaller plants, serving local markets. Thus the ramifications of the adjustments to a new pattern of production, work, and life, compelled in a sense by modern technology, have had a widespread effect on demand for products of the major sectors and even of the many more narrowly defined industrial divisions, raising the demand for some and perforce limiting it for others.

But there were also the inducing effects of innovations, which not only increased productivity in turning out old products (thus possibly reducing their relative prices) but created new consumer and capital goods. Every consumer good, old or new, can be related to some recognized and established category of human wants: television sets can be seen as a substitute for village feasts in the way of recreation, and railroads and automobiles as a substitute for horses in the way of transportation. Even if the structure of wants in their distribution among broad categories such as nourishment, clothing, shelter, recreation, transportation, and the like, had not changed—in the sense that the proportions of total product allocated to each remained constant—with the differential effect of technological innovations the same wants could have been satisfied in one period by products from the agriculture sector and in another by products from the industry sector. Furthermore, a greater degree of innovation with respect to one category of wants, e.g. recreation or transportation, than, say, clothing, could also have affected the structure, inducing consumers to allocate more of their expenditures to satisfying wants of one category than of another. The structure of human wants is not so invariant as to bar such changes in composition and priority—above some minimum for each.

The preceding comments are intended to emphasize the importance of changes on the production or supply side in explaining changes in the industrial distribution of total product among the major and minor sectors, even on the assumption of a closed economy. Such factors on the production side assume additional weight once we admit the possibility of foreign trade—for clearly the demand in a group of developed countries for a category of products with a low income elasticity would show a higher income elasticity of demand when the markets are expanded to include other countries with lower income levels, with an opposite effect on products with high income elasticity. This additional argument of comparative advantage reflects differences on the production side rather than on the demand side: it is the loss by developed countries of the differential advantage with respect to agriculture and gain with respect to industry that provides an additional explanation of trends in the distribution of product among the major sectors.

It is not the intention here to provide a full explanation of the changes in industrial structure summarized in Table 3.1. We shall add to the general comments above in the more detailed discussion of each major sector, although even then a complete and tested explanation is out of the question. Nor is it intended here to deny the constraints in the structure of human wants, which, however, are largely related to the indispensable minima involved. But it seemed proper to warn against too easy a reliance on the invariant structure of human wants as an exogenous variable presumably providing an adequate explanation of trends in industrial structure in modern economic growth. The danger of such a position lies in the neglect of the significant effects of changes on the production side—endogenous to economic growth—on the structure of final demand and consequently in the neglect of valuable directions of further analysis emphasizing the variety of interrelations in the process of growth.

We may turn now to the shares of the three major sectors in total productive resources used, the levels and trends of which need not be identical with those of the sector shares in total product. A decline in a sector's share in total product is not necessarily accompanied by a decline in its share in total labor force or total capital: if productivity or efficiency, reflected in output per unit of input, has risen *less* in a given sector than in others, the sector may have absorbed a constant or even rising proportion of total resources. And it may well be that the two sets of trends are interrelated: the lagging efficiency of a sector may have meant higher relative prices for its products and contributed to a decline in demand relative to the demand for the products of other, more "progressive" sectors in the economy. Similarly, a sector whose share in total product has risen may have increased its efficiency and produced more output per unit of input more rapidly than others; and its share in total resources may not have risen.

Table 3.2, which assembles data on long-term changes in the distribution of the labor force, here defined for almost all countries to exclude women in agriculture (which reduces the decline in the share of the agriculture sector), includes fourteen countries and provides fairly good coverage of developed countries. Table 3.3 shows the distribution of reproducible, material wealth among categories that can be related to the three major sectors only with some difficulty; it covers only four countries and is, in other respects, woefully inadequate. Neither table covers resource inputs adequately: hours and quality of labor are not considered and capital estimates are incomplete. Yet some major trends are apparent and can be briefly summarized.

1. The share of the agriculture sector in total labor force declined in every country in Table 3.2, even in Australia where the share in product was either constant or rose from the 1860s to the late 1930s. Depending upon the initial share recorded in Table 3.2, the absolute decline in the sector's share in the labor force was either small or large; but it was invariably large *relative* to the initial level. The share

TABLE 3.2

Distribution of Labor Force among Three Major Sectors, Selected Countries, Long Periods

Shares in total labor force (%)

| | Agriculture | | | Industry | | | Services | | |
|---|---|---|---|---|---|---|---|---|---|
| | Initial date (1) | Terminal date (2) | Change (3) | Initial date (4) | Terminal date (5) | Change (6) | Initial date (7) | Terminal date (8) | Change (9) |
| *Great Britain* | | | | | | | | | |
| 1. 1801 to 1841 | 35 | 23 | −12 | 29* | 39* | +10* | 36* | 38* | +2 |
| 2. 1841 to 1901 | 23 | 9 | −14 | 43(39*) | 54 | +11 | 34(38*) | 37 | +3 |
| 3. 1901 to 1921 | 9 | 7 | −2 | 54 | 55 | +1 | 37 | 38 | +1 |
| 4. 1921 to 1951 | 7 | 5 | −2 | 55 | 57 | +2 | 38 | 38 | 0 |
| *France* | | | | | | | | | |
| 5. 1866 to 1911 | 43 | 30 | −13 | 38* | 39* | +1* | 19* | 31* | +12* |
| 6. 1911 to 1951 | 30 | 20 | −10 | 43(39*) | 47 | +4 | 27(31*) | 33 | +6 |
| *Belgium* | | | | | | | | | |
| 7. 1880 to 1910 | 24 | 18 | −6 | 39* | 50* | +11* | 37* | 32* | −5* |
| 8. 1910 to 1947 | 18 | 11 | −7 | 56(50*) | 58 | +2 | 26(32*) | 31 | +5 |
| *Switzerland* | | | | | | | | | |
| 9. 1880 to 1910 | 33 | 22 | −11 | 48 | 54 | +6 | 19 | 24 | +5 |
| 10. 1910 to 1941 | 22 | 20 | −2 | 54 | 49 | −5 | 24 | 31 | +7 |
| *Netherlands* | | | | | | | | | |
| 11. 1899 to 1947 | 28 | 17 | −11 | 36* | 37* | +1* | 36* | 46* | +10* |
| *Denmark* | | | | | | | | | |
| 12. 1901 to 1952 | 42 | 19 | −23 | 28* | 38* | +10* | 30* | 43* | +13* |
| *Norway* | | | | | | | | | |
| 13. 1875 to 1910 | 49 | 38 | −11 | 33 | 41 | +8 | 18 | 21 | +3 |
| 14. 1910 to 1950 | 38 | 25 | −13 | 41 | 48 | +7 | 21 | 27 | +6 |

| | 1 | 2 | 3 | 4 | 5 | 6 | 7 | 8 | 9 |
|---|---|---|---|---|---|---|---|---|---|
| *Sweden* | | | | | | | | | |
| 15. 1870 to 1910 | 55 | 41 | −14 | 12* | 30* | +18* | 33* | 29* | −4* |
| 16. 1910 to 1950 | 41 | 19 | −22 | 36(30*) | 50 | +14 | 23(29*) | 31 | +8 |
| *Italy* | | | | | | | | | |
| 17. 1871 to 1911 | 51 | 45 | −6 | 35 | 36 | +1 | 14 | 19 | +5 |
| 18. 1911 to 1951 | 45 | 35 | −10 | 36 | 40 | +4 | 19 | 25 | +6 |
| *United States* | | | | | | | | | |
| 19. 1840 to 1870 | 68 | 51 | −17 | | | | | | |
| 20. 1870 to 1910 | 51 | 32 | −19 | 30 | 41 | +11 | 19 | 27 | +8 |
| 21. 1910 to 1950 | 32 | 12 | −20 | 41 | 45 | +4 | 27 | 43 | +16 |
| *Canada* | | | | | | | | | |
| 22. 1901 to 1951 | 44 | 19 | −25 | 33 | 44 | +11 | 23 | 37 | +14 |
| *Australia* | | | | | | | | | |
| 23. 1891 to 1947 | 26 | 17 | −9 | 43 | 48 | +5 | 31 | 35 | +4 |
| *Japan* | | | | | | | | | |
| 24. 1872 to 1925 | 85 | 52 | −33 | 6 | 24 | +18 | 9 | 24 | +15 |
| 25. 1925 to 1942 | 52 | 43 | −9 | 24 | 34 | +10 | 24 | 23 | −1 |
| 26. 1950 to 1960 | 48 | 33 | −15 | 27 | 35 | +8 | 25 | 32 | +7 |
| *U.S.S.R.* | | | | | | | | | |
| 27. 1928 to 1958 | 71 | 40 | −31 | 18 | 38 | +20 | 11 | 22 | +11 |

\* Transport and communication are included in cols. 7–9.

*Sources:* For all countries, except Great Britain, Japan, and the U.S.S.R., the entries are calculated from estimates for labor force excluding women in agriculture, in Clark, *Conditions of Economic Progress,* 3d ed., Table III, pp. 510–20.

*Lines 1–4:* From Deane and Cole, *British Economic Growth,* Table 30, p. 142.

*Lines 24–25:* From Ohkawa and others, *Growth Rate of the Japanese Economy,* App. Table 2, pp. 245–46.

*Line 26:* From Mataji Umemura, "An Analysis of the Employment Structure in Japan," *Hitotsubashi Journal of Economics,* 2 (March 1962), Table 9, p. 27.

*Line 27:* From Kuznets, "Comparative Appraisal," Table VIII-6, p. 344.

in the premodern phase was over 65 per cent in the United States in 1840 (line 19), Japan in 1872 (line 24), and the U.S.S.R. in 1928 (line 27), and in general it probably was not below 50 per cent. It then declined in most countries to below 20 per cent (and would be even lower if the records were carried to the late 1950s), with the significant exception of Japan and the U.S.S.R., the latecomers in the process of industrialization. One may conclude that, by and large, the declines in the share of the agriculture sector in labor force, ranging from well over 20 to more than 50 percentage points, were as large, absolutely and perhaps even proportionately, as those in the sector's share in total product.

2. The share of the agriculture sector in total reproducible wealth declined in all four countries in Table 3.3—moderately in Australia, rather markedly in the other three countries. For our purposes it would have been more appropriate to have the share of the sector in total wealth, including land and other nonreproducible resources. But we know that in all developed countries the share of land—which is largely in the agriculture sector—in total material wealth declined sharply in the course of economic growth. In Great Britain, the share of land in total capital, excluding movable property, declined from 54 per cent in 1832 to 4 per cent in 1927.[6] If land had been included, the decline in the share of the agriculture sector in total wealth of Great Britain would have been appreciably greater than it is in Table 3.3. For the United States, the share of the agriculture sector in total material wealth including land declined from 65 per cent in 1850 to 11 per cent in 1958.[7] In general, with land included, the share of the agriculture sector would be larger than its share in reproducible capital; and it also would decline more absolutely, although not necessarily proportionately. While available data bar any

6. See Deane and Cole, *British Economic Growth*, Table 70, p. 271.
7. See Goldsmith, "Growth of Reproducible Wealth," Tables I and II, pp. 307–10 and Goldsmith, *National Wealth in the Postwar Period*, Table A-20, pp. 147–48.

TABLE 3.3

Distribution of Reproducible Wealth among User Categories,
Selected Countries, Long Periods
(underlying totals in current prices)

| | Shares in reproducible wealth (%) | | |
| --- | --- | --- | --- |
| | Initial date (1) | Terminal date (2) | Change (3) |
| *Great Britain*, 1865 to 1933 | | | |
| 1. Farm | 16 | 2 | −14 |
| 2. Domestic railways, industrial, commercial | 49 | 64 | +15 |
| 3. Buildings | 28 | 24 | −4 |
| 4. Public property | 8 | 11 | +3 |
| *Norway*, 1900 to 1953 | | | |
| 5. Agriculture and related industries | 17 | 11 | −6 |
| 6. Industry (mining, manufacturing, electricity and gas, transport) | 19 | 40 | +21 |
| 7. Dwellings | 42 | 29 | −13 |
| 8. Commercial and finance | 7 | 7 | 0 |
| 9. Government | 15 | 13 | −2 |
| *United States*, 1850 to 1958 | | | |
| 10. Agriculture | 37 | 7 | −30 |
| 11. Business | 40 | 39 | −1 |
| 12. Residential | 20 | 40 | +20 |
| 13. Government | 3 | 14 | +11 |
| *Australia*, 1903 to 1956 | | | |
| 14. Agriculture (machinery and livestock) | 14 | 10 | −4 |
| 15. Other machinery and equip. | 7 | 14 | +7 |
| 16. Buildings | 38 | 39 | +1 |
| 17. Public assets | 41 | 38 | −3 |

*Sources: Lines 1–4:* From Deane and Cole, *British Economic Growth,* Table 81, p. 306.

*Lines 5–9:* From Aukrust and Bjerke, "Real Capital," Table III, p. 95. Covers structures and equipment.

*Lines 10–13:* From Goldsmith, "Growth of Reproducible Wealth," Table I, p. 306 and Goldsmith, *The National Wealth of the United States in the Postwar Period* (National Bureau of Economic Research, 1962), Table A-31, pp. 169–70. Covers reproducible wealth excluding consumer durables and military and foreign assets.

*Lines 14–17:* From J. M. Garland and R. W. Goldsmith, "The National Wealth of Australia," in Goldsmith and Saunders, eds., *Income and Wealth, Series VIII,* Table XIV, p. 356. Excludes inventories and bullion.

general conclusions, they do not deny the plausible conjecture that the relative declines in the share of the agriculture sector in total wealth were as great as those in its share in total product.

3. The share of the industry sector in total labor force rose in every country listed in Table 3.2. But in many the rise was absolutely and proportionately small—despite the long periods covered. In France, Switzerland, Belgium (1910–47), the Netherlands, Italy, and Australia the share rose just a few percentage points; and even the more substantial absolute rises in the other countries are not large relatively, certainly not as large as the relative rise in the sector's share in total product. If a rise from about 20 to over 40 per cent may be considered typical of the trend in the share of the industry sector in total product, such doubling or more than doubling of its share in total labor force is found only in Great Britain, Sweden, Japan, and the U.S.S.R. For other countries in Table 3.2, during periods as long as those in Table 3.1, the relative rise in the share of the industry sector in labor force appears to be significantly smaller than the relative rise in its share in total product.

4. Table 3.3 does not permit a clear identification even of reproducible capital used in the industry sector—except possibly for Norway. In the other countries, the distinguishable components either include capital in commerce and finance (as in the United States and Australia), or exclude buildings, or both. Using the given data as exceedingly crude approximations, one may conclude that the share of the industry sector in total reproducible capital rose and that the rise would be somewhat greater as a share in total material wealth, including nonreproducible resources. But we have no evidence that the relative rise in the share of the sector in either total or reproducible capital would even begin to approach the doubling or more than doubling observed for its share in total product.

5. The share of the services sector in total labor force

either is constant or changes relatively little in Great Britain, Belgium, the Netherlands, Sweden, and Australia. But in other countries there is a large absolute and relative rise, particularly marked in Switzerland, Denmark, Norway, Italy, the United States, Canada, Japan, and the U.S.S.R., where the initial share was low, ranging from about 10 to less than 20 per cent. Since the share of the services sector in total product either was constant or changed little (see Table 3.1), we may conclude that in many countries the absolute and relative rise in the share of the services sector in total labor force was significantly *greater* than the increase in its share in total product.

6. It is not easy to identify the share of the services sector in reproducible wealth. If we assign to this sector dwellings or buildings, commerce and finance (when given separately), and government, the share rises appreciably in the United States and declines slightly in Great Britain and Australia and markedly in Norway. No general conclusion can be drawn—although the shares in total wealth including land might show a somewhat greater tendency to rise. However, since the sector's share in the labor force has expanded appreciably in many countries, the share of the services in *total resources* might show a significant rise in a number of countries—compared with constancy or a minor movement in the sector's share in total product.[8]

One inference implicit in the findings above is noted before we turn to the discussion of each major sector separately. It relates to trends in sectoral productivity or efficiency, in output per unit of input. Let us designate:

8. This conclusion might require significant qualification if we were to take into account changes in man-hours and quality of labor—for the service and other sectors as well. For the service industries in particular, a recent survey for the United States covering 1929–61 indicated that quality of labor and amount of capital per worker rose less and man-hours declined less than in the commodity sectors. See Victor R. Fuchs, "Productivity Trends in the Goods and Services Sectors, 1929–61: A Preliminary Survey," National Bureau of Economic Research, *Occasional Paper 89* (New York, 1964).

T and $T_i$—total product and the product of sector i,
O and $O_i$—total resources and resources used in sector i
(labor, capital, or both),
$f_i$—the share of sector i in total product,
$g_i$—the share of sector i in total resources.

Then:

$$f_i/g_i = (T_i/O_i) : (T/O) \qquad (5)$$

In other words, the ratio of a sector's share in total product to its share in total resources describes the ratio of the sector's productivity (output per unit of resources in the sector) to countrywide productivity (total output per unit of total resources). If the shares change, and we express these changes as relatives of initial levels, designating the relative for $f_i$ as $k_i$, and that for $g_i$ as $m_i$, then the terminal shares at the end of the period are $f_i k_i$ and $g_i m_i$ respectively.

Toward the end of the period:

$$f_i k_i/g_i m_i = (T_i/O_i)(k_i/m_i) : (T/O) \qquad (6)$$

Thus if the proportional rise in the sector's share in total product $(k_i)$ is greater than that in its share in resources $(m_i)$, the sector's productivity *relative* to countrywide productivity rises; and the result will be the same if the share in product declines proportionately less than the share in resources. The *absolute* movement of the sector's productivity will, of course, depend also upon the rate of change in $(T/O)$, countrywide output per unit of resources.

If, as Tables 3.1 to 3.3 suggest, the relative decline in the share of the agriculture sector in total resources (labor, capital, or both) was, in most countries, almost as great as the relative decline in its share in total product, $k_i/m_i$ is about 1; the level of productivity in the sector, *relative* to countrywide, must have remained the same; and consequently, productivity in the agriculture sector must have grown as rapidly as productivity in the economy as a whole. Similarly, the evidence for the industry sector suggests that its share in total resources grew proportionately much less than its share in total product; and with $k_i/m_i$ well above 1, productivity in the industry sector must have grown at appreciably higher rates than productivity in the entire economy. Finally, the evidence suggests that the share of the services sector in total resources in a number of countries grew relatively more than its share in total product; and with $k_i/m_i$ distinctly below 1, the rate of growth in productivity in the services sector must have been distinctly below that in productivity in the economy as a whole.

Given the distribution of total product in current rather than in constant prices, the limitations on comparability of periods and estimates, the paucity of data on capital resources, the inability to adjust for changes in hours and quality of labor, and a host of other inadequacies, the broad conclusions and inferences are subject to serious qualifications. Although we may never be able to remove all such qualifications, the orders of magnitude suggested in the discussion are large enough to transcend many minor corrections, and the findings may be accepted, provisionally at least, as guides to thinking. They can be examined further, along with other aspects, in the separate discussion of each major sector.

### MOVEMENT AWAY FROM AGRICULTURE

The preceding comments suggest that the long-term decline in the share of the agriculture sector in total product could be explained by the low income elasticity of demand for its products, combined with the possible loss of advantage in that sector by developed countries. It was also indicated that the low income elasticity of demand, while reflecting the structure of human wants with respect to such items as food and clothing, may also be due in large part to the greater compulsion and inducement toward products of other sectors resulting from technological changes and shifts in patterns of work and life closely associated with modern economic growth.

Before turning to long-term trends in the share of the agriculture sector in resources—the main topic of this section—we consider briefly the *wide* prevalence of declines in the share in total product, under conditions of an open, not a closed, economy, since the latter would make the low income elasticity of domestic demand paramount. The question is why, with greater ease of foreign trade, international specialization was not greater. Why didn't some countries increasingly supply others with products of the A sector, thus retaining the high share of the latter in their total product, while permitting the share of that sector in the product of other countries to decline all the more precipitously? Why was the decline in the share of the A sector in total product widespread, rather than concentrated in some countries and absent in others?

The answer must be given in the light of conditions of economic growth which imply, as will be argued below, a marked rise of productivity in the A sector as well as in the other sectors. And, disregarding such noneconomic factors as nationalistically motivated urges for domestic manufactures and other conspicuous symbols of "modernity," we stress four arguments. First, with rising per capita income, there may be a proportionately greater demand for nonagricultural products—and for goods that can be imported only at prohibitive cost and perhaps not even then. A proportionately greater demand for education and health services could hardly be satisfied by imports; and neither could demand by ultimate consumers for more transport and distribution services within the country. There are thus limits on the extent to which international specialization can reduce the effects of different income elasticities of domestic demand on the structure of domestic output. Second, if the volume of agricultural production rises, as it must in response to increased population and per capita income, the widening domestic market for nonagricultural products, even if importable, reduces the earlier comparative disadvantages and thus widens the economic base for import-substitution industries outside the A sector. Third, we found widespread declines in the share of the A sector in total product in the *developed* countries (except Australia).

But the period when the declines occurred was one in which these countries came into closer contact—through increasingly improved means of transport and communication and in other ways—with previously isolated parts of the world. This may have meant that the earlier comparative advantage of the more developed countries in the A sector was adversely affected by the increasing exposure to competition from other less developed areas, while the comparative advantage in the non-A sectors (with the possible exception of natural resource-based subdivisions like mining) was not. Finally, the changes involved in much of modern technology, e.g. the substitution of mechanical for animal power, and eventually of synthetic for "natural" products, restricted agriculture even more—over and above the low income elasticity of ultimate demand for its finished products. The substitution of the tractor and the automobile for the horse, of chemical for natural fertilizers, and of coal and petroleum for wood are conspicuous illustrations of this trend.

We may turn now to long-term movements in the share of the agriculture sector in resources, particularly labor but also capital. Two main points are discussed: (1) the indispensability of a significant rise in productivity in the agriculture sector for the high overall rates of increase in productivity associated with modern economic growth (discussed in Chapter 2); and (2) the implication of the marked long-term decline in the share of the agriculture sector in total resources for the migration of these resources, particularly labor, to other sectors. Some other trends to which that decline contributes—the urbanization of the population and the shift in the labor force toward employee status and white-collar occupations—are best noted after we deal with the industry and services sectors, since changes within those sectors also contribute to these two broad trends.

1. As already indicated in the preceding section, the proportional changes in the share of the agriculture sector in total resources were, in many countries, as large as those in the sector's share in total product. Productivity in the agri-

culture sector, therefore, must have increased at a rate close to that for the country as a whole. We calculated the ratios of the shares in total product to those in total labor force—the resource for which we have data for most developed countries—at the two terminal points in a long period for twelve countries (Table 3.4). The shares are mostly from Tables 3.1 and 3.2, but in some cases the periods were changed for greater comparability of the time interval.

Since the underlying shares are rather crude, the ratios are indeed rough approximations. In general, a change of one decimal point in the ratio cannot be viewed as significant. Hence for four countries (Great Britain, Norway, the United States in constant prices, and Canada), we have no grounds for assuming a significant trend in the ratio of per worker product in the agriculture sector to countrywide per worker product. In the Netherlands, Denmark, and Australia, the ratios rise more than one decimal point, and perhaps in these three countries productivity in the agriculture sector increased at somewhat higher rates than countrywide. In France, Sweden, Italy, Japan, and the U.S.S.R. the ratios decline more than one decimal point, and in Italy and Japan from four to five tenths of the initial level. We may infer that even when the ratio of the share of the agriculture sector in product to its share in labor force declined, the decline was not more than a third of the initial level. This implies that the rate of growth in product per worker in the agriculture sector was at least two thirds of the rate of growth in product per worker for the entire economy. Considering the high levels of the latter—as suggested in Chapter 2, well above 10 and sometimes over 20 per cent per decade—the implied rates of growth for the agriculture sector in these countries must also have been quite high.

That in most countries the rate of increase in product per worker in the agriculture sector was as high as the countrywide cannot be due to a rise in the per worker supply of capital in this sector relative to the other sectors. In terms of total capital including land—the appropriate

116

TABLE 3.4

Ratio of Product per Worker in the Agricultural Sector to Countrywide Product per Worker, Selected Countries, Long Periods
(underlying product totals in current prices unless otherwise indicated)

| | Period covered | | Ratio of the sectoral to the countrywide product per worker | | |
|---|---|---|---|---|---|
| | Product (1) | Labor force (2) | Initial date (3) | Terminal date (4) | Change (5) |
| 1. Great Britain | 1801–1955 | 1801–1951 | 0.9 | 1.0 | +0.1 |
| 2. France | 1872/82–1954 | 1866–1951 | 1.0 | 0.6 | −0.4 |
| 3. Netherlands | 1913–50 | 1909–47 | 0.6 | 0.8 | +0.2 |
| 4. Denmark | 1900/04–1948/52 | 1901–52 | 0.7 | 1.0 | +0.3 |
| 4a. Denmark, constant prices | 1900/04–1948/52 | 1901–52 | 0.6 | 0.9 | +0.3 |
| 5. Norway | 1875–1950 | 1875–1950 | 0.7 | 0.6 | −0.1 |
| 6. Sweden | 1868/72–1949/53 | 1870–1950 | 0.7 | 0.5 | −0.2 |
| 7. Italy | 1871/75–1951/55 | 1871–1951 | 1.1 | 0.7 | −0.4 |
| 8. United States | 1869/79–1939/48 | 1870/80–1940/50 | 0.4 | 0.7 | +0.3 |
| 8a. United States, constant prices | 1869/79–1939/48 | 1870/80–1940/50 | 0.5 | 0.5 | 0 |
| 9. Canada | 1900–1950/51 | 1901–51 | 0.8 | 0.7 | −0.1 |
| 10. Australia | 1889/93–1934/38 | 1891–1939 | 0.9 | 1.1 | +0.2 |
| 10a. Australia, constant prices | 1889/93–1934/38 | 1891–1939 | 1.0 | 1.2 | +0.2 |
| 11. Japan | 1878/82–1962 | 1878/82–1960 | 0.8 | 0.4 | −0.4 |
| 12. U.S.S.R., constant prices | 1928–58 | 1928–58 | 0.7 | 0.5 | −0.2 |

*Sources:* All entries are calculated directly from Tables 3.1 and 3.2; or, when a different period is used, from the sources cited in the notes to Tables 3.1 and 3.2.

total here—the partial evidence in Table 3.3 and general reasoning suggest that the share of the agriculture sector must have declined proportionately at least as much as its share in labor force. With the weight of land in total capital declining, a rise in, or even maintenance of, per worker supply of total capital in the agriculture sector relative to the other sectors would have required an extremely large flow of reproducible capital into the sector. This is unlikely since the capital requirements of the other sectors, particularly rapidly growing industry, have been demanding through most of the period of modern economic growth. (It is only in later phases of growth that an accelerated flow of reproducible capital into agriculture becomes feasible.) Thus the shares of the agriculture sector in labor and in capital have, in most countries, probably declined as much as its share in total product; and if the former declined less than the latter in a few countries, we can still infer a substantial rise in the sector's productivity even in those.

Indeed, it is difficult to see how the countrywide rates of growth of productivity, suggested in Chapter 2, could have been attained *without* a marked rise in productivity in the agriculture sector. To begin with, if output per unit of resources in the agriculture sector had remained constant, the rates of increase of productivity in the other sectors would have had to be extremely high to yield the overall rates. If we assume that the overall rate of growth of productivity was, say, 15 per cent per decade, and the agriculture sector accounted in the early phases of growth for 50 per cent of total product, and if productivity in the agriculture sector were stagnant, the rate of growth in productivity in the other sectors would have to be 30 per cent. Since much of the nonagriculture residual is in the services sector where increases in productivity, although not easily measurable, could not have been high, the increase would have to be largely in the industry sector—which in the early phases accounted for no more than a fifth of total product (implying a rise in productivity of that one sector of 75 per cent per decade—if it were the only one with rising productivity).

But there is more to the argument than merely the dead-weight effects of a large sector on the overall rate of productivity growth—important as they are. If we assume that income per worker in sectors other than agriculture rises 30 per cent per decade, the demand for the products of the agriculture sector must also increase. If we assume that income elasticity of demand for such products is 0.6, a 30 per cent rise in per worker income in the industry and services sectors would mean an 18 per cent rise in their demand for the products of the agriculture sector—which would have to be provided either domestically or from foreign countries. If, to simplify the argument, we reason in terms of a closed economy, the 18 per cent rise in the demand of population outside the agriculture sector for that sector's product would, given no increase in its productivity, require additional labor and capital. And the *shares* of labor force and of capital devoted to the agriculture sector would have to increase—at the same time that its productivity, relative to the higher productivity in the other sectors, declined. Such a shift would reduce the overall rate of productivity growth, and the strain of forcing resources into less productive uses would exercise pressures not only on the price structure (raising prices of the agriculture sector's product relative to other) but also on the drive for increasing productivity in the agriculture sector.[9] And this

9. An illustrative calculation of the effects can be made if we assume, in addition to an income elasticity of 0.6, initial shares of the agriculture sector of, say, 0.7 in the labor force and 0.5 in total product. We can then derive the per worker demand for the products of the agriculture sector, separately for workers in the agriculture sector and in the others (assuming, for simplicity, that total product is the total income of the labor force or of the population associated with it, and that the proportion of labor force to population is constant). With per worker incomes of 0.714 and 1.667, respectively, for the agriculture and other sectors, the per unit demand for agricultural products will be 0.40 and 0.73, respectively. A 30 per cent rise in the incomes of workers outside the agriculture sector will raise their per unit demand for products of the agriculture sector from 0.73 to 0.86. The share $(x)$ in

drive would be reinforced by the effects of increased productivity in the nonagriculture sectors on the productive resources attached to the agriculture sector: all other conditions being equal, labor and capital would be induced to move *toward* the other sectors that enjoy higher returns. The outcome is likely to be increased productivity in the domestic agriculture sector. Even if we abandon the assumption of a closed economy and assume some difficulties in raising productivity in the domestic agriculture sector, greater reliance on imports of such products from abroad—with the wide foreign sources of supply commanded by the increased productivity of the domestic industry and services sectors—is also likely to result in a reduction of the resources devoted to the domestic agriculture sector and in increased productivity because of the elimination of the least productive uses.

2. One may conclude that a substantial rise in productivity of resources in the domestic agriculture sector is a condition of the large increase in overall productivity in modern economic growth. It is such a rise in productivity,

---

total labor force of the agriculture sector needed to satisfy total demand can then be derived from the equation: $0.714x = 0.40x + 0.86 (100 - x)$. With $x$ working out to $0.732$, the share of the labor force in the agriculture sector has to rise from 70 to 73.2 per cent; total output per worker, assuming per worker product of $0.714$ and $2.167$, respectively, would be $1.103$, a rise of about 10 per cent or only a third of that assumed for the labor force in the sectors outside of agriculture. The calculations apply to the decade with initial shares as given; as time passes and the shares shift away from the agriculture sector, the effects of a lag in its productivity diminish.

The argument is valid even if we assume that there is much unemployed or underemployed labor or capital attached to the agriculture sector. The requirement for increased productivity to permit an adequate rate of overall growth in productivity still remains. The one change may be the greater facility in attaining a rise in productivity in the agriculture sector: it may be easier when there is a plentiful supply of unemployed or underemployed labor. But, paradoxically, this does not necessarily follow—since conditions that create a labor surplus in the agriculture sector also present obstacles to increased productivity, even with an increased demand for the products of agriculture.

combined with the low income elasticity of demand for products of the agriculture sector, that accounts for the marked decline in the share of that sector in the total of labor and capital used.

Such a decline means that labor and capital employed in the agriculture sector grew at much lower rates than productive resources used in the other sectors. These differences in rates of growth of labor and capital between the agriculture and the other sectors may, theoretically, be attained in one of two ways. The rate of *natural* increase of capital and labor may be correspondingly lower in the agriculture sector, in the sense that net saving and capital accumulation rates relative to the stock of capital used and the rate of natural increase of population, and hence of labor force, in that sector may both be lower than in the other sectors. The other possibility is that if rates of natural increase of resources in the agriculture sector are higher, the same as, or only slightly lower than those in the other sectors, the shares of the former decline largely because of transfer of capital and migration of labor.

There is no easily available evidence on accumulation of savings and capital funds within the agriculture and other sectors to provide an answer to the question just raised. If we consider the early phases of modern economic growth, when the agriculture sector is still large, and assume for this sector shares in labor force and population of, say, 70 per cent, and shares in total product and in total capital of 50 per cent (the latter perhaps too low), it seems reasonable to argue that the new capital funds provided for the agriculture sector are appreciably less than 50 per cent of total capital funds—so that even with reinvestment of all these savings within the sector, its share in total capital would decline. With a per capita income of 0.714 in the agriculture sector and of 1.667 in the other sectors, the savings–income ratio should be appreciably lower in the agriculture sector than in the others—despite the higher savings propensities of the agricultural communities and the reduction of the income disparity for differential cost of living. Still, the

121

difference in the rate of accumulation between the agriculture and other sectors is probably not sufficient to account for the sharp decline in the share of the agriculture sector in total capital, and substantial transfers of capital may have to be assumed.[10]

In the case of labor, a variety of evidence suggests that the rate of natural increase of the rural or farm population—and hence of its potential labor force—was *greater* than the rate of natural increase of the urban or nonfarm population. By implication, the rate of natural increase of the population and labor force attached to the agriculture sector was greater than the rate of natural increase of population and labor force attached to the other sectors. The magnitudes involved are large, and their order should be taken into account—if only by means of illustrative data.

To begin with, for the modern period the birth rates, while declining for both groups of the population, have been persistently higher for the farm or rural population than for the nonfarm or urban. Thus, in the United States, the number of children under 5 years of age per thousand white women aged 20 to 44 (the childbearing ages) was, taking the average for 1830 and 1840, 1,162 for rural population and 705 for urban, a ratio of over 1.6 to 1; for 1940 and 1950, it was 612 for rural population and 395 for urban, both much lower than a century earlier, but with a ratio still close to 1.6 to 1.[11] When rural farm population is distinguished from rural nonfarm, the contrast between the

10. In Japan in the early development decades such transfers were accelerated by the tax system; government's main revenues were derived from taxes on agriculture and channeled largely into investment in other sectors (see Kazushi Ohkawa and Henry Rosovsky, "The Role of Agriculture in Modern Japanese Economic Development," *Economic Development and Cultural Change, 9,* October 1960, Part II, 50–63). It would be of interest to determine whether similar policies were followed in the early periods of modern growth by other countries.

11. See *Historical Statistics of the United States,* Series B 39–B 41, p. 24. The data are not adjusted for undercount of children, and the urban–rural classification is that of the Census of 1940 with urban limited to incorporated places of 2,500 inhabitants or more.

birth rate of the former and that of urban population is still sharper. Thus in the United States, the number of children ever born per thousand native white women aged 45–49 (by which age the childbearing life span is usually completed) was 3,587 for rural farm population and 2,096 for urban, a range of 1.7 to 1.[12] Similarly wide differences in fertility between the rural and urban population are found for recent years in many countries, industrialized or not.[13] And while in premodern days the birth rates in the cities were higher than in the countryside, they declined rapidly to below the countrywide levels. Thus in 1701–50, the crude birth rate in the London area was 38 per thousand, compared with 34 in England and Wales as a whole; by 1801–30 the two birth rates were 35 and 37, respectively—and in the earlier period the death rate in the London area was as high as 49 per thousand compared with 33 for the whole country, while in the later period the two rates were 27 and 23, respectively.[14] In short, for almost all the period associated with modern economic growth the crude birth rate was much higher for the population engaged in the agriculture sector than for that engaged in the other sectors.

Next, the death rate was no higher for the population engaged in the agriculture sector than for that engaged in the other sectors. In fact, it was much lower in the countryside than in the cities in premodern days; and the major technological changes in this field, while reducing the death rate in the cities much more than in the countryside, did not cause a significant reversal in position. If we assume the same crude death rate for both groups of the popula-

12. See Clyde V. Kiser, "Differential Fertility in the United States," in Universities–National Bureau of Economic Research Committee, *Demographic and Economic Change in Developed Countries* (Princeton, 1960), Table 2, p. 88. These figures are based on the 1950 Census definition of urban, which is somewhat different from that for earlier censuses in that it includes the urban fringes around cities of 50,000 or more.

13. See U.N., *Demographic Yearbook, 1952*, Table F, p. 17 and discussion in the text.

14. See Deane and Cole, *British Economic Growth*, Table 28, p. 127.

tion—an exaggeration that weakens our argument—we can illustrate the implications of the differences in the birth rates for the rate of natural increase—which, barring migration, determines the rate of population growth. A birth rate for the agricultural population 1.6 times higher than that for population engaged in other sectors, a ratio of the agricultural population to the total of 70 per cent, and a countrywide birth rate of 50 per thousand imply a birth rate for the agricultural population of 56 per thousand, and for the rest of the population of 35 per thousand. If we assume a death rate of 25 per thousand, the rate of natural increase for the agricultural population is 31 per thousand, and for the nonagricultural population, 10 per thousand, or only a third. If we keep all the other assumptions, but reduce the countrywide birth rate to 35 per thousand and the death rate to 20 per thousand, the implied rates of natural increase are 20 per thousand for the agricultural population and only 5 per thousand for the nonagricultural. The illustrations could be multiplied and modified, but the point is clear: differentials in birth rates between agricultural and other population, would, given the same death rate for both, yield rates of natural increase for the two components of total population with much larger *relative* disparities—an important consequence, provided that the agricultural population is a substantial segment of the total.

The inference for disparities in rate of natural increase between agricultural and other population also applies to a comparison of the two labor force components—for neither the magnitude nor the trends of the ratio of labor force to population in the two groups of sectors differ sufficiently to modify significantly the impact of the differential rates of natural increase on the labor force. Consequently, barring migration, the rate of natural increase of the labor force in the agriculture sector might keep the rate of growth of the sector's labor force as much as three times as high as that of the labor force in the other sectors. Clearly, if the share of the agriculture sector in total labor force showed the decline observed in Table 3.2, there must have been, in a closed population, massive internal migration—the transfer from the agriculture to other sectors, involving in most cases actual migration across space. If we allow for emigration and immigration, the outflow from the agriculture sector of some countries must have gone abroad, and the flow in some countries must have favored the nonagriculture sectors. But these flows only supplemented internal migration: for obvious reasons, international migration could not fully substitute for migration from sector to sector within a country.

Internal migration must have been a widespread and rapid process in most developed countries, considering the marked differentials in rates of natural increase of agricultural and other population and in rates of growth of economic opportunities within the two groups of sectors. It must also have had numerous effects on modern economic growth, but it is impossible to discuss these within the limits of the present monograph. However, three comments are added to those made in Chapter 2 concerning the effect of the detachment of a migrant from his early home surroundings on his adaptability to economic opportunities, and the effect of the cleavage between blood ties and origin and location of economic opportunities on increasing efficiency in modern economic growth.

First, migration is a process highly selective as to age and sex—if it is not forced but is a voluntary response to greater economic opportunities. The people who move are usually in prime working ages and until recent decades were preponderantly males. Thus, in the United States, interstate net migration per decade for 1870–1900 was, proportionately to the base population, highest among males aged 25–29 (close to 7 per cent); the proportion for all males was 4 per cent, that for all females 3.3 per cent.[15] International migration in the "free" decades was even more

15. See Dorothy Swaine Thomas, "Age and Economic Differentials in Interstate Migration," *Population Index, 24* (October 1958), Table 1, p. 315.

selectively concentrated in the prime working force ages. This meant that the migrants from agriculture to other sectors were workers probably born and raised in the countryside and ready for work; and regardless of transfers of capital funds from the agriculture sector to the others, the transfer of past investment in training and education of the migrants must have represented a large body of economic resources from which the other sectors benefited.

Second, as migration took place and the share of the agriculture sector in total population, capital, and labor force declined, its contribution in the form of capital transfers and internal migration to the capital and labor force in the other sectors diminished. As the nonagriculture sectors increased proportionately in the economy, the sources of their further growth lay more and more within themselves rather than in the transfer of capital and labor from the agriculture sector. This transfer process was, therefore, especially important in the early phases of modern economic growth and industrialization. The implications of this trend for the distribution of income by size will be noted in Chapter 4.

Finally, while internal (and to some extent foreign) migration from agriculture to the other sectors was among the largest streams, there were other disparities between the rates of natural increase of productive factors and of growth and employment potentials—within the agriculture sector proper, and within and between the industry and service sectors. While birth rates are higher for the farm population than for other groups, those for rural nonfarm tend to be higher than urban, and those for small city population higher than for big cities; and with the death rates showing far smaller differentials, the disparities in rates of natural increase among all these groups have been fairly wide and persistent. Insofar as associations differ between residence in these localities of varying size and economic opportunities—and opportunities do not necessarily grow more rapidly in localities with the highest rates of natural increase— the discussion of the shifts from agriculture to nonagriculture can be applied to shifts in *other* components within labor force and economic structure. It may well be that as the shifts arising from the contrasts between agriculture and nonagriculture diminished in relative importance, the scope and rate of internal migration of labor, and perhaps of capital, were sustained by the continued disparity between the rates of natural increase of these productive factors and those in economic growth potential for groups within the nonagricultural sectors proper. The disparities between demographic and economic trends in the increase of population and labor, and between internal capital accumulation and differentials in investment opportunities, are numerous and widespread; and the required transfers and migrations were far-reaching processes whose role in the rapid structural shifts and high rates of modern economic growth can hardly be exaggerated.

STRUCTURE OF THE INDUSTRY SECTOR AND OF MANUFACTURING

When the share of the industry sector in total product is related to its share in labor force, as was done for agriculture in Table 3.4, the ratios (not given in detail to conserve space) for Great Britain or the United Kingdom, France, the Netherlands, Norway, Italy, and Canada rise, some significantly; for Sweden, the United States, Australia, and the U.S.S.R. they are stable; and in none of the ten countries for which the comparison is possible does the ratio decline. One may conclude that output per worker in the industry sector rose at least as much as countrywide output per worker; and in many countries at appreciably higher rates. Probably a similar conclusion would be reached with respect to output per unit of all resources— if we could add capital; and this higher upward trend in the productivity of the industry sector, compared with the countrywide, would be more prominent if we could adjust properly for the decline in man-hours and hours of capital utilization.

But we are more concerned here with (1) the structure of the industry sector and (2) the structure of manufacturing, and with the changes in them associated with modern economic growth. As already indicated, the industry sector includes mining, electric power, gas, and water (sometimes included with manufacturing and sometimes under transportation and other public utilities), manufacturing, construction, and transportation and communication. It is of interest to observe both the levels and trends of the shares of these subdivisions of the industry sector in the sector's total output and resources, or in the countrywide totals.

We begin with the shares for recent years, because a fair amount of data is available for developed countries in the post-World War II years. For ten countries we derived the shares for 1954–56 in domestic product (at factor cost or at market prices); and the shares for the late 1940s or early 1950s in the labor force. The unweighted arithmetic means of the shares for individual countries are given in the following tabulation:

Shares in Total for the Industry Sector (%)*

| | Mining | Electric power, gas, water | Manu-facturing | Con-struction | Trans-portation and commu-nication | Share of sector in country-wide total (%) |
|---|---|---|---|---|---|---|
| Domestic product | 5 | 4 | 62 | 12 | 17 | 52 |
| Labor force | 5 | 2 | 63 | 15 | 15 | 44 |

* The countries included are the United Kingdom, France, Belgium, West Germany, the Netherlands, Denmark, Norway, the United States, Canada, and Japan. Product data are from U.N., *Yearbook of National Accounts Statistics, 1961;* labor force data, from U.N., *Demographic Yearbook, 1955,* Table 16.

While countries differ in the share of some subdivision of the industry sector—e.g. the share of mining is high in Canada (8.5 per cent of the sector total product) and low in Denmark (0.4 per cent)—the range is relatively narrow for the large subdivisions, particularly manufacturing.

Thus, in no country is the share of manufacturing in total product of the sector less than 50 per cent or over 70 per cent. For the share in the sector labor force, the range is even narrower: from 55 to 67.5 per cent. The averages, therefore, are fairly representative, and we may conclude that in recent years manufacturing has accounted for over six tenths of the industry sector's output and labor force; and the addition of electric power, gas, and water would raise the share to about two thirds. This means that shares in the countrywide product and labor force are between 30 and 35 per cent. The second largest subdivision is transport and communication, accounting for about a sixth of the sector's output and labor, and for about 7 to 9 per cent of the countrywide totals. The share of construction, which covers all construction other than that done for themselves by enterprises primarily engaged in other types of activity, is between a seventh and an eighth of the sector's output and labor force, and about 6 to 7 per cent of the country-wide totals. The share of mining in the industry sector of developed countries is quite small, only about 5 per cent of the sector totals and about 2.5 per cent of the countrywide totals.

The distribution of capital investment among the subdivisions of the industry sector is significantly different. Thus in the United Kingdom in 1953, of the total fixed assets in the industry sector (including trade), transport and communication accounted for 28 per cent—almost double their share in output in the mid-1950s;[16] whereas manufacturing, construction, and trade accounted for 54 per cent, compared with the share in total sectoral product (excluding trade) of about 75 per cent. In Norway in 1953, fixed assets for mining and manufacturing accounted for less than 40 per cent of total fixed assets in the industry sector,

16. All data on capital cited in this paragraph except those for the United States, are from Goldsmith and Saunders, eds., *Income and Wealth, Series VIII,* Table IV, pp. 20 ff.; those for the United States are from *Historical Statistics of the United States, Series* F 247–F 251, p. 152.

compared with 52 per cent in output; whereas electric power and transport and communication accounted for over 50 per cent of fixed assets, but only 35 per cent of product. In the United States at the end of 1948, the value of structures and equipment in the transportation and public utilities subdivision was over 50 per cent of the total for industry (the latter including mining and manufacturing but not construction), whereas the share in product was only about 20 per cent. In Canada in 1955 fixed assets in transportation and communication were about a quarter of those in total industry, and the share in product was less than a fifth. In general, transport and communication, electric light and power, gas, and water account for a far higher share in the industry sector's capital than in its product or labor force. Because they are more capital intensive than the other subdivisions, their shares in labor force may be expected to be somewhat lower than their shares in product.

By examining the long-term movements in the structure of the industry sector, we can ascertain the secular shifts, if any, in the composition of the industry sector. The scanty data that can be easily assembled on shares in product and in labor force, are summarized in Table 3.5.

With the necessary qualifications due to the limited coverage and the difficulty of assuring full comparability in the classification, several conclusions are suggested.

First, mining was always a relatively small subdivision of the industry sector, except in Australia in the early years, when it loomed large in what was an empty if rapidly growing country; and its shares in the sector's total product and labor force tended to decline. The shares of construction in the sector's product and labor force, substantially higher than those for mining, show, with some exceptions, the same downward trend. Both of these trends seem reasonable. The shares of mining in total industry, although not necessarily in countrywide total product and labor force, will decline as, with the exhaustion of resources, a country loses some of its comparative advantage—while the increasing demand for the products of manufacturing and for the services of

130

TABLE 3.5

Distribution of Product and Labor Force in the Industry Sector,
Selected Countries, Long Periods
(underlying totals in current prices unless otherwise indicated)

Shares in total for the industry sector (%)

| | Mining (1) | Manu-facturing (2) | Con-struction (3) | Trans-portation and commu-nication (4) | Share of sector in country-wide total (%) (5) |
|---|---|---|---|---|---|
| **A. PRODUCT** | | | | | |
| *United Kingdom* | | | | | |
| 1. 1907 | 13 | 59 | 8 | 20 | 46 |
| 2. 1924 | 10 | 61 | 6 | 23 | 52 |
| 3. 1955 | 6 | 69 | 10 | 15 | 56 |
| *Sweden* | | | | | |
| 4. 1861–65 | | 44 | 42 | 14 | 17 |
| 5. 1901–05 | | 64 | 18 | 18 | 38 |
| 6. 1949–53 | | 74 | 12 | 14 | 55 |
| *Norway* | | | | | |
| 7. 1910 | | 70 | | 30 | 37 |
| 8. 1956 | | 64 | | 36 | 53 |
| *Italy* | | | | | |
| 9. 1861–65 | 2 | 79 | 11 | 8 | 20 |
| 10. 1896–1900 | 4 | 69 | 9 | 18 | 22 |
| 11. 1951–55 | 2 | 74 | 11 | 13 | 48 |
| *United States* | | | | | |
| 12. 1869/79 | 5 | 42 | 16 | 36 | 33 |
| 13. 1919–28 | 6 | 57 | 11 | 26 | 39 |
| 14. 1929 | 5 | 59 | 10 | 26 | 42 |
| 15. 1961–63 | 3 | 66 | 12 | 19 | 43 |
| *Constant prices* | | | | | |
| 16. 1869–78 | 5 | 61 | 20 | 14 | 29 |
| 17. 1939–48 | 5 | 65 | 5 | 25 | 42 |
| *Australia* | | | | | |
| 18. 1861–65 | 46 | 14 | 29 | 11 | 31 |
| 19. 1934–38 | 9 | 51 | 20 | 20 | 33 |
| *Constant prices* | | | | | |
| 20. 1861–65 | 44 | 17 | 35 | 4 | 31 |
| 21. 1934–38 | 7 | 51 | 21 | 21 | 30 |
| **B. LABOR FORCE** | | | | | |
| *Great Britain* | | | | | |
| 22. 1841 | 6 | 75 | 11 | 8 | 43 |
| 23. 1901 | 10 | 61 | 14 | 15 | 54 |
| 24. 1921 | 14 | 65 | 8 | 13 | 55 |
| 25. 1951 | 7 | 69 | 11 | 13 | 57 |

131

TABLE 3.5—*Continued*

Shares in total for the industry sector (%)

| | Mining (1) | Manufacturing (2) | Construction (3) | Transportation and communication (4) | Share of sector in countrywide total (%) (5) |
|---|---|---|---|---|---|
| *Netherlands* | | | | | |
| 26. 1909 | 2 | 78 | | 20 | 46 |
| 27. 1947 | 3 | 81 | | 16 | 44 |
| *Switzerland* | | | | | |
| 28. 1880 | 0 | 94 | | 6 | 48 |
| 29. 1910 | 2 | 82 | | 16 | 54 |
| 30. 1941 | 1 | 91 | | 8 | 49 |
| *Denmark* | | | | | |
| 31. 1911 | 0 | 85 | | 15 | 32 |
| 32. 1952 | 0 | 85 | | 15 | 45 |
| *Norway* | | | | | |
| 33. 1875 | | 72 | | 28 | 33 |
| 34. 1910 | | 77 | | 23 | 41 |
| 35. 1950 | | 78 | | 22 | 48 |
| *Sweden* | | | | | |
| 36. 1910 | 2 | 82 | | 16 | 36 |
| 37. 1950 | 1 | 83 | | 16 | 50 |
| *Italy* | | | | | |
| 38. 1871 | 1 | 92 | | 7 | 35 |
| 39. 1911 | 2 | 87 | | 11 | 36 |
| 40. 1936 | 2 | 86 | | 12 | 37 |
| *United States* | | | | | |
| 41. 1870 | 5 | 58 | 20 | 17 | 30 |
| 42. 1910 | 7 | 56 | 16 | 21 | 41 |
| 43. 1950 | 4 | 65 | 14 | 17 | 45 |
| *Canada* | | | | | |
| 44. 1901 | 7 | 42 | 36 | 15 | 33 |
| 45. 1951 | 5 | 62 | 15 | 18 | 44 |
| *Australia* | | | | | |
| 46. 1891 | 13 | 41 | 30 | 16 | 43 |
| 47. 1947 | 4 | 59 | 16 | 21 | 48 |
| *Japan* | | | | | |
| 48. 1872 | 1 | 74 | 13 | 12 | 6 |
| 49. 1925 | 5 | 67 | 12 | 15 | 24 |
| 50. 1950 | 6 | 59 | 16 | 19 | 27 |
| 51. 1960 | 3 | 63 | 18 | 16 | 35 |

*Sources:* Cited in notes to Tables 3.1 and 3.2.

the transportation and communication system make for a more rapid growth of these subdivisions. The shares of construction in the industry product and labor force, and perhaps even in the countrywide totals, will decline as the rate of population growth and the demand for new residential construction slackens, as more construction is done not within the contract construction industry but by enterprises primarily engaged in other activities, and as capital investment shifts away from construction of plants, offices, etc. toward equipment—a trend to be discussed in Chapter 5.

Second, the share of manufacturing, including or excluding electric power, gas, and water, in the total product of the industry sector rose. Such an upward trend is less apparent for the share in labor force: in Great Britain it declined, but in the other three countries for which it is available it rose. Since the share of the industry sector in countrywide total product rose, the share of manufacturing in countrywide total product must have increased markedly in all developed countries; and its share in countrywide labor force must also have risen in many developed countries, if not in all. Thus, at least with respect to product, and in many countries with respect to labor force, manufacturing was the major rapidly rising division in the economy.

Third, the share of transportation and communication in product apparently reflects differential price movements. The prices of transportation and communication services must have declined drastically, probably more than the prices of many other goods. Hence constancy or even a mild decline in their share in product in current prices may conceal a substantial rise in their share adjusted for differential changes in prices (compare lines 12–15 with lines 16–17). By and large, the share of the transport and communication subdivision in industry product in constant prices rose, which would indicate an even greater rise in the share in countrywide product. The share in the sector's labor force was either constant or rising; and there must also have been a rise in the share in countrywide labor force. Thus, like manufacturing, transport and communication was among the rapidly rising subsectors in the total economy's product and labor force—although the shares were not as high as those of manufacturing.

Data on the shares of the subdivisions of the industry sector in total capital are exceedingly scanty. And the difficulty is compounded because the trends in the structure of capital within the industry sector depend upon the period covered by the estimates: if it were to include the early phases of economic growth, when the transportation and communication network was being constructed (e.g. for railroads, the most capital-demanding branch in the United States between 1840 and 1890), we would observe a rise in the share of transport and communication (and related public utilities) in total capital in the industry sector, and probably in total capital of the economy; if it were to cover only the later phases, after the public utility network had practically been completed, we would observe a decline in the share of transport and communication in total capital of the industry sector—and a rise in the shares of other subdivisions, particularly manufacturing.[17] In view of the large capital investment in the transport, communication, and other public utilities networks in the early phases of modern economic growth, it is a pity that no detailed studies are available on the timing of these trends in relation to capital investment and rate of growth of product and labor force in other sectors. For the present we must be satisfied with the meager conclusion that the more rapid growth of product and labor force in the manufacturing and transport and

17. In the United States in 1880, transport, communication, and other public utilities accounted for 83 per cent of the total stock of structures and equipment for industry (mining, manufacturing, and public utilities); by 1948, this share had declined to 53 per cent. In the same period, the share of manufacturing rose from 13 to 41 per cent (see *Historical Statistics of the United States*, Series F 249–F 251, p. 152). Similar trends can be found for similar or even later periods for a number of countries in Goldsmith and Saunders, eds., *Income and Wealth, Series VIII*. But in all these cases the early periods of growth when the transport, communication, and other public utility networks were in the process of construction are not covered.

communication subdivisions of the industry sector—which made for a rise in the shares of these two subdivisions in the industry sector and in the countrywide totals of product and labor—was probably accompanied by shifts in the structure of capital investment that had distinctive time patterns, different for the two subdivisions. The rise in the share of the transport and communication subdivision in sectoral or countrywide capital stock emerged first, that in the share of manufacturing appearing later. Perhaps the combined shares of the two subdivisions in the total capital of the sector and of the country would show a fairly continuous upward trend, but this conjecture cannot be checked for lack of data.

2. Since manufacturing is among the most rapidly growing subsectors in the course of modern economic growth, and its share in total product in most developed countries is almost a third, great interest attaches to trends in its *structure*—in the distribution of its output and resources among the various branches. But available and comparable long-term data are scanty, and we present the evidence in some detail for only two countries, the United States and Sweden, referring in the text to findings for other countries.[18]

Table 3.6 summarizes the distribution in the United

18. Data for recent (or earlier) years, on structure of manufacturing in association with per capita product (or any other measure of economic growth), are an unreliable indicator of long-term trends. Forestalling discussion on this point in Chaps. 5 and 8, one may mention here that the danger lies in the failure of cross-section data to reflect changes in technology and tastes. If these changes run counter to the income effects (e.g. the above-average rate of growth of frozen foods contrasted with income elasticities in cross-section analysis that are probably less than 1), cross-section data will suggest trends with the wrong sign (i.e. declines rather than rises); and in other cases, such data will yield incorrect coefficients, even if they have the right sign. Such failure of cross-section data could be overcome if the trends in technology and tastes were known and could be embodied in a distinction within the cross-section data at a point of time between old and new, modern and obsolescent, and the like. But if we had such direct knowledge of past trends, there would be no need for cross-section data in this connection—however useful they may be for short-term analysis and policy.

**TABLE 3.6**

Structure of Manufacturing, United States, 1880–1948*

| | Food, beverages, tobacco (1) | Textile products (2) | Leather and rubber (3) | Forest products (4) | Paper and printing (5) | Stone, clay, and glass (6) | Chemicals and petroleum (7) | Metal products (8) | Miscellaneous (9) |
|---|---|---|---|---|---|---|---|---|---|
| *Shares in value of output (%)* | | | | | | | | | |
| *Current prices* | | | | | | | | | |
| 1. 1880 (5.1) | 28 | 19 | 10 | 11 | 4 | 2 | 5 | 19 | 2 |
| 2. 1948 (213.3) | 21 | 12 | 3 | 4 | 6 | 2 | 16 | 32 | 3 |
| *1929 prices* | | | | | | | | | |
| 3. 1880 (8.8) | 28 | 18 | 12 | 18 | 3.5 | 2 | 3.5 | 13 | 2 |
| 4. 1948 (128.1) | 20.5 | 12 | 4 | 3 | 5 | 2 | 17 | 33.5 | 3 |
| *Shares in value added (%)* | | | | | | | | | |
| 5. 1880 (1.8) | 16 | 22 | 7 | 11 | 6 | 4 | 3 | 23 | 8 |
| 6. 1947 (74.4) | 13 | 13 | 4 | 5 | 10 | 3 | 10 | 39 | 3 |
| *Shares in net income originating (%)* | | | | | | | | | |
| 7. 1947 (58.7) | 10 | 14 | 4 | 6 | 9 | 3 | 10 | 41 | 3 |
| *Shares in number engaged (%)* | | | | | | | | | |
| 8. 1880 (employees, 2.6) | 12 | 28 | 7 | 12 | 5 | 5 | 2 | 22 | 7 |
| 9. 1947 (15.4) | 11 | 16 | 4 | 8 | 8 | 3 | 6 | 40 | 4 |
| *Shares in total capital (%)* | | | | | | | | | |
| *Book values* | | | | | | | | | |
| 10. 1880 (2.7) | 18 | 22 | 6 | 13 | 5 | 6 | 3 | 24 | 2 |
| 11. 1948 (113.4) | 14 | 9 | 3 | 4 | 7 | 3 | 22 | 35 | 3 |
| *1929 values* | | | | | | | | | |
| 12. 1880 (4.8) | 19 | 21 | 7 | 17 | 5 | 3 | 5 | 21 | 2 |
| 13. 1948 (78.0) | 13 | 9 | 3 | 4 | 6 | 3 | 23 | 36 | 3 |

| Shares in fixed capital (%) | | | | | | | | | |
|---|---|---|---|---|---|---|---|---|---|
| 14. 1948, book values (45.7) | 12 | 6.5 | 2 | 4.5 | 7 | 3 | 29 | 33.5 | 2.5 |
| 15. 1948, 1929 values (36.5) | 12 | 7 | 2 | 4.5 | 7 | 3 | 29 | 33.5 | 2 |
| Number engaged per establishment | | | | | | | | | |
| 16. 1947 (average for mfg., 60) | 39 | 63 | 91 | 30 | 36 | 40 | 73 | 120 | 42 |

* Unless otherwise indicated, the underlying totals are the absolute volumes—output, value added, income, and capital in billions of dollars; total number engaged in millions.

Sources: Lines 1–4, 10–15: From Daniel Creamer, Sergei P. Dobrovolsky, and Israel Borenstein, *Capital in Manufacturing and Mining: Its Formation and Financing* (National Bureau of Economic Research, 1960), Table A-8, pp. 241–47; Table A-9, pp. 248–51; and Table A-10, pp. 252–58.

Lines 5 and 8: From United States, Bureau of the Census, *12th Census of the United States, 7, Manufactures, Part I* (Washington, 1902), Table LVIII, p. cxliv.

Line 6: From U.S., Bureau of the Census, *Census of Manufactures, 1947, 1* (Washington, 1950), Table 2, p. 24.

Line 7: From U.S., Department of Commerce, *U.S. Income and Output*, Table I-10, p. 130.

Line 9: From U.S., Department of Commerce, *National Income, 1954 Edition* (Washington, 1954), Table 28, p. 202.

Line 16: From U.N., *Patterns of Industrial Growth, 1938–1958* (New York, 1960), p. 414.

States of various measures of output, number engaged, and capital invested among broad manufacturing groups, some of which could be broken down further. Table 3.7 covers the structure of manufacturing in Sweden, emphasizing the distribution of finished output, and the three components within the latter. These estimates suggest not only the major trends in the structure of manufacturing but also the characteristics of the industry groups.

First, we note the differences in the shares of the various industries for different measures of manufacturing output. The shares of the food and the chemical industries (the latter including petroleum and coal products) in total output, which includes unfinished products consumed within manufacturing and the value of materials and fuel purchased from others, are distinctly larger than the shares in value added or in net income originating (Table 3.6, lines 1–2, 5–7).[19] By contrast, the shares of paper and printing and the large metal products group in value of output are distinctly lower than those in value added or income originating. The differences in the shares of various industries are even wider when we compare the total of *finished* commodities with the value of output including unfinished commodities (Table 3.7, lines 1–4). Thus the share of food in the total of finished commodities is distinctly larger than its share in total output, and the same is true, to some extent, of the textile products group; whereas the shares of chemicals and metal products in finished output are distinctly lower than those in total output. These differences would be even wider if we compared shares in finished output with those in value added or in net income origi-

19. Value added is the difference between value of products and cost of materials and fuel (including cost of containers, electric energy consumed, and freight and haulage). Net income originating is the contribution to national income and thus represents the sum of factor costs incurred by the industry in production. It differs from value added in that it is net of depreciation charges and payments to other sectors for goods other than materials and fuels.

## TABLE 3.7

Structure of Manufacturing, Sweden, 1873–1948 (underlying product totals in 1913 prices)

| | Food (1) | Textile products (2) | Leather and rubber (3) | Wood products (4) | Paper and printing (5) | Stone, clay, and glass (6) | Chemicals (7) | Mining and metal (8) | Total (9) |
|---|---|---|---|---|---|---|---|---|---|
| *Shares in value of output (%)* | | | | | | | | | |
| 1. 1873 | 29 | 11 | 6 | 24 | 1 | 2 | 7 | 20 | 491 |
| 2. 1948 | 19 | 11 | 7 | 3 | 13 | 4 | 4 | 40 | 9,094 |
| *Shares in finished output (%)* | | | | | | | | | |
| 3. 1873 | 37 | 11 | 5 | 29 | 1 | 1 | 2 | 14 | 370 |
| 4. 1948 | 25 | 14 | 7 | 3 | 12 | 1 | 2 | 36 | 5,735 |
| *Shares in finished consumer goods (%)* | | | | | | | | | |
| 5. 1873 | 63 | 19 | 9 | 3 | 1 | 2 | 2 | 1 | 206 |
| 6. 1948 | 44 | 24 | 12.5 | 3 | 4 | 1.5 | 2.5 | 8.5 | 3,214 |
| *Shares in finished investment goods (%)* | | | | | | | | | |
| 7. 1873 | 0 | 6 | 0 | 6 | 0 | 0 | 0 | 88 | 17 |
| 8. 1948 | 0 | 0.3 | 0.3 | 0.4 | 0 | 0.2 | 0 | 99 | 1,090 |
| *Shares in exports (%)* | | | | | | | | | |
| 9. 1873 | 6 | 1.5 | 0.5 | 66 | 1.5 | 0.5 | 3 | 21.5 | 147 |
| 10. 1948 | 1.5 | 0.5 | 0.5 | 5 | 40 | 1 | 2.5 | 49 | 1,431 |
| *Number engaged per establishment* | | | | | | | | | |
| 11. 1951 | 9 | 9 | 15 | 8 | 37 | 13 | 34 | 23 | 14 |

Sources: *Lines 1–10:* From Johansson, "Economic Growth and Structure in Sweden," Table 10. The entries in col. 9 are totals in millions of kronor.

*Line 11:* From U.N., *Patterns of Industrial Growth*, p. 375.

nating.[20] One important inference follows. Changes in demand are directly connected with *finished* output; and in terms of shares in the unduplicated total of value added or, still better, of net income originating, changes in the structure of manufacturing can occur independently of changes in demand for finished product—in the sense that, with technological and related changes, similar finished products can represent different degrees of fabrication.

Second, the United States data suggest that the shares of the various groups in number engaged do not differ significantly from those in value added or income originating. To be sure, the share of the textile products group in number engaged is distinctly higher and that of the chemical group distinctly lower than the corresponding shares in value added; but for the other branches the two shares are fairly close. The same is true when we compare the shares in value added with those in capital invested, whether total or fixed. This suggests that there are no major differences among industry groups, at least for the broad distribution in Table 3.6, in capital intensity, whether measured by capital per engaged or per unit of value added. In particular, the notion that consumer goods industries, such as food products or textiles, are less capital intensive than producers' goods, such as metal products, is not supported by the evidence in Table 3.6. The only exception is the chemical–petroleum group, accounted for largely by the high capital intensity of the petroleum refining branch, which is largely a consumer goods industry in a modern economy.[21] Undoubtedly, a more detailed classification

20. In the United States, the share of manufactured food products in the total of finished manufactured commodities was over 40 per cent in 1879, compared with their shares of 28 per cent in total output and of 16 per cent in value added. The first figure is derived from William H. Shaw, *Value of Commodity Output since 1869* (National Bureau of Economic Research, 1947), pp. 110 and 152; the other two are from Table 3.6, lines 1 and 5.

21. The distinction must be based on the ultimate destination of the preponderant output of a given industry group—i.e. whether the finished product flows into household consumption, fixed capital, or exports.

would reveal other capital–intensive subgroups: tobacco within the food group, paper within the paper and printing group, and basic metals within the metal products group— none of which is more preponderantly producer than consumer goods. And while the metal products group is larger than average in terms of number engaged (Table 3.6, line 16 and Table 3.7, line 11), other branches which produce consumer goods are also larger.

Third, in both the United States and Sweden, the shifts in the structure of manufacturing—revealed by shares in total or finished output, value added, number engaged, and capital invested—are quite similar. The shares of both the food industries and the wood products group declined. The shares of textiles and leather products (even with the latter including rubber) declined in the United States but not in Sweden; yet the decline in the share of textile products can be observed in many other countries.[22] Of the remaining major groups, the shares of paper and printing, chemicals and petroleum, and metal products rose; and for the latter two branches we find ample confirmation in the shares in value added in the Hoffmann monograph.[23]

With the share of metal products rising substantially and those of the food and textile groups declining markedly,

22. See Hoffmann, *The Growth of Industrial Economies,* Tables XL-XLII, pp. 161–65. Hoffmann's data show a decline in the share of textile products in value added in Great Britain (from 43 per cent in 1871 to 17 per cent in 1948), in France (from 34 per cent in 1861–65 to less than 20 per cent in 1921), in Switzerland (from 55 per cent in 1882 to 22 per cent in 1929), and in Canada (from 20 per cent in 1901 to 12 per cent in 1950). The decline in the share of food industries in manufacturing value added was not as widely observed—although the downward trends might have been more conspicuous in the shares in total or finished output. This may be due to the increasing importance of fabrication in finished food output.

23. The changes in the shares in value added are as follows: Great Britain—a rise in the share of metal products from 12 per cent in 1871 to 40 per cent in 1948, in the share of chemicals from 2 to 5 per cent; Belgium—a rise in the share of metal products from 13 per cent in 1846 to 26 per cent in 1926, of chemicals from 2 to 6 per cent. The shares of these groups in France, Switzerland, Denmark, Canada, Australia, and New Zealand also rose but not as much.

one is tempted to interpret the changes as shifts in the structure of manufacturing from consumer to producer goods and to associate the "advanced" structure of manufacturing industries with emphasis on producer goods.[24] But this is a misleading oversimplification. Two other groups whose shares usually rise—paper and printing, and chemicals—are largely consumer goods; and within the metal products group itself, the share of consumer goods has increased and must have accounted in part for the rise in the share of the group.

The data in Table 3.7 are of particular interest in this connection. The share of the metal products group in total finished output (lines 3 and 4) increased but its share in each component of finished output (consumer goods, investment goods, and exports) also rose. This means that the rise in the share of metal products was not the result of a greater emphasis on investment goods; it was due in substantial part to the substitution of metals for other materials within final household consumption and within exports. Thus, if we assume that only the relative magnitudes of consumption, exports, and investment manufactured goods changed from 1873 to 1948 as they did (i.e. the share of exports de-

24. This is the main argument of Hoffmann's monograph. He classifies chemicals and metal products as producer goods branches, compares their shares with those of food, textile products, and leather and furniture as consumer goods branches—all in manufacturing value added—and derives a "law" stating the systematic decline in the ratio of consumer to producer goods from 4 to 1 to 1 to 1 (or less). Since the chemical industries, with their concentration on fertilizers, drugs, textile dyes, gasoline, and residual fuel oil, and the industries omitted from Hoffmann's comparison (such as paper and printing, and other wood products) are essentially consumer goods branches, adjustment for them would materially change the level and trends of the ratio of consumer to producer goods. Therefore the coefficients and the formulation of the "law" propounded by Hoffmann would have to be drastically revised.

For a more detailed discussion of the data for the United States and Sweden and critical evaluation of the Hoffmann data, see Yichi Shionoya, "Patterns of Industrial Growth in the United States and Sweden: A Critique of Hoffmann's Hypothesis," *Hitotsubashi Journal of Economics, 5* (June 1964).

clining, that of investment goods rising, and that of consumption goods remaining relatively constant), while the percentage shares of metal products *within* each finished output component remained the same, the rise in the share of metal products in total finished manufacturing output would have been only 9 percentage points, not 22 points as shown in Table 3.7. Of the 13 points unaccounted for, 4 points were contributed by the rise of metal products within consumer goods, 2 points by the rise of metal products within investment goods, and 7 points by the rise of metal products within exports. The conclusion to be emphasized is that the shift of countrywide output toward producer goods (to be discussed in Chapter 5) was rather moderate; and the large rise in the share of metal products was due less to the countrywide shift toward producer goods than to the technological changes that stimulated the use of metal products within ultimate consumption by households and as substitutes for other materials and goods within producer goods.

STRUCTURE OF THE SERVICES SECTOR

The services sector comprises a variety of economic activities, ranging from professional pursuits demanding high skill and large investment in training to domestic service and other unskilled personal services; from activities with large capital investment, such as residential housing, to those requiring no material capital; from pursuits closely connected with the private market, such as trade, banking, and related financial and business services, to government activities, including defense, in which market considerations are limited. They have one basic feature in common: none of the activities represents in any significant way the *production of commodities;* each renders a product that is intangible and not easily embodied in a lasting and measurable form. For this reason, and despite the magnitude of the services sector, the measurement of its output is most subject to error, and data and knowledge are far too scanty to permit adequate analysis. It may seem ironic that we know less about this sector which includes groups engaged in the production and spread of basic and applied knowledge, as well as those concerned with major political and social decisions, than about the other sectors; but it is not surprising, for activities that are not within the repetitive patterns of large-scale operation are for that reason not readily subject to measurement or analysis. Whatever the reason, the easily available data provide only general orders of magnitude; and they are not necessarily the most revealing with respect to some of the smaller, but in other respects most important, subdivisions of the sector.

If we begin with the structure for recent years, 1954–56 for shares in gross domestic product and 1950 for shares in labor force, the average shares for nine developed countries are given in the following tabulation.

Shares in Total for the Services Sector (%)*

|  | Whole-sale and retail trade | Banking, insur-ance, real estate | Owner-ship of dwellings | Public agencies and defense | Other private services | Share of sector in country-wide total (%) |
|---|---|---|---|---|---|---|
| Domestic product | 35 | 8 | 9 | 20 | 28 | 37 |
| Labor force | 41 | | | 59 | | 34 |

* From the sources cited for the industry sector on p. 128 for the same countries except Japan.

Commerce, i.e. trade and finance, accounts for over four tenths of the total output and labor force of the sector, implying a share in the countrywide total of some 14 to 15 per cent. The share of ownership of dwellings, reduced for post-World War II years by rent control and similar limitations, is about a tenth of the sector's output, or less than 4 per cent of countrywide product; its share in labor force must clearly be negligible. The share of government and

144

defense, unusually high in post-World War II years compared with the long-term past, is a fifth of the sector's output, and hence over 7 per cent of the countrywide product; its share in labor force is probably at least as large as its share in product, perhaps somewhat larger. All other private services—professional, personal, business—account for over a quarter of the sector's output and thus for about 10 per cent of countrywide product; and the share in labor force is likely to be the same or somewhat higher.

Capital invested in the services sector is dominated by residential housing and government capital. For a post-World War II year, in the early or mid-1950s, we have a distribution of reproducible capital for ten developed countries which, despite the limitation on coverage and comparability of the underlying estimates, suggests the orders of magnitude.[25] For these countries the average share (unweighted arithmetic mean of shares computed for individual countries) of residential dwellings (excluding agricultural) in total reproducible tangible assets was about 27 per cent; of government capital (excluding public enterprises), about 16 per cent; and of *all* nonagricultural inventories, about 14 per cent. If we assume that only about half of the inventories is to be assigned to trade and other subdivisions of the services sector, the capital invested in that sector is about 50 per cent of total reproducible capital—a significantly higher share than that in countrywide output or labor force. Of this capital stock within the services sector, residential housing would account for over half and government for over three tenths. The two subdivisions that loom large in output and labor force—commerce and private services—account for only a small share of material capital.

No data are available that might indicate long-term trends in the distribution of capital among the various sub-

25. The data are from Goldsmith and Saunders, eds., *Income and Wealth, Series VIII*, Table I, pp. 8–11. The countries included in the averages are: Belgium, the Netherlands, West Germany, France, the United Kingdom, Norway, Canada, the United States, Australia, and Japan.

divisions of the services sector. The only plausible suggestion is that the share of government in total capital in the sector and in the economy has possibly risen, since its shares in output and labor force have increased.

The evidence on trends in the distribution of output and labor force is summarized in Table 3.8. While the coverage in terms of countries and subdivisions distinguished is not too revealing, some trends are apparent. First, the shares of commerce (or trade) in the sector product and labor force both show an upward trend—more marked in the latter than in the former—in all countries for which we have shares in product except the United States, and in all countries for which we have shares in labor force except Japan. Since commerce is the largest single subdivision in the services sector—between a third and a half of the sector's output and labor force—these trends are important. But, as we noted in the preceding discussion, the share of the services sector in countrywide product was either constant or declined (see Table 3.1), whereas its share in countrywide labor force rose in a number of countries (see Table 3.2); and this conclusion is only confirmed by data for fewer countries in Table 3.8. Thus the upward trend in the share of commerce in the sector's product means, in most cases, constancy or only an insignificant rise in the share of commerce in countrywide product, while the upward trend in the share of commerce in the sector's labor force means an even greater rise in its share in countrywide labor force. It follows that for a number of countries, with the share of commerce in countrywide output rising so much less than its share in labor force, the ratio of the product per worker in commerce to countrywide product per worker, must have declined substantially; and it thus contributed to the downward trend, in the same countries, in the relative product per worker in the service sector as a whole. However, difficulties in measuring the product of commerce, as well as of other service sector components, must be borne in mind.

A few other trends, revealed largely by the distribution of product, deserve note. As could be expected, the shares

TABLE 3.8

Distribution of Product and Labor Force in the Services Sector,
Selected Countries, Long Periods
(underlying product totals in current prices unless otherwise indicated)

Shares in total for services sector (%)

| | Trade or commerce (1) | Services of dwellings (2) | Domestic service (3) | Other private service (4) | Government (5) | Share of sector in country-wide total (%) (6) |
|---|---|---|---|---|---|---|
| **A. PRODUCT** | | | | | | |
| *United Kingdom* | | | | | | |
| 1. 1841 | 35 | 21 | 15[a] | 28[b] | | 44 |
| 2. 1907 | 36 | 15 | 8[a] | 35[b] | 6 | 48 |
| 3. 1924 | 41 | 15 | 8 | 26[b] | 10 | 44 |
| 4. 1955 | 40 | 8 | 2 | 26[b] | 24 | 39 |
| *Sweden* | | | | | | |
| 5. 1861–65 | 48 | 34 | 9 | c | 9 | 44 |
| 6. 1901–05 | 61 | 24 | 4 | c | 10 | 27 |
| 7. 1949–53 | 67 | 11 | 2 | c | 20 | 35 |
| *Norway* | | | | | | |
| 8. 1910 | 46 | 24 | 11 | 19 | | 39 |
| 9. 1956 | 52 | 12 | 3 | 33 | | 34 |
| *United States* | | | | | | |
| 10. 1869/79 | 34 | | 57 | | 9 | 47 |
| 11. 1919–28 | 27 | | 54 | | 19 | 50 |
| 12. 1929 | 32 | d | 8 | 48 | 12 | 49 |
| 13. 1961–63 | 31 | d | 5 | 39 | 25 | 53 |
| *Australia* | | | | | | |
| 14. 1861–65 | 28 | 25 | 34 | | 13 | 47 |
| 15. 1934–38 | 41 | 20 | 29 | | 10 | 44 |
| *1910/11 prices* | | | | | | |
| 16. 1861–65 | 24 | 19 | 41 | | 16 | 51 |
| 17. 1934–38 | 42 | 22 | 27 | | 10 | 46 |
| **B. LABOR FORCE** | | | | | | |
| *Great Britain* | | | | | | |
| 18. 1841 | 31 | | 59 | | 10e | 34 |
| 19. 1901 | 37 | | 42 | | 21e | 37 |
| 20. 1921 | 36 | | 35 | | 29e | 38 |
| 21. 1951 | 37 | | 25 | | 38 | 38 |
| *France* | | | | | | |
| 22. 1911 | 43 | | 38 | | 19 | 27 |
| 23. 1951 | 51 | | 49 | | | 33 |
| *Switzerland* | | | | | | |
| 24. 1880 | 26 | | 74 | | | 19 |
| 25. 1910 | 29 | | 71 | | | 24 |
| 26. 1941 | 33 | | 67 | | | 31 |

TABLE 3.8—*Continued*

Shares in total for services sector (%)

| | Trade or commerce (1) | Services of dwellings (2) | Domestic service (3) | Other private service (4) | Government (5) | Share of sector in country-wide total (%) (6) |
|---|---|---|---|---|---|---|
| *Denmark* | | | | | | |
| 27. 1911 | 39 | | 54 | | 7 | 30 |
| 28. 1952 | 41 | | 59 | | | 36 |
| *Norway* | | | | | | |
| 29. 1875 | 25 | | 75 | | | 18 |
| 30. 1910 | 35 | | 65 | | | 21 |
| 31. 1950 | 40 | | 60 | | | 27 |
| *Sweden* | | | | | | |
| 32. 1910 | 29 | | 60 | | 11 | 23 |
| 33. 1950 | 43 | | 57 | | | 31 |
| *United States* | | | | | | |
| 34. 1870 | 34 | | 62 | | 4 | 19 |
| 35. 1910 | 40 | | 54 | | 6 | 27 |
| 36. 1950 | 45 | | 35 | | 21 | 43 |
| *Canada* | | | | | | |
| 37. 1901 | 39 | | 57 | | 4 | 23 |
| 38. 1951 | 44 | | 56 | | | 37 |
| *Australia* | | | | | | |
| 39. 1891 | 37 | | 63 | | | 31 |
| 40. 1947 | 45 | | 39 | | 16 | 35 |
| *Japan* | | | | | | |
| 41. 1872 | 58 | | 42 | | | 9 |
| 42. 1925 | 55 | | 45 | | | 24 |
| 43. 1950 | 49 | | 35 | | 16 | 25 |
| 44. 1960 | 54 | | 37 | | 9 | 32 |

a. Includes personal service.
b. Includes income from foreign investments.
c. Included in col. 1.
d. Included in col. 4.
e. Includes professional service.
*Sources:* As cited in notes to Tables 3.1 and 3.2. For Great Britain the estimate for 1841 of the share of trade and transportation in product was adjusted to exclude transportation on the basis of the distribution for the labor force.

of domestic service in the sector's product, in countrywide product, and probably also in the labor force, show drastic declines. In contrast, the shares of government (excluding public enterprises) in output and labor force, both of the sector and of the country, rose (except for Japan, with reduction of military activities after World War II); and while the rise was accelerated by World War II, in the United States at least there was some rise even in the earlier decades from the very low levels of the nineteenth century. But the data do not yield much beyond these familiar trends; and in particular, we have no evidence on the structure of the large and diversified subdivision of "other" services. Probably skilled and professionally trained labor, and perhaps their product, have increased proportionately to labor and product in the services sector and in the economy. Thus, in the United States, the proportion of "professional, technical, and kindred workers" in total gainfully occupied population rose from about 4 per cent in 1900 to over 8 per cent in 1950; and the single professional group of engineers multiplied over 14-fold during the half century, while total labor force merely doubled.[26] But a comparative study of this aspect of the services sector would require an intensive analysis of detailed data far beyond the scope of the present summary, although some evidence will be cited in Chapter 4.

Even so, some aspects of the trends revealed in Table 3.8, and inferable from the current structure of the services sector, raise intriguing questions. Why should the sector have absorbed rising proportions of the labor force, and grown to the point where in the more advanced countries, like the United States, it accounts for well over 40 per cent of all workers? What are the factors behind the combination of rising shares in labor force and constant or declining shares in countrywide product, true both of the services sector as a whole and of the large trade and commerce subdivision within it?

26. See *Historical Statistics of the United States,* Series D 72, D 74, and D 145, pp. 74–75.

Answers to these questions are necessarily speculative; but we formulate them because they suggest some important interrelations in the process of modern economic growth.

If we begin with the shares in product, several explanatory observations come to mind—some already noted. The territorial concentration of commodity production and the increase in the scale of the producing units (and of their fixed capital investment) imply localization of output and pressure to maintain production at a steady rate—regardless of the territorial dispersion of ultimate consumers and of any temporal (seasonal or other short-term) variations in demand. The role of trade, and finance to some extent, in bridging the gap between centralized and steady production and dispersed and variable demand, has obviously increased, while the higher per capita consumer income has added to the demand for labor-consuming services, particularly in retail trade. The relation between the changing structure of commodity production and the mushrooming of advertising, financial, and similar services should also be noted. The growing urbanization of the developed economies has meant much greater demand for labor-consuming services of urban governments (in police, sanitation, public health, education, and the like), while the growing complexity of the country's productive system has led to an increase in the supervisory and regulatory functions of central governments—well before the two world wars raised the proportion of the labor force engaged in the military forces. The rise in per capita consumer income has also increased the demand for recreation, health, educational, and other professional services, a demand that is income elastic; and the greater use of consumer durable commodities has meant an enormous increase in the demand for labor-intensive repair and servicing activities. The two latter trends probably more than outweigh the decline in the supply and use of paid domestic service. In short, secular shifts in commodity production and in associated patterns of living combined with differing income elasticity of demand for different services have greatly augmented the demand for the products of the services sector, many of them labor intensive.

But this increased demand for the products of the sector, when measured in money terms, yields either a roughly constant or a declining share of total demand (i.e. of total product). And the rise of the sector's share in labor force would not have been so significant if the productivity of labor in the sector had displayed a steeply rising secular trend. The complete answer to the question under discussion could be given only if productivity in the sector were to be effectively measured, permitting a linkage between the demand for the product of the sector and its share in inputs—largely labor. Offhand it may seem that for some large subdivisions of the services sector—retail trade, the numerous clerical jobs in the business service firms and in government—secular rates of growth in productivity have been appreciably lower than those in agriculture and the industry sector; and the same or even a lower rate of growth of demand for the products of the services sector would imply a rise in the share of labor force attached to the sector. But plausible as the conjecture is, we must not overlook the benefits of mechanization, even in service activities, or the rapidly growing professional and other highly skilled groups within the services sector whose product is difficult to measure but whose productivity rise could hardly be inferior to that in the agriculture or the industry sector. Our estimates of product in the services sector are so crude that we dare not use them as direct evidence of productivity. A lag in productivity in the services sector compared with the others, in terms of the rise in comparable product per worker, may well be a plausible assumption. But it is not more than that, pending improvement in the measures of the product of service activities.[27]

27. An intensive study of the service industries in the United States has been initiated by the National Bureau of Economic Research. In addition to the paper cited in note 8, see Victor R. Fuchs, "The Growing Importance of the Service Industries," *The Journal of Business of the University of Chicago, 38* (October 1965).

These comments also answer implicitly the question regarding the factors that might have contributed to a combination of the rise of the services sector's share in labor force with constancy or decline of its share in countrywide product. Only two additional points are noted. First, further study of the structure of the services sector may provide more information on a dilution of labor and of capital that would constitute indirect but telling evidence on productivity, in terms of product per worker. The greater growth of retail than of wholesale trade, the increased use of female labor force in clerical and related jobs, the increasing weight of the more moderately paid employees in the business and government service subdivisions, all may have contributed to a labor mix with respect to skill and income level that would have kept the average in the services sector growing at a lower rate than in the agriculture and the industry sectors in which such dilution of the labor mix was not as marked. The same effect for the services sector as a whole would be produced by the decline in the share of income from residential housing, which, being largely capital income, yields a high ratio per unit of the small number of workers engaged in the subdivision. Second, there may well have been larger monopoly elements in the incomes in the services sector during the early phases of economic growth than during the later phases. In the early phases, when capital funds were scarce and predominantly in the hands of the trading and financial community, rather than of the commodity producing and transportation enterprises, the incomes of these capital-owning groups may well have been relatively higher than in later phases—a differential that could hardly be eliminated by the customary adjustment for price changes. In the early phases of growth, when education was scarce and professionally trained members of the services sector were almost in the position of monopolists, the low per capita income itself might have meant professional incomes that were large multiples of the countrywide average—much higher than in the later phases when education was more widespread and per capita income much higher.[28]

The industrial structure of national output and productive resources is a key aspect of an economy in the process of growth because it permits us to observe the impact of the advance in technological knowledge, the differential response of demand to increased productive capacity and rise in per capita income, and the shifts in the size and location of groups in society associated with the different industries. Industries are distinguished from each other by the raw materials that they use, by the productive process in which they engage (and hence by the technological constraint on size of plant), by the skill-mix of the labor force, by the capital intensity, etc. imposed by the specific production process employed, and by the finished product, and hence by the market that is being served. Indeed, an industry is *defined* by these characteristics of material, process, and product; and a marked change in one, often but not necessarily accompanied by changes in the others, is usually a basis for distinguishing and defining a new industry. Thus the emergence of rayon brought into being a new industry, even though the product was similar in many ways to that of the old established cotton textiles industry; and the introduction of the quick-freezing process gave rise to a new branch within the old established food industries group. Granted the interrelations among industries, their dependence upon common pools of productive resources, and their competitiveness and complementarity in the markets for finished products, each industry represents a distinctive bundle of activities subject to distinctive short-term responses and long-term growth patterns; and the classification by industries provides a basis for distinguishing groups

28. See Kuznets, "Quantitative Aspects: II," in this connection and on other points touched upon in the text.

in economic society whose positions in the process of growth are also subject to different patterns of movement.

Since an industry is a complex that reflects determining factors on the production–supply and output–demand sides, an adequate account of causes and consequences of trends in industrial structure will also constitute an account of much of the economic growth process. This is all the more true, the greater the detail in distinguishing industries and the more comprehensive the account of the technological constraints on the production side and of the specific responses on the demand side. The discussion above is merely a beginning, since it distinguishes only the broader groups; emphasizes only the main trends, without a detailed analysis of determinants and consequences; and is limited in coverage of countries and hence of varieties of growth experience. Some conclusions have been suggested with respect to the downward trend in the shares of the agriculture sector in countrywide output, labor force, and capital, and the marked rise in productivity in the sector as a necessary condition of modern economic growth; the upward trend in the share of the industry sector—particularly manufacturing and transport and communication—in national output, and the marked rise in productivity that limited the absorption of labor (and probably of capital) in the sector; and the combination of constancy or a decline in the share of the services sector, and of trade (its major subdivision), in national output with a distinct rise in the share in labor force in a number of countries (combined with a large share of the sector in the countrywide stock of reproducible capital). But, clearly, a more detailed classification of each sector or each major subdivision would reveal trends in shares in output and resources different from those for the sector or subdivision as a whole—as can easily be seen in some rapidly growing subdivisions of agriculture and in the lagging and declining industries within manufacturing. Also, groupings different from those followed above might emphasize other aspects of trends in industrial structure not stressed in our discussion. Thus, adding mining to the agriculture sector

154

would emphasize the decline in the share of the extractive industries as a whole, i.e. of those closely dependent upon natural resources within the country.

But only a summary treatment is possible within the limits of the present monograph, and it must be selective, omitting much valuable detail. Yet it may be of value to conclude the chapter with a few supplementary comments on some aspects of the long-term trends in industrial structure not touched upon above.

Beginning with determinants of the shifts in industrial structure, we should note first that technological change is clearly a major source of these shifts. This is obvious when additions to useful knowledge result in the creation of a new product, of a new process, or of a new way of using raw materials and thus provide the basis for a new industry. The emergence of a new industry means, ipso facto, a change in the industrial distribution of national output and productive resources; and since a new industry usually grows for a long while at rates much higher than those of older industries, the shifts in industrial structure also continue. But even if technological changes involve only cost reductions and productivity increases in existing industries, these cost-reducing and productivity-increasing changes in the established industries would very likely affect differently the rates of growth in output of the several industries and in the volumes of productive resources used by them. For at any given time, the existing industries are at different stages of their life-cycles of development and represent different opportunities for technological and economic improvement as well as different potentials for further growth in output or in resources absorbed. The locus of technological change constantly shifts, and its concentrated impact is felt in different industries at different times, affecting them unequally at any one time because an industry, having once benefited from the modern technological revolution, offers diminishing opportunities for further major economic improvements since by definition it is limited to a given complex of materials, processes, and products. It is therefore highly unlikely that the effects of technological change, even if cost-reducing and productivity-increasing rather than new-product creating, would be the same on all existing industries.[29]

Second, the higher the rate of technological change, the greater should be the shifts in industrial structure. Unfortunately, it is not easy to measure the rate of technological change directly. But another, closely related, association can be studied, even if the data are limited. This is the association between the rate of growth of an economy, measured by its per capita income, and the extent of shifts in industrial structure. Such data are available, particularly on the industrial structure of the labor force; and we would expect that the higher the rate of growth in per capita national product in constant prices, the greater the shift in industrial structure. The higher rate of growth of income per capita not only reflects a higher rate of technological change, which should produce greater shifts in industrial structure, but, as already indicated, also causes greater shifts in the structure of demand, which should also be reflected in greater shifts in industrial structure. The test, for eighteen countries (some less developed but none truly underdeveloped) and using total displacement in the distribution of the labor force (sum of changes in sectoral shares, signs disregarded) among three major industrial sectors, shows a significant positive association.[30] But this association is due partly to technological change and partly to shifts in structure in demand—although, to repeat, the two

29. For a discussion of the pattern of technological change and growth of output in individual industries see Simon Kuznets, *Secular Movements in Production and Prices* (Boston, 1930), the main conclusions of which were summarized in "Retardation of Industrial Growth," in Kuznets, *Economic Change* (New York, 1953), and Arthur F. Burns, *Production Trends in the United States since 1870* (National Bureau of Economic Research, 1934), Chap. 4.

30. See Kuznets, "Quantitative Aspects: II," Table 24 and discussion on pp. 52–55. The coefficient of rank correlation is 0.54. The definitions of the industry and service sectors differ from those used here, in that the former exclude and the latter include the transport and communication subdivision. But this would have no significant effect on the association.

are in a sense interrelated. Perhaps a better measure for the present purposes would be changes in distribution of product or labor force among sectors classified by the level of technological change in them—in the crudest form, distinguishing "new" industries created by new technological inventions from older branches not affected by them. While such data are not available, if only because it is difficult to decide how long "new" remains "new," the obvious conjunction of high rates of growth in per capita product with the continuous emergence of new industries in the developed countries, which automatically means shifts in industrial distribution of product and labor force, does not require confirmation by elaborate statistics.

Third, insofar as the overall rate of growth, in terms of per capita income, and technological change necessitate marked shifts in the industrial structure of product and resources, obstacles to such shifts constitute impediments to economic growth. This point was made in our discussion of the internal migration of labor (and capital) from the agriculture sector to others, involved in modern economic growth. The observation has far-reaching implications, since changes in industrial structure involve shifts of people to new pursuits and often new places of work and residence; the declining importance of industries that sustain losses in the share of output and resources may mean the painful displacement of people attached to them, and resistance is naturally generated—not infrequently by means of political pressure. To the extent that this resistance to shift succeeds, some resources that should flow to industries with a greater growth potential will continue to be attached to the less productive and stagnant industries. In short, a high rate of modern economic growth is attainable only if the required marked shifts in industrial structure are not too impeded by resistance—of labor and of capital, of people and their resources in the old and accustomed grooves. One basic requirement of modern economic growth is therefore the capacity of society to accommodate itself to the shifts and displacement involved in the trends in industrial structure of labor and capital, without putting so high a price on this adjustment as to starve the growing industries of the resources needed for growth.

The consequences of shifts in industrial structure—even those limited to changes in the distribution of the labor force—are numerous; some have already been touched upon in earlier discussion. In general, engagement in different industries implies distinctive patterns of work and life, because of the interrelation between the technical constraints of an industry and the mode and locus of its operation. Different industries compel different forms of organization of the operating unit—ranging from the small-scale, individually managed farm or retail store to the large corporation, controlling productive establishments equipped with large stocks of fixed capital and employing thousands of workers; from the private market-oriented firm to the nonprofit association and the government agency. Some industries are necessarily urban because the economies of scale are so large that it would be extremely costly to limit the size of the plant and disperse the people engaged over the countryside; and the requirements for urbanization differ in degree, in that some activities (e.g. large-scale insurance and financial operations) can be carried on only in metropolitan centers. Other industries, because of the extensive use of land, compel the people engaged in them to reside in the countryside. Some industries require labor of high skill and advanced education; others do not. Insofar as shifts in industrial structure require changes in labor skills, in amounts of capital investment, in size of economic units, and in place of residence—rural or urban—there are many far-reaching consequences of trends in industrial structure for the patterns of work and life of people in modern society and for the channeling of their capital into productive use.

These consequences—increasing urbanization, growing size of producing establishments and of corporate units that control them, and shifts in the labor force from independent entrepreneurial status toward employee status, from emphasis on manual work toward emphasis on white-collar skills, among others—can only be mentioned here and not treated in detail, even though, while familiar, they have not been adequately measured and analyzed. Many of these trends will be noted again in connection with the structural aspects of economic growth upon which they bear most directly. They are mentioned here only to stress the wide ramifications of the trends in industrial structure which should be kept in mind when we discuss the other aspects of economic growth. They provide the important links in the interrelation between production, distribution, and use of the national product in the course of its rapid growth in modern times.

159

# 4 DISTRIBUTION OF PRODUCT AND INCOME

National product, whose aggregate growth and industrial structure were discussed in the preceding two chapters, can be viewed as the total at market value of a congeries of finished goods turned out during the year. Corresponding to this total is a total of income shares or other claims distributed. Some of these finished goods are retained by producers for their own consumption, and for this small share of the national product of developed economies we can assume the fiction of "sales to themselves," i.e. that the money value of the goods retained is actually received by the producers as income. The preponderant part of the finished goods is sold to others; and from the proceeds income payments are made to factors engaged in producing the goods—directly as compensation of employees, income of entrepreneurs, returns on assets engaged at the final stage of production; or indirectly as payments for materials, which are in turn distributed to factors engaged in producing these materials. Furthermore, some of the proceeds go to governments. In short, national output represents a total of claims originated in the process of production—most of it distributed as service and property income of households, but some retained as profits of corporations and governments and some paid as taxes to governments.

The present chapter deals primarily with two sets of

trends associated with modern economic growth: (1) in the distribution of national income by factor shares, with some reference to distinctions within each share; and (2) in the distribution of income among households by size of income. But we shall first clarify the relation between total output and income distribution.

Table 4.1, which utilizes the customary social accounts, indicates, on the basis of recent data for developed countries, the typical relations among various national product totals and the distribution of income. The items in the stubs require only three comments. The transfers to households (line 14) are largely from government, exclude interest on public debt (which is included in line 13), and represent relief, unemployment insurance payments, pensions, etc. The final services of government (line 15) are treated as income in kind and refer largely to educational, health, and recreational services provided directly by governments to households (*not* money payments for this purpose).[1] Finally, capital consumption (line 3) covers capital in the hands of corporations, government, and households and, unlike the other items, cannot be allocated among the three recipient groups distinguished.

Three major conclusions are suggested by Table 4.1.[2] First, in order to account completely for all receipts in a distribution of any national product total, we must include all three groups of recipients—households, corporations, and governments (the first including, as they always do, unincorporated, individual entrepreneurs). Even national income at factor cost, the total underlying column 2, con-

1. For a discussion of this item see Kuznets, "Quantitative Aspects: VII," pp. 8–11.

2. Table 4.1 contains an element of duplication in both personal and disposable income. If these totals include, as they should, money transfers (largely from government) and also government final services, they should be net of contributions for social insurance which should be another deduction from line 6. But the duplication is relatively minor, amounting to a small percentage of national income, and could not be easily distinguished for many of the countries in Table 4.1.

TABLE 4.1

Relation of Gross National Product to Disposable Income, Averages for 12 Developed Countries, 1954–60

| | % Shares in | | | | |
|---|---|---|---|---|---|
| | Gross national product (1) | National income, including interest on government debt (2) | Personal income, including government final services (3) | Disposable income (4) | Disposable income, direct taxes allocated (5) |
| 1. Gross national product | 100.0 | (82.5) | (88.2) | (76.3) | (76.3) |
| 2. Indirect taxes less subsidies | 10.7 | | | | |
| 3. Capital consumption | 8.6(11) | | | | |
| 4. National income (line 1 − line 2 − line 3) | 80.5(11) | | | | |
| 5. Interest on public debt | 1.9 | | | | |
| 6. National income, including interest on public debt (line 4 + line 5) | 82.5(11) | 100.0 | | | |
| 7. Corporate savings, after taxes | 3.2(11) | 3.8 | | | |
| 8. Corporate taxes | 3.5 | 4.3 | | | |
| 9. Government income from property and entrepreneurship | 1.8 | 2.0 | | | |
| 10. Service and property income of households (line 6 − line 7 − line 8 − line 9) | 74.2 | 89.9 | 84.2 | 97.2 | 81.7 |
| 11. Employee compensation | 50.6 | 60.0 | 57.6 | 66.6 | 58.9 |
| 12. Income of entrepreneurs | 16.9 | 21.3 | 19.1 | 22.0 | 16.8 |
| 13. Property income of households | 6.7 | 8.6 | 7.5 | 8.7 | 6.0 |
| 14. Money transfers to households | 8.0 | 9.8 | 9.0 | 10.4 | 10.4 |

| | | | | | |
|---|---|---|---|---|---|
| 15. Government final services | 6.0 | 7.3 | 6.8 | 7.9 | 7.9 |
| 16. Personal income, including government final services (line 10 + line 14 + line 15) | 88.2 | 106.9 | 100.0 | 100.0 | 115.6 |
| 17. Direct taxes on households | 11.8 | 13.8 | 13.4 | | 15.6 |
| 18. Disposable income (line 16 − line 17) | 76.3 | 93.1 | 86.6 | 100.0 | 100.0 |
| 19. Service income (line 11 + line 12) | 67.5 | 81.3 | 76.7 | 75.7 | 88.5 |
| 20. Income from assets | 15.8[a] | 18.7[a] | 7.5[b] | 6.0[b] | 8.7[b] |
| 21. Remainder to 100 | 16.7[c] | 0 | 15.8[d] | 18.3[d] | 2.8[e] |

a. Sum of lines 7, 8, 9, and 13.    b. Line 13.

c. Line 2 + line 3 − line 5.    d. Line 14 + line 15.

e. Line 14 + line 15 − line 17.

*Sources:* The basic data are from U.N., *Yearbook of National Accounts Statistics, 1961.* The countries included are: Australia, Belgium, Canada, New Zealand, Sweden (except in col. 2), the United Kingdom, the United States (except in line 9), France, Finland, the Netherlands, Japan, and West Germany.

The entries are unweighted arithmetic means of shares in cumulated totals for 1954–60, in current prices, calculated separately for each country.

The figures in parentheses in line 1, cols. 2–5 are percentages that the totals designated in the column headings are of gross national product.

For the estimate of the share of government final services see Kuznets, "Quantitative Aspects: VII," Table 6, p. 12 and accompanying text.

In col. 5 direct taxes for each country were allocated among the type of income shares on the assumption that none fall on transfers or government final services (lines 14 and 15), that the burden on property income of households is twice the average rate on all nontransfer incomes (e.g. $2 \times 15.6/97.2$), and that on income of entrepreneurs is 1.5 times that ratio. Taxes on compensation of employees are derived as a residual.

tains items that are *not* received by households, but are either retained by corporations or flow to government (lines 7, 8, and 9). Hence when we ask "who gets what," in reference to the changing output of a nation in the course of economic growth, a complete answer involves the shares of such incongruous entities as these: households, which comprise the human members of the society; corporations, whether private or public, which are artificial units with a life of their own; and governments. Conversely, when we limit our attention to the shares of the households, we must recognize that the total of these shares flowing out of the production process falls short of the output turned out. The share of personal income, including government final services, is about 88 per cent of gross national product in Table 4.1 (line 16, column 1).[3] Furthermore, in the course of economic growth, the share of personal income in total output may be changing.

Second, in studying the distribution among households, our interest is in those flows to them that originate in the process of producing the nation's output, not in any and all receipts; and it is often difficult to specify them. Service and property income of households, even including interest on public debt, falls short of total receipts: it excludes money transfers (largely from government but also some from business and the rest of the world) and direct services of governments (see lines 10, 14, and 15). On the other hand, it is subject to a compulsory draft in the form of direct taxes. Should we view these transfers and taxes as *redistribution* of incomes received, or as an integral part of income distribution, even if incomes are limited to

3. In Communist countries the differential is even greater. For the U.S.S.R., the share of household income, including transfer receipts, in gross national product was 74 per cent in 1928, 65 per cent in 1940, and 62 per cent in 1958 (see Abram Bergson, Hans Heymann, Jr., and Oleg Hoeffding, *Soviet National Income and Product, 1928–48: Revised Data*, Rand RM-2544, November 15, 1960 and Nancy Nimitz, *Soviet National Income and Product, 1956–58*, Rand RM-3112, Prel., June 1962). Thus the income distributed among persons is a much smaller share of total output in the U.S.S.R. than in the countries included in Table 4.1.

those originating in the process of production? If persons engaged in production demand higher returns in expectation of the burden of a progressive income tax, or accept lower returns in expectation of assured transfers from government or other agencies, should the receipt, and costs of the factor, be limited to compensation of employees (and other factor income) or should it include transfers and exclude direct taxes? While the proper answer may be debatable, a variant of the distribution that takes account of both transfers and taxes should have some significance for our analysis.

Third, decisions must be made concerning the scope of the income distribution—for instance, whether to limit it to households or include nonpersonal organizational units, and whether to limit it to primary factor incomes or include transfers and exclude taxes—and these will obviously have significant effect on the results, whether we deal with the allocation between labor and capital or with the distribution of income by size among households. Therefore, in considering these two aspects of income distribution, we must sharply define the scope and level of the income distribution.

Before turning to these topics, we comment on the likely trend in the relation of such fully distributable totals as national income at factor cost, personal income, and disposable income, to the aggregate output measures used in earlier chapters, particularly gross national product. If we accept the finding that national income at factor cost was, in recent years, between 80 and 83 per cent of gross national product (Table 4.1, lines 4 and 6), can we say that the share has risen or fallen in the course of economic growth? If service and property income of households in recent years was 74 per cent of gross national product (line 10) and disposable income little more (line 18), what was the trend in these shares in the long-term growth process?

Only limited direct evidence is available on these questions, yet most of the answers can be inferred. The proportion of capital consumption to gross national product probably has risen, partly because the ratio of depreciable reproducible assets to total output has risen, partly because the shift in fixed capital formation from construction to producers' durable equipment has reduced the life span and hence raised the capital consumption charges relative to output (see Chapter 5). The share of indirect taxes net of subsidies in gross national product has probably also increased.[4] One may reasonably assume that in the earlier periods, say at mid-nineteenth century for most of the presently developed countries, the share of capital consumption and indirect taxes was closer to 10 than to 20 per cent of gross national product; and consequently national income at factor cost accounted for 90 per cent or more of gross national product compared with 80 to 83 per cent in recent years. Likewise, the shares of corporations (net savings plus taxes) and of property and entrepreneurial income of governments must have increased—the former with the growing importance of corporations in economic life, the latter with the growing share of capital assets of governments in total assets in the economy. If we assume that a century ago the share of these two items was closer to 5 per cent of gross national product than to the 8 per cent shown in Table 4.1, the service and property income of households must have accounted for over 85 per cent of gross national product compared with 75 per cent in recent years. The addition to such service and property income of transfers (in money and kind) must have been proportionately much smaller, perhaps no more than 5 per cent of gross national product; but the deduction of direct taxes on households must also have been proportionately smaller so that the

4. For three countries direct evidence is available. In Italy the share rose from 6.7 per cent in 1861–65 to 12.1 per cent in 1954–60; in the United States from 6.8 per cent in 1899–1901 to 8.5 per cent in 1954–60; in Australia from 3.6 per cent in 1861–65 to 11.3 per cent in 1954–60. The data for recent years are from U.N., *Yearbook of National Accounts Statistics, 1961*. For the earlier years the data are from Italy, Istituto Centrale di Statistica, *Indagine Statistica*, Table 36, p. 249; Raymond W. Goldsmith and others, *A Study of Saving in the United States*, III (Princeton, 1956), Table N-1, pp. 427 ff. and Table N-5, pp. 435 ff., and Butlin, *Australian Domestic Product, Investment and Foreign Borrowing, 1861–1938/39*, Table 1, p. 6.

share of disposable income was probably not much different from that of service and property income of households—roughly 85 per cent of gross national product compared with the 76 per cent share of recent years.

On the basis of these conjectures we can infer that the shares of national income, personal income, and disposable income in gross national product declined in the course of economic growth—that of personal income less than the others since it was bolstered by a rising contribution of transfers. But these trends, although perceptible and clear, are slight compared with the sustained rises in total and per capita product. The quadrupling over a century of per capita gross national product—a not uncommon occurrence in the course of modern economic growth—can be translated into a rise from 90 to 325 in per capita national income or from 85 to 300 in per capita disposable income—enormous increases in the per capita availability of distributable or allocable income. It can therefore be argued that in the long run, incomes subject to distribution increased almost as much as the total output represented by gross national product.

### SHARE OF INCOME FROM ASSETS

The long-term changes in the shares of employee compensation, income of entrepreneurs, and income from assets in national income at factor cost (including interest on public debt) are summarized, for the few countries for which records are available, in Table 4.2. We deal first with the share of income from assets (column 3).

This category includes: property income of households—dividends, interest, and rent (both money rent received and rent imputed on owner-occupied housing); net profits of corporations, after payment of dividends but before payment of direct taxes; and property and entrepreneurial incomes of governments. It excludes any income from assets that accrues to individual entrepreneurs and the self-employed on their equity, which is included in total income of entrepreneurs in column 2.

167

**TABLE 4.2**

Distribution of National Income among Factor Shares, Selected Countries, Long Periods (underlying totals in current prices)

| | Shares in national income (%) | | | Per cent of entrepreneurs and self-employed in labor force (4) | Share in national income (%) | | | |
| | | | | | Assumption 1 | | Assumption 2 | |
| | Compensation of employees (1) | Income of entrepreneurs and self-employed (2) | Income from assets (3) | | Return on entrep. equity (5) | Total income from assets (3 + 5) (6) | Return on entrep. equity (7) | Total income from assets (3 + 7) (8) |
|---|---|---|---|---|---|---|---|---|
| *United Kingdom* | | | | | | | | |
| 1. 1860–69 | 47 | 17 | 36 | 13 | 10 | 46 | 5 | 41 |
| 2. 1905–14 | 47 | 16 | 37 | 13 | 9 | 46 | 6 | 43 |
| 3. 1920–29 | 59 | 15 | 26 | 10 | 8 | 34 | 3 | 29 |
| 4. 1954–60 | 70 | 9 | 21 | 6 | 4 | 25 | 1 | 22 |
| *France* | | | | | | | | |
| 5. 1853 (excluding corporate savings) | 36 | 46 | 18 | 36 | 26 | 44 | 10 | 28 |
| 6. 1911 (excluding corporate savings) | 44 | 32 | 24 | 33 | 10 | 34 | 12 | 36 |
| 7. 1911 total | 43 | 31 | 26 | 33 | 10 | 36 | 13 | 39 |
| 8. 1913 | 45 | 33 | 22 | 33 | 11 | 33 | 11 | 33 |
| 9. 1920–29 | 50 | 29 | 21 | 30 | 8 | 29 | 9 | 30 |
| 10. 1954–60 | 59 | 29 | 12 | 27 | 7 | 19 | 4 | 16 |
| *Germany* | | | | | | | | |
| 11. 1895 | 39 | 45 | 16 | 26 | 31 | 47 | 6 | 22 |
| 12. 1913 | 47 | 35 | 18 | 21 | 22 | 40 | 5 | 23 |
| 13. 1913 | 48 | 33 | 19 | 21 | 20 | 39 | 5 | 24 |

| | | | | | | | | |
|---|---|---|---|---|---|---|---|---|
| 14. 1925–29 | 64 | 26 | 10 | 19 | 11 | 21 | 2 | 12 |
| 15. 1954–60 (FR) | 60 | 22 | 18 | 16 | 11 | 29 | 3 | 21 |
| *Switzerland* | | | | | | | | |
| 16. 1913 | | 66 | 34 | na | na | na | na | na |
| 17. 1924 | 49 | 25 | 26 | 25 | 9 | 35 | 9 | 35 |
| 18. 1954–60 | 60 | 18 | 22 | 19 | 4 | 26 | 5 | 27 |
| *Canada* | | | | | | | | |
| 19. 1926–29 | 59 | 25 | 16 | 28 | 2 | 19 | 6 | 22 |
| 20. 1954–60 | 66 | 13 | 21 | 18 | −2 | 19 | 5 | 26 |
| *United States* | | | | | | | | |
| 21. 1899–1908 | 54 | 24 | 22 | 28.5 | 2 | 24 | 9 | 31 |
| 22. 1919–28 | 58 | 18 | 24 | 21.5 | 2 | 26 | 7 | 31 |
| 23. 1929 | 58 | 17 | 25 | 21 | 2 | 27 | 7 | 32 |
| 24. 1954–60 | 69 | 12 | 19 | 15 | 0 | 19 | 3 | 22 |

*Sources: Cols. 1–3:*

*Lines 1–3:* From Kuznets, "Quantitative Aspects: IV," App. Table 9, pp. 86–87.

*Lines 4, 10, 15, 18, 20, and 24:* From U.N., *Yearbook of National Accounts Statistics, 1961.*

*Lines 5–9:* From "Quantitative Aspects: IV," App. Table 10, p. 88.

*Lines 11–14:* From ibid., App. Table 12, p. 90.

*Lines 16–17:* From ibid., App. Table 14, p. 92.

*Line 19:* From Dominion Bureau of Statistics, *National Accounts, Income and Expenditures, 1926–56,* Table 1, p. 32.

*Lines 21–22:* Extrapolated from Department of Commerce estimate for 1929–38 by series for earlier years, both given in "Quantitative Aspects: IV," App. Table 17, p. 94.

*Line 23:* From Department of Commerce, *U.S. Income and Output,* Table I-8, pp. 126–27 and Table I-17, pp. 138–39 (for interest on public debt).

*Col. 4:*

*Line 1:* Assumed the same as line 2.

*Lines 2–4:* From Deane and Cole, *Economic Growth,* Table 66, p. 248 for 1911, 1931, and rough extrapolation from 1951.

TABLE 4.2—*Continued*

*Lines 5–10:* From "Quantitative Aspects: IV," App. Table 11, p. 89. The Pupin estimates were extrapolated by those shown for later years.

*Lines 11–14:* From ibid., App. Table 13, p. 91.

*Line 15:* Rough extrapolation from 1950, given in ibid., App. Table 7, p. 81.

*Lines 17–18:* Rough estimates based on ibid., App. Table 15, p. 92.

*Line 19:* Estimated from Dominion Bureau of Statistics, *Seventh Census of Canada, 1931, Occupations and Industries,* 7 (Ottawa, 1934), Table 50, p. 558.

*Line 20:* Rough extrapolation from 1951, given in "Quantitative Aspects: IV," App. Table 7, p. 82.

*Line 21:* Rough extrapolation from line 22.

*Line 22:* Average for 1919–28 in ibid., App. Table 18, p. 96.

*Lines 23–24:* Extrapolated from line 22 by estimates in Department of Commerce, *U.S. Income and Output,* Table VI-13, p. 211 and Table VI-16, p. 215 and in Department of Commerce, *Survey of Current Business,* July 1962, Tables 52 and 55, p. 29.

*Col. 5:* Col. 2 − [col. 4 ÷ (100 − col. 4) × col. 1], on the assumption that the labor component of income per entrepreneur and self-employed equals per worker income of all employees.

*Col. 7:* Col. 3 × [col. 4 ÷ (100 − col. 4)], on the assumption that the rate of return on the equity of entrepreneurs and self-employed equals that on all other equity and that their equity is in the same proportion to all income-yielding wealth as their number is to the labor force.

170

In interpreting the levels of and trends in the share of income from assets, in column 3, it may help to view such income as the product of three fractions.[5] The first, $R$, is the ratio of income-yielding wealth ($W$) to national income ($I$); and $W$ includes all material wealth within the country (and the net balance of wealth owned abroad), whether it is a natural resource, e.g. land, or a reproducible asset, e.g. buildings or producers' equipment, so long as it is a possible source of property income. The second, $S$, is the fraction of $W$ that is outside the equity of the entrepreneurs and self-employed. The third, $Y$, is the rate of yield on $WS$—including not only the interest, dividends, and rent paid out, but also all the retained profits of both corporations and government.[6] If for illustrative purposes, we assume that $R$ varies between 4 and 6, $S$ between 0.25 and 0.75, and $Y$ between 6 and 12 per cent, the share of income from assets can presumably vary from 6 per cent at the lowest ($4 \times 0.25 \times 0.06$) to 54 per cent at the highest ($6 \times 0.75 \times 0.12$). This range, much wider than that observed in the estimated share of income from assets in Table 4.2, may be due in part to the use of unrealistic values in the illustration, but it is probably the result of the interrelations implicitly assumed among $R$, $S$, and $Y$. If $R$ is high, i.e. if the

5. For a more detailed discussion of these fractions, in particular application to developed and underdeveloped countries, see Kuznets, "Quantitative Aspects: IV," pp. 15–23.

6. All the ratios must be for totals in current prices. If the current value of wealth ($W$) is determined as the discounted total of future yields, and if the current net income from wealth is the only base for such an estimate of future yields, then $Y$ is the rate of discount, i.e. the rate at which current yield is converted into the value of wealth. Whether the estimates of wealth at current value do in fact reflect current yields alone, combined with some discount rate, is a question to which no easy answer can be given. If the answer is in the affirmative, and if the general assumption of a downward trend in discount rates in the process of economic growth suggested in the text below is valid, the decline observed in $R$ is even more significant because it indicates a greater decline in yield on wealth as a proportion of national income. But we cannot be sure of the answer, and it is safer not to identify $Y$ too closely with the rate of discount, although the latter obviously is a major component.

supply of wealth per unit of income is large, $Y$ is likely to be low. If $S$ is low, i.e. if the share represented by equity of entrepreneurs is high—a condition usually associated with the limited role of corporations and government characteristic of pre-industrial, less developed economies—$Y$ is likely to be high. If then we associate high $R$ and $S$ with low $Y$, and low $R$ and $S$ with high $Y$, the range is narrowed to 15 percentage points: from 12 per cent ($4 \times 0.25 \times 0.12$) to 27 per cent ($6 \times 0.75 \times 0.06$).

But as we shall see, even this result does not quite correspond with the estimates given. An adequate interpretation of their levels and movements would require a more intensive study of the values of $R$, $S$, and $Y$—a closer scrutiny of the supply of material capital, of the ownership, and financial and credit structures that determine the equity of individual entrepreneurs (the difference between total asset uses and indebtedness), and of the rate of yield on capital—than has been or can be done here. However, some fairly plausible suggestions concerning the trends in these fractions can be made, and they may help to explain the trends indicated in Table 4.2.

First, as already noted in Chapter 2, the general trend in $R$, the ratio of total wealth to national product, has been downward, particularly in Great Britain, Belgium, Japan, the United States, and Australia (see Table 2.7). These declines were observed for the total wealth–national product ratios, but are also true of the ratios to national income at factor cost. Although the data do not indicate perfect consistency of trend within the long periods set by the terminal dates, they do suggest the general direction.

Second, it is reasonable to assume that $S$, the fraction of $W$ outside the equity of unincorporated enterprises (but including individually held residential housing) has risen in the course of economic growth, reflecting the rise in the shares of corporations and governments in the economy. The magnitude of this rise cannot be estimated adequately because long-term records of entrepreneurial equity as a share of total wealth are lacking; but since the shares of agriculture and of the unincorporated nonagricultural sector in the economy have declined markedly in the long period of modern growth, we may assume that $S$ has at least doubled and may even have tripled.

Finally, the most reasonable conjecture concerning $Y$, the rate of yield on $WS$, is that it has declined—for most countries. This is the rate of return on capital which, in addition to that invested in residential housing, is used for investment in the new and growing sectors of an economy. The demand for such capital in the early phases of development, particularly in a follower country, would be high while the supply of capital funds would be limited (a characteristic of the premodern growth era); and with a low per capita income the rate of discounting the future would be high. All this should mean high rates of return on $WS$ in the early phases of a country's development, compared with later phases when the opportunities afforded by "backwardness" are fewer and the rate of discount is lower. To be sure, a downward trend in $Y$ may be qualified by other factors, e.g. difficulties in the early phases that may cause losses on the initial applications of capital to modern uses, and revolutionary expansion of investment opportunities in the later phases; and the trend may therefore not be continuous. But on balance and over long periods of *successful* economic growth the trend in $Y$ should be downward.

With long-term declines in $R$ and $Y$, and long-term rises in $S$, we can derive many diverse trends for the share of income from assets, depending upon the levels and rates of change assigned to the three variables. The findings in Table 4.2 can be briefly stated: (1) up to World War I, the share of income from assets was stable, in the United Kingdom and the United States, or was rising, appreciably in France and slightly in Germany; (2) between the two World Wars the share declined in the United Kingdom, Germany, and Switzerland but not in France and the United States; (3) after World War II the share declined widely in all countries except Canada. The downward movement after World War II is also observed in Belgium, Norway, Japan, Australia, and New Zealand.[7]

7. See Kuznets, "Quantitative Aspects: IV," Table 9, p. 48.

The stability of the share of income from assets in Table 4.2 could be explained by rises in $S$ being offset by declines in either $R$ or $Y$; and the rises in the share could be credited to rises in $S$. It is no accident that the increase in the share in France from 1853 to 1911 (lines 5 and 6), in Germany from 1895 to 1913 (lines 11 and 12), and in Canada from 1926–29 to 1954–60 (lines 19 and 20) is associated with a marked decline in the share of income of unincorporated enterprises (column 2). And the more prevalent downward trend in the share of income from assets after World War I, and particularly after World War II, can presumably be attributed to the declines in $R$ and $Y$, the latter intensified in recent decades by government controls of residential rent and of the interest rate in the long-term markets. Since, as already indicated, we do not have the necessary independent data, on a comprehensive and long-term basis, for $R$, $S$, and $Y$, the discussion above only suggests the directions in which study can be pursued and does not provide an adequate explanatory hypothesis.

Two further aspects of the trends in the share of income from assets should be noted. First, for 1954–60, the distribution of income from assets by type, for ten developed countries, was as follows:

Shares in Total Income from Assets,
Ten Developed Countries, 1954–60 (%)*

| Rent (1) | Interest (2) | Dividends (3) | Property income of households (4) = (1 + 2 + 3) | Corporate net profits (5) | Corporate direct tax (6) | Property and entrepreneurial income of government (7) |
|---|---|---|---|---|---|---|
| 16 | 17 | 13 | 46 | 21 | 22 | 12 |

* The countries included are the United Kingdom, Belgium, France, Switzerland, Finland, Japan, Canada, the United States, Australia, and New Zealand and the data are from U.N., *Yearbook of National Accounts Statistics, 1961*. The averages do not add to 100 because detail given varies from country to country.

Property income of households accounts for only half of all income from assets; and *private* income from assets, net of corporate tax, is only about seven tenths of the total. Since all income from assets is about 19 per cent of national income for the eleven developed countries in Table 4.1, private income from assets is only about 13 per cent of national income. Furthermore, direct taxes on property income of households must be deducted: and if we follow the assumption used in Table 4.1, that the tax rate on property income is double that on all nontransfer income, the direct tax burden on property income of households is about 31 per cent, or about 3 per cent ($0.31 \times 0.086$) of national income—leaving only 10 per cent of national income for private income from assets net of direct taxes. For the post-World War II period, the proportion to net national product of net domestic (or national) capital formation was between 14 and 16 per cent while the proportion to total capital formation of that under the auspices of public administration was about a tenth[8]—so that the share of private net capital formation in net product was between 12.5 and 14.5 per cent. Thus even if we assume that *all* private income from assets, net of taxes, is saved to finance private capital formation, it falls short of the latter by a significant margin. Furthermore, much of the interest and rent receipts, and even of dividends, flows to income groups well below the top; while income from assets accounts for only a moderate fraction of the total income of the upper income groups.[9] It may, therefore, be argued that a large proportion of savings to finance private (and other) capital formation origi-

8. See Kuznets, "Quantitative Aspects: V," Table 4, p. 13 and Table 7, p. 37.

9. In the United States, in 1948, the top 10 per cent of population received 73 per cent of all dividends, but only 30 per cent of interest, 25 per cent of rent, and 47 per cent of all property income of households (see Simon Kuznets, *Shares of Upper Income Groups in Income and Savings*, National Bureau of Economic Research, 1953, Table 124, p. 664). Of the total income of the top 10 per cent group in the same year, property income receipts accounted for only 16.7 per cent (ibid., Table 125, p. 675). Both estimates refer to income before taxes.

nates not in the income from assets (too often viewed as the *only* source of national savings) but in compensation of employees and income of entrepreneurs, particularly the former. Indeed, judging by the estimates for recent years, no more than half of the household savings to finance capital formation can be credited to household income from assets net of taxes.

Second, this recent structure of income from assets reflects movements that have occurred over the long period of growth—the rise in the shares of corporate net profits and of corporate direct taxes, the decline in the share of property income of households, and the shifts within the latter among rent, interest, and dividends. While data are at hand only for the United States, a brief summary of these may be of some interest and may possibly be representative of other countries (Table 4.3).

TABLE 4.3

Structure of Income from Assets, United States, 1899–1908 to 1954–60

|  | 1899–1908 (1) | 1919–28 (2) | 1929 (3) | 1954–60 (4) |
|---|---|---|---|---|
| 1. Share of income from assets in national income (%) | 22 | 24 | 25 | 19 |
| *Shares in total income from assets (%)* | | | | |
| 2. Rent | 32 | 29 | 24 | 17 |
| 3. Interest | 26 | 25 | 32 | 21 |
| 4. Dividends | 26 | 21 | 25 | 18 |
| 5. Property income of households (excluding corporate transfers) | 84 | 75 | 81 | 56 |
| 6. Corporate net profits | 16 | 17 | 13 | 12 |
| 7. Corporate taxes | 0 | 8 | 6 | 30 |

*Sources: Cols. 1 and 2:* See Kuznets, "Quantitative Aspects: IV," App. Table 17, p. 94 and Simon Kuznets, "Long-Term Changes in the National Income of the United States of America since 1870," in Kuznets, ed., *Income and Wealth, Series II*, Table 27, p. 136.
*Cols. 3 and 4:* See the notes to Table 4.2.

Allowing for the crudity of the estimates and the peculiar features of the single prosperous year 1929, the trends are as expected: a rise in the share of the combined total of corporate undistributed profits and corporate taxes, and a decline in the shares of rent, dividends, and interest, with the share of the latter bolstered by greater concentration of households' savings in various types of contractual arrangements. The share of household property income in total income from assets declines significantly. The implication is that in the earlier periods, e.g. the middle to late nineteenth or early twentieth century, when the share of property income of households was much greater and the impact of progressive direct taxes much weaker, private income from assets in the hands of households could have provided a greater proportion of private savings than it has in the recent post-World II period. However in those earlier times the share of income of entrepreneurs in national income was also appreciably greater and that of total income from assets somewhat smaller—so that an additional large source of private savings existed then. Therefore, we cannot assume that income from assets, as defined in column 3 of Table 4.2, was—during any long period—the only significant source of private savings and of private financing of capital formation.

### ALLOCATION OF INCOME OF ENTREPRENEURS AND THE SHARES OF CAPITAL AND LABOR

Income from assets, as measured in column 3 of Table 4.2, does not include returns on the equity of unincorporated enterprises and thus falls short of the total return on wealth. Attempts to secure a complete measure of the latter, and thus ascertain the shares of capital and labor, have led to various allocations of total income of entrepreneurs, as covered in column 2 of Table 4.2, between the component representing compensation of entrepreneurial labor and that constituting a return on equity and thus on capital.[10]

One approach to the allocation between the two com-

10. For a review of these allocations and a discussion of the conflicting results, particularly when applied to entrepreneurial income in underdeveloped countries, see Kuznets, "Quantitative Aspects: IV," pp. 23–28.

ponents begins with an estimate of the labor component of entrepreneurial income, usually by assigning to entrepreneurs a per capita labor income equal to per worker compensation of employees, either in the country as a whole or in the several sectors; the return on equity is then obtained as the difference between total entrepreneurial income and the labor component as estimated. This procedure was followed in the derivation of columns 5 and 6 of Table 4.2, where we applied the average countrywide compensation per employee to all entrepreneurs to estimate the labor component of their income. The residual return on equity (as a share of national income) appears in column 5, which, when added to the share of income from assets in column 3, yields the share of the return on all capital (column 6). While theoretically it may have been preferable to apply sectoral compensation per employee to the number of entrepreneurs in the respective sectors, the necessary data are not at hand. Moreover, the assumption that the labor service of an entrepreneur equals that of an average employee, even in the same sector, is far too crude to warrant the refinement in calculation—even if the requisite data were available.

The second type of allocation begins with an approximation to the equity of unincorporated enterprises and applies to it an appropriate rate of return to arrive at an estimate of the capital income component of entrepreneurial income directly. The main difficulty with this approach is in securing data on entrepreneurial equity. In Table 4.2, columns 7 and 8, to compensate for the lack of relevant data, we assume that the equity of entrepreneurs is in the same proportion to total income-yielding wealth as the number of entrepreneurs is to total labor force; and that the rate of return on that equity is the same as the rate on all other wealth. The first assumption is not unreasonable, at least for the United States: the ratio of the sum of the equities of the farm sector and of unincorporated nonfarm business to total equity is about 25 per cent at the end of 1900 and 1912 and declines to 17 per cent at the end of

1949;[11] the share of entrepreneurs in total labor force is about 28.5 per cent in 1899–1908 and 15 per cent in 1954–60 (Table 4.2, column 4, lines 22 and 25); and the two sets of shares are quite similar.

The alternative allocations of the income of entrepreneurs between the labor and property income components yield results in Table 4.2 that differ significantly—and not in the same direction for all countries. In the United Kingdom throughout, in France in 1853 and 1954–60, and in Germany in 1895, 1913, and 1954–60, the deduction of the labor service component leaves a return on equity substantially larger than that derived directly. In these cases, either the labor component of entrepreneurial income is underestimated, or equity per entrepreneur is larger than other capital per employee, or the return on the equity is higher. In Germany in 1925–29, Switzerland in 1954–60, and Canada and the United States throughout, the deduction of the labor component from total entrepreneurial income leaves a return on equity below that estimated directly; and, in fact, in Canada in 1954–60 and in the United States in 1869–79 there is a loss, and in the United States in 1954–60 there is no return. These differences among countries and periods may well reflect genuine differences in the labor–property income composition of entrepreneurial income, but a proper test of the results requires data not presently available.

Of the two assumptions the first seems more acceptable. To begin with, the argument that per worker income of employees is a minimum standard to apply in estimating the labor income of entrepreneurs has some validity. Also,

11. See Goldsmith, *A Study of Saving*, Table W-9, pp. 42 ff. The sum of the equities for individual sectors is somewhat larger than total wealth estimated directly, because of errors of estimation of sectoral assets and liabilities. On the basis of total wealth, the percentages in the text would be 32 and 22 per cent, respectively.

In calculating the equity of the farm sector we excluded government and similar security holdings and life insurance reserves from the assets, since they are not relevant to the origin of entrepreneurial income from agriculture included in column 2 of Table 4.2.

at least according to data for the early 1950s for five developed countries, the total number of self-employed constituted 18 per cent, on the average, of the total labor force (excluding unpaid family labor, armed services, and unclassified), but only 6 per cent were classified as employers, i.e. employing at least one worker; the remaining 12 per cent were classified as workers on own account, i.e. people who worked independently in business or the professions and employed no paid labor.[12] The data thus indicate that the predominant majority of entrepreneurs are self-employed workers and that the major proportion of their income is derived from their labor. That the entries in Table 4.2 based on this assumption use per worker compensation of employees for the country, rather than by sector, has some advantages: if it thereby attributes too high a labor income to independent farmers, who constitute a large proportion of entrepreneurs even in developed countries, it also allows implicitly for the greater responsibility of entrepreneurial than employee labor.

If then we concentrate on the results of this approach we find that in all countries except Canada, the share of total income from assets or capital declined—in the United Kingdom only after 1905–14 and in the United States only since World War II, but in all other countries from the earliest period shown (column 6). Canada is the only country that fails to show a downward trend in the share of income from capital, but despite this failure its share is among the lowest in 1954–60.

The sample of countries in Table 4.2 is distressingly small, and the estimates leave much to be desired. But if any general conclusion is justified, it is that the share in national income of returns on capital declined over time in almost all countries—in some from almost a half to about a fifth or a quarter; and the share of "labor" must correspondingly have risen. If we accept the long-term upward

12. See U.N., *Demographic Yearbook, 1956*, Tables 14 and 15. The countries included are: Canada, the United Kingdom, Australia, New Zealand, and Sweden.

trend in the share of labor in national income and the downward trend in the share of capital, we must recognize that these developments occurred under conditions in which man-hours of labor, taken as such, were growing at far lower rates than capital stock, at constant prices—a point already made in Chapter 2, where it was shown that man-hours per capita in most countries declined over the long period of growth, while capital per capita grew at substantial rates. What then is the explanation of the rising share of labor in national income? Is it that with slow growth of the labor inputs relative to the capital inputs there was a marked increase in labor's relative marginal productivity and therefore in its relative price; and that the price shift has been more than sufficient to offset the relatively smaller quantity of labor in use? Or must we also consider different impacts of technological change and of changes in structure of final use on the relative demand for labor and capital?

It may be useful to suggest some of the factors involved by drawing again upon the results of the recent analysis for the United States by Edward F. Denison.[13] According to Denison, the shares of land and reproducible capital in national income, in current prices, were 8.9 and 21.6 per cent, respectively, for 1909–13, leaving 69.5 per cent for the share of labor; the former two shares declined to 3.0 and 19.7 per cent, respectively, in 1954–58, and the share of labor rose correspondingly to 77.3 per cent (Denison, Table 4, p. 30). The decline in the share of income from all capital of some 8 percentage points in 45 years is greater than that shown in Table 4.2, column 6, but this stems largely from differences in the procedure used to allocate entrepreneurial income between labor and capital.

Between 1909 and 1957—a period of 48 years quite close to the 45 years from the middle of 1909–13 to the middle of 1954–58—labor input, in terms of man-hours, grew at the rate of 0.87 per cent per year (calculated from Denison, Table 19, p. 148 and Table 13, p. 102); land did not grow

13 See Denison, "The Sources of Economic Growth."

at all; and reproducible capital grew at a rate of 2.41 per cent per year (Denison, Table 13, p. 102). If we allow for no differential changes in the prices of labor (i.e. man-hours) and capital services, and combine the growth of man-hours with that of capital input, at the weights of labor, land, and reproducible capital in 1909–13, by 1954–58 the share of labor declines to 58.8 per cent, that of land to 5.1 per cent, and that of reproducible capital rises to 36.1 per cent.

But the share of labor in national income in current prices rose to 77.3 per cent in 1954–58. To attain this level, the share in 1909–13 (69.5 per cent) should have grown 2.84, not 0.87, per cent per year—to exceed by an adequate margin the rate of growth of the combined total of land and reproducible capital. In other words, the price per man-hour of labor *relative* to the price per service unit of capital had to rise by the difference between 2.84 and 0.87 per cent per year; or the relative price differential of labor man-hours had to increase 2.41 times between 1909–13 and 1954–58. That this change in relative prices did in fact take place in the United States economy is suggested by other data. The most comprehensive measure of wages per man-hour available—that for all production workers in manufacturing—rose 9.5 times from the average of 1909 and 1914 to 1955–57; while the most comprehensive measure of prices of reproducible capital (and some land)—prices implicit in domestic gross capital formation—achieved a less than fourfold rise from 1909–13 to 1955–57.[14] If we "deflate" the wage per man-hour by prices of capital goods, which we take here as prices of capital services (implying a constant rate of return), wage per man-hour so deflated would have multiplied 2.44 times—an

14. The series on wages per man-hour is from *Historical Statistics of the United States*, Series D 626, p. 92. The prices of gross capital formation are derived from Kuznets, *Capital in the American Economy*, Table R-29, pp. 572 ff. (through 1953) and extrapolated to 1955–57 by the indexes derived from U.S., Department of Commerce, *U.S. Income and Output*, Tables VII-5 and VII-6, p. 224.

increase quite close to that in the price differential in favor of labor services of 2.41 times suggested above.

The question is then why price per man-hour of labor should rise so much more than price per unit of capital services—and thus increase the share of labor in national income, despite the lower rate of growth in man-hours than in capital stock, even including land. Denison provides some partial answers, in the suggested sources of improvement in the "quality of labor." One important source is education, and Denison sets the rate of rise in educational levels of the labor force at 0.78 per cent per year (comparable to the rate of growth of total man-hours of 0.87 per cent). Other sources are improvement in efficiency of labor associated directly with reduction in working hours (0.43 per cent growth in quality of labor), and improvement in efficiency of female labor (0.14 per cent). These improvements raise the rate of growth of labor input from 0.87 per cent, in terms of man-hours, to 2.22 per cent per year, in terms of labor "adjusted for quality." Whether or not we accept Denison's estimates, the general import of his analysis is clear. Among the factors that raised the price of labor per man-hour were increased investment in education, greater general efficiency of labor because of shorter man-hours, and the like. None of these factors directly affects the price of material capital and its services, since it is *live* labor that is the carrier of these improvements.

If we accept Denison's estimates of the increased quality of labor and raise its price (per man-hour) relative to capital services by the amount he suggests, the rate of growth in labor inputs becomes 2.22 per cent per year, the rate of growth in reproducible capital remains 2.41 per cent per year, and that in land, zero. These rates, applied over a 45-year period to the shares in national income in 1909–13, yield a share of labor equal to 72.2 per cent in 1954–58, in a total national income that is 158.6 per cent higher. One can put the explanation of the rising share of labor in either of two ways: (1) The share of labor increased slightly from 1909–13 to 1954–58 because the price per man-hour

183

of labor relative to price per unit of capital services advanced as a result of the increased quality per man-hour, and consequently the rate of growth in labor input at these higher prices exceeded the rate of growth of capital services at their prices. (2) The share increased because, with constant prices per unit of labor service of standard quality and per unit of capital service, the rate of growth in labor input, reduced to standard quality, was greater than the rate of growth in capital input.

But we still must consider residual efficiency, i.e. the growth in output per unit of total input, which amounted to about a third of the rate of growth in total input for the period 1909–57.[15] If we assume this proportion applicable to the period 1909–13 to 1954–58, with total growth in inputs of 158.6 per cent, total growth in national income would be 211.5 per cent. Since national income is allocated to capital or labor and since the estimate of capital input assumes implicitly that capital input and total return on capital are the same (since the weight used is the share in national income), Denison's estimates implicitly and my calculations above explicitly assign the gains in efficiency to the labor share. As a result, the share of labor in 1954–58 is over 76.9 per cent, quite close to the actual share of 77.3 per cent.

Whether or not the magnitudes used here are valid, the general implication of the argument is obvious. The price per man-hour of labor relative to price per unit of capital service rose not only because of quality improvements credited to labor man-hours (but not to capital) but also because of the gains in residual efficiency—which are, indeed, components of the rise in total output not accounted for by measured inputs.

The validity of the line of distinction drawn between im-

15. See Denison, Table 19, p. 148. We use the term "residual efficiency" to distinguish this concept from the wider one in Chap. 2, which allowed for inputs of labor and capital in simple units disregarding quality changes.

provements in the quality of labor and gains in efficiency is a matter for further consideration, but beyond the limits of discussion feasible here. It might be more useful to distinguish between improvements in quality of labor reflected by measurable investment on the part of labor—e.g. in education or in some elements of a higher standard of living indispensable for the performance of more highly skilled functions within urban conditions imposed by the changing industrial structure associated with modern economic growth—and *net* gains in efficiency, after these investments and higher costs of living and functioning on the part of labor (costs not measured in the usual price and cost of living indexes) have been taken into account.

If we allow for increased investment in the education of labor (using the term "education" in its widest sense) and increased costs of living and functioning required by the changing productive system, and some gain remains in residual efficiency, i.e. output per unit of resources rises, it may be allocated either to capital or to labor. If to capital, the price of capital relative to labor services, the latter properly adjusted for education and higher hidden costs, will rise; if to labor, as was done for the United States, the relative price of labor will rise. By making this distinction we can separate the inputs of factors judged by their cost from gains in efficiency—which can then be allocated without affecting the replacement needs of the two factors.

Except for some further discussion of related topics in Chapter 5, which deals with capital formation and consumption, we shall not try to develop the discussion further; and, indeed, it may require data not now available.

To conclude: the share of labor in growing net output has increased, particularly in recent decades, because greater investment has been made in maintaining and increasing the quality of labor; also, a larger proportional share of the net gains, after the input of resources adjusted for quality has been taken into account, has gone to labor—possibly an expression of the higher priority increasingly assigned by society, at least in the free market economies, to the claims of living members than to the claims of their material capital.

## COMPENSATION OF EMPLOYEES

The share of compensation of employees in total income rose in all six countries in Table 4.2—from below 40 per cent in the early periods to between 60 and 70 per cent in recent years. This upward trend can be observed in several other countries for shorter recent periods. The share of wages and salaries in total factor income in Norway rose from 48.5 per cent in 1930 to 55.2 per cent in 1955.[16] From 1938 to 1955 the share of wages and salaries in national income rose in Belgium (from 46 to 54 per cent), Finland (from 50 to 61 per cent), Italy (from 40–42 to 48–50 per cent), the Netherlands (from 51 to 54 per cent), and Sweden (from 52 to 63 per cent).[17]

The data are too limited to reveal possible exceptions, but the general evidence suggests a marked rise in the share of compensation of employees in national income. Consequently, it is difficult to assign much weight to statements claiming constancy of the "wage share," if they are taken to mean, as clearly intended, a long-term stability of the share of compensation of employees (or wages and salaries) in national income. Such stability can be observed in Table 4.2 only for the United Kingdom from 1860–69 to 1901–14, and it may have been the result of the stability of the share of entrepreneurs and self-employed in the labor force and the maintenance of a constant share of income from assets during that period.[18]

Since the share of income from assets, observed in Table

16. See Odd Aukrust, "Trends and Cycles in Norwegian Income Shares," in Milton Gilbert and Richard Stone, eds., *Income and Wealth, Series VI* (London, 1957), Table IV, pp. 304–05.

17. See U.N., *Economic Survey of Europe in 1956* (Geneva, 1957), Chap. 8, Table 1, p. 3.

18. For references to the literature on the "wage share" and a brief discussion see Kuznets, "Quantitative Aspects: IV," pp. 55–56.

4.2, was constant or rose slightly in the periods preceding the recent one (when it declined) the major factor in the expanded share of compensation of employees was probably the rise in the share of employees in the total labor force. For unless income per employee declined relative to income per entrepreneur, the rise in the share of employees in total labor force would mean a rise in the share of compensation of employees in total participation income (the sum of employee compensation and income of entrepreneurs); and since the share of the latter in national income was constant or declined only slightly, this would mean a rise in the share of employee compensation in national income. The evidence in Table 4.2 suggests that income per employee did not decline relative to income per entrepreneur and self-employed, but rather rose: compare the ratio of income of entrepreneurs (column 2) to total participation income (sum of columns 1 and 2) with the ratio of entrepreneurs to total labor force (column 4). But even if income per employee relative to income per entrepreneur had remained constant, the marked rise in the share of employees in total labor force would have meant a marked rise in the share of employee compensation in participation income as well as in national income—particularly during the recent period when the share of income from assets declined.

This trend in the distribution of the labor force—a drop in the share of entrepreneurs and self-employed from over 35 to less than 20 per cent, and an increase in the share of employees from less than 65 to over 80 per cent of the total labor force (and the shifts would have been greater for records reaching further back)—was due, at least in the free market economies, partly to shifts in industrial structure and partly to changes in status within specific industrial sectors. Agriculture and related industries have always been characterized by small-scale firms and a higher proportion of entrepreneurs and self-employed to the labor force attached to the sector—particularly if we exclude, as we should, unpaid family labor. Thus, in recent years, even in the underdeveloped countries, the proportion of entrepreneurs to the total sectoral labor force is significantly higher for agriculture than for the industry and services sectors— 66, 31, and 35 per cent respectively; and the contrast is naturally more marked for developed countries—61, 11, and 17 per cent, respectively.[19] The decline in the share of agriculture in the labor force in itself meant a substantial drop in the share of entrepreneurs and self-employed in total labor force. Furthermore, even in the industry and services sectors, producing units tended to increase in scale and shift from unincorporated status, and thus reduce the ratio of entrepreneurs and self-employed to labor force. No relevant long-term records are at hand, but in the post-World War II years the proportion of entrepreneurs and self-employed in the labor force attached to these sectors is smaller in the developed than in the underdeveloped countries. A variety of evidence relating to the shift to large-scale, corporate enterprise in many nonagricultural sectors in the course of modern economic growth would lead us to expect a marked trend within these sectors toward a higher share of employees in the labor force.

This trend toward employee status is one aspect of a widely ramified process of change in scale and organization of the economic enterprise that accompanies economic growth in the free market economies and is, of course, the distinctive hallmark of the revolutionary and violent breaks that usher in authoritarian economies under the guidance of a monolithic minority party. The importance of this process for the free economies is suggested by the voluminous literature on industrial organization, corporate structure, economies of scale, and a variety of other related topics. An analysis of the changes in shares of enterprises grouped by *size* or scale of firm unit in the discussion of structural changes in national product would have immediately contributed to our understanding of both the shift to employee status and other changing aspects of factor shares. Unfortunately no data for such a quantitative analysis are readily available. We note this complex of changes here primarily to

19. See Table 8.1, pp. 404–05.

stress the point that the rise in the share of compensation of employees in national income—insofar as it was due to the marked rise in the proportion of employees in the labor force—was a reflection of far-reaching trends not only in industrial structure but also in the scale and character of the economic unit.

Another aspect of this trend within the labor force toward employee status is closely related to both our preceding and subsequent discussion. A shift from being one's own boss—whether a small farmer, shopkeeper, or craftsman (let alone a rich merchant or broker)—to the status of an employee means a change in the basis of economic life and planning; and the difference in status is likely to be associated with differences in attitudes toward family and children, in patterns of consumption, and in propensity to invest in education and training relative to inclination to save for investment in one's business and elsewhere. All these interrelations bear upon some demographic patterns already considered in Chapter 2 and upon capital investment, savings, and consumption, to be discussed in Chapter 5. To put it more generally, trends in the relative shares of compensation of employees and of income of entrepreneurs reflect shifts in the distribution of labor force by status—and the latter reflect changes in the economic base of life of the persons involved and hence changes in the likely patterns of behavior affected by economic status.

Does the factor share of compensation of employees, the major income of the predominant proportion of the labor force in the developed countries, reveal any marked trends in structure? This question has already been partly answered, since changes in the industrial structure of the labor force, discussed in Chapter 3, are bound to be reflected in the industrial distribution of compensation of employees—implying declines in the shares of compensation of employees originating in agriculture, domestic service, and other lagging sectors; and rises in the share originating in the industry sector. It should also be clear from the discussion of Table 4.1 that payments other than wages and salaries (i.e. contributions to Social Security and the like) have constituted a rising share of total compensation of employees—although the fraction is not large even in recent years.

Other distinctions within compensation of employees are of primary interest here. For example, what are the trends in the share of wages compared with those in the share of salaries, on the assumption that we can draw an effective distinction between the two? Or what is the trend in the share of compensation of employees that could be interpreted as return on investment in education and training? Or finally, what are the trends of compensation of employees in large-scale firms and in small-scale economic units?

No data are available on these long-term movements, and we mention them only to indicate the possible value of explorations in these directions. Here we can refer only to some observable changes in the structure of the employed labor force—by age, occupational status, and sex—that do not directly reveal the changing structure of compensation of employees over time, but may nevertheless be suggestive.

1. In general, modern economic growth has been accompanied by a substantial rise in the age of entry into the labor force and by a reduction in the age of retirement. For labor force as a whole (including entrepreneurs), the proportion of the younger age groups (under 18 in Great Britain and under 20 in four other countries) declined in the countries covered in a study by Clarence D. Long. These declines were in large part due to a sharp fall in the rate of labor force participation of the age groups in question.[20] The decline in the share in the labor force of persons 65 years old and over was less widespread, because the proportion of the aged in total population increased so markedly. But the combined share in the labor force of the very young and of the old, of the groups below and above the prime ages, de-

20. See *The Labor Force under Changing Income and Employment* (National Bureau of Economic Research, 1958), appendix tables for Great Britain, 1911–51; Germany, 1895–1939; the United States, 1890–150; Canada, 1911–51; and New Zealand, 1896–1951.

clined. This finding suggests that in the course of economic growth the labor force, and presumably employees, were increasingly concentrated in the prime labor ages—thus contributing both to higher general efficiency and to a narrower spread in age-determined ability.

2. The changes in occupational status and in sex distribution are illustrated by data for the United States in Table 4.4. The proportion of manual labor (line 11) declined sharply from 1900 to 1960; and the decline is equally marked if the distribution is restricted to nonagricultural employees. By contrast, the shares of the white-collar and highly trained occupations rose (lines 2–6). Furthermore, even within manual labor there was a definite shift away from unskilled labor (line 9) toward skilled labor (lines 7 and 8).

Some of these trends were no doubt more conspicuous in the United States than in other countries, but there are obvious grounds for assuming that the occupational shifts in other developed countries were similar. To begin with, they reflect the widely observed and common changes in industrial structure—an increase in the share in the labor force of the service sector and a decline in the share of the commodity producing sectors. Second, the greater demand for professional and technical labor, for managers and officials in the growing large-scale public and private enterprises, and for clerical labor is a common feature in modern economic growth in all developed countries. Finally, the demand for greater skill and the fewer opportunities for unskilled manual labor are the results of increasing mechanization, while the reduced supply of household workers is a common consequence of rising per capita income in all developed countries.

These comments on the relevance of the occupational shifts in Table 4.4 suggest that there has been a general shift in the distribution of employees from wage-earners (or blue-collar workers) to salaried people (or white-collar workers). Implicit in the present discussion is the distinction between the two groups, based upon the degree of contact with

191

TABLE 4.4

Occupational Structure of Employees, United States, 1900 and 1960

| | Share of occupational groups in total (%) | | Share of females in occupational group (%) | |
|---|---|---|---|---|
| | 1900 (1) | 1960 (2) | 1900 (3) | 1960 (4) |
| 1. Share of employees in total labor force (%) | 74.9 | 93.0 | 22.7* | 34.3* |
| *Occupational groups* | | | | |
| 2. Professional, technical, and kindred workers | 5.7 | 12.2 | 35.2 | 38.1 |
| 3. Managers and officials | 0.8 | 5.8 | 0.4 | 14.4 |
| 4. Clerical and kindred workers | 4.0 | 16.0 | 24.2 | 67.6 |
| 5. Sales workers | 6.0 | 8.0 | 17.4 | 36.4 |
| 6. White-collar workers (lines 2–5) | 16.6 | 42.0 | 24.5 | 45.7 |
| 7. Craftsmen, foremen, and kindred workers | 14.1 | 15.4 | 2.5 | 2.9 |
| 8. Operatives and kindred workers | 17.1 | 21.5 | 34.0 | 28.1 |
| 9. Laborers except farm and mine | 16.6 | 5.9 | 3.8 | 3.5 |
| 10. Farm laborers and foremen | 23.6 | 2.6 | 13.6 | 17.3 |
| 11. Manual workers (lines 7–10) | 71.4 | 45.4 | 14.0 | 15.7 |
| 12. Service workers except household | 4.8 | 9.6 | 34.3 | 52.4 |
| 13. Household workers | 7.3 | 3.0 | 96.6 | 96.4 |
| 14. Service workers, total (lines 12–13) | 12.1 | 12.6 | 71.8 | 63.0 |

* Share of females in total number of employees.

*Sources: Cols. 1 and 3:* Underlying data are from *Historical Statistics of the United States*, Series D 72–D 122, p. 74 and Series D 123–D 572, pp. 75 ff. The group in line 3 is derived by subtracting managers, officials, and proprietors, n.e.c. (Series D 204) from a larger group which includes proprietors (Series D 79), on the assumption that the former is dominated by individual entrepreneurs and self-employed. We assumed that the proportion of females for the group in line 3 is the same as for the larger group including proprietors.

*Cols. 2 and 4:* Underlying data are from U.S. Bureau of the Census, *Statistical Abstract of the United States, 1964*, Table 308, pp. 229 ff. From the total for the experienced civilian labor force we excluded farmers and self-employed managers and officials, and those with occupation unknown.

the manual operations and thus the degree to which a worker's employment is dependent upon the current volume of production. Industry sectors differ widely in the distribution of their employees between wage-earners and salaried workers—the proportions of the latter being lowest in agriculture (from 4 to 13 per cent), next in industry (from 11 to 18 per cent), and highest in services (from 42 to 63 per cent).[21] Hence, the mere shift in the labor force away from agriculture and toward the service sector would raise the overall share of salaried workers among all employees; and this trend would be intensified by shifts toward greater proportions of salaried workers within the industry sector. In fact, in France, Germany, Switzerland, the United States, and a few other countries, we find a marked rise in the share of salaried among all employees, from a few percentage points in the earlier years to between 20 and 30 per cent in recent years (see Kuznets, "Quantitative Aspects: IV," pp. 53–54). And unless compensation per salaried employee declined enormously relative to compensation per wage-earner, the share of salaries in total compensation of employees also must have risen in the long run.

3. The proportion of women among employees in the United States increased significantly—from 23 to 34 per cent over the sixty years covered in Table 4.4. Clarence D. Long's data relate to total labor force, including entrepreneurs and self-employed; but since employees predominate, the findings suggest trends in the distribution of employees by sex. The proportion of women in the labor force of the United States increased from 17 per cent in 1890 to 27 per cent in 1950; in Canada from 13 per cent in 1911 to 22 per cent in 1951; in New Zealand from 18 per cent in 1896 to 23 per cent in 1951; in Germany (pre-World War II territory) from 30 per cent in 1895 to 36 per cent in 1939; and in Great Britain only slightly, from 30 per cent in 1911 to 31 per cent in 1951.[22]

In general, the reduction in birth rates that began in the older European countries in the last quarter of the nineteenth century, the shift of employment opportunities from

21. See Kuznets, "Quantitative Aspects: IV," Table 7, p. 43.
22. See *The Labor Force*, Table A-2, p. 286; Table A-9, p. 302; Table A-11, p. 305; Table A-14, p. 309; and Table A-16, p. 312.

manual to clerical and sales positions, and the urbanization of the population which placed women within closer reach of organized labor markets and growing job opportunities, all combined to permit more active participation by women in the developed countries. It is significant that in Table 4.4 the occupational groups that showed the greatest increase within the total body of employees—professional and technical, clerical, sales, and service workers other than household (lines 2, 4, 5, and 12)—were all characterized by large proportions of females. Moreover, the proportion of females within each occupational group in which they were at all important increased (or was stable at high levels), with the one exception of operatives (line 8) and that decline reflects the contraction in the relative shares of textiles, clothing, and similar industries in which the proportions of women among all workers were traditionally higher than in other industries.

Two concluding comments can be made concerning the trends in the age, occupation, and sex structure of the employed labor force. First, the trends reflect the increasing demands of modern economic growth for education, training, and greater skills in the labor force—as well as the feasibility, given the higher income per capita, of making the investments required to attain these higher levels of education and skill. They also reflect the basic changes in demographic patterns accompanying modern economic growth, particularly the reduction in birth rates and the increasing urbanization. Since all these interrelations are evident whenever there is economic growth, we should expect to find similar changes in the Communist countries in the age, sex, and occupational structure of the population.

Second, the changes briefly noted contrast sharply with the trends in the character of the employed labor force envisioned by the Classical economists, and even more by the Marxian School. The shift toward employed status, the "proletarianization" of the small entrepreneurs and self-employed, was expected to be accompanied by the maintenance of the employees, the workers, at an "iron law of wage" minimum, by a continuously intensified feeling of low class position in economic society, by an increasing cleavage between this growing body of employees and, depending upon the theory, either a body of landlords drawing increased shares of product as rent or a diminishing body of capitalists controlling an increased proportion of capital (if not necessarily of income) in the economy. Instead, there has been a marked reduction in the share of unskilled workers among employees and implicitly a greater investment in education and training; an increase in the proportion of employees some steps removed from the material production process and in positions of quasi-control, at high or low levels of professional and educational attainment; and an increasing share of women, who to a great extent are only temporary participants in the production process and who form an effective but secondary labor force, scarcely likely to develop the class consciousness that was expected of the industrial proletariat. Obviously the actual experience was the result of technological changes that could not easily be foreseen in the early phases of modern economic growth, and that affected the organizational structure of economic units and the mode of life of an increasing proportion of total and active population—inducing growth in the proportion of white-collar workers in employed labor, greater skill mixture even of production labor, and an increase of employees in the service sector.

### DISTRIBUTION OF INCOME BY SIZE: PROBLEMS OF DEFINITION

We turn now to the distribution of income among individuals and households, the major recipients in the economy, by size of income per receiving unit—and we thus concentrate on the equality or inequality of the shares. Our main interest is to observe whether, in association with the growth of per capita income, changes in industrial structure, trends in factor shares, and other trends within modern economic growth, there have also been changes in the distribution of income by size, which in turn would have affected the uses of income for savings and investment, or for different categories of consumption. But at this point, when we are trying to trace the flow of income to households, a variety of definitional problems arise; and while it is impossible to discuss them in detail here, it is indispensable to deal with them briefly to permit clear understanding of the few findings in the field.[23]

*Income Shares*—Since we wish to study the effects of economic growth—conceived as changes in the production process—on the size distribution of income, the income shares needed are presumably those that flow directly out of participation in the production process: wages, salaries, and other compensation of employees, entrepreneurial income, and returns on property invested by households in the production process. Any subsequent redistribution of these primary shares that is unrelated to the production process—gambling gains, gifts, and the like—should be of no concern. Once we agree on what the production process is, definition of income shares should directly follow.

But as already suggested in the discussion of Table 4.1 this conclusion is immediately disturbed since the compensation of the people (or of their capital) directly engaged in production may be affected by differential conditions of employment or redistributions that are unavoidable concomitants of participation in the production process. Consider the possible effect of a progressive income tax on the compensation of employees with differing degrees of training and skill. Once the tax has been in effect for some time and is accepted as a form of redistribution, the range of employees' compensation flowing directly from the productive process is likely to be at least partly adjusted to it—so that the after-tax income of the higher skill groups will still reflect the differential compensation for the greater ability. Similarly, after the establishment of free benefits,

23. Most of the subsequent discussion in this chapter is taken directly from Kuznets, "Quantitative Aspects: VIII," pp. 2–10 and 58–67.

such as state-paid medical and educational services, which accrue mostly to the lower income groups (or at least are of proportionately greater value to them), there may be more ready acceptance of low rates of compensation flowing out of the production process. Thus inequality in the distribution of employee compensation as it originates in the production process may be wider merely because of the extension of progressive income taxation at one end and the provision of free benefits at the other, i.e. because of the expected "redistribution," not because of any change within the production process itself. If so, the income shares that properly reflect the changes in the production process are compensation of employees and other payments, *excluding* income taxes and *including* free benefits.

That the point is of considerable weight is suggested in Table 4.1. Service and property incomes constitute the income shares of households as they flow directly from the production process. Their redistribution through direct taxes, transfers, and direct services by government is a third of the original shares in the developed countries (the ratio in column 3 or 4 of the sum of lines 13, 14, and 17 to line 10). The growth over time in the relative weight of these taxes, transfers, and direct services by government in the developed countries would—other factors remaining equal— tend to widen inequality of service and property incomes originating in the production process; but such a trend would be properly attributable to expected redistribution and might not be apparent in the more suitable base series, i.e. income after taxes and including benefits.[24]

Consider next the effect of conditions of participation in the productive process. If earning a high income requires living in urban communities, with higher prices than in

24. An adjustment for redistribution through taxes and benefits reduces the share of the top 5 per cent of consuming units in Great Britain (for 1948/49) from 23 to 18 per cent of total income and in the United States (for 1949/50) from 24 to 22 per cent; and the concentration ratios for the total distribution are reduced from 0.31 to 0.25 for Great Britain and from 0.34 to 0.31 for the United States (see ibid., Table 7, p. 26).

the countryside for identical goods, the comparison of income shares should adjust for differences in the cost of living. This problem will be discussed in Chapter 5 in connection with the maintenance of the share of consumption with the rise in per capita income in the course of economic growth, but it is also relevant here. The production process reflects the different conditions of life associated with different roles and status levels; any changes in the size distribution of income that reflects such differentials in associated and indispensable costs must be adjusted for the effects of the latter. Thus if, in the process of economic growth, the inequality in shares flowing from the productive process widens (or narrows) because differential costs widen (or narrow), these changes cannot be interpreted as meaningful trends in the distribution of income.

*Recipient Units*—Since it is individuals who participate directly in the productive process, the income recipient unit, for our purposes, may seem to be the individual rather than the family consuming unit or any larger group. But the difficulties of securing a meaningful distribution of income among individual income recipients prove, in fact, to be discouragingly great.

To begin with, little meaning can be attached to a distribution among individuals of property income or of income that originates within households from unpaid family labor. In the former case, most of the underlying ownership claims are held by family units, not by distinct individuals. In the latter case, a given individual's participation in the production process is not clearly distinguishable from that of other members of the family. The proportions of total income accruing to the population that cannot thus be distributed among individuals are far from negligible. The share of property income rises to over 20 per cent of total personal income, and the contribution of agriculture, and of similarly traditional sectors in which unpaid family labor is prevalent, is significant even in developed economies; and it was much greater in the earlier periods of growth.

## Distribution of Product and Income

But even if we exclude property income and treat the product of unpaid family labor as part of the individual income of the family head (which makes the latter less comparable with individual incomes of heads of families with no unpaid family labor and of other family members who may be receiving income), other difficulties remain. In observing the distribution of participation or earned income among individuals, do we include only those who received *some* income during the time period covered, or do we also include those who should have received some through gainful employment but did not because of the limitations of the production system (rather than through some fault of their own)? Presumably the latter should also be included, with zero or negligible incomes (the same reasoning applies to both); yet it would be extremely difficult, if not impossible, to define this missing group properly under changing conditions of social organization and economic development, for it involves the normative concept of the groups within the population that are entitled to effective, income-earning opportunities within the country's productive system. The same problem emerges within the active, and presumably income-receiving, labor force, which includes some marginal or at least secondary groups—a result of age and, in some occupations, of sex. The relative importance of these secondary groups varies over time with differences or changes in family and social organization, since the latter lead to differences or changes in accepted views regarding who is to be considered a member of the active labor force. The numbers of individual income recipients given in the labor force data (which presumably comprise all potential earned-income recipients) include large groups of marginal cases in some periods that are not included in other periods; and size distributions of income among individual recipients are affected by these differences in the extent to which society permits labor force participation by marginal groups, a decision that may have little *direct* relation to the constraints of the productive system, which adapts itself to different conditions and compositions of labor supply.

199

For the present purpose, the individual income-recipient unit, while possibly more useful than other units in reflecting differences in contribution to the production process, is unsuitable because it bars a complete distribution of personal income among the total population and because the distributions based on it are affected too much by differences over time in the selection of those who can claim individual engagement in the production process. This selection is, in essence, determined by the relation to needs, i.e. by the degree of dependence of the consuming unit—largely the family—upon the contribution of the individual member through his participation in the labor force. The needs, however, are those of consuming or family units. Indeed, size distribution of income assumes full meaning only when it is related to population needs, not merely to the intrinsic productive properties of the individual members of the population. For this reason meaningful size distributions must use a basic consuming unit whose needs determine choices with respect not only to *use* of income but to *receipt* of income.

Two major questions in connection with distributions among family units should be noted. Disregarding technical details of definition (whether the family unit is limited to persons related by blood and residing together—the usual definition—or includes some nonrelated co-residents, or dependent relatives residing elsewhere), one may observe first that even separate families or households may be related— so that the economic fortunes of one are the concern of another. For example, the family unit of a parent couple and the family units of their married children, all living in separate households, presumably have a community of interest: the economic resources of all may be pooled for some special purposes and the economic success or failure of one is of consequence to all. The size distribution of income should reflect the changing shares of units that have such strong community of interest, and it would be of value to study the distribution not merely among separate families or households, but among clusters of households with that community of interest. Such an approach is not permitted by the available data, but its relevance must be borne in mind in the interpretation of existing distributions. Thus, if small, nuclear families, characteristic of the developed countries in recent years, are more subject to combination in such related clusters than the larger extended families of earlier periods, the distribution of income based on the common definition of the family or consuming unit might show wider inequality in the later than in the earlier periods. But this difference would be an exaggeration of that shown by distributions taking account of ties of interest among separate but related households.

The other question arises from the differing size of family or household units. The larger incomes of some may be due to a larger number of income earners and may be associated with a larger number of persons for whose consumption and savings the total family income provides. Some adjustment for the size of the family or household unit is therefore advisable—by relating total income to total number of persons, or to some type of adult equivalent.[25]

*Period of Income Cumulation*—Income may be modified by short-term factors, whether they are of a type to affect large numbers of family units almost equally (e.g. a crop failure or an unusually large crop) or to have a different impact on different units (e.g. sickness or a turn of personal fortune). These short-term effects may be nearly random, i.e. reflect a multiplicity of causes, none great enough to stand out; or they may be systematic, as in business cycles during which some income types respond more sensitively than others (e.g. entrepreneurial incomes in trade compared with salaries in government)—with consequent effects on the size distribution of income among families dependent upon different types of income.

25. A full allowance for number of persons per family and a regrouping of the units by scale of per capita income often yields a distribution with wider inequality. This was true of Great Britain in 1951/52, the Netherlands in 1954, and the United States in 1952 (see Kuznets, "Quantitative Aspects: VIII," Table 9, p. 32).

Short-term variability of income can be viewed as a consequence, at least in part, of the factors involved in economic growth. Thus, dominance of agriculture may mean that the incomes of a large proportion of families are subject to effects of marked fluctuations in crops; while in the industrialized countries with the free organization of the market, business cycles may dominate short-term movements. Nevertheless, we should distinguish between the short- and long-term components of income, since they might have different sources in the productive system in the course of growth and would have different impacts on the disposition of income by recipients, on their responses to income as an incentive. Unfortunately, it is not easy to adjust the income distribution for the effect of short-term income variability.

Ideally, one should have for this purpose long records of income receipts for each family or household unit, so that the secular paths rather than the fluctuating annual amounts could be traced. If such records were available for all units in the population, we could set up a size distribution of secular income ordinates rather than of given year values. And if lifetime cycles of income could be established, an alternative distribution of secular values, *adjusted* for the particular phase of the life cycle occupied by a given family unit in a given year, might be secured. If income recipients tend to evaluate their incomes within the perspective of the life earnings cycle based on current or recent experience, a distribution of what might be called secular-life-cycle-relatives of income might give us an insight not provided otherwise.

But no long-time records of income for separate family units are available on an adequate scale, and we must use more practical devices, while keeping the wider problem in mind. One practical approach has been suggested by the illuminating analysis by Milton Friedman in *A Theory of the Consumption Function* (National Bureau of Economic Research, 1957). For our purposes, the major conclusion of Friedman's analysis is that, on some reasonable assumptions, the size distribution of household consumption (or the variance of household consumption for family units grouped by size of family income) is a far better approximation to the size distribution of what he calls "permanent" (i.e. long-term) income than the size distribution of measured annual income (the income distributions usually provided). To be sure, the distinction is based largely on the implicit treatment of income by the income recipient as the basis for decisions concerning consumption and savings—not on the evaluation of income with reference to different criteria (e.g. phase of lifetime progression, or standing relative to incomes of other groups).[26]

Another practical alternative is to study income differentials not among discrete households, but among groups of them—particularly among groups distinguished by attachment of the household head to different industrial sectors. Such a grouping will not eliminate short-term changes in income which are common to all or most units within a group, and it may still leave some cyclical elements in the income differentials. But it should minimize the short-term effects on income that are different for different units within the group, e.g. those that are largely random, or those associated with different phases in the life cycle of earnings; and these may be the more important components in the short-term disturbances of income values. At any rate, the relevant data on intersectoral income differentials should be utilized to supplement the conventional size distributions among discrete family or household units.

*Rates of Income Mobility*—Two size distributions of income, even if they relate to long-term income levels of family units, may differ greatly in meaning because of different degrees of internal mobility. If in one distribution

26. The shift to distribution of consumption expenditures from that of income received naturally reduces the inequality in the distribution by eliminating progressive direct taxes and savings that are proportionally higher in the upper income brackets, as observed in data on annual income (see the result for Great Britain in 1951/52 and the United States in 1950 in Kuznets, "Quantitative Aspects: VIII," Table 8, p. 28).

the given family units remain at the same long-term income position, absolute or relative, while in another the long-term income level of some families involves marked shifts upward and downward, the responses of the household units to income level as well as their ties with the productive system are likely to be quite different. Yet the two size distributions of family income may be quite similar with respect to income, recipient unit, and period of income cumulation as defined above. While reduction of transient income elements naturally reduces income mobility, the use of long-term income levels (even related to position in the life cycle of earnings) does not bar extensive and significant mobility due to long-term, "permanent," differences in the endowments of different families relative to secularly changing opportunities afforded by the productive system in the process of growth. Nor would such mobility be reduced to insignificance for clusters of family units related by ties of common interest: even for these there may be upward or downward mobility, not only in absolute long-term income but also in income relative to those of other family clusters in the country.

Since, as already indicated, we have no long-term income records for families, the extent of income mobility cannot be studied on a scale even remotely adequate for our purposes. Yet the point must be stressed because it directs our attention to the implications of some basic characteristics of economic growth for the interpretation of the conventional measures of the size distribution of income. Sustained and marked increases in per capita income are a constituent feature of economic growth. It follows that, barring factors to the contrary, the incomes of a much greater proportion of families will rise more in a country sustaining economic growth than in a stagnant or slowly growing country. Thus absolute upward income mobility, at least, is a direct function of economic growth. Furthermore, if such growth takes place under relatively free market conditions, the rise must affect the personal income of families—since the accompanying changes in industrial structure cannot be made without the inducement of higher incomes in those sectors of the economy that are the carriers of growth. Given more structural shifts accompanying vigorous economic growth, and hence significantly greater internal mobility, there is likely to be more income mobility—not only absolute, with a balance toward rises, but also relative; some groups, perhaps previously low on the scale, may be rising, and others, perhaps previously high on the scale, may be declining. One would tend to assume that internal income mobility is more limited in stagnant or slowly growing countries than in those showing rapid growth; and there are implications also for the trends in income mobility over the long time span of growth within a country.

The importance of this aspect of the income distribution can hardly be overemphasized. Indeed, extreme mobility would rob the size distribution of income of much of its present meaning. If the groups of family clusters originally in the upper brackets have moved, with the passage of a generation, to the bottom of the array and have been replaced by groups of clusters whose immediate forebears began at the bottom, and if the identity of the groups in the size distribution of income has changed markedly, the differences revealed by the latter have no cumulative impact; there is no persistent economic class consciousness; and there is little meaning to the question whether the poor are getting poorer and the rich richer. Of course, for purely technical analysis of the effect of economic growth on income size and change, and of effects of the latter on economic groups, it should still be of interest to distinguish high and low income groups, while separating within each those who are recent additions from above or below. But with complete mobility—a shift from top to bottom and from bottom to top within a generation or some such reasonably limited period—the impact of the size distribution of income and of the problems created by income differentials would be much reduced, if not completely canceled. Actually, mobility has not been so extreme; and wealth and poverty, or more precisely, high and low relative income positions have tended to be transmitted within one group to its descendants. Yet to the extent that modern economic growth has been accompanied by wider structural shifts and greater economic and income mobility than in the more slowly growing or stagnant societies, size distributions of current or even of secular long-term income levels have lost much of their meaning as pictures of the shares of relatively stable groups within the population.

### DISTRIBUTION OF INCOME BY SIZE: LONG-TERM TRENDS

The data demanded by the definitional problems above obviously are not available for long periods for any country; and if we are to observe trends in the size distribution of income, we must, while respecting the comments as cautionary, use the few crude series that do exist. We have figures for only a few developed countries; and they permit only some approximations to shares of ordinal groups in the distributions of tax units (usually families) or consuming units; no allowance can be made (except in rare cases) for the size of the family unit or any other variant suggested as relevant in the preceding discussion.

In view of the difficulties of properly measuring the size distribution of income, it is hardly surprising that many of the estimates used below are crude approximations. They are derived from comparisons of data reported on tax returns with total income received by households, and they are subject to all the possible errors inherent in the biases of the tax data and the difficulty of reducing them to units comparable with those in total population and income. However, the estimates used here do possess the great advantage of relating to shares in total population and income —they are not the widely used and rather misleading measures of the distribution of tax return groups with an unknown relation to the rest of a country's income-receiving population. The broad trends suggested by these data merit emphasis, particularly if they are observed for a number of countries.

Distribution of Product and Income

The original sources of the data in Table 4.5 provide information on the units for which the shares of ordinal groups are estimated. The table covers nine countries (counting Prussia, Saxony, and Germany–West Germany as three), and only the records for four reach back into the nineteenth century. Nevertheless, some trends are indicated.

First, for the period through the post-World War II years, there is a perceptible narrowing in inequality in the size distribution of income if judged by the declines in the shares of upper ordinal groups; less marked if judged by the rise in the shares of the lower ordinal groups. In most countries, the share of the top 5 per cent group in income before taxes was 20 per cent or less in the post-World War II years. In the 1920s or the 1930s the share of the top 5 per cent group in income before taxes was about 30 per cent. Likewise, the share of the top 20 per cent group in income before taxes in post-World War II years was between 40 and 45 per cent; whereas in the 1920s and the 1930s it was well above 50 per cent. The evidence on the share of the lowest 60 per cent group is much more scanty, but there is some indication that it was below 30 per cent in the 1920s and the 1930s and rose to well above 30 per cent in the post-World War II years. But according to the evidence, the rise in the share of the lower brackets was less conspicuous than the decline in the shares of the upper groups.

Second, for the three countries for which shares in income before and after taxes can be compared (the United Kingdom, Sweden, the United States), the decline in the shares of upper groups and the rise in the shares of the lower groups are somewhat greater for the shares in income after taxes. This finding is not surprising: given the generally growing impact of progressive taxes in most developed countries in recent years, the trends toward equality should be more conspicuous in the shares in income after taxes. Another point to be noted is that the measures in Table 4.5 do not reflect services in kind (education, health, etc.) provided directly by government to ultimate consumers. Their inclusion, with the primary contribution to the

## TABLE 4.5

Shares in National Income of Ordinal Groups, Tax Units or Consuming Units, Selected Countries, Long Periods

*Successive dates and entries*

**UNITED KINGDOM**

| | Bowley | | Clark | | Seers | Lydall | | |
|---|---|---|---|---|---|---|---|---|
| 1. Dates | 1880 | 1913 | 1929 | 1938 | 1947 | 1938 | 1949 | 1957 |
| *Income before tax* | | | | | | | | |
| 2. Top 5% | 48 | 43 | 33 | 31 | 24 | 29 | 23.5 | 18 |
| 3. Top 20% | 58 | 59 | 51 | 52 | 46 | 50 | 47.5 | 41.5 |
| *Income after tax* | | | | | | | | |
| 4. Top 5% | | | | 26 | 17 | 24 | 17 | 14 |
| 5. Top 20% | | | | 48 | 39 | 46 | 42 | 38 |

**PRUSSIA**

| | Procopovitch | | | | Reich Statistical Office | |
|---|---|---|---|---|---|---|
| 6. Dates | 1854 | 1875 | 1896 | 1913 | 1913 | 1928 |
| 7. Top 5% | 21 | 26 | 27 | 30 | 31 | 26 |
| 8. Top 20% | | 48 | 45 | 50 | 50 | 49 |
| 9. Lowest 60% | | 34 | | 33 | 32 | 31 |

**Mueller**

| 10. Dates | 1873–80 | 1881–90 | 1891–1900 | 1901–10 | 1911–13 |
|---|---|---|---|---|---|
| 11. Top 5% | 28 | 30 | 32 | 32 | 31 |

**SAXONY**

| | Procopovitch | | | Reich Statistical Office | |
|---|---|---|---|---|---|
| 12. Dates | *1880* | *1896* | *1912* | *1913* | *1928* |
| 13. Top 5% | 34 | 36 | 33 | 33 | 28 |
| 14. Top 20% | 56 | 57 | 55 | 54 | 50 |
| 15. Lowest 60% | 27 | 26.5 | 27 | 28 | 31 |

**GERMANY—WEST GERMANY**

| | Reich Statistical Office | | | Mueller | | United Nations | | Wochenbericht | |
|---|---|---|---|---|---|---|---|---|---|
| 16. Dates | *1913* | *1928* | *1928(adj.)* | *1928* | *1936* | *1936* | *1950* | *1955* | *1959* |
| 17. Top 5% | 31 | 27 | 21 | 20 | 23 | 28 | 24 | 18 | 18 |
| 18. Top 20% | 50 | 49 | 45 | | | 53 | 48 | 43 | 43 |
| 19. Lowest 60% | 32 | 31 | 34 | | | 26.5 | 29 | 34 | 34 |

**NETHERLANDS**

| | | | |
|---|---|---|---|
| 20. Dates | *1938* | *1949* | *1954* |
| 21. Top 5% | 19 | 17 | 13 |
| 22. Top 20% | 49 | 45.5 | 38.5 |
| 23. Lowest 60% | 31 | 34 | 40 |

**DENMARK**

| | Zeuthen I | | | Zeuthen II | | | Bjerke | |
|---|---|---|---|---|---|---|---|---|
| 24. Dates | *1870* | *1903* | *1925* | *1908* | *1925* | *1939* | *1949* | *1955* |
| 25. Top 5% | 36.5 | 28 | 26 | 30 | 26 | 24.5 | 19 | 17.5 |
| 26. Top 10% | 50 | 38 | 36 | 39 | 37 | 35 | 29.5 | 27.4 |
| 27. Top 20% | | | | 55 | 53 | 51 | 45 | 44 |
| 28. Lowest 60% | | | | 31 | 25 | 27 | 32 | 32 |

TABLE 4.5—*Continued*

*Successive dates and entries*

**NORWAY**

| | 1907 | 1938 | 1948 |
|---|---|---|---|
| 29. Dates | | | |
| 30. Top 5%, country districts | 27 | 20 | 14 |
| 31. Top 5%, cities | 28–32 | 22 | 19 |

**SWEDEN**

*Earned income before tax* — Bentzel

| | 1930 | 1935 | 1945 |
|---|---|---|---|
| 32. Dates | | | |
| 33. Top 5% | 30 | 28 | 24 |
| 34. Top 20% | 59 | 58 | 52 |
| 35. Lowest 60% | 19 | 19 | 23 |

*Total income before tax* — United Nations

| | 1935 | 1945 | 1948 | 1954 |
|---|---|---|---|---|
| 36. Dates | | | | |
| 37. Top 5% | 28 | 23.5 | 20 | 17 |
| 38. Top 20% | 56 | 51 | 45 | 43 |
| 39. Lowest 60% | 23 | 26 | 32 | 34 |

*Total income after tax*

| | 1935 | 1945 | 1948 |
|---|---|---|---|
| 40. Top 5% | 25.5 | 21 | 17 |
| 41. Top 20% | 54 | 48 | 43 |
| 42. Lowest 60% | 23 | 28 | 32 |

UNITED STATES

|  | Kuznets | | | | |
|---|---|---|---|---|---|
| 43. Dates | 1913–19 | 1919–28 | 1929–38 | 1939–43 | 1944–48 |
| *Income before tax* | | | | | |
| 44. Top 1% | 14 | 14 | 13 | 11 | 9 |
| 45. Top 5% | 24 (1917–19) | 25 | 25 | 21 | 17 |
| *Income after federal tax* | | | | | |
| 46. Top 1% | 13 | 13 | 12 | 9 | 6 |
| 47. Top 5% | 22 (1917–19) | 24 | 24 | 18 | 14 |

|  | Department of Commerce | | | | | |
|---|---|---|---|---|---|---|
| 48. Dates | 1929 | 1935–36 | 1941 | 1944–47 | 1950–54 | 1955–59 |
| *Income before tax* | | | | | | |
| 49. Top 5% | 30 | 26.5 | 24 | 21 | 21 | 20 |
| 50. Top 20% | 54 | 52 | 49 | 46 | 45 | 45 |
| 51. Lowest 60% | 26 | 27 | 29 | 32 | 33 | 32 |
| *Income after federal tax* | | | | | | |
| 52. Top 5% | 29.5 | | 21.5 | | 18 | 18 |
| 53. Top 20% | 54 | | 47 | | 43 | 44 |
| 54. Lowest 60% | 26.5 | | 30 | | 34 | 34 |

*Source:* Kuznets, "Quantitative Aspects: VIII," Table 16, pp. 60 ff.

211

lower income brackets and their increased weight in total income in recent years, would also accentuate the decline in the shares of upper income groups and the rise in the shares of the lower brackets.

Third, if we were to ask when this trend toward narrower inequality in the size distribution of income in the developed countries began, the evidence in Table 4.5 provides no clear answer. Even the few records that reach back before the 1920s show different patterns for different countries. In the United Kingdom, there is little decline in the shares of the upper brackets between 1880 and 1913; but by the 1920s the drop is significant compared with pre-World War I levels, and then the decline is resumed with World War II and subsequent years (lines 1–2). In Prussia the share of the top 5 per cent seems to rise from 1854 to 1875 to 1913, markedly according to Procopovitch (line 7), but less so from 1873–80 on, according to Mueller (line 11). In any case, the decline in the upper shares—after a long period of constancy or rise—comes only after World War I, as it does for Saxony and possibly Germany as a whole. In the United States, the shares of the top groups seem to be constant from the few years before World War I through the 1920s; and the decline begins in earnest only with World War II. Only in Denmark is there a clear reduction in inequality, shown by the shares of the top 5 and 10 per cent groups, from 1870 to the beginning of the present century; but we cannot say when this narrowing in inequality began (lines 25 and 26). In short, the narrowing of inequality in the size distribution of income in many developed countries may have started after World War I or with World War II; but the records are far too scanty for the earlier periods to make an empirical generalization feasible.

In considering the factors that may have affected the long-term trends in the size distribution of income in developed countries, we face a difficulty not uncommon in attempts to explain economic trends, particularly in distributive or allocational rather than aggregative aspects of the economy. A variety of factors can be discerned, some inducing movements in one direction, others pushing the process in the opposite direction. The resulting trends are a net balance of these conflicting effects of different factors and can properly be explained only if each factor is observed and its possibly changing effects gauged over the period covered by the long-term trends under investigation.

Thus, in the present connection, it is easy to recognize changes in the process of growth of developed economies that should reduce the inequality in the size distribution of income. One of these is the narrowing inequality in product per worker among major industry sectors.[27] If differentials between the A and the non-A sectors in product per worker loom large, we should expect the range of the resulting differentials to become narrower as the result and accompaniment of the mere decline in the share of the labor force in the A sector—the usual "industrialization" concomitant of modern economic growth. For if the share of the labor force in the A sector declines, and if the usually initially low ratio of product per worker in the A sector to that in the non-A sector does not drop further, intersectoral inequality must contract. Furthermore, in the process of growth, product per worker in the A sector usually rises relatively to product per worker in the non-A sector—if the initial ratio of the former to the latter is low.

The movements of the per worker product in the M and S sectors similarly tend to reduce income inequality. As shown in Kuznets, "Quantitative Aspects: II," the initially low ratio of product per worker in the M sector to that in the S sector tends to rise. And while in many countries the proportion of the labor force in the S sector tends to rise more than that in the M sector, any widening of inequality produced thereby is more than offset by the convergence in the per worker products of the two sectors.

Second, trends in the distribution of the labor force by status, discussed above, may also be viewed as reducing income inequality in the size distribution. The reduced proportion in the labor force of independent entrepreneurs

27. See Kuznets, "Quantitative Aspects: II," pp. 45–50.

means a reduction in the weight of a group whose income, even when adjusted for transient elements, shows wider inequality than that of employees—for the income inequality of entrepreneurs produced by differences in ability, in monopoly positions, or in accumulation of capital, tends to be much wider than that of employees, whose compensation is subject to narrower institutionally imposed limits. It may well be that a parallel trend toward a rise in the share of salaried workers among all employees has also contributed to the narrowing inequality in the total size distribution, since the decline in the share of wage earners means a reduction in weight of the low-income, unskilled labor components in the total; and the addition to the lower income clerical group is of less consequence, since this group, more than unskilled labor, tends to be recruited from the secondary labor supply, the auxiliary earners in any size distribution among families or consuming units.

Third, as indicated earlier in the chapter, the share of property income in total household income declined. Unlike the trends in intersectoral inequality in product per worker and in the status structure of the labor force, which emerged early in the process of modern industrialization, the decline in the share of property income is apparently a recent development that began in some European countries after World War I, and spread more generally among developed countries only between the pre- and post-World War II years. In view of the concentration of property income in the hands of upper ordinal groups, the decline in its share in the total income of households should have made for narrower inequality in the size distribution of income.

Finally, in addition to the statistical determinants, i.e. the quantified structural changes listed above, a variety of other factors, some measurable and others only describable, may have contributed to the narrowing inequality in the size distribution of income in the developed countries. For obvious reasons the distribution of income among various groups in society is a matter of perennial interest and passionate concern; and the egalitarian philosophy that accompanies modern economic growth exercises continuous pressure to limit income inequality as much as considerations of productivity and the resistance of tradition permit. It is scarcely an accident that legal equality, political equality, and finally economic equality were the successive goals of modern society. And, more specifically, the legislative decisions—with respect to education and health services, inheritance and income taxation, social security, full employment, and economic relief—can be viewed as manifestations of the general decision to minimize economic inequalities by equalizing as much as possible economic opportunities and compensating for failures that could be debited to defects in the economic and social structures, not to the voluntary action of individuals. In this connection, it is noteworthy that the trends toward income equality received a strong push during and immediately after the two world wars. For the wars destroyed some long-established positions that may have been sources of high income and demonstrated the capacity of governments to exercise greater control over economic life than had previously been practiced in the free, market-oriented economies. And the continuation of international tensions even after the armed conflicts were over made it difficult, if not impossible, for income inequalities to remain as wide as they had been. For the groups in the lower income brackets the earlier promise of possible gain in the long run was qualified too much by the danger that faced societies in that long run; and the conviction that such inequalities were necessitated—and justified—by long-term economic growth had lost much of its strength. Whatever the reasons for the low levels of unemployment and the rise in the ratio of unskilled to skilled labor wage rates in post-World War II years, the effects contributed to narrowing the inequality in the size distribution of income since the 1930s.

In short, we could easily list a number of factors that should have made for narrower inequality in the size distribution of income in developed countries—some inducing such a trend in the earlier phases of the modern growth process, others emerging only more recently. On the other hand, we could also list changes that should have made for *wider* inequality in the size distribution of income. The size distribution of income within the non-A sector was, in the earlier periods, much more unequal than that within the A sector—as the present patterns for underdeveloped (and many developed) countries suggest—and the very rise in the share of the non-A sector, other conditions remaining equal, should have widened total inequality in the size distribution of income.[28] Furthermore, within the A and non-A sectors separately, there may have been forces making for wider rather than narrower inequality in the distribution of income. The rise in productivity within the A sector, indispensable for modern economic growth, may have been associated with technological changes that raised the scale of production on farms and introduced a cleavage between the large commercial farms in the progressive part of agriculture and the small units lagging behind—which would make for wider inequality of income within the A sector, at least until the process of modernization had spread throughout the sector. Within the non-A sector the continuous migration to the cities, from the countryside or from abroad, may have added to the lower income brackets, and this, combined with the growth in relative importance of occupations with a long training period and wider inequality through the life cycle (such as the professions), may have contributed to widening the inequality—possibly within the M and the S sectors taken separately—and offsetting, or more than offsetting, the opposite effects of the convergence of the per worker products of the two sectors. Finally, the increasing separation of economically less productive family units, either too young or too old, may have contributed to wider inequality in many developed countries in recent years.

Thus, to repeat the comment made at the beginning of this discussion, the size distribution of income in the de-

28. See Kuznets, "Quantitative Aspects: VIII," pp. 45–52.

veloped countries is subject to a variety of factors, some making for narrower inequality, others for wider. The actual trends are a net balance of these forces, and to account for them one should be able to measure the changing effects of pushes upward and of pulls downward. This we cannot do without data that are not now available. It seems plausible to assume that in the process of growth, the earlier periods are characterized by a balance of counteracting forces that may have widened the inequality in the size distribution of total income for a while because of the rapid growth of the non-A sector and wider inequality within it. It is even more plausible to argue that the recent narrowing in income inequality observed in the developed countries was due to a combination of the narrowing intersectoral inequalities in product per worker, the decline in the share of property incomes in total incomes of households, and the institutional changes that reflect decisions concerning social security and full employment. But these are conjectures that, while consistent with the existing data, have so far only an imprecise empirical base.

### FOUR MAJOR TRENDS

Aware that we may be overstating the long-term movements in the distribution of income and limiting them to the free market economies, we summarize the discussion in terms of four major trends.

First, the proportion in gross national product of income distributed as factor shares to households, in direct return for the current participation of their labor or their capital in the process of production, has declined, probably from 85 to 90 per cent in the mid-nineteenth century to 75 per cent in recent years. There has been an increase in shares flowing directly to nonpersonal organizations, such as governments and public or private corporations, in the form of capital consumption charges, indirect taxes less subsidies, and corporate income before taxes and after payment of dividends. On the other hand, the incomes of households

217

have been bolstered by transfers, from government or from business, and by direct services of government, which may have risen from a few percentage points of gross national product in the mid-nineteenth century to between 10 and 15 per cent in recent years. This complex of trends reflects the changing organizational structure of developed economies, characterized by increasing participation by corporations and governments in economic activity.

Second, the proportion of property income in national income (excluding the equity of individual entrepreneurs), which ranged between 20 and 40 per cent in the mid-nineteenth century, has, after a long period of stability or slight rise, declined—in some countries beginning with the post-World War I period, in others beginning with World War II—and is now at or below 20 per cent. Even more clearly discernible is the decline in the share of income from capital, including that on equity of individual entrepreneurs, from almost a half to about 20 per cent—although the allocation of the income of entrepreneurs between service and property components has many elements of arbitrariness.

Third, the rise in the share of labor, the counterpart of the decline in the share of capital, can be explained in terms of the greater investment in the training and education of labor, the increased real cost of living not being properly reflected in national product in constant prices, and the allocation to labor of the gains attributable to residual efficiency—over and above the measurable input of resources, i.e. of capital and of labor, allowing for quality rise in the latter associated with greater education and skill.

Fourth, for the period of observation, the distribution of income by size among individuals and households, after showing stability or perhaps a slight widening in pre-World War I years, has shown a marked reduction in inequality. This reduction would have been more evident if full allowance could have been made for changes in the distribution due to increased direct taxes and to the increased contribution of transfers and of direct services of governments. Since per capita real income has increased at rates almost as high as per capita gross national product, the trend toward reduced income inequality meant that real income grew even more at the lower levels of the income distribution than at the upper levels.

One further qualification must be attached to the findings: the underlying records extend only to the later phases in the growth of the presently developed countries. The earlier periods are inadequately covered; and it is possible that these earlier periods were not characterized by the trends toward a reduction in the share of income from capital and toward narrower inequality in the size distribution of income. We can only speculate on the movement during these periods of the share of property income and the change in the inequality of the size distribution of income.

Many of the aspects of the rather complex changes in the organizational structure of economic units and of income distribution in the process of economic growth could be noted only briefly, and others were not mentioned. In the present discussion, emphasis was placed on the quantitatively measurable trends; and the findings and analysis were limited because the available data fail to cover some important structural divisions within the economy. In consequence, the account is incomplete, and in many ways it is only a bare beginning. Moreover, much of it is not directly relevant to the experience of authoritarian economies, in which the relations between the impersonal economic units, governments, and the living members of society are quite different from those of the free market economies. In Communist countries today income distributed to households constitutes a relatively low proportion of total gross national product; direct services of governments are a large share; income from assets is almost entirely in the hands of governments; and the size distribution of income cannot easily be discerned.

# 5 TRENDS IN THE PATTERNS OF PRODUCT USE

PATTERNS OF USE: SOME BROAD DISTINCTIONS

The countrywide product originates in the various sectors of the economy (discussed in Chapter 3), and the claims to it are distributed to various groups in the form of income and related shares (discussed in Chapter 4); it is then used—consumed, added to stocks of capital within the country, or added to economic claims against other countries. The accepted national accounts procedures distribute the countrywide product fully among these uses. But a number of conceptual problems arise in such an allocation; and before examining the long-term trends in this pattern of use that accompany economic growth, we must consider these problems explicitly.

Such consideration is facilitated by Table 5.1, which summarizes the average pattern of use for almost all the developed countries in the post-World War II years, excluding the U.S.S.R. The basic distinction is among three broad categories. The first, private consumption expenditures, covers purchases of all consumer goods, excluding land and dwellings, including receipt of income in kind, net gifts from abroad, and net of sales of such consumer goods—purchases and receipts by households and nonprofit institutions. The latter—trade unions, charitable bodies, certain sports associations, private research institutions, and some private schools and universities—are defined as units "which are not established primarily with the aim of earning a

220

## TABLE 5.1

Distribution of National Product by Final Use, Developed Countries, Post-World War II Years*

(percentages based on totals in current prices)

| Share in: | Private consumption expenditures (1) | Government consumption (2) | Gross domestic capital formation (3) |
|---|---|---|---|
| 1. Gross national product (15) | 63.6 (63.8) | 13.4 (14.1) | 22.7 (22.3) |
| 2. Total domestic uses (15) | 63.7 (63.7) | 13.5 (14.1) | 22.8 (22.2) |

*Structure of the three components above*

| (1a) | (1b) | (2a) | (2b) | (3a) | (3b) |
|---|---|---|---|---|---|
| 3. Food, beverages, tobacco (10) | 30.0; 5.3; 3.4 — 38.8 | Civil (10) | 64 | Fixed capital (14) | 92.1 |
| 4. Clothing (10) | 13.3 | Defense (10) | 36 | Net change in inventories (14) | 7.9 |
| 5. Rent, fuel and light, household operation (10) | 8.9; 3.9; 3.6 — 16.4 | Education and health (included in line 3) | 28 | Residential construction (9) | 20.2 |
| 6. Furniture and furnishings (10) | 7.0 | | | Other construction (9) | 30.0 |
| 7. Transport and communication (10) | 8.1 | | | Producers' equipment (9) | 43.3 |
| 8. Personal care and health, recreation, and amusement (9) | 4.9; 6.6 — 11.4 | | | Net change in inventories (9) | 6.5 |
| 9. Other services (10) | 5.6 | | | | |
| 10. Expenditures of residents abroad minus expenditures of foreigners in country (10) | 1.9; —1.3 — 0.6 | | | | |

* Figures in parentheses in stubs and cols. 1a, 2a, and 3a show the number of countries included in the averages. The entries are unweighted arithmetic means of shares for individual countries for eight or nine years (usually 1950–58). The entries above the line in col. 1b, lines 3, 5, 8, and 10 are the shares of the subgroups listed in col. 1a, in the order indicated; the entry below the line is the share for the group as a whole.

*Sources: Lines 1 and 2:* From Kuznets, "Quantitative Aspects: VII," App. Table 1, pp. 62–63 for countries in Group I, in Group II (except Venezuela), and Japan. The entries in parentheses are the average shares for the smaller number of countries for which the structure of private consumption, government consumption, and gross domestic capital formation is shown in lines 3–10.

*Lines 3–10, cols. 1a and 1b:* From ibid., App. Table 5, pp. 76–79 (Groups I and II).

*Lines 3 and 4, cols. 2a and 2b:* From ibid., App. Table 3, pp. 68–70 (Groups I and II).

*Line 5, col. 2b:* Based on ibid., Table 5, p. 11.

*Lines 3–4, cols. 3a and 3b:* From "Quantitative Aspects: V," App. Table 1, pp. 77–78 for Groups I and II (omitting Switzerland and Venezuela), and Japan.

*Lines 5–8, cols. 3a and 3b:* From ibid., App. Table 2, pp. 80–83 for Canada, Belgium, Sweden, the United Kingdom, the United States, Denmark, France, the Netherlands, and Norway.

profit and are not mainly rendering services to enterprises." [1] Private consumption expenditures, by far the largest of the three categories, accounted in recent years for almost two thirds of the GNP of the developed countries, and for about the same share of total domestic uses (TDU)—the sum of private consumption expenditures, government consumption, and gross domestic capital formation or alternatively, GNP minus the net balance of exports over imports and minus the net flow of factor payments abroad, the sum of the latter two being capital exports or imports.

The second broad category, government consumption, includes current expenditures on commodities and services (net of sales of such goods) by *general* government, excluding government enterprises and public corporations (which are included under "enterprises")—with the important proviso that "expenditures for defence purposes, excluding civilian defence, is treated as consumption expenditures" and is consequently excluded from capital formation.[2] This category accounted for almost a seventh of GNP or TDU.

Gross domestic capital formation, the third major use category, is the gross value of goods added to the capital stock within the country—excluding defense equipment but including residential construction. Gross of current consumption of fixed capital, this category accounted for between a fifth and a quarter of GNP or TDU. As will be shown below (Table 5.4), capital consumption charges in recent years were about four tenths of gross domestic capital formation. With an allowance for these charges, *net* domestic capital formation would account for about 15 per cent, private consumption expenditures for about 70 per cent, and government consumption for 14.7 per cent of net national product.

Finally, the balance of exports and of foreign factor payments—one use component of gross national product not

1. See U.N., *Studies in Methods, Series F, No. 2, Rev. 1* (New York, 1960), par. 85, p. 11. For detailed notes on the items included in the various components of national product see this source.

2. See ibid., par. 138, p. 26.

shown in Table 5.1—averaged about 0.2 per cent of GNP in recent years, although, as indicated below, it ranged from a much larger positive percentage (i.e. capital exports) in some developed countries to even larger negative percentages (i.e. capital imports) in others.

Lines 3–10 provide distributions of the three major use components of countrywide product by subcategories—the detail depending largely upon the available data. These more detailed distributions indicate the types of goods included, and they facilitate the discussion of some of the broader aspects of the allocation by use—to which we now turn.

First, allocation of the type summarized in Table 5.1 is the end product of numerous transactions, in the course of which the income and related shares received by various groups are combined with transfers, credits, claims, and counterclaims. Hence even for large groups, e.g. all households, there is no simple relation between what they *receive* in the process of the income distribution (discussed in the preceding chapter) and what they *use*. Some of the characteristic shifts were noted at the outset of Chapter 4, in the discussion of the taxes and transfers that modify the income claims as they flow out of the production process; others due to the channeling of gross and net savings will be touched upon below. But in fact the available data, except for a country or two (and even then only for a short period), do not cover fully the total flow of transactions that intervene between income distribution and income use; and we are therefore compelled to deal with the net unduplicated results of this whole process, without tracing the antecedent complex of transactions.

Second, and perhaps more important, the items included under the various uses of countrywide product show that the criteria employed in defining an economic final good (rather than an intermediate one) affect not only the magnitude of countrywide product but also the allocations, whether by industrial origin, type of income, or final use—a general point made in Chapter 1. Thus illegal activities (prostitution, drug peddling, etc.) are excluded by definition from output in countrywide product, from any industry sector distinguished, from income payments, and from consumption, private or government. Proceeds from legal but noneconomic activities, e.g. licensed gambling, are also omitted, on the reasonable view that gains by the successful gambler represent no real service to the persons who suffer the losses—unlike the fees received by a physician from his patients. Quantitatively more important, goods produced and used by enterprises—except capital goods with a fairly long life (which include *net* changes in stocks)—are excluded from the countrywide product total since the value of such intermediate goods enters the value of the final product, and thus their factor contributions are already accounted for.

Third, the line of distinction between consumption, i.e. the use of goods to satisfy the wants of ultimate consumers, and capital formation, i.e. addition to the stock of tools used to produce other goods, may be drawn differently within one and the same aggregate product. The differences reflect different possible interpretations of the use of a given good, whether to satisfy consumers' wants or to further production.

To illustrate these problems of distinction between final and intermediate products and between consumption and capital formation, we begin with the former. Turning first to government consumption, we find that this component is a hybrid with respect to "finality" of the products included. The educational, health, and recreational services rendered to households are in the nature of a final product —directly satisfying the needs of the human beings who comprise society. This part should be added to private consumption expenditures to form what might be called "total consumption." Services by government to the enterprise sector (e.g. marketing services to farmers or to nonagricultural business) are clearly an intermediate product and should be excluded. Services in the way of general administration, legislation, adjudication, and defense, which are needed to maintain the internal structure and external safety of the society, while subject to conflicting interpretation, can most reasonably be classified as general maintenance costs—neither consumption nor capital formation. The entries in lines 3–5, columns 2a and 2b of Table 5.1, suggest that the final product part of government consumption accounted in recent years for about three tenths of the total; and consequently some 9 per cent of GNP or 10 per cent of NNP is really intermediate and should be excluded.

When we come to consider private consumption expenditures or, still better, total consumption including the final product of government, similar questions emerge. Offhand, one would be inclined to treat all such consumption as final product, on the general premise that the uses of goods by households and nonprofit associations are final and not offsets to some cost of production. But can this premise be applied to the full range of uses included under private or total consumption expenditures? If a household is located in a big city and therefore makes larger consumption outlays than a rural household to satisfy the same needs (larger in terms of greater real inputs of resources) and does so only because the head of the household must live there in order to have a job, is the extra consumption real net product, or is it greater cost of production and consequently intermediate product? If a business executive joins a golf club and is an active member only because he is required to do so for reasons of public relations, is this consumption of final product or the use of an intermediate product, a cost of production?

These questions may overemphasize the motivational aspect of consumption expenditures, but they are relevant regardless of the possible satisfaction consumers derive from the expenditures in question. There is an objective connection between industrial and occupational changes in the process of economic growth and the pattern of life—urban, white-collar, or other—that is thus imposed upon large groups in the population as a condition of effective participation in the economy. Granted this close, and apparently indispensable, connection between basic aspects of the modern production system and some aspects of consumption, there is a question whether substantial parts of product now included under total consumption should not be classified as intermediate rather than final product, i.e. as extra costs of modern economic growth, and be excluded from both consumption and unduplicated product totals.

The components of consumption that can thus be viewed as intermediate product are far from negligible. For the United States in 1941 the difference between the country-side and the cities in prices for roughly identical goods was estimated to be somewhat more than 20 per cent:[3] and to this must be added outlays in the cities on commodities and services not needed in the countryside but desired in the cities to offset the peculiar problems of urban life (e.g. transportation, extra sanitation, and the like)—even if we set aside a specific standard of living often required by the occupational status of urban workers. With the proportion of nonfarm population in the United States in the 1950s about 90 per cent,[4] the adjustment for the rural–urban price differentials alone would mean extra costs equivalent to 18 per cent of total consumption; and this figure would be raised substantially by other allowances, which cannot be made without intensive analysis of consumption expenditures (excluding those considered capital investment) that would distinguish between outlays required by the conditions of gainful employment and those that represent free choices by individuals as ultimate consumers. If we allow a minimum of 20 per cent of total consumption for the extra costs involved, gross national product excluding government intermediate products will be reduced proportionately.

Furthermore, if consumption—government, private, or

3. See Nathan Koffsky, "Farm and Urban Purchasing Power," in National Bureau of Economic Research, *Studies in Income and Wealth*, Vol. 11 (New York, 1949), Table 8, p. 170. The figure was derived as a geometric mean of the differences based on farm and city expenditure weights.

4. See U.S., *Economic Report of the President, January 1963*, Table C-76, p. 260.

total—contains intermediate products that represent costs, it might be argued that the capital goods used to produce these elements of consumption should also be excluded—just as standard national accounting procedures exclude military capital, on the ground that it does not produce final goods. But the argument is not consistent with treatment of capital investment in general: such investment is included whether it is used to turn out final or intermediate products, for in either case it represents a facility that, given final output and existing technology, would have to be provided. So long as we include capital formation at all, which, in the *very* long run, does represent duplication with final consumption, all of it must be included—whether used for intermediate or final product.

Elimination of the intermediate products included in gross national product as defined in accepted national accounts procedures, reduces the total some 23 per cent; and a more detailed analysis of private and government consumption might well result in a larger reduction. The effect on the apportionment between total consumption and capital formation is naturally to raise the share of the latter, from slightly less than a quarter to three tenths.

We turn now to the distinction between consumption and capital formation. The first question that arises concerns inclusion of residential construction under capital formation, particularly of owner-occupied dwellings. The owner-resident is now treated as an "enterprise," managing his house and deriving business income from it in the form of net imputed rent. If owner-residents of dwellings are so treated, why not owners of other consumer durable goods, such as passenger cars, refrigerators, furniture, and even clothing? Indeed, one may push the analogy further and treat the purchases of all consumer goods by households as capital goods, in which case the final product is not the goods themselves but the services to be derived from them.

The analogy is not followed in the direction suggested presumably because it has little value as an operating hypothesis. There is no evidence that households calculate the service yields of the goods they purchase and distinguish between the purchase of goods and the purchase of services; it is impossible, therefore, to test the hypothesis in terms of the long-term behavior of households. The choice between purchasing the good and purchasing the services is, however, clear in the case of residential dwellings, where one can either buy or rent; and the magnitude of the expenditures on such goods forces their treatment as a major capital outlay. This treatment probably need not be extended to other consumer durable goods, since unit values are so much lower, and the distinction between the commodity and its services is difficult to draw.

However, other components now included under consumption could be viewed as capital investment, not because the expenditure is on durable goods with large unit value, but because the use of the good is closely related to the efficiency of the consumer as a producer. The main item in question is outlays on education (formal or on-the-job training) and there are some related outlays on health care and recreation.

These components are far from negligible. T. W. Schultz estimated that in the United States, in 1956, total outlay on formal education was $28.7 billion, of which, however, $12.4 billion was income foregone.[5] If we omit the latter, the residual $16.3 billion can be compared with a total gross material capital formation for that year of $79.5 billion (United Nations definition, see U.N., *Yearbook of National Accounts Statistics, 1962*). If direct costs of formal education alone are over 20 per cent of gross capital formation, outlays on education, health, and recreation, treatable as investment in man, may well be as high as four tenths of capital formation.[6] If so, the distribution of gross national

5. See T. W. Schultz, "Capital Formation by Education," *Journal of Political Economy, 68* (December 1960), Tables 5, 6, and 7, pp. 580 and 582.

6. In our discussion above we set the final product of government consumption, largely educational and health outlays, at 4.5 per cent of the conventional gross national product total, i.e. about 6 per cent of

product, net of intermediate products, would be not 70 per cent for consumption and 30 per cent for capital formation, but perhaps 58 per cent and 42 per cent, respectively.

Further adjustments in the magnitude of total product and in its allocation between consumption and capital formation will occur when we take account of costs of income foregone, and, more generally, of the uses of time not committed to gainful work (or so committed at lower-than-possible compensation for the sake of learning). Two approaches can be followed. First, we can merely add the cost of income foregone in formal education and in on-the-job training to both countrywide product and educational investment in man. In 1957, investment in formal education net of income foregone and investment in on-the-job training of males in the labor force, all of which is income foregone, were about the same, $18.2 and $18.6 billion, respectively.[7] Consequently, the total value of income foregone can be set at 1.67—(0.60 + 0.40) ÷ 0.60—times investment in formal education, net of income foregone; or, using 20 per cent of gross capital formation as indicated in note 5, about 10 per cent of the "pure" GNP total. If, then, we add 10 per cent to "pure" GNP and to the capital formation component, the distribution between total consumption and capital formation, put at 58 and 42 per cent respectively at the end of the preceding paragraph, now becomes 53 per cent for consumption and 47 per cent for capital formation.

---

the "pure" total (which is 23 per cent less). *Private* outlays in the United States in 1956 on health and education amounted to $14.0 and $2.8 billion, respectively, according to *U.S. Income and Output*, Table II-4, p. 150; or together to about 5 per cent of the pure GNP. Thus public and private expenditures on health and education alone account for 11 per cent of the pure GNP, compared with 30 per cent allocated to gross domestic capital formation.

7. See T. W. Schultz, "Reflections on Investment in Man," *Journal of Political Economy,* 70 (October 1962 Supplement), Table 1, p. 6. Using the Schultz estimates in "Capital Formation by Education," we set the proportion of income foregone to total outlays on formal education at 40 per cent; and by applying this proportion to the increment to educational capital in population obtained $18.2 billion for investment in education in 1957, net of income foregone.

The second approach requires the addition of the value of all time released by the reduction in working hours accompanying economic growth, and of the income foregone in on-the-job training, to countrywide product and to the relevant components. The full value of released time should be included because this released time is a major result of economic growth and because much of the allocation of consumption, and even the use of the time for further education, is not comprehensible unless some magnitude is assigned to the increased leisure. A rough calculation for the United States, which sets the value of an hour released from work at the average labor product per work hour in the economy, yields a magnitude for 1939–48 that is as much as 40 per cent of GNP.[8] If we assume the same proportional magnitude to "pure" GNP (i.e. excluding intermediate products in government and private consumption) and add 6 per cent for income foregone in on-the-job training, the revised countrywide product total becomes 146—of which consumption including leisure accounts for 58 points (as indicated above) plus 40 points for total leisure minus 4 points representing time spent and income foregone in formal education, or a total of 94 points; whereas capital formation, which amounted to 42 points, is augmented by the 10 points allowed for income foregone in formal education and on-the-job training—and the final allocation is 64 per cent for total consumption including leisure and 36 per cent for total capital formation including costs of income foregone.

The calculations are restated in the form of a summary table, retracing the steps in the preceding discussion (Table 5.2). Several observations can be made in concluding this exercise, which may seem at first to be a numbers game but in fact deals with some fundamental issues in the analysis and definition of an economy's product and its uses in the course of economic growth.

First, despite the crudity of the assumptions and of the re-

8. See Kuznets, "Long-Term Changes," in Kuznets, ed., *Income and Wealth, Series II,* Table 7, p. 65 and Table 1, p. 30.

## TABLE 5.2

Illustrative Calculation of Gross National Product and Its Use Structure, with Various Assumptions Concerning "Finality" and the Distinction between Consumption and Capital Formation*

| | Shares of use components (%) | | | |
| --- | --- | --- | --- | --- |
| | Private or total consumption (1) | Government consumption (2) | Gross capital formation (3) | GNP (4) |
| 1. National accounts definition (line 1, Table 5.1) | 63.5 | 13.5 | 23.0 | 100 |
| 2. Omitting intermediate products in government consumption (9%) and shifting balance to col. 1 | 68 | 0 | 23 | 91 |
| 3. Omitting intermediate products in total consumption (20% of line 2, col. 1) | 54 | 0 | 23 | 77 |
| 4. Line 3, GNP shifted to 100 | 70 | 0 | 30 | 100(77) |
| 5. Allowing for investment in man, excluding cost of income foregone (0.4 of line 4, col. 3) | 58 | 0 | 42 | 100(77) |
| 6. Adding income foregone in formal education and in on-the-job training (10% of total in line 5) | 58 | 0 | 52 | 110(85) |
| 7. Line 6, GNP shifted to 100 | 53 | 0 | 47 | 100(85) |
| 8. Adding to line 5 full value of leisure and of income foregone in on-the-job training | 98 | 0 | 48 | 146(112) |
| 9. Shifting part of leisure in line 8, col. 1 to col. 3 (income foregone in formal education) | 94 | 0 | 52 | 146(112) |
| 10. Line 9, GNP shifted to 100 | 64 | 0 | 36 | 100(112) |

* Entries in parentheses in col. 4 are percentages of the adjusted GNP total to the standard national accounting total in line 1.

sulting estimates, the main points in the analyis should be clear. Given the close association between the structural changes accompanying economic growth on the production side and the many components of consumption required (either as extra costs or as extra investment in human beings) to assure effective participation of people in the productive process, the presently accepted national accounting definitions of the net totals and the distinctions between consumption and capital formation leave much to be desired. The accepted definitions and distinctions are based upon the purpose for which a good is purchased and on the status of the purchaser as an "enterprise"—a unit bent largely on profit. If a good is *not* purchased for resale (with or without some transformation), it is defined as a "final" product, even if it is used by the purchaser (household or government) to cover costs connected with the operation of the economy, or as investment in education. If a good is purchased by an enterprise but has a long life and is not intended for *immediate* resale, then it is a final capital good. But the resale principle, while suitable for the analysis of short-term changes with particular emphasis on possible shortages or excesses of purchasing power, is hardly a useful criterion in the analysis of long-term trends and structural changes involved in economic growth. The connection between the use of a good and its effect on long-term trends in output and efficiency is poorly defined by resale; and in view of the importance of quality of human beings as a factor in economic growth, total consumption as now defined cannot be considered completely free of elements of investment in human beings, or of elements of additional costs imposed upon people by the changing conditions of participation in economic production.

Second, if investment in human beings and foregone income are recognized, the whole pattern of use of time—in addition to the use of goods—must be considered. For, after all, time at the disposal of human beings is a basic and limited resource. It must therefore be explicitly understood that the release of more time from engagement in direct production of commodities and services is an important aspect of economic growth, an important part of its total product; and regardless of the difficulties involved, it must be given an explicit weight. Consequently, we cannot limit measurement to what has actually been produced but must attempt to estimate what might have been produced if the drain upon a basic limited resource had remained unchanged.

Third, to return to the problems of distinction and estimation, calculations like those summarized in Table 5.2 are obviously crude guesses, whose primary value lies largely in indicating minimal orders of magnitude. More useful measures would require an intensive analysis of consumption, capital formation, and time use by the human beings who comprise the economic society. In the process, such difficult problems as distinguishing between education as investment and education as consumption, or between consumption demanded by a job and consumption to satisfy personal needs, would have to be faced and satisfactory operating and empirically testable answers sought for. Furthermore, the definition and valuation of time released from direct engagement in producing commodities and services would have to be sharpened and tested.

The attempt to distinguish clearly between intermediate and final products by criteria other than those of the market requires a scale of human wants independent of the requirements for and influence of engagement in the changing structure of economic production. The formulation of an acceptable scale, one testable by objective means, may not be within reach; and the criteria actually used may consequently reflect too strongly an analyst's predilections and views, a danger that perhaps has not been avoided in the discussion here. Furthermore, if the use of consumption goods seems to be closely related to man's productive efficiency, there may be grounds for extending investment in man beyond such items as education and health care to include consumption outlays on other goods. If extra food, special clothing, or particular housing increases a consumer's efficiency, should it not also be considered investment in man? In that case much of consumption, net of intermediate products and over and above the minimum needed for holding body and soul together, would be classified as investment in man. This possibility, which would have a marked effect on the distribution of final product between consumption and capital formation, need not be ruled out.

At any rate, little work has been done along such lines, and the results accumulated are too few to provide a basis for summary discussion of the type to which the present monograph is devoted. We shall, therefore, no longer pursue such analysis in dealing with long-term trends in the use pattern of income. The very line of distinction between economic and noneconomic is bound to become blurred, unless the criteria used in following up these problems can be given greater support than is feasible at present. The arguments so far developed will be used, however, to qualify the conclusions suggested by the available but not fully revealing and relevant measures; and some illustrative figures for one or two countries, when available, will be presented.

### TRENDS IN BROAD PATTERN OF USE

In trying to discern the trends in the structure of gross national product that accompanied economic growth, we have sufficiently long records for ten developed countries and a much shorter series for the U.S.S.R. (Table 5.3). The estimates generally correspond to standard national accounting procedures, although, as usual, they are less reliable for the earlier periods.

The post-World War II decade was characterized, in the free developed countries, by a rather distinctive structure in which the shares of government consumption and of gross capital formation, domestic or national, were markedly higher than the pre-World War II levels, and those of private consumption expenditures correspondingly lower. Whether this structure represents a lasting shift to new secular levels, or reflects large transient elements of recovery from the war or of passing Cold War pressures, is a question that could perhaps be answered by detailed analysis not feasible here; even with such analysis a firm answer might not be possible. At any rate, in presenting the long-term trends it may be safer to assign a somewhat lesser weight to the post-World War II decade than that suggested by the actual magnitudes.

Even with due regard for these complexities, the long-term changes in the shares of the three major use components in gross countrywide product still stand out quite clearly. First, the share of government consumption rises—from 3.5 to 5 per cent of gross product in the mid-nineteenth century in the free market economies to an average of about 14 per cent in recent years. The sharp rise in many countries after World War II is due clearly to a marked increase in defense expenditures. But even if we limit the record to the period before the post-World War II years, the share of government consumption in gross product rose in all countries, as much as 8 or 9 percentage points if we include defense outlays and perhaps 4 to 5 percentage points for the share of civilian outlays alone.

In discussing the share of gross capital formation, we must distinguish between national capital formation (column 5), which represents the country's savings, and domestic capital formation (column 3), which represents additions to capital stock within the country, whether financed by the country's savings or by foreign funds. In most countries the gross national capital formation proportion, i.e. the share of gross savings, rose in the long run—even if we discount the high share in the post-World War II decade. From less than 10 per cent for some countries in the earliest periods the share rose to between 12 and 20 per cent even before World War II.

But there are some significant deviations from a generally upward trend in the share of gross savings—a trend that we would expect with a general rise in product per capita.

TABLE 5.3

Distribution of Gross National Product by Final Use, Selected Countries, Long Periods
(based on totals in current prices)

Share in GNP (%)

| | Private consumption (1) | Government consumption (2) | Gross domestic capital formation (3) | Capital exports or imports (−) (4) | Gross national capital formation (5) |
|---|---|---|---|---|---|
| *United Kingdom* | | | | | |
| 1. 1860–79 | 82.7 | 4.8 | 9.4 | 3.1 | 12.5 |
| 2. 1880–99 | 81.9 | 5.8 | 8.4 | 3.9 | 12.3 |
| 3. 1900–14 | 78.6 | 7.4 | 8.7 | 5.3 | 14.0 |
| 4. 1921–29 | 82.0 | 8.9 | 6.8 | 2.3 | 9.1 |
| 5. 1950–58 | 66.9 | 16.9 (9.4) | 15.5 | 0.7 | 16.2 |
| *Germany* (boundaries of the period) | | | | | |
| 6. 1851–70 | 81.6 | 4.0 | 13.7 | 0.7 | 14.4 |
| 7. 1871–90 | 73.1 | 5.9 | 18.9 | 2.1 | 21.0 |
| 8. 1891–1913 | 68.7 | 7.1 | 23.0 | 1.1 | 24.1 |
| 9. 1928 | 76.1 | 7.2 | 18.2 | −1.5 | 16.7 |
| 10. 1950–59 | 58.7 | 14.4 | 23.7 | 3.1 | 26.8 |
| *Italy* | | | | | |
| 11. 1861–80 | 87.3 | 4.2 | 10.0 | −1.5 | 8.5 |
| 12. 1881–1900 | 84.4 | 4.8 | 10.8 | 0 | 10.8 |
| 13. 1901–10 | 78.4 | 4.2 | 15.9 | 1.4 | 17.3 |
| 14. 1921–30 | 78.5 | 5.6 | 18.1 | −2.2 | 15.9 |
| 15. 1950–59 | 68.2 | 12.0 | 20.8 | −1.0 | 19.8 |

236

| | | | | | |
|---|---|---|---|---|---|
| *Denmark* | | | | | |
| 16. 1870–89 | 92.0 | | 9.8 | −1.8 | 8.0 |
| 17. 1890–1909 | 88.8 | | 13.5 | −2.3 | 11.2 |
| 18. 1921–30 | 87.8 | | 11.9 | 0.3 | 12.2 |
| 19. 1950–59 | 68.6 | 12.5 (9.6) | 18.9 | 0 | 18.9 |
| *Norway* | | | | | |
| 20. 1865–74 | 83.8 | 3.8 | 11.3 | 1.2 | 12.5 |
| 21. 1875–94 | 84.7 | 4.8 | 11.9 | −1.4 | 10.5 |
| 22. 1895–1914 | 83.6 | 6.6 | 14.7 | −4.9 | 9.8 |
| 23. 1915–24 | 78.1 | 8.5 | 18.9 | −5.5 | 13.4 |
| 24. 1925–34 | 77.5 | 8.7 | 14.4 | −0.6 | 13.8 |
| 25. 1950–59 | 60.0 | 12.5 (8.9) | 29.9 | −2.4 | 27.5 |
| *Sweden* | | | | | |
| 26. 1861–80 | 85.3 | 4.4 | 10.8 | −0.5 | 10.3 |
| 27. 1881–1900 | 85.0 | 5.4 | 11.2 | −1.6 | 9.6 |
| 28. 1901–20 | 81.6 | 5.8 | 13.1 | −0.5 | 12.6 |
| 29. 1921–40 | 75.0 | 8.6 | 15.8 | 0.6 | 16.4 |
| 30. 1941–59 | 64.8 | 14.3 | 21.0 | −0.1 | 20.9 |
| 31. 1950–59 | 61.9 | 16.8 (11.9) | 21.2 | 0.2 | 21.4 |
| *United States* (official concept) | | | | | |
| 32. 1869–88 | 76.7 | 3.6 | 20.6 | −0.9 | 19.7 |
| 33. 1889–1908 | 73.6 | 4.4 | 21.4 | 0.5 | 21.9 |
| 34. 1909–28 | 74.7 | 4.9 | 18.4 | 2.0 | 20.4 |
| 35. 1929–38 | 77.9 | 9.4 | 12.3 | 0.4 | 12.7 |
| 36. 1946–55 | 66.4 | 15.4 | 17.3 | 0.9 | 18.2 |
| 37. 1950–59 | 63.7 | 17.9 (7.5) | 17.9 | 0.5 | 18.4 |

TABLE 5.3—Continued

Share in GNP (%)

| | Private consumption (1) | Government consumption (2) | Gross domestic capital formation (3) | Capital exports or imports (−) (4) | Gross national capital formation (5) |
|---|---|---|---|---|---|
| *Canada* | | | | | |
| 38. 1870 and 1890 | 86.5 | 5.6 | 15.2 | −7.3 | 7.9 |
| 39. 1890, 1900, 1910 | 82.1 | 7.4 | 18.5 | −8.0 | 10.5 |
| 40. 1920, 1929 | 71.5 | 10.5 | 22.9 | −5.0 | 17.9 |
| 41. 1926–30 | 73.0 | 7.5 | 21.5 | −2.0 | 19.5 |
| 42. 1950–59 | 63.5 | 14.1 (7.9) | 25.0 | −2.6 | 22.4 |
| *Australia* | | | | | |
| 43. 1861–80 | 88.8 | | 16.1 | −4.9 | 11.2 |
| 44. 1881–1900 | 90.0 | | 17.1 | −7.1 | 10.0 |
| 45. 1900/01–1919/20 | 87.1 | | 14.7 | −1.8 | 12.9 |
| 46. 1919/20–1938/39 | 84.7 | | 17.4 | −2.1 | 15.3 |
| 47. 1950/51–1959/60 | 63.9 | 9.9 (6.5) | 28.6 | −2.4 | 26.2 |
| *Japan* | | | | | |
| 48. 1887–1906 | 92.0 | | 10.1 | −2.1 | 8.0 |
| 49. 1907–26 | 86.5 | | 14.1 | −0.6 | 13.5 |
| 50. 1927–36 | 84.7 | | 15.9 | −0.6 | 15.3 |
| 51. 1950–59 | 59.5 | 10.3 | 29.4 | 0.8 | 30.2 |

U.S.S.R.

| | | | |
|---|---|---|---|
| 52. 1928 | 84.1 (4.6) | 3.4 | 12.5 |
| 53. 1937 | 63.0 (10.5) | 11.1 | 25.9 |
| 54. 1950 | 55.9 (10.2) | 17.2 | 26.9 |
| 55. 1955 | 56.7 (8.7) | 15.2 | 28.1 |
| 56. 1960 | 47.1 | 20.3 (10.1) | 32.6 |

*Sources: Lines 1–31, 35–51:* From Kuznets, "Quantitative Aspects: VII," App. Table 4, pp. 72–75. Figures in parentheses in col. 2 are for civilian consumption and are from ibid., App. Table 3, pp. 68–71.

*Lines 32–34:* Share of government consumption extrapolated to 1909–28 from line 35 by share of government in gross national product, derived from U.S. Department of Commerce, *U.S. Income and Output,* Table I-12, pp. 134–35 and Table I-16, pp. 138–39; and to 1869–88 by the share of government in national income or aggregate payments, given in Kuznets, "Long-Term Changes," Table 14, p. 89.

*Lines 52–55:* Estimates based on 1937 ruble factor costs, given in "Quantitative Aspects: VII," Table 8, p. 17. Figures in parentheses in col. 1 are for communal services, included in figures without parentheses.

*Line 56:* From Stanley Cohn, "The Gross National Product in the Soviet Union: Comparative Growth Rates," in *Dimensions of Soviet Economic Power,* Joint Economic Committee Hearings, December 10–11, 1962 (Washington, 1962), Part II, Table 1, p. 72.

239

In the United Kingdom and the United States the share has not risen since the mid-nineteenth century; and while we would have found such a rise if we extended our records further back—in the United Kingdom back to the late eighteenth century, in the United States back to the 1840s[9] —it is noteworthy that in these two countries and for a period of almost a century, the gross savings proportion failed to rise, although product per capita was growing at a significant rate. In other countries, the expected rise in the gross savings proportion was delayed: in Norway and Sweden there is no clear evidence of a rise until about World War I, and in Australia not until 1900; yet the four or five decades covered by the records before these dates were marked by substantial rises in real product per capita.

The share of capital export or import relative to gross national or gross domestic capital formation was important only in the one large creditor country, the United Kingdom, and in small borrower countries, particularly Canada and Australia, which in their early colonial decades were favored recipients of capital funds from their metropolitan country (but see also Norway for 1895–1924). Hence, the shift from the national capital formation, or gross savings, rate to the domestic capital proportion yields trends not much different from those already observed. The share of gross domestic capital formation in GNP rose in most countries, again with the significant exception of the United Kingdom and United States for the periods covered. Again the rise in the domestic capital formation proportion was delayed in some countries, beginning only after a fairly long period of substantial growth: in Italy after 1900; in Norway after 1894; in Sweden after 1900. And for most countries the upward movement was less marked in the gross domestic capital formation proportion than in the national capital formation share since most countries were capital borrowers in the early decades of their growth, tending to reduce their

9. See Kuznets, "Quantitative Aspects: VI," Table UK-1, p. 58 and Table US-3, p. 94.

dependence on foreign financing or ceasing to rely on it as they grew.

With the share of government consumption rising and that of gross national capital formation constant or rising, the movement in the share of private consumption expenditures in GNP was necessarily downward. From over 80 per cent in the early decades, the share declined to about 60 per cent in the post-World War II decade; and even if we discount for the unusual characteristics of the latter period, the share of private consumption expenditures as measured in standard national accounting declined at least about a fifth. This, of course, means that the rate of growth of total household consumption was significantly lower than the rate of growth of total national product.

The estimates for the U.S.S.R. are interesting in that they reproduce, in compressed form, the trends in the structure of national product in the free market countries: the decline in the share of household consumption and the rise in the shares of government consumption and gross capital formation. All these shifts, larger absolutely than those for other countries, have been achieved in the U.S.S.R. in a period only a third as long.

How would the trends in the use structure of country-wide product observed for the free developed countries in Table 5.3 be affected if allowances were made for the extra costs and different distinctions between consumption and capital formation discussed in the preceding section? While no firm answer can be given, it will be helpful at least to speculate, using some data available for the United States to illustrate.

The proportion of intermediate product represented by defense and general government administration must have increased over time—although not markedly if we exclude defense. Likewise, with increasing urbanization and rising consumption requirements of the job in the course of economic growth the proportion of intermediate products to private consumption should also have risen. Thus, if the recent differential in prices of final goods to farmers and nonfarmers, 20 per cent, is assumed to be applicable in 1870, and population on farms declined from 55.7 per cent of total population in 1870 to 8.7 per cent in 1960, the extra costs included in private consumption were at least 9 per cent in the earlier year and about 18 per cent in the later year.[10] If in recent years an allowance of almost one fourth of conventional GNP should be made for intermediate products, an allowance of about a tenth in the 1870s seems reasonable; and the growth of conventional GNP was about two tenths greater than that of the pure total, adjusted to exclude intermediate products.[11] Such an adjustment would have little effect on the distribution between consumption and capital formation.

On the other hand, the growth of conventional GNP should be adjusted upward for the value of the time released from gainful work by the marked reduction in working hours. According to Kuznets, "Long-term Changes," for the 1870s the value of time released from work in the United States can be put roughly at about 10 per cent of conventional GNP, compared with about 40 per cent in the 1940s, and perhaps a higher proportion in the 1950s. This allowance, in and of itself, would have permitted a greater volume of investment in education, if only in the form of income foregone; and Professor Schultz's estimates of the total cost of formal education (no estimates are available for in-

10. The proportion of farm population in 1960 is from U.S., *Economic Report of the President, January 1963*, Table C-76, p. 260. The proportion in 1870 was derived by extrapolating the 1920 proportion to 1910 by the proportion of farm to nonfarm households, and to 1870 by dividing total rural population between nonfarm and farm on the assumption that the proportion of the nonfarm population in 1870 was 25 per cent, compared with 40 per cent for 1910 and 63 per cent for 1950. The data on farm and nonfarm households, total rural population, and nonfarm and farm population are from *Historical Statistics of the United States,* Series A 242–A 244, p. 15, and A 36–A 38, p. 9.

11. According to Kuznets, *Capital in the American Economy,* Table R-26, pp. 563–64, conventional GNP increased from $9.1 billion in 1871 to $186.5 billion in 1953, or 19.5 times. Pure GNP would therefore have increased from $(0.9 \times 9.1)$ to $(0.75 \times 186.5)$, or 16.1 times.

vestment in on-the-job training for early years) suggest a rise in the ratio to gross capital formation (conventional definition) from about 9 per cent in 1900 to over 38 per cent in the 1950s. At the same time, the proportion of income foregone in total costs of education also rises from 26 per cent in 1900 to over 43 per cent in 1956.[12]

The general impression then is that while the allowance for intermediate products would reduce the rate of growth of GNP, perhaps as much as a fifth, and would leave the distribution between consumption and capital formation unchanged, the allowance for increased leisure would more than offset this downward adjustment and would tend to reduce the decline in the share of consumption, even with an allowance for increased investment in education—since only a limited fraction of the increased uncommitted time would appear under costs of income foregone in the total cost of education. But the measures of the effects of these adjustments that we can now make are far too crude to warrant presentation here.

### FINANCING AND STRUCTURE OF CAPITAL FORMATION

In considering capital formation as the embodiment of savings, we turn first to the structure of financing in a recent post-World War II period (Table 5.4). Since replacement of capital often involves a marked rise in productive capacity, gross capital formation is probably more directly relevant than net to economic growth. We therefore concentrate our attention on gross rather than net savings flows.

Of gross national savings, which in all developed countries almost equaled gross domestic capital formation (see line 1), the public sector, including public corporations, accounted for about a fifth (see lines 6 and 9). The remainder was accounted for by private corporations and households, the latter including nonprofit associations and all individual

12. For the costs of education see Schultz, "Capital Formation." For the conventional estimates of gross capital formation in 1900 see Kuznets, *Capital in the American Economy*, Table R-29, pp. 572–74.

TABLE 5.4

Structure of Gross Domestic Capital Formation Financing,
Developed Countries, 1956–60
(based on totals in current prices)

| | Inclusive sample | | Omitting exceptional cases | |
|---|---|---|---|---|
| | Number of countries (1) | Average (2) | Number of countries (3) | Average (4) |
| 1. Ratio, gross national savings to GDCF (%) | 14 | 99.4 | 11 | 101.9 |
| 2. Ratio, capital consumption to GDCF (%) | 13 | 39.8 | 10 | 41.5 |
| 3. Ratio, net national savings to NDCF (%) | 13 | 99.4 | 10 | 104.1 |
| *Share of public sector (%)* | | | | |
| *Including public corporations* | | | | |
| 4. In capital consumption | 7 | 16.1 | 6 | 12.2 |
| 5. In net national savings | 7 | 24.7 | 6 | 28.5 |
| 6. In gross national savings | 7 | 22.2 | 6 | 22.6 |
| *Excluding public corporations* | | | | |
| 7. In capital consumption | 8 | 7.1 | 7 | 5.3 |
| 8. In net national savings | 8 | 25.7 | 7 | 27.9 |
| 9. In gross national savings | 8 | 18.5 | 7 | 19.0 |
| *Share in net national savings (%)* | | | | |
| 10. Private corporations | 7 | 29.2 | 6 | 23.2 |
| 11. Households | 7 | 46.0 | 6 | 48.3 |
| 12. Households (more inclusive sample) | 10 | 52.4 | 8 | 48.8 |

*Sources:* Underlying data are from U.N., *Yearbook of National Account Statistics, 1962.* Entries are unweighted arithmetic means of shares derived for each country from cumulative totals for 1956–60.

*Lines 1–3:* Cols. 1 and 2 cover the United Kingdom, France, Germany, Italy, Denmark, Norway, Sweden (line 1 only), Belgium, the Netherlands, the United States, Canada, Australia, New Zealand, and Japan; cols. 3 and 4 exclude Canada, Australia, and New Zealand.

*Lines 4–6:* Cols. 1 and 2 cover the United Kingdom, the Netherlands, the United States, Canada, Australia, New Zealand, and Japan; cols. 3 and 4 exclude the United Kingdom.

*Lines 7–9:* Cols. 1 and 2 cover the United Kingdom, France, Germany, Italy, Belgium, Denmark, Norway, and the Netherlands; cols. 3 and 4 exclude the United Kingdom.

*Lines 10 and 11:* Cols. 1 and 2 cover the United Kingdom, the Netherlands, the United States, Canada, Australia, New Zealand, and Japan; cols. 3 and 4 exclude the United Kingdom.

*Line 12:* Cols. 1 and 2 cover the countries listed for lines 10 and 11, cols. 1 and 2, and Belgium, France, and Germany; cols. 3 and 4 exclude the United Kingdom (very low) and Belgium (very high).

proprietors of unincorporated enterprises. We have no breakdown of the *gross* savings of the private sector between private corporations and households. But according to Table 5.4, capital consumption charges assignable to the private sector constitute 36.4 per cent of gross domestic capital formation—line 2, column 4 × (1 − line 4, column 4)—or 35.7 per cent of gross national savings; and private corporations, which dominate mining, manufacturing, and transport and public utilities (and are quite prominent in construction, trade, and finance) must account in developed countries for at least half of this total. Using this latter proportion, we can calculate the share of private corporations in gross national savings to be about 31.6 per cent, and that of households about 46.5 per cent (which together with some 22 per cent for the public sector equal 100). The apportionment of net national savings, given in Table 5.4, column 4, is not too different: 28.5 per cent for the public sector, about 23 per cent for private corporations, and 48.5 per cent for households.

The one finding that deserves emphasis is that households, even including individual proprietors, contribute only about a half of either gross or net savings. Thus, in terms of sheer weight, the savings propensity of the public sector and the private corporate sector combined is at least as important as that of households and individual entrepreneurs. Furthermore, since households and individuals have demonstrated a growing tendency to channel their savings into capital formation indirectly through financial intermediaries (banks, insurance companies, pension funds, etc.), leaving to these agencies the choice of investment opportunities to be financed, one may conclude that the role of households in financing capital formation and influencing choices within it is far less dominant than is generally assumed.[13]

13. In the United States, the proportion of net domestic capital formation financed directly by individuals, excluding flow through financial intermediaries, declined from 0.4 in 1900–19 to 0.2 in 1945–55 (see Kuznets, "Quantitative Aspects: VI," App. Table US-9, p. 101).

Could the structure of financing in the recent period, as revealed in Table 5.4, be the end result of long-term rises in the shares of the public and private corporate sectors and declines in the share of the household sector? If so, a few decades back the share of households in gross and net savings might have been much larger than half. Several trends accompanying economic growth might have contributed to such a decline in the share of households. First, the relative rise of the government sector should have meant an increasing share in capital consumption charges; and, in times free from wars and other events that magnify current expenditures, it should also have meant an increasing share of net savings flowing from government enterprises and public corporations, or from the excess of current revenues over current expenditures (the latter including transfers). Second, the share of private corporations in total output must have increased—partly because of the more rapid rise of industrial divisions with large-scale and necessarily corporate units and partly because of the spread of the corporate form of organization to other branches of the economy (e.g. construction, trade, and finance). The increase in the share of private corporations in output should have been accompanied by an increase in their shares in capital, capital consumption, and net savings. Third, the proportion of capital consumption charges to gross savings or to gross domestic capital formation may have risen—partly because the proportion of fixed depreciable to total capital may have risen, partly because within fixed capital the average useful life has declined with the relative rise of the shorter-lived equipment compared with the longer-lived construction (both of these trends suggested by Table 5.6, below). Furthermore, the average useful life of fixed capital may have declined, also because of the increased pace of technological progress and hence of obsolescence and of increased shifts in location and tastes, and partly because in some countries the rate of growth of gross domestic capital formation may have declined (which would make for a rising share of capital consumption in current capital formation). If the proportion of capital consumption to gross savings did rise, the relatively low share of households in capital consumption charges should have made for a decline in their share in *gross* (but not net) savings.

Unfortunately, we have no data at hand to substantiate these suggested trends, or to indicate the actual shares of households, private corporations, and the public sector in gross and net savings over the past decades. Table 5.5 provides some estimates of the share of capital consumption charges in gross national savings; and here the findings are rather mixed. In the United Kingdom and the United States the share of capital consumption in gross savings rose markedly, despite the reduction effected by the unusually large current capital formation in the 1950s. In the other countries, no clear trend in the share of capital consumption in gross saving is apparent, except that in Japan there is some evidence of a decline. On the other hand, the rises in the proportions of the government and of private corporations are trends that are sufficiently established to support the assumption that the share of households in gross and net savings must have declined from the mid-nineteenth century.[14]

Table 5.5 suggests another interesting finding, that relating to the trend in the share of net national savings (column 6). In connection with Table 5.3 we observed that the *gross* savings proportion rose in most countries except the United Kingdom and the United States, even if we discount the high shares in the post-World War II decade; but that in some countries these increases began only after several decades of fairly vigorous growth and rising per capita income.

14. According to R. W. Goldsmith's estimates of *net* savings (excluding consumer durable goods) in the United States, the share of personal savings (identical with that of households) declined from 70 per cent in 1897–1914 to 64 per cent in 1920–29, that of private corporations dropped from 23 to 21 per cent, and that of government rose from 7 to 15 per cent (see *Historical Statistics of the United States,* Series F 304–F 315, p. 155). Estimates for later years are affected too much by the depression and war to be useful.

## TABLE 5.5

### Financing Ratios, Selected Countries, Long Periods

| | % of GDCF | | | Net national savings as % of NDCF (4) | NDCF as % of NDP or NNP (5) | Net national savings as % of NDP or NNP (6) |
|---|---|---|---|---|---|---|
| | Gross national savings (1) | Capital consumption (2) | Net national savings (1–2) (3) | | | |
| *United Kingdom* | | | | | | |
| 1. 1860–79 | 133.0 | 20.0 | 113.0 | 141.2 | 7.7 | 10.9 |
| 2. 1880–99 | 146.4 | 21.6 | 124.8 | 159.2 | 6.9 | 11.0 |
| 3. 1900–14 | 160.9 | 19.7 | 141.2 | 175.8 | 7.5 | 13.2 |
| 4. 1921–29 | 133.8 | 55.5 | 78.3 | 176.0 | 3.3 | 5.8 |
| 5. 1950–58 | 104.5 | 53.0 | 51.5 | 109.6 | 7.9 | 8.7 |
| *Italy* | | | | | | |
| 6. 1861–80 | 85.0 | 55.2 | 29.8 | 66.5 | 4.6 | 3.1 |
| 7. 1881–1900 | 100.0 | 56.9 | 43.1 | 100.0 | 5.0 | 5.0 |
| 8. 1901–10 | 108.8 | 44.2 | 64.6 | 115.8 | 9.9 | 11.5 |
| 9. 1921–30 | 87.8 | 49.0 | 38.8 | 76.1 | 10.3 | 7.8 |
| 10. 1950–59 | 95.2 | 42.4 | 52.8 | 91.7 | 13.3 | 12.2 |
| *Denmark* | | | | | | |
| 11. 1870–89 | 81.6 | 51.2 | 30.4 | 62.3 | 5.1 | 3.2 |
| 12. 1890–1909 | 83.0 | 39.5 | 43.5 | 71.9 | 8.6 | 6.2 |
| 13. 1921–30 | 102.5 | 48.1 | 54.4 | 104.8 | 6.5 | 6.8 |
| 14. 1950–59 | 100.0 | 34.5 | 65.5 | 100.0 | 12.9 | 12.9 |

| | | | | | | |
|---|---|---|---|---|---|---|
| *Norway* | | | | | | |
| 15. 1865–74 | 110.6 | 41.9 | 68.7 | 118.2 | 6.8 | 8.0 |
| 16. 1875–94 | 88.2 | 44.6 | 43.6 | 78.7 | 7.0 | 5.5 |
| 17. 1895–1914 | 66.7 | 38.6 | 28.1 | 45.8 | 9.4 | 4.3 |
| 18. 1915–24 | 70.9 | 39.0 | 31.9 | 52.3 | 12.4 | 6.5 |
| 19. 1925–34 | 95.8 | 43.3 | 52.5 | 92.6 | 8.6 | 8.0 |
| 20. 1950–59 | 92.0 | 33.5 | 58.5 | 88.0 | 22.2 | 19.5 |
| *United States* | | | | | | |
| 21. 1869–88 | 95.6 | 39.5 | 56.1 | 92.7 | 14.1 | 13.1 |
| 22. 1889–1908 | 102.3 | 47.2 | 55.1 | 104.4 | 13.3 | 13.9 |
| 23. 1909–28 | 110.9 | 58.8 | 52.1 | 126.5 | 9.1 | 11.5 |
| 24. 1929–38 | 103.3 | 89.1 | 14.2 | 130.3 | 1.9 | 2.5 |
| 25. 1946–55 | 105.2 | 66.2 | 39.0 | 115.4 | 8.5 | 9.8 |
| 26. 1950–59 | 102.8 | 52.3 | 50.5 | 105.9 | 9.3 | 9.8 |
| *Canada* | | | | | | |
| 27. 1870 and 1890 | 52.0 | 54.2 | –2.2 | –4.8 | 7.3 | –0.4 |
| 28. 1890, 1900, 1910 | 56.8 | 54.7 | 2.1 | 4.6 | 9.6 | 0.4 |
| 29. 1920, 1929 | 78.2 | 41.4 | 36.8 | 62.8 | 14.2 | 8.9 |
| 30. 1926–30 | 90.7 | 58.2 | 32.5 | 77.8 | 9.7 | 7.5 |
| 31. 1950–59 | 89.6 | 46.0 | 43.6 | 80.7 | 15.1 | 12.2 |
| *Australia* | | | | | | |
| 32. 1861–80 | 69.6 | 26.5 | 43.1 | 58.6 | 12.0 | 7.0 |
| 33. 1881–1900 | 58.5 | 39.5 | 19.0 | 31.4 | 10.8 | 3.4 |
| 34. 1900/01–1919/20 | 87.8 | 37.6 | 50.2 | 80.4 | 9.2 | 7.4 |
| 35. 1919/20–1938/39 | 87.9 | 39.5 | 48.4 | 80.0 | 10.8 | 8.6 |
| 36. 1950/51–1959/60 | 91.6 | 23.5 | 68.1 | 89.0 | 21.6 | 19.2 |

TABLE 5.5—*Continued*

% of GDCF

| | Gross national savings (1) | Capital consumption (2) | Net national savings (1−2) (3) | Net national savings as % of NDCF (4) | NDCF as % of NDP or NNP (5) | Net national savings as % of NDP or NNP (6) |
|---|---|---|---|---|---|---|
| *Japan* (excluding military) | | | | | | |
| 37. 1887–1906 | 79.2 | 48.0 | 31.2 | 60.0 | 5.6 | 3.4 |
| 38. 1907–26 | 95.7 | 41.3 | 54.4 | 92.7 | 8.9 | 8.3 |
| 39. 1927–36 | 96.2 | 39.2 | 57.0 | 93.8 | 10.3 | 9.7 |
| 40. 1950–59 | 102.7 | 28.6 | 74.1 | 103.8 | 21.8 | 22.6 |

*Sources: Col. 1:* From Table 5.3, col. 5 ÷ col. 3 × 100.
*Cols. 2 and 5:* From Kuznets, "Quantitative Aspects: VI," appendix tables for individual countries except for the U.S., line 26. The latter, for 1953–59 is from U.N, *Yearbook of National Accounts Statistics, 1960.* The recent period is slightly different from the one indicated in the stub.
*Col. 4:* Col. 3 ÷ (1 − col. 2) × 100.
*Col. 6:* Col. 4 × col. 5 ÷ 100.

The same findings are suggested by Table 5.5, but in an accentuated form. In the United Kingdom and United States the *net* savings proportion declined significantly; in Norway it showed no definite trend over the period preceding World War II, and there is some question as to the existence of a rising trend in Australia. In the remaining four countries—Italy, Denmark, Canada, and Japan—the net national savings proportion rose. But it is curious that in Italy before 1900, in Denmark before 1890, in Canada before 1910, and in Japan before 1906, the net national savings proportion was 5 per cent or less (in Canada actually negative in the first period), while per capita real income rose markedly in the preceding decades. Too heavy a burden of interpretation should not be put on the *net* savings ratio, given the necessarily problematical basis of the estimates of capital consumption. But if the net savings measures can be accepted as having some significance, why have the ratios declined or failed to rise in some countries, and why were they so low in others—all in periods of rather vigorous growth and marked rise in real income per capita? Was the pressure for increased consumption associated with industrialization and urbanization so great as to bar a prompt rise of savings proportions with a rise in per capita product? Were the capital imports so heavy that they raised domestic price levels, and inhibited real, as distinct from money, savings? Was the relative "backwardness" such that capital-saving types of investment were widely available, and hence there was no great pressure for domestic savings? These and other questions can be raised, but we are not in a position to explore them.

We now consider capital formation as additions to material capital stock and observe the trends in its distribution by type of good—the only distribution available for a number of countries (Table 5.6, columns 1–4). With due allowance for the possibly exceptional character of the post-World War II decade, the long-term changes in this structure of gross domestic capital formation can be easily discerned.

TABLE 5.6

Distribution of Gross Domestic Capital Formation by Type of Goods (Current Price Totals) and Incremental Capital–Output Ratio, Selected Countries, Long Periods

| Country and period (for cols. 1–4) | Share in GDCF (%) | | | | Period (5) | Rate of growth, GDP (%) (6) | Incremental C/O ratio (gross) | |
|---|---|---|---|---|---|---|---|---|
| | Residential construction (1) | Other construction (2) | Producer equipment (3) | Change in inventories (4) | | | Ratio, current prices (7) | Ratio, constant prices (8) |
| *United Kingdom* | | | | | | | | |
| 1. 1860–79 | 14.8 | 31.4ᵃ | 35.4 | 18.4 | 1860/69 to 1880/89 | 2.97 | 3.1 | 3.5 |
| 2. 1880–99 | 15.0 | 30.8ᵃ | 33.3 | 20.9 | 1880/89 to 1900/09 | 2.24 | 4.0 | 4.1 |
| 3. 1900–14 | 12.8 | 29.5ᵃ | 37.5 | 20.2 | 1885/94 to 1905/14 | 1.52 | 6.1 | 6.2 |
| 4. 1921–38 | | 76.6 | 47.0 | −23.6 | 1921/29 to 1930/38 | 2.55 | 3.4 | |
| 5. 1952–58 | 19.8 | 25.9 | 48.6 | 5.7 | 1952–58 | 2.36 | 6.6 | |
| *Germany* (NDCF and NNP; 1913 territory) | | | | | | | | |
| 6. 1851–70 | 29 | 36ᵇ | 20 | 15 | 1851/60 to 1871–80 | 2.7 | 3.4 | 3.5 |
| 7. 1871–90 | 32 | 38ᵇ | 24 | 6 | 1871/80 to 1891/1900 | 2.7 | 4.4 | 4.5 |
| 8. 1891–1913 | 31 | 30ᵇ | 34 | 5 | 1881/90 to 1901/13 | 2.9 | 4.7 | 4.8 |

| | | | | | | | | |
|---|---|---|---|---|---|---|---|---|
| *Italy* | | | | | | | | |
| 9. 1861–80 | 17.5 | | 69.5 | 13.0 | 1861/70 to 1881/90 | 0.75 | 13.7 | 11.9 |
| 10. 1881–1900 | 22.4 | | 75.9 | 1.7 | 1881/90 to 1901/10 | 1.49 | 8.0 | 7.3 |
| 11. 1901–10 | 17.9 | | 71.9 | 10.2 | | | 7.5 | 7.0 |
| 12. 1921–30 | 13.1 | | 84.9 | 2.0 | 1921–39 | 2.42 | 3.7 | |
| 13. 1952–58 | 24.6 | | 72.7 | 2.7 | 1952–58 | 5.65 | | |
| *Denmark* | | | | | | | | |
| 14. 1870–89 | | 56.0 | 32.8 | 11.2 | 1870/79 to 1890/99 | 2.97 | 3.6 | 3.8 |
| 15. 1890–1909 | | 55.5 | 34.4 | 10.1 | 1890/99 to 1900/09 | 3.38 | 4.0 | 4.0 |
| 16. 1921–30 | | 46.7 | 41.0 | 12.3 | 1921/30 to 1931/39 | 2.45 | 5.1 | 4.8 |
| 17. 1952–58 | | 40.3 | 55.4 | 4.3 | 1952–58 | 2.86 | 6.4 | |
| *Norway* | | | | | | | | |
| 18. 1865–99 | 41.3 | 39.1 | 19.6 | | 1865/74 to 1885/94 | 1.66 | 7.0 | 7.9 |
| 19. 1899–1939 | 27.2 | 47.6 | 25.2 | | 1885/94 to 1905/14 | 2.24 | 6.1 | 6.8 |
| 20. 1939–53 | 16.6 | 48.6 | 34.8 | | 1905/14 to 1925/34 | 2.75 | 6.1 | 6.3 |
| 21. | | | | | 1952–58 | 3.11 | 9.6 | |

TABLE 5.6—*Continued*

| Country and period (for cols. 1–4) | Share in GDCF (%) | | | | Incremental C/O ratio (gross) | | | |
|---|---|---|---|---|---|---|---|---|
| | Residential construction (1) | Other construction (2) | Producer equipment (3) | Change in inventories (4) | Period (5) | Rate of growth, GDP (%) (6) | Ratio, current prices (7) | Ratio, constant prices (8) |
| *Sweden* | | | | | | | | |
| 22. 1861–80 | 66.5 | | 22.0 | 11.5 | 1861/70 to 1881/90 | 2.96 | 3.7 | 4.6 |
| 23. 1881–1900 | 60.5 | | 30.0 | 9.5 | 1881/90 to 1901/10 | 3.06 | 3.9 | 4.2 |
| 24. 1901–20 | 54.6 | | 38.3 | 7.1 | 1901/10 to 1921/30 | 2.63 | 5.1 | 4.7 |
| 25. 1921–40 | 54.4 | | 38.2 | 7.4 | 1921/30 to 1941/50 | 3.41 | 5.2 | 4.9 |
| 26. 1941–50 | 45.5 | | 44.1 | 10.4 | | | | |
| 27. 1952–58 | 60.6 | | 34.4 | 5.0 | 1952–58 | 3.52 | 6.1 | |
| *United States* | | | | | | | | |
| 28. 1869–88 | 20.0 | 35.4 | 23.8 | 20.8 | 1869/78 to 1889/98 | 4.91 | 4.4 | 4.9 |
| 29. 1889–1908 | 21.5 | 46.9 | 23.6 | 8.0 | 1879/98 to 1899/08 | 3.91 | 5.7 | 6.3 |
| 30. 1909–28 | 18.6 | 38.2 | 32.6 | 10.6 | 1899/08 to 1919/28 | 3.14 | 6.3 | 6.7 |
| 31. 1929–48 | 14.1 | 40.1 | 42.5 | 3.3 | 1919/28 to 1939/48 | 2.02 | 8.2 | 7.8 |
| 32. 1946–55 | 18.6 | 34.3 | 41.6 | 5.5 | 1939/48 to 1948/57 | 4.25 | 4.7 | 4.0 |

*Canada*

| | 54 | | 23 | 23 | | | |
|---|---|---|---|---|---|---|---|
| 33. 1870 and 1890 | | | | | 1870 to 1898/02 | 3.36 | 4.2 |
| 34. 1896–1910 | 18.2 | 43.2 | 23.8 | 14.8 | 1898/02 to 1928/30 | 3.51 | 5.9 |
| 35. 1911–30 | 16.7 | 45.2 | 27.1 | 11.0 | 1919/23 to 1939/43 | 3.42 | 6.3 |
| 36. 1926–40 | 18.9 | 41.5 | 32.8 | 6.8 | 1944/48 to 1954/58 | 3.84 | 6.1 |
| 37. 1941–55 | 19.8 | 39.4 | 37.7 | 3.1 | | | |
| 38. 1952–58 | 19.1 | 43.8 | 33.3 | 3.8 | 1952–58 | 2.86 | 8.6 |
| *Australia* | | | | | | | |
| 39. | | | | | 1861/70 to 1881/90 | 5.2 | 3.3 |
| 40. | | | | | 1881/90 to 1901/10 | 2.2 | 6.7 |
| 41. | | | | | 1901/10 to 1921/30 | 2.5 | 6.1 |
| 42. | | | | | 1952/53 to 1958/59 | 3.6 | 7.3 |
| *Japan* | | | | | | | |
| 43. 1887–1906 | 24.8 | 53.6 | 21.6 | | 1885/89 to 1905/09 | 3.8 | 2.8 |
| 44. 1907–26 | 11.9 | 54.6 | 33.5 | | 1905/09 to 1925/29 | 4.6 | 3.0 |

TABLE 5.6—*Continued*

| | Share in GDCF (%) | | | | Incremental C/O ratio (gross) | | | |
|---|---|---|---|---|---|---|---|---|
| Country and period (for cols. 1–4) | Residential construction (1) | Other construction (2) | Producer equipment (3) | Change in inventories (4) | Period (5) | Rate of growth, GDP (%) (6) | Ratio, current prices (7) | Ratio, constant prices (8) |
| *Japan–cont.* | | | | | | | | |
| 45. 1927–36 | 7.6 | 55.4 | 37.0 | | 1925/29 to 1935/39 | 5.1 | 3.1 | |
| 46. 1952–58 | 8.3 | | | | 1952–58 | 6.8 | 4.2 | |

a. Includes other construction and mixed fixed capital formation, the latter covering expenditures of railroads, local authorities, and telephone and telegraph companies.

b. Includes other construction, canals, roads, and railroads.

*Source:* All data are from Kuznets, "Quantitative Aspects: VI," appendix tables for individual countries. For the ratios in cols. 7 and 8, the capital formation proportions for the periods including three decades (when the span covered was 20 years) were weighted 1, 2, and 1, respectively.

First, the share of fixed capital in the total tends to rise and that of net changes in inventories to decline. The estimates of net changes in inventories are none too firm, and they are available for only seven countries. But in all seven the share declines, from as high as a fifth of total capital formation (in the United Kingdom and the United States) in the earlier decades to a few percentage points in the recent period. Such a decline is plausible in view of the marked improvement in means of transport and communication, the reduction in the share of the agriculture sector which is characterized by seasonally large inventories, and the possibly increasing use of productive capacity instead of inventories to absorb short-term variations in demand.

Second, the share of construction in both fixed capital formation and total capital formation declined and that of producers' equipment rose. The rise in the share of the latter in total capital formation can be observed in all eight countries for which this component is distinguished—from as low as a fifth of total capital formation in the earlier years to well over a third in recent years in most countries. These shares are based on totals in current prices; and a shift to a constant price base would result in an even greater rise of the share of producers' equipment, since the prices of the latter declined more or rose less than prices implicit in construction (where costs remained high because of a lag in efficiency).[15] This upward trend in the share of producers' equipment is also plausible, in view of the deceleration in the rate of growth of population which should have restricted growth in residential construction; the extensive buildup of the basic network of plants, railroads, and public utilities in the earlier phases of economic growth of the presently developed countries; and the advance of technology, which may have placed greater emphasis on in-

15. See Kuznets, "Quantitative Aspects: VI," Table 14, p. 41 and R. A. Gordon, "Differential Changes in the Prices of Consumers' and Capital Goods," *American Economic Review*, 51 (December 1961).

creasingly elaborate machinery than on the construction shell within which it was to be housed.

Third, within total construction, which amounted to between a half and two thirds of gross domestic capital formation, residential construction accounted usually for no more than a third, i.e. between a sixth and a fifth of gross capital formation. With some exceptions, the share of residential construction, like that of total construction, failed to show any distinct trend; but in the three Scandinavian countries—Denmark, Norway, and Sweden—the share of total construction did drop, as did the share in Japan, but only because of the decline in the share of residential construction. It may well be that the shares of total and residential construction in gross capital formation based on constant price values would show a more prevalent decline than is observed in Table 5.6.

If material capital were the only factor contributing to the value of output, or if there were no significant correlation between the contribution of capital and that of other factors, changes in the structure of gross domestic capital formation would have a direct bearing on the ratio of gross increment to capital stock to increase in gross domestic product. With the useful life of construction set at 50 years, that of producers' equipment at 10 years (these figures, while realistic, are merely illustrative), and that of net changes in inventories eternal, the implicit incremental gross capital–output ratio—allowing for the calculation of capital consumption charges along a straight line, a net return on capital of 6 per cent, and gross product equal to the sum of capital consumption charges and net return on capital—would be $100/(2 + 6)$, or 12.5 for construction; $100/(10 + 6)$, or 6.25 for producers' equipment; and $100/6$, or 16.7 for net changes in inventories. If the structure of gross domestic capital formation in the early years covered by Table 5.6 is assumed to be 60 per cent for construction, 20 per cent for producers' equipment, and 20 per cent for net changes in inventories, the implicit incremental capital–output ratio for the economy, on the premises stated, would be about 11. With a shift in structure to, say, 55 per cent for construction, 40 per cent for producers' equipment, and 5 per cent for net changes in inventories, in recent years the incremental capital–output ratio for the economy, on the same assumptions of useful life and net return, would decline to 9. If we assume that at both points of time the share of labor and other factors in gross product was, say, 0.6, the gross incremental capital–output ratio would become 4.3 for the earlier period and 3.6 for the later period.

But, in fact, the directly measurable contribution of material capital is only a small part of total product, and it is not necessarily fixed over time even for the broad categories distinguished in Table 5.6. Long-term changes in the actual gross incremental capital–output ratios are given in columns 7 and 8. The entries in column 7 were computed by dividing the average proportion of gross domestic capital formation to gross domestic product (both in current prices) by the rate of growth of gross domestic product in constant prices (given in column 6); for those in column 8, the capital formation proportions were based on totals in constant prices, the base used to measure growth of gross domestic product in column 6.[16] In general, prices of capital goods embodied in gross domestic capital formation declined less or rose more than those of countrywide product—largely because of the effect of construction costs, already mentioned. But the shift of the capital formation proportion from current to constant prices significantly affects the trend of the incremental capital–output ratio only in Sweden.

The trends in these ratios are quite different from those

16. The capital formation proportion based on totals in current prices may be designated $(dK)'/Y'$, where the numerator is gross addition to capital stock, in current prices, and the denominator is gross domestic product, also in current prices. The rate of growth of gross domestic product can be expressed as $dY/Y$, where both $dY$ and $Y$ are in constant prices. Dividing the first ratio by the second, we get: $((dK)'/dY):Y'/Y$. If prices of $dK$ and $Y$ change in the same fashion, the latter expression reduces to $dK/dY$, the incremental capital–output ratio in constant prices.

suggested by the illustrative calculation above, based on presumptive effects of the shifts in structure shown in columns 1–4. In Italy a distinct decline in the capital–output ratios accompanies a marked acceleration in the rate of growth of product in column 6. In Norway there is a slight decline in the ratios if we discount the high ratio in the post-World War II decade. But in all other countries—the United Kingdom, Germany, Denmark, Sweden, the United States, Canada, Australia, and Japan—the gross incremental capital–output ratios rose, and in some fairly steeply from between 3 and 4.5 in the early periods to between 4 and 6 in recent periods. These trends would not change if we were to shift to a net basis, i.e. exclude capital consumption from both the capital formation proportions and domestic product. The level of the ratios would be reduced about four tenths, and the rise in the ratio would be substantially less for the United Kingdom and the United States. But the rise in the ratio would still be pronounced, especially for the United States. In all other countries, the rise would be as steep in the net as in the gross incremental capital–output ratios.[17]

If these rises in the incremental capital–output ratios were not due to shifts in the structure of gross domestic capital formation, shown in columns 1–4 of Table 5.6, neither were they due to shifts in the structure of capital formation by industrial channels of destination (i.e. agriculture, mining, manufacturing, etc.)—if we can judge by the results for the few countries with relevant data (see "Quantitative Aspects: VI," Table 15, pp. 46–47 and the discussion of the results). Nor can the variation over time in these incremental capital–output ratios be explained by variation in the input of labor, at least in terms of number of workers, on the theory that capital–output ratios rise when the rate of growth of the labor force declines and vice versa (see ibid., pp. 27–33). The explanation for these rising and rather variable capital–output ratios, as well as for the dif-

17. Further detail on these and other aspects of the capital–output ratios is given in Kuznets, "Quantitative Aspects: VI."

ferences in their level among countries, must be sought in the diverse conditions that influence the use of material capital—investment in man, technological peculiarities of the detailed industry-mix, relative supplies of capital and labor, and organizational structure of economic units and country—and permit the attainment of the same product by different combinations of labor and capital, total or incremental. It would be a gross oversimplification to assume that purely technical constraints make for a fixed capital–output ratio, even within narrowly defined industrial subdivisions, let alone a complex and changing mixture like a country's economy.[18]

The interrelation of capital formation proportions, rates of growth of product and population, and changes in the capital–output ratios must be emphasized. We observed earlier that capital formation proportions, gross or net, rose in most countries, the significant exceptions being the United Kingdom and the United States. If capital formation proportions rise, incremental capital–output ratios can remain constant only if the rate of growth of countrywide product rises proportionately. If population grows at a decreasing rate, as it has in many developed countries, product per capita grows at an increasing rate even if total product grows at a constant rate; and if the total product has to accelerate to keep the capital–output ratio constant, with

18. It should be emphasized that the discussion dealt with *incremental*, not average, capital–output ratios, and that capital was limited to *reproducible* material capital goods, excluding land and other non-reproducible material capital. While the incremental capital–output ratio for reproducible capital, and perhaps the corresponding average ratio, did rise in a number of countries, the ratio of total material capital to output, the former including land and other nonreproducible assets, declined (see Table 2.7 and the accompanying discussion). If investment in man were also included, the total capital–output ratio, average or incremental, might well show a long-term upward trend. But this possibility does not invalidate the discussion in Chapter 2 which emphasized the importance of additions to knowledge, over and beyond input of material capital, in accounting for increased efficiency in modern economic growth in terms of increase of output per unit of simple labor input.

rising capital formation proportions, acceleration in the rate of growth of per capita product must be all the more marked. Such accelerated growth in per capita product should result in higher savings and hence in higher capital formation proportions—which means that the rate of growth of total and per capita product must accelerate further, if the incremental capital–output ratio is to be kept from rising. Since the extent of such self-acceleration is limited in conditions of a declining rate of growth of population, and since the increased supply of capital funds makes for a larger stock of long-lived goods and a lower marginal yield of capital, a *rising* incremental capital–output ratio, gross or net, is plausible in the course of economic growth. Such a rise would be even more prominent if we were to add investment in man to capital formation, for then the capital formation proportion would be rising even more appreciably while the rate of growth of countrywide product would be unaffected.

### STRUCTURE OF CONSUMPTION

Before we consider trends in the structure of consumption, it is of interest to note the share of personal savings in total or disposable income of households and to observe the long-term trends in these personal savings–disposable income ratios.

Table 5.4 indicated that in recent years households have accounted on the average for almost half (48 to 49 per cent) of net national savings. Since net national savings were 60 per cent of gross national savings and these in turn were close to 23 per cent of GNP, the share of net savings of households in gross national product was (0.485 × 0.6 × 0.23), or 6.7 per cent. Disposable income of households, including money transfers but excluding direct services by government, has amounted in recent years to 70.3 per cent of GNP (see Table 4.1). Hence, net personal savings averaged 6.7/70.3, or 9.5 per cent of disposable income.[19]

19. This estimate is supported by a direct calculation of the ratio of personal savings to disposable income (essentially a sum of consumer

In recent years, then, the savings–disposable income ratio has been close to 10 per cent and the share of consumer outlays over 90 per cent. Were there any changes in this distribution over the decades since the mid-nineteenth century? Several conflicting trends are relevant to this question. The proportion of net national savings to NDP or NNP rose in about half of the countries in our small sample (the significant exceptions were the United Kingdom and the United States, and possibly Norway and Australia; see Table 5.5); and if *all* these were net savings of households, they would have to be related to disposable income, which constituted a diminishing proportion of NDP or NNP (see pp. 165–67). Thus the rise in the ratio of savings to disposable income would be more pronounced than that in the net savings proportion in NDP or NNP. But with the rise in the shares of private corporations and the public sector, the share of households in net national savings may well have declined. If disposable income was, say, 90 per cent of NNP in earlier periods and declined to about 85 per cent in the recent period, a constant share of net savings in NNP of 15 per cent would mean a rise in the share in disposable income from 16.7 to 17.6 per cent. But if the share of household savings in total net savings dropped from 75 to 50 per cent, the personal savings–disposable income ratio would decline from about 12.5 to less than 9 per cent.

It is plausible to assume that the share of household savings in total net savings declined proportionately more than the share of disposable income in NDP or NNP. Hence, whenever the share of net national savings in NDP or NNP declined, remained stable, or rose only slightly, one may infer that the implicit share of personal savings in disposable income drifted downward. The entries in column 6 of Table 5.5 suggest that this inference is true of the United

expenditures and personal saving) for 1957–58 for eleven developed countries from data in U.N., *Yearbook of National Accounts Statistics, 1962*. The arithmetic mean ratio for these countries (the United Kingdom, France, Germany, the Netherlands, Belgium, Sweden, the United States, Canada, Australia, New Zealand, and Japan) is 9.6 per cent.

Kingdom and the United States. In Italy, Denmark, Canada, and Japan, the rise in the net national savings proportion was quite striking, and the personal savings–disposable income ratio must have risen. Perhaps the same was true of Germany before World War I and of Sweden, judging by the movement of the gross savings proportion in Table 5.3.

But whatever the trends in the personal savings–disposable income ratios, the absolute range could have been no wider than from 2 to 5 to about 10 per cent. One important implication follows. In Chapter 4 we observed that the proportion of personal disposable income to gross national product declined, but probably not more than from about 85 per cent in the earlier decades to about 76 per cent in recent years. This means that the rate of growth of real disposable income per capita was about 13 per cent below the rate of growth of gross national product per capita; and the latter was shown in Table 2.5 to be quite high, the rise ranging from 250 to 400 per cent over a century. It thus appears that disposable income per capita also grew at rates that meant rises over a century to between 3 and 4.5 times the initial level. Yet such marked rises in disposable income per capita were accompanied by rather limited savings proportions, which meant that the preponderant part of the increase in disposable income went into larger consumption expenditures per capita. If we assume that personal savings rates were, say, 3 per cent of diposable income at the beginning of the last century and rose to 10 per cent at the end of the century,[20] while disposable income per capita quadrupled (i.e. rose 300 per cent), the marginal propensity to spend (i.e. the proportion of the increase in consumption expenditures to the increase in disposable income) was 0.88 over the century, and the marginal propensity to save was 0.12.

20. This checks roughly with the decline in the share of consumption in GNP suggested in connection with Table 5.3 above. A decline of 13 per cent in the share of disposable income brings it down to 87; and subtracting 3 per cent and 10 per cent (the share of savings) from 100 and 87, respectively, yields 97 and 78, or about a fifth lower.

Some reasons for a high propensity to consume have already been suggested in the discussion of the sizable amounts of intermediate products now included in consumption that reflect extra costs of living under conditions imposed by the changing, urbanized structure of modern economic production; and of the increased investment in man in the way of education and health care. But obviously other factors tend to raise the high level of consumer expenditures per capita. As we turn now to the long-term changes in the structure of consumption, we should attempt to discern the changing conditions that limited the rate of savings by inducing a high rate of growth of consumer expenditures per capita, and thus explain the high propensity to consume.

Table 5.7 summarizes changes in the structure of consumer expenditures by five broad categories. The estimates exclude educational, health, and other services rendered directly by governments to households and ultimate consumers, which should theoretically be included under household consumption. Their inclusion would raise the proportion of "other" and diminish those of the accompanying four categories. While the additions for recent years would be no more than 10 percentage points, they would accentuate the rise in the share of "other."

The estimates suggest some findings that accord with our expectations, and others that do not. In all countries and periods covered in the table, expenditures per capita in constant prices rose markedly. We would, therefore, expect the share of food in total consumption outlay to decline— since cross-section comparisons indicate an inverse relation between per capita expenditures and the proportion of total expenditures spent on food.[21] On similar grounds, we would expect the share of clothing to rise. The asso-

21. For this and other associations between per capita expenditures and the shares of various categories in consumer expenditures see the discussion in Kuznets, "Quantitative Aspects: VII," pp. 23–28. The negative relation between per capita income and the proportion spent on food is known familiarly as Engel's Law.

TABLE 5.7

Structure of Consumer Expenditures, Selected Countries, Long Periods

Shares in total consumer expenditures (%)

| | Current prices | | | | | Constant prices | | | | |
|---|---|---|---|---|---|---|---|---|---|---|
| | Food (1) | Beverages and tobacco (2) | Clothing (3) | Housing (4) | Other (5) | Food (6) | Beverages and tobacco (7) | Clothing (8) | Housing (9) | Other (10) |
| *United Kingdom* | | | | | | | | | | |
| 1. 1880–99 | 34.2 | 13.8 | | 10.7 | (41.3) | | | | | |
| 2. 1900–19 | 34.7 | 11.2 | 9.8 | 14.7 | 29.7 | 28.2 | 17.8 | 10.1 | 14.0 | 29.9 |
| 3. 1920–39 | 31.9 | 11.2 | 10.7 | 13.9 | 32.3 | 30.2 | 11.6 | 10.3 | 15.1 | 32.8 |
| 4. 1940–49 | 29.1 | 19.2 | 10.0 | 13.1 | 28.6 | 31.4 | 12.3 | 8.5 | 17.8 | 30.0 |
| 5. 1950–59 | 31.3 | 14.1 | 11.7 | 12.8 | 30.1 | | | | | |
| *Germany* | | | | | | | | | | |
| 6. 1851–70 | | | | | | 44.8 | 18.8 | 12.5 | 19.0 | 4.9 |
| 7. 1871–90 | | | | | | 39.9 | 19.3 | 14.4 | 20.5 | 5.9 |
| 8. 1891–1910 | | | | | | 38.5 | 15.8 | 15.0 | 23.0 | 7.7 |
| *Italy* | | | | | | | | | | |
| 9. 1861–80 | 52.0 | 17.2 | | 5.8 | (25.0) | | | | | |
| 10. 1881–1900 | 47.3 | 21.0 | | 7.9 | (23.8) | | | | | |
| 11. 1901–20 | 49.7 | 17.3 | | 6.6 | (26.4) | | | | | |
| 12. 1921–40 | 47.8 | 12.9 | | 7.9 | (31.4) | | | | | |
| 13. 1941–50 | 52.6 | 11.2 | | 1.2 | (35.0) | | | | | |
| 14. 1950–59 | 46.6 | 10.7 | 11.5 | 5.2 | 26.0 | | | | | |

| | (1) | (2) | (3) | (4) | (5) | (6) | (7) | (8) | (9) |
|---|---|---|---|---|---|---|---|---|---|
| *Norway* | | | | | | | | | |
| 15. 1865 and 1875 | 45.2 | 7.0 | 10.9 | 19.8 | 17.1 | | | | |
| 16. 1890 and 1900 | 42.6 | 6.7 | 11.8 | 16.6 | 22.3 | | | | |
| 17. 1910 and 1930 | 37.2 | 6.1 | 13.3 | 15.6 | 27.8 | | | | |
| 18. 1950 | 28.2 | 8.6 | 18.1 | 9.7 | 35.4 | | | | |
| 19. 1950–59 | 30.3 | 8.1 | 16.7 | 10.2 | 34.7 | | | | |
| *Sweden* | | | | | | | | | |
| 20. 1864, '73, '82 | 38.7 | | 5.2 | 26.3 | 29.8 | 36.3 | 29.9 | 4.9 | 28.9 |
| 21. 1889, '97, '06 | 36.5 | | 8.5 | 19.4 | 35.6 | 35.7 | 20.0 | 9.5 | 34.8 |
| 22. 1906, '13, '26 | 35.6 | | 10.0 | 14.8 | 39.6 | 36.6 | 14.2 | 10.4 | 38.8 |
| 23. 1938–48 | 25.2 | | 12.6 | 11.0 | 51.2 | 28.2 | 9.4 | 13.6 | 48.8 |
| 24. 1950–59 | 29.4 | 9.2 | 13.9 | 13.9 | 33.6 | | | | |
| *United States* | | | | | | | | | |
| 25. 1869, '79, '89 | 39.3 | | 17.0 | 16.9 | 26.8 | 39.6 | 18.6 | 15.1 | 26.7 |
| 26. 1889–1908 | 37.7 | | 14.7 | 18.0 | 29.6 | 39.2 | 16.7 | 14.2 | 29.9 |
| 27. 1909–28 | 33.1 | | 13.0 | 18.0 | 35.9 | 31.0 | | 10.9 | |
| 28. 1909, '14, '19 | 35.5 | | 14.3 | 20.0 | 30.2 | | | | |
| 29. 1919, '23/25, '29 | 31.7 | | 14.7 | 16.8 | 36.8 | | | | |
| 30. 1929–48 | 31.8 | | 13.6 | 14.8 | 39.8 | | | | |
| 31. 1950–59 | 23.7 | 5.7 | 10.1 | 15.7 | 44.8 | | | | |
| *Canada* | | | | | | | | | |
| 32. 1870 and 1890 | 32.2 | 5.7 | 16.9 | 26.7 | 18.5 | | | | |
| 33. 1900 and 1910 | 30.0 | 6.5 | 17.0 | 24.8 | 21.7 | | | | |
| 34. 1920 and 1930 | 29.8 | 5.7 | 15.0 | 26.0 | 23.5 | | | | |
| 35. 1926–30 | 26.4 | 5.2 | 13.8 | 28.2 | 26.4 | | | | |
| 36. 1941–50 | 27.1 | 8.2 | 14.2 | 24.5 | 26.0 | | | | |
| 37. 1950–59 | 23.7 | 8.3 | 10.2 | 21.2 | 36.6 | | | | |

*Source:* From Kuznets, "Quantitative Aspects: VII," App. Tables 5 and 6, pp. 76–92. For the United Kingdom, the shares before 1900 were spliced with those for later years on the basis of the overlap for 1900–09; and housing in 1880–99 covers rent only. For Canada, col. 4 includes house operation.

ciation between per capita expenditures and the share spent on housing is not as clear-cut. But within "other," the weight of such components as house furniture and equipment, transportation (particularly the passenger car), medical care, recreation, and the like, should lead one to expect that, as per capita expenditures increase, the share of these goods with high demand elasticity would rise.

Some of the trends indicated in Table 5.7 confirm our expectations. In several countries—Germany, Norway, Sweden, the United States, and Canada—the share of food, including or excluding beverages and tobacco, in total expenditures declines. But in the United Kingdom and Italy no significant drop can be observed before the post-World War II decade; and even in the other countries, where the trends are on the whole downward, for long periods the share fails to decline while per capita expenditures and income are presumably rising at marked rates. Thus in Germany between 1871–90 and 1891–1910, in Sweden between 1864 and 1926, at least for totals in constant prices, and in Canada between 1900–10 and 1941–50 the share of food hardly changes.

The deviations from expectations are even more conspicuous for the share of clothing. In only three of the six countries for which this share can be distinguished—Germany, Norway, and Sweden—does it rise significantly. In the United Kingdom the share of clothing in the total in current prices is rather stable and the share in the total in constant prices declines; whereas in the United States and Canada the share definitely declines.

The share of housing in total expenditures differs among the eight countries more than do those of other categories, suggesting that the definitions may differ in scope. Moreover, rent control in the post-World War II decade may have depressed the share unduly. At any rate, the estimates indicate that in Norway, Sweden, and probably the United Kingdom the share of housing declined; in the United States, Canada, and Italy it tended to be constant, at least before World War II; and in Germany before World War I it definitely rose.

These brief comments on the findings in Table 5.7 leave us with the conclusion that not only did consumer expenditures keep pace with the rise in disposable income per capita, but that expenditures on some categories (such as food), whose share in total outlay was expected to decline, failed to do so, thus implying a growth in expenditures per capita no lower than that in total consumption per capita; whereas other categories (such as clothing), whose shares in total outlays were expected to rise, also failed to do so in several countries. It need hardly be mentioned that if more subgroups could be distinguished within consumer expenditures, there would have been more disagreements between the trends in shares shown over time and the expectations based on cross-section comparisons of consumer expenditures, whether within or among countries (and this is what we will find for the United States in Table 5.10). Hence any analysis of the trends in the level and structure of consumer expenditures in the course of modern economic growth should account for both the high propensity to consume and the numerous disagreements between the trends in the shares of the subgroups and those expected on the basis of cross-section analysis.

While it is impossible to present such an analysis here, some suggestions of the major explanatory factors may be of value.[22] These factors can be grouped under three heads: (1) changes in living conditions, imposed by shifts in the production structure of the modern economy which in turn impose higher levels and a changing structure of consumption expenditures; (2) technological changes, particularly in the field of consumer goods, inducing higher consumption levels—more for some subgroups in consumer expenditures than for others; and (3) changes in occupational composition of the active population and in various aspects

22. Much of the discussion that follows is based on Kuznets, "Quantitative Aspects: VII," pp. 36–60.

of the income distribution, which accompany economic growth and which may affect both the propensity to consume and the shares of various subgroups within total consumption. The three groups of factors, although interrelated, are best treated separately.

1. Of the changes in living conditions, and hence in consumption, imposed by structural changes in production, the most conspicuous is, of course, urbanization—the movement of an increasing proportion of the population in developed countries to urban areas. This process has been so common in the course of modern economic growth that urbanization has become a widely recognized feature of modern life and perhaps no statistical elaboration is needed. Yet it must be recognized that although cities make for economies of scale in production, they do not constitute an indispensable condition for such economies; and it may be of value to present a summary of available data—if only to reveal the rapidity of the process even in the last half century, at least in those developed countries that, unlike the United Kingdom, still had substantial proportions of rural population at the beginning of the century (Table 5.8). It should also be emphasized that urbanization is not simply a process of shifting across some fixed dividing line between rural and urban population. Urban communities differ widely in size, and a town of a few thousand inhabitants is much less urban than a metropolis of several million. Furthermore, although residents in metropolitan suburbs may be a large component of rural nonfarm population, they are far more urbanized than those of small cities. Even the detailed data for the United States in lines 13–19 of Table 5.8 do not reveal the full extent of urbanization, although they do show that the proportional increase in the share in total population was positively associated with the size of the community (with the greatest proportional rise in the share of urban communities of 500,000 and over). In general, data like those summarized in Table 5.8 understate the extent of urbanization since they do not reflect shifts within

the urban population to the larger communities and the possibly increasing share within rural population of the "dormitory" suburbs of metropolitan centers.

Several aspects of the urbanization process bear upon trends in the level and structure of consumer expenditures. First, urbanization means an increasing division of labor within the country, growing specialization, and the shift of many activities from nonmarket-oriented pursuit within the family or the village to specialized market-oriented business firms. Much food processing, tailoring, dressmaking, and even building and repairing of houses, was at one time done within the household or by communal efforts within the village; and today a large part is performed by business firms within the urbanized modern society. Moreover, this earlier activity within the household or the village community is not fully reflected in national income accounts, while the market-oriented specialized substitutes for them are more likely to be recorded. This shift does not necessarily raise the proportion of consumer expenditures relative to capital formation, since in the past nonspecialized family or community production of capital goods may have been relatively as large as that of consumer goods. But it is likely to affect the trends in the structure of consumer expenditures as reported. The shares of groups of consumer goods in which home production was particularly large in the past (e.g. foods and clothing) are more likely to be sustained by the shift toward commercialization and urbanization than the shares of other consumer goods.

Second, the shift toward increasingly dense urban communities meant that the satisfaction of an increasing number of wants became more costly—in terms of resources required to provide the same satisfaction as in the less dense countryside. This extra cost of urban life, already noted, may be caused either by the greater difficulties imposed by urban density—with respect to housing, sanitation, water, intracity transportation, and similar basic requirements—or by the need to transport to the cities a variety of goods, par-

TABLE 5.8

Proportion of Urban Population, Developed Countries, Long Periods

A. COMPARATIVE DATA, SELECTED COUNTRIES

| | Early date | | Late date | | Definition of urban |
|---|---|---|---|---|---|
| | Year (1) | % (2) | Year (3) | % (4) | (5) |
| 1. United Kingdom | 1901 | 77.0 | 1951 | 80.7 | Urban status, regardless of size |
| 2. France | 1901 | 41.0 | 1946 | 52.9 | Communities of more than 2,000 inhabitants |
| 3. Germany | 1900 | 56.1 | 1939 | 69.9 | Communities of more than 2,000 inhabitants |
| 4. Netherlands | 1909 | 40.5 | 1947 | 54.6 | Communities of 20,000 or more |
| 5. Switzerland | 1900 | 22.0 | 1950 | 36.5 | Communities of more than 10,000 |
| 6. Denmark | 1901 | 38.2 | 1950 | 67.3 | Towns including suburbs; other agglomerations of 250 inhabitants or more |
| 7. Norway | 1900 | 28.0 | 1950 | 50.5 | 1900: urban status; 1950: also including suburbs and agglomerations of 100 or more |
| 8. Sweden | 1900 | 21.5 | 1950 | 56.3 | 1900: urban status; 1950: also including suburbs, and agglomerations of 100 or more |
| 9. United States | 1900 | 39.7 | 1950 | 59.0 | Including places of 2,500 and more (some townships) |
| 10. Canada | 1901 | 37.5 | 1951 | 62.1 | Including cities and villages of 1,000 or more |
| 11. Japan | 1920 | 18.1 | 1950 | 37.5 | Municipalities, and other agglomerations of 30,000 or more |
| 12. New Zealand | 1901 | 43.1 | 1951 | 61.3 | Cities and boroughs regardless of size |

272

| | 1870[a]<br>(1) | 1960[b]<br>(2) |
|---|---|---|
| 13. Total urban | 25.7 | 63.0 |
| 14. 2,500 to 50,000 | 13.0 | 26.9 |
| 15. 50,000 to 500,000 | 8.5 | 20.2 |
| 16. 500,000 and over | 4.2 | 15.9 |
| 17. Total rural | 74.3 | 37.0 |
| 18. Farm | 55.7 | 8.7 |
| 19. Rural nonfarm | 18.6 | 28.3 |

a. Percentages of unrevised total.

b. The definition of urban used before 1950, to retain comparability.

*Sources: Lines 1–12:* From U.N., *Demographic Yearbook, 1952*, Table 6, except for the United States for 1950 for which see sources below.

*Lines 13–19:* For 1870 from *Historical Statistics of the United States*, Series A 195–A 209, p. 14, and A 36–A 38, p. 9. For 1960 see *Statistical Abstract of the United States, 1962*, Table 13, p. 21. For farm population in both years see note 10.

ticularly foods, that require extensive cultivation and must therefore be produced beyond urban boundaries. These extra costs of urban life affect the level of consumer expenditures relative to savings and capital formation and are likely to have a different impact on different groups of consumer goods; for example, the effect on expenditures by the urban population on agricultural products is greater than that on expenditures on city-produced commodities that are needed and used in the countryside.

Finally, urban life, with the anonymity of its dense population masses, with the detachment from earlier roots of the large immigrant component, and with the ease of observation and imitation of consumption patterns, may facilitate higher consumption levels by permitting greater play of the demonstration effect and by increasing sensitivity to new consumer goods. Here again the effects may be reflected in the trends in consumer expenditures relative to those of savings and capital formation, and in some components of total consumer expenditures more than others.

The effects of these aspects of urbanization on the level and structure of private consumption cannot be measured with the present data. But for expenditures on food in Sweden and the United States, the primary cost—its value at the door of the farm producer or at entry into the country (in the case of imports)—can be distinguished from its full cost to ultimate consumers, including additional charges for processing, transportation, and distribution (Table 5.9).

For our purposes the scope of the PTD component (processing, transportation, and distribution), as measured in Table 5.9, is too wide because it may include some processing that is not used within the household but may be desired and therefore may constitute an addition to *real* income rather than replacement of family labor, or extra cost. But the P part of the PTD component is relatively small, and the estimates do at least indicate the order of magnitude of

# TABLE 5.9

Shares of Primary Input; Processing, Transportation, and Distribution; and Final Cost of Food in Private Consumption Expenditures, Sweden and United States, Long Periods

| | Ratio, final cost to primary input, food (1) | Share of food in PCE, current prices (%) | | | Food expenditures per capita, constant prices | | | |
|---|---|---|---|---|---|---|---|---|
| | | Total (2) | Primary input (col. 2 ÷ col. 1) (3) | PTD (col. 2 − col. 3) (4) | PCE per capita, constant prices (5) | Total (col. 5 × col. 2) (6) | Primary input (col. 5 × col. 3) (7) | PTD (col. 5 × col. 4) (8) |
| *Sweden* | | | | | | | | |
| 1. 1871–80 | 1.40 | 46.4 | 33.1 | 13.3 | 49.5 | 23.0 | 16.4 | 6.6 |
| 2. 1881–90 | 1.43 | 44.0 | 30.8 | 13.2 | 57.3 | 25.2 | 17.6 | 7.6 |
| 3. 1891–1900 | 1.57 | 43.5 | 27.7 | 15.8 | 69.3 | 30.1 | 19.2 | 10.9 |
| 4. 1901–10 | 1.69 | 44.9 | 26.6 | 18.3 | 88.0 | 39.5 | 23.4 | 16.1 |
| 5. 1911–20 | 1.64 | 44.2 | 27.0 | 17.2 | 103.9 | 45.9 | 28.0 | 17.9 |
| 6. 1921–30 | 1.89 | 36.8 | 19.5 | 17.3 | 118.5 | 43.6 | 23.1 | 20.5 |
| *United States* | | | | | | | | |
| 7. 1869 | 1.41 | 32.6 | 23.1 | 9.5 | 157 | 51.2 | 36.3 | 14.9 |
| 8. 1879 | 1.44 | 29.5 | 20.5 | 9.0 | 248 | 73.2 | 50.8 | 22.3 |
| 9. 1889 | 1.45 | 28.6 | 19.7 | 8.9 | 289 | 82.6 | 56.9 | 25.7 |
| 10. 1899 | 1.46 | 28.2 | 19.3 | 8.9 | 361 | 101.8 | 69.7 | 32.1 |
| 11. 1909 | 1.47 | 27.6 | 18.8 | 8.8 | 454 | 125.0 | 85.4 | 39.9 |
| 12. 1909–14 | 1.53 | 28.1 | 18.4 | 9.7 | 463 | 130.1 | 85.2 | 44.9 |
| 13. 1919–29 | 1.79 | 26.8 | 15.0 | 11.8 | 575 | 154.1 | 86.2 | 67.9 |
| 14. 1929–38 | 2.05 | 23.9 | 11.7 | 12.2 | 592 | 141.5 | 69.3 | 72.2 |
| 15. 1939–48 | 1.95 | 25.6 | 13.1 | 12.5 | 771 | 197.4 | 101.0 | 96.4 |
| 16. 1949–57 | 2.28 | 23.6 | 10.4 | 13.2 | 922* | 217.6 | 95.9 | 121.7 |

* Average for 1949–55.

*Source:* See Kuznets, "Quantitative Aspects: VII," Table 13, pp. 43–45. Col. 5 for Sweden is an index (1913 = 100); for the United States it is in 1929 dollars.

the effect of shifts toward commercialization and the extra costs of urbanization on the cost of food.

In both countries the share of food in total consumer expenditures declined, although slightly in Sweden through 1920 and although there was some stability in the United States between 1889 and 1909–14 (column 2). But the share of the primary cost of food in consumer expenditures declined far more consistently and sharply (column 3). By contrast, the share of the PTD component in total consumer expenditures (and even more so in total food outlays) rose, and the rise was particularly marked in the more recent periods—in Sweden after 1890 and in the United States after 1909 (column 4). Clearly, the share of the outlay on food in consumer expenditures was sustained by the increasing proportion contributed by the costs of processing, transportation, and distribution; and with increasing per capita expenditures and urbanization, the primary input into food—largely the part received by agriculture—accounted for a sharply declining proportion of consumer expenditures (and of national product), while the PTD component accounted for a rising share of consumer expenditures, and probably also of national product.

2. Technological changes, the main source of modern economic growth, affect consumer goods by the creation of new types and by major changes in the old. Even in the case of food, modern canning, freezing, etc. are new processes that affect the total demand for food and its distribution among various categories and must be reflected in the processing part of the PTD component in Table 5.9. Such technological changes are even more conspicuous when they lead to entirely new consumer goods—synthetic fiber textiles, household electric appliances, radio and television sets, passenger cars, airplane transportation, and the like. The relative technological impact on consumer goods and on capital goods is difficult to measure, but this is not important in the present connection. However, it is important to recognize the continuous and far-reaching effect of technological changes on consumer goods—as would be revealed by a

brief glance at the variety of consumer goods used in presently developed countries and resulting from relatively recent technological progress.

Increases in the stock of useful knowledge may affect consumer preferences even for old consumer goods; for example, preferences for foods have changed as a result of increased knowledge of nutrition and its effects on health. And there may be other shifts in consumer preferences due to technological progress and independent of the introduction of new consumer goods or of major changes in old. But, setting aside shifts in preferences caused by changes in conditions of life and work, it may be argued that technological changes have been a dominant factor—both in inducing a much higher level of consumption expenditures per capita than would otherwise have been the case and in changing materially the distribution of consumer expenditures among various subgroups.

In this connection Table 5.10, which presents a summary of changes in consumer expenditures in the United States over the last half century that is more detailed than that in Table 5.7, may be of interest. Even this distribution is too broad, and moreover it does not distinguish between new goods attributable, in part or whole, to technological changes and other goods not so affected. Yet, limited as it is, Table 5.10 reveals the sharp rise in the shares of expenditures on some newer products—in particular, house furnishings and appliances (line 11), communications and telephone (line 9), automobile and other user-transportation (line 13), and medical and health care (line 16). These four categories, which reflect more than others the effects of new technology, taken together rose 13.4 percentage points between 1909 and 1957, which, considering their combined proportion in 1957 of 24.9 per cent, means that over half of their recent share was gained within the last half century. The only other distinguishable category in Table 5.10 whose share definitely rose, although not as much, was recreation and reading (line 17), a reflection of the growing demand for commercialized recreation in conditions of urban life.

Changes over time in consumer preferences may be seen

TABLE 5.10

Structure of Consumer Expenditures, 1909–57, and Cross-section Expenditure Elasticity of Demand, 1901 and 1950, United States

| | Share in consumer expenditures (%) | | | | Elasticity of demand | |
|---|---|---|---|---|---|---|
| | 1909 (1) | 1929 (2) | 1929 (3) | 1957 (4) | 1950 (5) | 1901 (6) |
| 1. Food and nonalcoholic beverages | 25.6 | 24.4 | 24.7 | 23.4 | 0.59 | |
| 2. Alcoholic beverages | 6.2 | 2.5 | 0 | 3.2 | 1.94 | |
| 3. Tobacco | 2.2 | 2.1 | 2.2 | 2.1 | 0.22 | |
| 4. Food, beverages, and tobacco (lines 1–3) | 34.0 | 29.0 | 26.9 | 28.7 | 0.62 | 0.61 |
| 5. Clothing and related products | 13.9 | 13.4 | 14.2 | 10.5 | 1.70 | 1.76 |
| 6. Personal care | 0.9 | 1.4 | 1.4 | 1.4 | 0.77 | |
| 7. Housing (rent) | 19.3 | 14.1 | 14.2 | 12.0 | 0.60 | 0.78 |
| 8. Fuel, light, water (including electricity and gas) | 4.7 | 3.8 | 3.9 | 3.8 | 0.30 | 0.34 |
| 9. Communications (telephone, etc.) | 0.6 | 1.1 | 0.7 | 1.2 | | |
| 10. House operation (domestic service, etc.) | 3.4 | 2.9 | 3.2 | 2.7 | 1.86 | |
| 11. House furnishings and equipment | 4.8 | 5.5 | 5.8 | 6.3 | 1.14 | |
| 12. Total house (lines 7–11) | 32.8 | 27.4 | 27.8 | 26.0 | | |
| 13. Auto and other vehicles for user transport (including operation) | 2.3 | 7.2 | 7.5 | 11.6 | 1.82 | |
| 14. Public transport | 2.9 | 2.7 | 2.1 | 1.2 | 1.27 | |
| 15. Personal business (insurance, fees, etc.) | 3.3 | 7.1 | 6.4 | 5.5 | | |
| 16. Medical and health | 2.7 | 3.6 | 4.5 | 5.8 | 0.70 | |
| 17. Recreation and reading | 3.0 | 4.7 | 5.8 | 6.0 | 1.56 | |

18. Other (including private education)     4.2     3.5     3.4     3.2     2.38

19. All excluding food (line 4), clothing (line 5),
    housing (line 7), and fuel, light, etc. (line 8)     28.1     39.7     40.8     45.0     1.41     1.99

*Sources: Cols. 1–4:* From *Historical Statistics of the United States,* Series G 219–G 243, p. 179, and G 191–G 218, p. 178. Recreation includes housing cost of transients in hotels and other accommodations.

*Col. 5:* Derived from a summary of consumption expenditures for 1950 for families of 2 or more persons in cities of 2,500 and over, by family income classes (ibid., Series G 353–G 372, p. 182). The ratios of percentage differences in per capita expenditures on a given group of items (food, alcoholic beverages, etc.) to percentage differences in total per capita expenditures were derived for four pairs of income classes (omitting the lowest family income group), the income classes being paired first at the extreme; then next to the extreme; and so on. The entries are arithmetic means of the four elasticity coefficients for each group of items. It would have been more proper to use geometric means; but the differences are only a couple of points in the second decimal place, and for one commodity (tobacco) the coefficient was negative in one comparison.

*Col. 6:* Based on data for a sample of some 11,000 families in 1901 (ibid., Series G 303–G 312, p. 180) again limited to the urban and largely wage-earning population. The groups of items distinguished are food, clothing, rent, fuel and light, and sundries. The procedure used to derive the average elasticity coefficients was analogous to that used for col. 5, except that five pairs of income classes were used, and again the lowest income class was excluded.

to be caused largely by technological achievements creating new or changed consumer goods and in part by additions to the stock of useful knowledge on the properties and effects of consumption and by changes in conditions of life and work. Given these changes over time, trends in the structure of consumer expenditures accompanying economic growth and increased expenditures per capita may show numerous deviations from trends suggested by expenditure elasticity coefficients of demand derived from cross-section studies. A consumer good with low elasticity of demand, e.g. margarine, may nevertheless account for a rising share of total consumer expenditures because technological improvements, unaccompanied by significant differential price declines, induce large increases in volumes of per capita consumption in current dollars. A consumer good with high elasticity of demand, e.g. clothing, may account for a declining share of total consumer expenditures because consumer preferences can shift toward other consumer goods.

Columns 5 and 6 of Table 5.10 provide approximate coefficients of expenditure elasticity of demand for various subgroups of consumer goods, derived from consumer expenditure studies for urban families in the United States in 1950 and in 1901. The measures are means of elasticities calculated separately for pairs of income classes—beginning with the extremes and converging toward the middle of the income distribution (four pairs for 1950 and five pairs for 1901). It should be noted that the cross-section data are limited to urban families, the subgroups of goods distinguished in the cross-section studies may not be strictly comparable with those in the distribution of aggregate consumer expenditures, and the effects of differential price trends on movements of shares over time may differ from those on cross-section comparisons. These factors obviously qualify the comparison of the coefficients in columns 5 and 6 with the movements of the shares over time in columns 1–4. Yet the measures in columns 5 and 6 differ from 1.0 in the direction expected from a variety of other cross-section studies; and the comparison, crude as it is, seems warranted.

In general, an elasticity coefficient below 1 would lead us to expect a decline in the share of the relevant subgroup in total consumer expenditures; a coefficient above 1 would lead us to expect a rise in the share. And if we use the actual coefficients, we can, given the rise in per capita total expenditures in constant prices, calculate the expected change in the share (on the assumption that differential price movements among the subgroups are not significantly large). The rise in per capita consumer expenditures between 1909 and 1929 can be estimated to be 33.1 per cent; between 1929 and 1957, 50.4 per cent.[23] If, for clothing, we use the elasticity coefficient of 1.76 (line 5, column 6), and a share for 1909 of 13.9 per cent, the expected value of the share in 1929 should be 16.5 per cent, not 13.4, as entered in line 5, column 2. If for the change from 1929 to 1957 we use the elasticity coefficient of 1.70 (line 5, column 5) and an initial share in 1929 of 14.2 per cent, the expected share in 1957 would be 17.6 per cent; if we begin with a share in 1929 of 16.5 per cent, derived from the expectancy for the period 1909–29, the expected share in 1957 would be 20.3 per cent—almost double the 10.5 per cent actually shown for 1957 in line 5, column 4. Similar calculations can be made for other subgroups of consumer goods; but no great reliance should be placed on the precise magnitudes of the coefficients in columns 5 and 6.

For several subgroups of consumer goods, the movement of the shares in total expenditures in columns 1–4 is opposite from that expected on the basis of the cross-section elasticity coefficients. According to column 5, the elasticity coefficient is above 1 for clothing (line 5), household operation (heavily weighted by domestic service, line 10), public transportation (line 14), and "other" (line 18)—but the shares of these four subgroups in total expenditures de-

23. For the rise between 1909 and 1929 see Kuznets, "Quantitative Aspects: VII," App. Table 6, line 146, pp. 86–87. The rise between 1929 and 1957 was calculated from the same source supplemented by series in the *Economic Report of the President, January 1963*, Table C-16, p. 191.

clined from 1929 to 1957; whereas the elasticity coefficient is below 1 for tobacco (line 3), personal care (line 6), fuel, light, and water (line 8), and, surprisingly, medical and health care (line 16)—but the shares of the first three of these subgroups were practically constant, and that of the last—medical care—rose fairly substantially. Thus 8 of the 14 possible comparisons between column 5 and changes from column 3 to column 4, show disagreement in direction between the actual and the expected trends. In view of the minor effect on structure of consumption of differences in trends among consumer goods prices, indicated in Table 5.7, these trends probably did not contribute much to the disagreement noted. It is rather due to changes in consumer preferences over time, traceable to the factors noted above.

The absolute number of disagreements, although not necessarily the proportion, could easily be increased by the use of an even more detailed distribution of consumer goods. For example, the share of foods in total consumer expenditures (line 1) declined roughly 2.5 percentage points from 1909 to 1957, from 25.6 per cent in 1909. Since per capita expenditures in constant prices doubled in that period, the implicit ratio of the proportional increase in food outlays to the proportional increase in per capita expenditures was 0.80, significantly above the cross-section elasticity coefficient in column 5 even for total food. But on the basis of apparent civilian consumption per capita of specific food products in quantity terms, between 1909–13 and 1953–57 the consumption of margarine rose to over 6 times its initial level; of canned fruit to almost 6 times; of canned fruit juice to over 40 times; and of ice cream to about 8 times.[24] The shares of expenditures on these products in total consumption must have increased markedly, even if we allow for differential price declines relative to prices of other foods. Yet in family expenditure studies in cross-section analysis, expenditure elasticity coefficients for

24. For the underlying data see *Historical Statistics of the United States,* Series G 558, G 562, G 563, and G 577, pp. 186–87.

margarine, canned fruit, canned fruit juice, and ice cream all would surely be below 1.0.

3. Finally, we come to employment status and occupational changes and to related shifts in the distribution of income, both associated with economic growth and commented upon at length in Chapter 4. If the structure of the active labor force shifts away from individual employers and entrepreneurs and the proportion of workers with employee status increases, the distribution between consumer expenditures and savings may be affected. Individual entrepreneurs (farmers, small industrialists, merchants, etc.) presumably have a high propensity to save, since additions to their capital are a major means of attaining successful growth of their own firms; employees have no such extra incentive toward financial savings, although they may be motivated to increase their investment in man—in the way of their own education and that of their children. Similarly, a shift within the labor force from occupations with low levels of skill, training, and education to the white-collar jobs that demand more training and education is likely to affect the structure of consumer expenditures in the relevant direction; and with a growing number of managerial and professional workers demanding a minimum standard of living and associated consumer expenditures far higher than those of individual businessmen with the same income, there would be significant effects on the level and structure of consumer expenditures.

Like trends in the structure of labor force by employment status and occupational distribution, which affect both levels and structure of consumer expenditures by the members of the labor force and their families, changes in the distribution of income by size help to sustain the growth of consumer expenditures relative to savings (both conventionally defined) and to change the structure of consumption in the direction of education and other appurtenances of a higher standard of living. Other conditions being equal, a narrowing of inequality in the size distribution of income tends to raise the proportion of consumer expenditures relative to savings and to increase within total consumer expenditures the shares of consumer goods with income elasticity below 1 and to reduce the shares of consumer goods with income elasticity above 1. (A widening of income inequality would have the opposite effects, again ceteris paribus.) Thus the narrowing inequality in the size distribution of income in a number of developed countries since World War I or World War II, commented upon in Chapter 4, has probably helped to sustain the share of consumer expenditures in disposable income (and total product) and the shares of food and similar goods with low income elasticity of demand within consumer expenditures.

Other factors associated with modern economic growth and not mentioned explicitly thus far may also have affected the level and structure of ultimate consumption—in particular, changes in values that may have put a higher priority on material satisfaction in the present world, via consumption expenditures, than on other types of satisfaction relevant to the future or to another world. But the possible relevance of such factors hardly needs elaboration. The use of income for savings or ultimate consumption is an integral part of the daily life of the millions of households involved. The trends in the level and structure of such consumption are necessarily affected by the complex interplay of changes not only in conditions of living and working, in the stock of useful knowledge and technology, and in social and economic groupings and their shares in income, but also in the overriding values that set the basic pattern of life.

# 6 TRENDS IN INTERNATIONAL INTERDEPENDENCE

In Chapters 2–5 we dealt with the internal characteristics of modern economic growth of individual countries, disregarding for the most part the fact that no nation lives alone but is a member of a concert of nations and has many ties with others that bear directly on economic growth. To be sure, there was a brief discussion of international migration in Chapter 2 and of the foreign component of capital formation in Chapter 5, but we have not yet focused on the dependence of any one nation's economic growth on the rest of the world, from which it can learn, with which it can trade, and to which it can be tied through cooperation, exchange, or conflict.

Among the external sources of a nation's economic growth we may distinguish: first, the worldwide stock of useful knowledge, to which the given nation may have contributed but necessarily only in part; second, the various international flows of economic resources or goods, either in exchange as in the case of foreign trade, in borrowing and lending as in the case of capital flows, or in unilateral receipts or payments as in the case of grants or, more important, immigration and emigration; third, acts of aggression by the given nation against some other part of the world, whether such acts constitute extraction of special privileges, exercise of colonial domination, or outright annexation. This classification suggests a wide variety of international ties and of the lines of dependence of a given nation's economic growth upon the rest of the world;

285

many of these ties are beyond the competence of economic analysis, are not susceptible of measurement or firm empirical observation, and could hardly be dealt with within the compass of the present monograph. Yet all affect the rate and structure of the economic growth of developed nations, their relations to the rest of the world, and the position of the underdeveloped countries today. Even a tentative and selective discussion of these trends in the worldwide framework of economic growth is warranted despite the fact that it must necessarily rest on a more tenuous basis than that in the four preceding chapters.

## TRANSNATIONAL STOCK OF KNOWLEDGE

In Chapter 1 we argued that modern economic growth, as observable for a substantial number of currently developed countries, could best be viewed as a process based on an epochal innovation—a complex of additions to useful knowledge which raises sharply the stock of technological and social knowledge in the world, and which when exploited is the source of the high rate of aggregate increase and of the high rate of structural shifts that characterize modern economies. Whether this basic source is best described as the increasing application of science to problems of economic production and organization—with the stimulus coming from the exogenous growth of science, basic and applied—or whether the emphasis should be on changes in men's views and social institutions which, at one and the same time, stimulate the growth of science and of its useful applications is an important question, but it need not concern us here. Whatever the source, the increase in the stock of useful knowledge and the extension of its application are of the essence in modern economic growth; and the rate and locus of the increase in knowledge markedly affect the rate and structure of economic growth. If the development of steam power, first for stationary use and then for transportation, can be identified as an early installment in the modern growth of science and technology,

286

then its emergence in the late eighteenth century and spread through the nineteenth century certainly affected the rate and structure of economic growth in many developed countries; and so have electric power, the internal combustion engine, and atomic power, on the technological side, and such inventions as the modern corporation, central banking, security exchanges, and modern trade unions, on the social side.

No matter where these technological and social innovations emerge—and they are largely the product of the developed countries—the economic growth of any given nation depends upon their adoption. In that sense, whatever the national affiliation of resources used, any single nation's economic growth has its base somewhere outside its boundaries—with the single exception of the pioneering nation, and no nation remains the pioneer for long. Indeed, this dependence of a single nation's growth on the transnational stock of useful knowledge is implicit in the concept of an economic epoch—in the sense that the epoch is distinguished by a complex of major innovations common to *many* nations and hence the exclusive preserve of none. This is particularly true of modern economic growth, in that the underlying epochal innovation, however defined, implies tested additions to knowledge that are invariant to personal traits or talents and to institutional vagaries and hence are fully transmissible on a worldwide scale, in ways in which, say, handicraft techniques in traditional agriculture and industry were not, because they were based on personal knowledge of conditions specific to a given country and could be effectively transmitted only through master–apprentice relations. Given this worldwide validity and transmissibility of modern additions to knowledge, the transnational character of this stock of knowledge and the dependence on it of any single nation in the course of its modern economic growth become apparent.

One easily observable corollary of such dependence is the spread in developed nations of modern education, particularly at the higher levels that supply a rapidly growing number of workers capable of mastering modern knowledge and of adding to it. The reduction of illiteracy is one obvious indication of a country's growing capacity to utilize and absorb modern knowledge. Thus it is hardly surprising that, at the turn of the century, the four developed countries for which we have data (the United States, Canada, France, and Belgium) show illiteracy ratios of between 10 and 20 per cent, whereas the ratios for less developed countries range from 50 to 94 per cent (the lowest being for Italy and the highest for Egypt and India).[1] And the spread of basic education has been a recent process even in developed countries, as shown by the trends in the proportion of illiterates for these countries. Thus, the proportion of illiterates in 1875 among recruits into the armed forces, one of the more literate groups in the population, was as high as 24 per cent in Germany, 18 per cent in France, about 25 per cent in Belgium, and 12 per cent in the Netherlands; and it was 52 per cent in Italy and 79 per cent in Russia.[2]

Perhaps in some ways more important was the rapid rise in the proportion of population enrolled in institutions of higher education. In Germany this proportion (per 10,000 of total population) was below 4 from the 1830s to the 1860s and rose to about 16 in the 1920s; in the United States it rose from 14 in 1869/70 to 155 in 1953/54; and in Japan from 1 in 1873 to 70 in 1956.[3] Similarly spectacular rises were observed for shorter periods in other developed countries: in France (native students only) from 7 in 1900 to 34 in 1956; in the Netherlands from 6 in 1900 to 28 in 1956; and in Switzerland (native students only) from 9 in 1900/01 to 23 in 1956/57. Furthermore, within higher edu-

1. The ratios—mostly to population 15 years of age and over, although for some countries to population 10 years of age and over—are from UNESCO, "Progress of Literacy in Various Countries," *Monographs on Fundamental Education, 6* (Paris, 1953).

2. See W. S. Woytinsky, *Die Welt in Zahlen, 7* (Berlin 1928), 255.

3. These and the data in the next sentence in the text are from Friedrich Edding, "Internationale Tendenzen in der Entwicklung des Ausgaben für Schulen und Hochschulen," *Kieler Studien, 47* (Kiel, 1958).

cation, the number of students of modern specialties increased more rapidly than the total; and more advanced types increased more rapidly than the less advanced. Thus in Sweden, between 1871–75 and 1921–25 the number of students in the faculty of theology actually declined while those in the historico-mathematical, medicine, and law faculties more than tripled.[4] In the United States the number of bachelor's degrees conferred rose some 24 times from 1879/80 to 1955/56; master's degrees, some 68 times; and doctorates, about 180 times.[5]

The rapid spread of modern education must have been a basic element in increasing the capacity of developed nations to exploit and contribute to the available stock of tested and useful knowledge. It provided a common language for increasingly large groups in the developed countries and thus a widening basis for sharing in and contributing to a common body of knowledge and techniques. Insofar as proportions of literate and educated to total population rose rapidly in the developed nations and literacy and education meant sharing a body of basic and applied knowledge, for any one nation modern economic growth meant an increasing use of and participation in a wide body of knowledge that transcended national origin and attachment. While this dependence did not mean that such use and participation were subject to the decisions of others, it did mean that a given nation's growth was increasingly affected by new contributions to tested knowledge made elsewhere, just as the growth of other countries was increasingly affected by contributions to knowledge by the given nation. In short, it was dependence in free cooperation rather than in trade, competition, or conflict, although the directions of effort in additions to applied knowledge, in particular, may have reflected some specific conditions in a given nation, which may or may not have been shared with others.

Because the scientific basis became increasingly important

4. Woytinsky, *Die Welt in Zahlen*, 7, 285.
5. See Edding, "Internationale Tendenzen," p. 142+.

in the transnational complex of tested knowledge, and because the proportion of human resources in the developed countries devoted to the acquisition and mastery of such knowledge grew rapidly, a number of consequences followed for the rate and structure of modern economic growth. Clearly, the high rate of aggregate growth was associated with the capacity of this scientific knowledge to augment productivity, to increase the command of labor over resources. Furthermore, aggregate growth benefited from the easily *cumulative* character of modern tested knowledge. Handicraft skills embodied in mortal human beings cannot be accumulated as easily as modern technological knowledge embodied in quantitative formulations and innovations based on overtly measurable and testable characteristics of natural and social processes. It is the very overtness and easy embodiment of tested knowledge and of its scientific base in a variety of durable forms independent of the personal skills of human beings that make both for its easy communicability and worldwide availability, and for the steadily cumulative results.

Combined with this cumulative character of the transnational stock of tested and useful knowledge was the continuous shift in the locus of its growth from one area of knowledge to another, from one complex of basic application to another—so that the highest rates of technological and social innovations were in different areas of production and economic organization in successive periods. Our discussion in Chapter 3 noted these shifts in the locus of technological and social change from one sector to another over time and the contribution thus made to the high rate of structural shifts accompanying modern economic growth. But this statement must be repeated here, because shifts in the locus of additions to useful knowledge, like the high cumulative impact of these additions on the rate of aggregate growth, have a bearing on the dependence of any one nation's growth on the changing transnational stock of knowledge. Some consequences of this dependence can be suggested, although it is impossible here to analyze or even list them fully.

First, given the high rate of growth of both the stock of knowledge and of those nations that managed to take advantage of it and attain modern economic growth, the relative position of any given nation when it enters into modern economic growth clearly depends upon the date of entry. The later the date, the longer the delay, and the larger the unutilized accumulation of technological and social knowledge, the greater the economic inferiority to the developed nations reflected in a lower relative position in per capita income and in the command over modern economic resources. The effects of this inferior position on the rate and other characteristics of the given nation's growth once it enters into the phase of modern economic growth, are a matter for investigation.[6] One might, in general, assume that the later the entry the higher the initial rates of growth should be, reflecting the existence of a greater stock of technological and social innovation to choose from and the pressure of greater backwardness. And indeed there is some semblance of such acceleration as we move from the growth of Great Britain, to that of the United States and France, to that of Germany, then of Japan, and finally of the U.S.S.R., using as a criterion the rate of increase in per capita product. The duration of this initial period of growth and the degree to which it is sustained must also be examined, but since the cases are far too few and conditions far too varied, this inference can be viewed only as a plausible suggestion subject to further testing.

Second, if the locus of recent rapid additions to useful

6. The possible consequences of backwardness, once economic growth begins, are illuminatingly explored in Alexander Gerschenkron, *Economic Backwardness in Historical Perspective* (Cambridge, Mass., 1962), particularly in the title essay, pp. 5–30, and in the postscript, pp. 353–64, with special reference to European industrialization. For the application of these hypotheses to the case of Japan, see Henry Rosovsky, *Capital Formation in Japan, 1868–1940* (New York, 1961), Chap. 4.

knowledge and of technological and social change shifts from period to period, the timing of entry of a nation into the process of modern economic growth may induce an association with a particular phase in the progress of knowledge and technology: it may be feasible and desirable to take advantage of the most recent phase rather than of an earlier one. For example, if a nation enters its modern growth process after both railroads and motor transport have become available, it may find it feasible and desirable to take more advantage of the currently rapidly growing motor trucking facilities than of railroad transport, whose growth has occurred in the past—provided that all considerations other than current availability are in balance; and, of course, even more so if they favor the new technology in the long run. Thus, whenever alternative technologies are available, the shifting focus of technological and social change on different innovations over time means that the timing of the entry of a given nation into the process of modern economic growth may affect not only its aggregate rate of growth but also the particular technological and social choices that will be made. And this constitutes another line of dependence of a single nation's growth on the changing transnational stock of technological and social knowledge that exists outside that nation's boundaries.

The discussion so far has been overly simplified, in two ways. First, we considered the possibility of a given nation *learning* from the rest of the world and making use of the transnational stock of useful knowledge, and we directed attention only to the changes in that stock itself, to the cumulative character of its rapid growth and to the shift in the locus of the technological and social innovations from one sector to another. We ignored the original historical heritage of the given nation—its size, resources, and economic and political institutions; yet all of these modify not only the timing of entry into modern economic growth, but also the particular ways in which that nation takes advantage of the worldwide stock of knowledge—a selection process that emphasizes some items and neglects others. Such a process does, of course, allow some choice; and with the spread of modern economic growth and the tremendous increase in the stock of technological and social knowledge, the range of choice becomes wider. As we have seen, some general features of the modern growth process are observed fairly widely wherever the process occurs: for example the accelerated rate of aggregate growth, the shift away from agriculture, the changes in size and character of enterprise. Yet the precise nature of these shifts may still differ from developed nation to developed nation with respect to the relative shares of various nonagricultural industries, the relative weights of various forms of enterprise organization, and so on. Thus while modern economic growth does mean increasing participation of those nations that experience growth in the use of a common stock of knowledge, the selections made by any one nation depend not only upon time of entry but also upon the characteristics specific to that nation with respect to size, natural resources, and historical heritage. The prominent position of shipping in the economic growth of Norway, of such natural resource products as paper and iron in Sweden, and of agricultural products in Australia and New Zealand are clear illustrations; and similar distinctions can be cited for all developed countries, large and small.

Second, we discussed participation by a given country in modern economic growth as a matter of learning, by direct use of the transnational stock of technological and social knowledge mastered by the educated members of the country's population and provided with the necessary institutional and economic auspices that would supply the drive and the necessary resources. But the extent of direct use also depends partly on the possibility of trade and partly on other aspects of international relations that are dominated by political power. To put it more precisely, the possibility of foreign trade and other peaceful international flows increases the variety of choices available as to the sectors and means by which the modern economic growth of a given nation will be induced; while the possibility of aggression provides noneconomic political ways of furthering economic growth and may even induce the lagging nations to accelerate the adoption of economic modernization if only for long-term security and no matter how heavy the economic and human costs may be.

## INTERNATIONAL FLOWS OF RESOURCES AND GOODS

The international flows that, unlike those of knowledge and ideas touched upon in the preceding section, find material embodiment and can, in fact, be measured, comprise the movements of men, goods, and capital. The long-term patterns of such flows to and from the developed nations in the course of their growth since the early nineteenth century have differed from those in which developed nations contributed to and drew upon the transnational stock of knowledge. The stock of knowledge has grown at a high rate and the number of developed nations contributing to and drawing upon it has increased. The spreading utilization of this stock of knowledge is of the very essence of modern economic growth and is also involved wherever elements of modernity are introduced, even in underdeveloped countries. It is, therefore, hard to visualize any marked retardation in the spreading use of, and contributions to, the transnational stock of knowledge. This, of course, is true of the concert of nations, of all developed nations taken as a group: a single developed nation may begin to lag behind, though even then the lag is only relative to the more vigorous members of the developed group and does not necessarily imply retardation over time.

The time pattern of the international flows of resources and goods contrasts sharply with this movement: the rapid acceleration in the rate of increase of these flows that began in the 1820s was followed by the markedly disrupting effects of the two world wars of this century and of the political institutional changes that were the consequence partly of these wars, partly of the spread of modern economic growth under auspices that militated against the widening of peaceful international economic flows. The decline in the rate of increase of such flows that began with World War I, extended to the end of World War II, and only currently is being compensated for by the high rate of some of these flows since the early 1950s, is in contrast with the apparently continuous and perhaps accelerated rise in the transnational stock of useful knowledge and in its utilization by an increasing number of developed nations and even by many less developed ones.

While the pattern just suggested—marked acceleration in volume over the century preceding World War I, and reduction in this growth over the last half century—is common to the international flows of men, goods, and capital, each of these has a specific impact upon the growth of the developed countries. Hence, each is discussed separately to suggest the variations and differences in the growth patterns that they imply for different groups of developed countries.

*International Migration*—These movements have already been considered briefly in Chapter 2. A more detailed description of the time patterns is provided in Table 6.1,

TABLE 6.1

Gross Migration from Europe, and Total Intercontinental
Migration, 1846–1955
(thousands, average per year)

A. OVERSEAS EMIGRATION FROM EUROPE

| Period | Total (1) | Region of "old emigration" (northwest) (2) | Region of "new emigration" (east and south) (3) |
|---|---|---|---|
| 1. 1846–50 | 257 | 254 | 2 |
| 2. 1851–60 | 270 | 258 | 12 |
| 3. 1861–70 | 283 | 256 | 27 |
| 4. 1871–80 | 314 | 251 | 63 |
| 5. 1881–90 | 700 | 444 | 256 |
| 6. 1891–1900 | 609 | 206 | 403 |
| 7. 1901–10 | 1,238 | 288 | 950 |
| 8. 1911–15 | 1,365 | 326 | 1,039 |
| (8a. 1911–20) | (885) | (225` | (660) |
| 9. 1921–30 | 592 | 274 | 318 |
| 10. 1931–39 | 139 | 55 | 84 |
| 11. 1946–55 | 436 | 155 | 281 |

| Period | Total (1) | United States (2) | Canada (3) | Australia and New Zealand (4) | Latin America (5) | Other (6) |
|---|---|---|---|---|---|---|
| 12. 1846–50 | 318 | 250 | 49 | neg. | 11 | 8 |
| 13. 1851–60 | 339 | 260 | 31 | 3[a] | 27 | 18 |
| 14. 1861–70 | 337 | 232 | 29 | 19 | 41 | 16 |
| 15. 1871–80 | 399 | 281 | 22 | 22 | 70 | 4 |
| 16. 1881–90 | 752 | 525 | 36 | 28 | 159 | 4 |
| 17. 1891–1900 | 642 | 369 | 24 | 45 | 194 | 10 |
| 18. 1901–10 | 1,494 | 880 | 114 | 161 | 289 | 50 |
| 19. 1911–20 | 1,111 | 574 | 106 | 99 | 299 | 33 |
| 20. 1921–30 | 871 | 411 | 99 | 67 | 264 | 30 |
| 21. 1931–40 | 188 | 53 | 8 | 12 | 75 | 40 |
| 22. 1946–55[b] | 436 | 124 | 95 | 87 | 119 | 11 |

a. New Zealand only.
b. European only.
Sources: *Lines 1–10:* From Kirk, *Europe's Population in the Interwar Years*, Table 1, p. 279. Col. 2 includes the British Isles, Germany, Norway, Sweden, Denmark, France, Switzerland, and the Low Countries; col. 3 includes Italy, Austria-Hungary, Czechoslovakia, Russia (including Finland, Poland, Lithuania, and Estonia), Spain and Portugal, and the Balkans.
    *Lines 11 and 22:* from Kirk, "Major Migrations since World War II," Table 1, pp. 18–19.
    *Lines 12–21:* From W. S. and E. S. Woytinsky, *World Commerce and Governments* (New York, 1955), Table 36, p. 77. The entries are assumed to cover all immigrants in intercontinental migration.

which can be viewed as a supplement to Table 2.4; and we now emphasize the distinction between the older developed countries—in Europe and Japan—that grew without immigration and the younger countries overseas where it was a major factor.

The flows in Table 6.1 are all gross, and reference may be made to the net flows in Table 2.4 in the interpretation. But clearly the picture of the rapid acceleration in volume beginning in the 1880s (for the early rise from the 1820s to the 1850s see Table 2.4) and continuing to World War I, the sharp contraction thereafter, and the incomplete recovery in the 1950s would persist even if we dealt with net immigration. And the decline in magnitudes *proportional* to the growing population would be much greater.

However, in its bearing upon the patterns of modern economic growth studied in the preceding chapters, the cumulative and increasing volume of migration during the three quarters of a century preceding World War I is perhaps more important than the reduction thereafter. The acceleration was due partly to the easing of intercontinental transportation by steamships and of intracontinental migration in Europe—from east to west and later from south to north —by railways. But in large part it was due to the spread of economic modernization and industrialization, which by its dislocating effects on southern and eastern Europe induced emigration from the large population stocks outside the northwest region of "old" emigration.

While the older developed countries in northwestern Europe were the destination of some migrants from the eastern and southern regions, the contrast between them and North America, some countries in Latin America (particularly Argentina and Uruguay), and Australia and New Zealand, was marked. On the eve of World War I, the proportions of foreign-born to total population were as high as 22 per cent in Canada (in 1911), 15 per cent in the United States (white population only, in 1910), 30 per cent in Argentina (in 1914), 15.5 per cent in Australia (in 1921, and probably higher in 1913), and 26 per cent in New Zealand (in 1921, and probably higher a decade earlier).[7] In the United States, the population of native stock (native born of native parents) grew from 14.2 million in 1840 to 82.7 million in 1930, less than 6 times the initial number; the population of foreign stock (foreign born and native born of foreign or mixed parentage) grew from somewhat less than 3 million to over 40 million, or over 13 times the initial number; and in 1930, about a third of the country's total population was of foreign stock.[8] An even more extreme

7. The data, except for the United States, are from Walter F. Willcox, ed., *International Migrations. II. Interpretations* (New York, 1931), pp. 130–31, 151, 173, and 188. For the United States see *Historical Statistics of the United States,* Series A 51–A 58, p. 9.

8. See Simon Kuznets, "Notes on the Pattern of U.S. Economic Growth," in Edgar O. Edwards, ed., *The Nation's Economic Objectives* (Chicago, 1964), pp. 21–22.

case is represented by Argentina, until recently the country in Latin America with by far the highest per capita income. According to the census for the middle of 1914, "about three-tenths [of total population] were of foreign birth. . . . In the group of males over 20 years of age the foreign-born were 52 percent and in the federal capital, for each native Argentinian over 20 years of age, there were almost three foreign-born of like age; 72 percent of the business heads and 75 percent of the owners of business houses were of foreign birth." [9] No such rates of immigration could be found in any of the older developed countries or in Japan.

The far more rapid rate of aggregate growth of the overseas offshoots of Europe, particularly in North America but also in Oceania and in some countries of Latin America; the much greater contribution from immigration; and a variety of effects on the structure of growth that such immigration, combined usually with a higher rate of natural increase, exercises, make it important to distinguish within the developed countries these overseas offshoots from the older units. It must be remembered that among the developed, high income countries, the European offshoots—Canada, the United States, Australia, New Zealand, and possibly the Union of South Africa, Argentina, and Uruguay —loom quite large, with the United States outstanding both with respect to its total economic magnitude and its per capita income. And in a more detailed analysis of the quantitative characteristics of modern economic growth than is possible here, this distinction might suggest some significant differences in pattern, and would therefore merit careful investigation.[10] It need hardly be argued that the sharp contraction in migration to these countries overseas must have affected the pattern and structure of their growth—so that comparisons of the recent half century with the pre-World War I decades would, in a detailed analysis, be directed to a search for these effects.

9. See Willcox, *International Migrations, II,* 151.

10. Some comparisons between the United States and the older larger developed countries are drawn in Kuznets, "Notes on the Pattern of U.S. Economic Growth."

Two other observations bear upon the economic growth of the overseas offshoots of Europe. The first relates to the great power of attraction of the United States on the available supply of intercontinental migrants. In 1840, the total United States population was some 17 million; that of Latin America must have been about 30 million.[11] Yet, as Panel B of Table 6.1 shows, gross immigration to the United States over the decades preceding World War I was many times that flowing to Latin America; and the reason could hardly have been a greater relative supply of natural resources, considering the present supplies of such resources in some areas of Latin America. The reasons lay more likely in a combination of the relatively low aboriginal population density in the United States; its political stability and independence; the kinship of its original settlers with the population of northwestern Europe—the origin of "early" emigration; and its capacity to absorb, in addition, other national streams as they began to flow in later decades from Italy and Eastern Europe. Whatever the reasons, it was an extraordinary case of rapid growth of an economic giant, fed by a wide diversity of national streams from Europe, and based upon an area far from the locus of early modern economic growth in Europe.

Second, the national origins of the immigration flow to the United States, limited to be sure largely to Europe but including in earlier days slave immigration from Africa and some immigration from Asia, were far more varied than those of the immigration flows to other overseas countries. Thus, of the 4.5 million Europeans residing in Latin America in the interwar years, about 45 per cent were from Spain and Portugal and another 40 per cent from Italy.[12] The British origin of immigration to Australia and New Zealand (diluted somewhat only in the post-World War II years) is well known. Hence, to the differences among the

11. It was estimated to be 19 million in 1800 and 33 million in 1850, according to U.N., *Determinants and Consequences of Population Trends,* Table 2, p. 11.

12. See Kirk, *Europe's Population,* Table 3, p. 281.

developed offshoots of Europe in their capacity to attract overseas emigrants, we must add differences in degree of regional and national divergence of sources and in the identity of the latter. These aspects of the movement, suggesting transfer of diverse values and social patterns from the different homelands, have a possible bearing upon divergences in some aspects of economic growth among the developed overseas countries.

*Foreign Trade*—The flows among nations of goods, as distinct from claims, comprise commodities and services, which together account for the overwhelming proportion of all receipts (exports) and of all payments (imports). The other items in receipts and payments in current international transactions—factor incomes and transfers—constitute changes in claims originating from current use of income and resources rather than from capital movements, and for developed countries they are minor proportions of all receipts and payments.[13] In any case, our concern now is with flows of goods.

Here the most important finding in the present connection is the marked difference among developed countries in the proportion of total foreign trade (exports and imports added) to gross national product (or any other aggregate measure of a country's economic performance)—a difference in some ways as important as that between the old nonimmigrant and the young immigrant countries. In Table 6.2, in which the 15 developed countries are arranged in descending order of gross national product, the ratios in columns 1 and 2 tend to rise as GNP drops. The simple arithmetic means of the proportions for the first five, second five, and last five countries for commodities and services trade (column 1) are 32.5, 55.7, and 86.2 per cent respectively; for commodity trade alone (column 2) they are 24.0,

13. See Kuznets, "Quantitative Aspects: IX," App. Table 2, pp. 82–83 for data for a post-World War II period. Much of the discussion that follows is based on that paper. The major source to be referred to here is Charles P. Kindleberger, *Foreign Trade and the National Economy* (New Haven, 1962).

TABLE 6.2

Proportions of Foreign Trade to Gross National Product,
Developed Countries, Post-World War II Year

| Countries in descending order of GNP | Exports plus imports as % of GNP | | Commodities as % of commodities and services (col. 2 ÷ col. 1) |
|---|---|---|---|
| | Commodities and services (1) | Commodities only (2) | (3) |
| 1. United States | 9.6 | 7.3 | 76 |
| 2. United Kingdom | 41.7 | 30.4 | 73 |
| 3. France | 26.5 | 19.0* | 72 |
| 4. West Germany | 44.5 | 29.2* | 66 |
| 5. Canada | 40.4 | 34.3 | 85 |
| 6. Japan | 27.3 | 21.6 | 79 |
| 7. Australia | 33.6 | 30.1 | 90 |
| 8. Belgium | 65.5 | 57.5 | 88 |
| 9. Sweden | 55.4 | 49.8 | 90 |
| 10. Netherlands | 96.8 | 83.6 | 86 |
| 11. Switzerland | 60.6 | 46.4* | 77 |
| 12. Denmark | 67.3 | 53.1 | 79 |
| 13. Norway | 88.7 | 52.9 | 60 |
| 14. New Zealand | 53.0 | 46.1 | 87 |
| 15. Luxembourg | 161.5 | 157.0 | 97 |

*Sources:* All ratios in cols. 1 and 2 relate average foreign trade for 1957–59 to GNP for 1958. Except for the starred items, the data are from U.N. *Yearbook of National Accounts Statistics*, various years. For the starred items the foreign trade data are from U.N., *Yearbook of International Trade Statistics, 1960*. For details see Kuznets, "Quantitative Aspects: IX," App. Table 3, pp. 84–85. Commodities include all merchandise, nonmonetary gold, and freight and insurance income where given. Services include all other current items, except factor income and transfers.

48.5, and 71.1 per cent. To be sure, there are some deviations from the association that reflect distance from world markets or degrees of development even within the generally developed group. But the tendency for the foreign trade proportions to be the larger, the smaller the country's GNP, dominates the arrays.

The proportion of foreign trade to national product is only a crude measure of a country's dependence upon the markets and supplies of the rest of the world; for its dependence is likely to be greater if its exports and imports are concentrated in a few key sectors rather than distributed equally among all. Furthermore, the foreign trade proportion is only a crude measure of the proportional advantages that a country derives from the international division of labor, for much depends also upon the substitutability of goods imported and the internal mobility of factor inputs into the goods exported—the gains being greater with low substitutability and mobility. But barring more detailed measurement, not feasible here and in any case quite difficult, one may accept the foreign trade proportion as a rough gauge of dependence of a country's overall performance upon material flows from and to the rest of the world and of the proportional advantages that it derives from international trade.

It follows that the smaller countries must rely far more heavily on foreign trade than the larger countries. Moreover, the finding in Kuznets, "Quantitative Aspects: IX" that foreign trade proportions are positively correlated with the level of economic development as measured by per capita income, once the size factor is taken into account, lends further support to the inference that small countries can attain economic growth *only* through heavy reliance on foreign trade, as indicated by high proportions to national product—although clearly this is a necessary but not sufficient condition; whereas the larger countries can attain economic growth with much lower foreign trade proportions, so that reliance on proportionally large material flows to and from the rest of the world is not a necessary condition, although it may occur (as it did in the United Kingdom). The implication is that small countries differ from large, both in the mechanism of economic growth and in an important aspect of the structure of national product, i.e. in the proportions within various sectors of foreign and domestic contributions and drafts.

The negative correlation between foreign trade proportions and the size of the country as measured by its GNP may seem to be merely an arithmetic truism, since for any two countries the volume of bilateral trade is the same and the proportion of the latter to GNP would be inverse to the proportion of the two national product totals. But even such an arithmetic truism has economic meaning if the proportions involved are not minuscule. If in the bilateral trade of two countries, one with a GNP 50 times as large as the other, the trade flows form 1 per cent of the larger and hence 50 per cent of the smaller GNP, one may still attribute economic significance to this high proportion and ask how in the process of growth the smaller country manages to generate this relatively large volume of exports and to absorb the relatively large volume of imports. Furthermore, it can be demonstrated that the arithmetic truism for trade proportions of two countries engaged in bilateral trade does not necessarily hold for trade proportions of $n$ countries; that, given the simple and plausible assumption that the propensity to enter foreign trade for a standard unit of goods of any country is the same whether it trades with a large or small partner, the formula for differences in foreign trade proportions shows the latter to be quite insensitive to even major differences in size of GNP.[14] In other words, when we deal with trade among $n$ countries, the negative association between foreign trade proportions and size of GNP requires an explanation. It emerges from the arithmetic only if we add a crucial and specific assumption: that the probability of a unit of goods entering foreign trade becomes greater for any country when it trades with a larger country than when it trades with a partner of equal or smaller size. To put it differently, the small countries, since most of their trade is with large countries, somehow attain higher foreign trade propensities than the assumption of equal per unit foreign trade probabilities would generate.

Obviously, if the small countries are to realize advantages of specialization and economies of scale, both indispensable prerequisites to higher per capita economic performance, they *must* rely more heavily on foreign trade than the large countries, whose internal markets and volumes of domestic resources in themselves permit such specialization and scale. But this obvious comment does not reveal the possible va-

14. For the detailed analysis see Kuznets, "Quantitative Aspects: IX," pp. 7–25.

riety of specialization; nor does it hint at the problems of the geographic and commodity concentration that is much more characteristic of the exports of small countries, even those developed, than of exports of the large, developed countries. Since many small, even developed, countries trade mainly with one or two large developed units—and the disparity in size is striking—satellite relations are likely to emerge. In the general analysis of economic growth, the heavy dependence of some of the smaller developed nations —particularly those at the extreme lower end of the range —makes their growth so interwoven with that of their larger partners that one may question their independence as units for analysis. For this reason we omitted from the tables in the preceding chapters the really small developed units (like Luxembourg, included in Table 6.2 to show the extremes of the range). And even the growth of Denmark or Norway is clearly more dependent upon the larger countries with which they trade, and that of Canada is more dependent upon the United States, than is the growth of one of the larger countries upon the others—at least as far as the peaceful flows of international trade are concerned.

These comments on the far-reaching significance of the higher foreign trade proportions in the small countries for the analysis of modern economic growth, and the emphasis on the distinction between small and large countries, bear on a wide theme which cannot be pursued further here. We now turn to the trends over time in the volume of international trade and the implied long-term trends in the foreign trade proportions in the developed countries in the course of their growth.

Table 6.3 presents a summary of the volume of world foreign trade in commodities over a long period extending back to the mid-eighteenth century. Similar estimates for foreign trade including services are available for only a few countries, but they indicate that the trends are not much different from those for commodity trade alone; although the share of services in the total tends to grow, this movement is not sufficient to change the basic time pattern. Even for commodity trade the estimates for the earlier years are approximate, although the absolute volumes in current prices for the 1880s check closely with the far more elaborate estimates of the League of Nations (Panel B); and while they omit any trade that may have taken place among the less developed and more isolated parts of the world, as well as all smuggling—not inconsiderable in the eighteenth century—the omissions are unlikely to affect the broader trends.

Two major findings are suggested by Table 6.3. The first is the high rate of growth of world trade over the century between the 1820s and the onset of World War I. The rate of growth, by roughly 30-year periods, was 50 per cent per decade between 1820–30 and 1850–60 and between 1850–60 and 1880–89, and about 37 per cent per decade between 1881–85 and 1911–13. For this long period as a whole, the rate of growth was 46 per cent per decade, only slightly below that of the United States, which showed the highest rate of aggregate growth over the century; and it was distinctly higher than the rates of growth of GNP for other major developed countries, such as the United Kingdom, France, or Germany, which, for long 30-year periods, ranged between less than 20 and slightly over 30 per cent per decade. Furthermore, this high rate of growth of foreign trade between the 1820s and 1913 was in sharp contrast to the much lower rate of slightly over 10 per cent shown for the period back to the mid-eighteenth century; and it dropped sharply over the five decades that followed 1913, to about 21 per cent per decade—despite the remarkably high rate for the 1950s (see Panel C, line 2, column 5). Even if we omit the World War I interval, for the period from 1928 to 1960 the rate of growth is only 27 per cent per decade, or six-tenths of the rate that prevailed from the 1820s to 1913.

Second, the share in world foreign trade of the few developed countries has been high throughout the long period since the 1820s. Northwest Europe and the United States accounted for six tenths in 1820–30 and about two thirds in 1880–89 (Panel A, line 20); the share of the same countries, with Canada and Australia added, was roughly two thirds

## TABLE 6.3

### World Foreign Trade and Its Distribution by Countries, Long Periods

#### A. 18TH CENTURY TO 1880-89, MULHALL DATA

| | 1720, 1750, 1780 (1) | 1820, 1830 (2) | 1830, 1840 (3) | 1840, 1850 (4) | 1850, 1860 (5) | 1860, 1870 (6) | 1870, 1880 (7) | 1880, 1889 (8) |
|---|---|---|---|---|---|---|---|---|
| 1. World trade, 1865–85 prices (millions of £) | 153 | 315 | 410 | 662 | 1,058 | 1,616 | 2,483 | 3,497 |
| 2. Rate of growth per decade, successive periods (%) | | 10.1 | 30.2 | 61.5 | 59.8 | 52.7 | 53.7 | 43.4 |
| *Shares of selected countries in world total, current prices (%)* | | | | | | | | |
| 3. United Kingdom | 14.1 | 21.6 | 20.8 | 20.1 | 22.7 | 25.1 | 24.0 | 22.4 |
| 4. France | 9.7 | 9.9 | 10.8 | 11.4 | 11.3 | 10.8 | 10.8 | 10.2 |
| 5. Germany | 10.2 | 11.5 | 10.2 | 8.8 | 8.6 | 9.2 | 9.7 | 10.3 |
| 6. Holland and Belgium | 4.4 | 7.2 | 7.6 | 7.6 | 6.6 | 6.0 | 7.0 | 8.5 |
| 7. Switzerland | 1.4 | 1.9 | 1.9 | 2.1 | 2.2 | 2.0 | 2.0 | 1.9 |
| 8. Scandinavia | 2.4 | 1.9 | 2.0 | 2.1 | 2.2 | 2.0 | 2.1 | 2.1 |
| 9. Italy | 3.6 | 4.6 | 5.0 | 4.9 | 4.0 | 3.2 | 3.0 | 2.9 |
| 10. Austria-Hungary | 2.8 | 3.3 | 3.8 | 3.7 | 3.3 | 3.5 | 3.6 | 3.1 |
| 11. Spain | 10.4 | 2.3 | 1.7 | 1.5 | 1.5 | 1.8 | 1.7 | 1.7 |
| 12. Russia | 9.4 | 6.7 | 6.4 | 5.3 | 4.0 | 4.0 | 4.5 | 3.9 |
| 13. Other Europe | 4.4 | 2.6 | 2.4 | 2.7 | 2.7 | 2.7 | 2.6 | 2.4 |
| 14. Europe | 72.6 | 73.5 | 72.6 | 70.2 | 69.0 | 70.3 | 71.0 | 69.4 |
| 15. United States | (1.0) | 6.0 | 6.3 | 7.3 | 8.3 | 8.3 | 8.8 | 9.8 |
| 16. Latin America | 11.0 | 8.7 | 8.5 | 8.4 | 7.4 | 6.3 | 5.7 | 5.1 |
| 17. British colonies | (1.6) | 1.6 | 2.9 | 4.5 | 6.1 | 6.3 | 6.3 | 7.7 |
| 18. India | 7.3 | 2.8 | 3.0 | 3.5 | 3.7 | 3.7 | 3.7 | 3.8 |
| 19. Others | 7.0 | 7.3 | 6.8 | 6.1 | 5.7 | 5.1 | 4.4 | 4.2 |
| 20. Sum of lines 3–8 and 15 | 43.2 | 60.0 | 59.6 | 59.4 | 61.7 | 63.4 | 64.4 | 65.2 |

| | 1881–85 (1) | 1886–90 (2) | 1891–95 (3) | 1896–1900 (4) | 1901–05 (5) | 1906–10 (6) | 1911–13 (7) | 1913 (8) |
|---|---|---|---|---|---|---|---|---|
| 1. World trade, 1913 prices (billions of $) | 15.69 | 18.13 | 19.97 | 22.54 | 27.52 | 32.88 | 39.07 | 40.50 |
| 2. Rate of growth per decade, decade periods (%) | | 42.0 | 27.3 | 24.2 | 37.8 | 45.9 | 47.6 | |
| *Shares of selected countries in world trade, current prices (%)* | | | | | | | | |
| 3. United Kingdom | 19.1 | 18.5 | 18.0 | 17.5 | 16.4 | 12.2 | 14.1 | 42.2 |
| 4. France | 10.7 | 10.0 | 9.2 | 8.5 | 7.6 | 7.6 | 7.5 | 7.4 |
| 5. Germany | 10.4 | 10.9 | 11.0 | 11.9 | 11.6 | 12.1 | 12.2 | 12.3 |
| 6. Holland and Belgium | 8.5 | 9.8 | 10.2 | 11.0 | 11.4 | 11.1 | 11.1 | 11.0 |
| 7. Switzerland | (2.0) | 2.0 | 1.9 | 1.9 | 1.7 | 1.7 | 1.6 | 1.6 |
| 8. Scandinavia | 2.2 | 2.4 | 2.6 | 2.8 | 2.8 | 2.6 | 2.5 | 2.7 |
| 9. Italy | 3.3 | 3.1 | 2.6 | 2.8 | 2.8 | 3.1 | 3.0 | 3.0 |
| 10. Austria-Hungary | 3.8 | 3.5 | 3.7 | 3.6 | 3.5 | 3.3 | 3.2 | 3.1 |
| 11. Spain | 1.7 | 2.0 | 2.0 | 1.7 | 1.5 | 1.2 | 1.1 | 1.1 |
| 12. Russia | 3.7 | 3.5 | 3.4 | 3.6 | 3.5 | 3.6 | 3.7 | 3.7 |
| 13. United States | 10.0 | 9.7 | 10.5 | 10.2 | 10.5 | 10.3 | 10.1 | 10.5 |
| 14. Canada | 1.4 | 1.4 | 1.5 | 1.7 | 2.0 | 2.2 | 2.6 | 2.9 |
| 15. Australia | 1.9 | 1.8 | 1.8 | 1.8 | 1.5 | 1.7 | 1.8 | 1.8 |
| 16. Sum of lines 3–8 and 13 | 62.9 | 63.3 | 63.4 | 63.8 | 62.0 | 57.6 | 59.1 | 59.7 |
| 17. Sum of lines 14, 15, and 16 | 66.4 | 66.5 | 66.7 | 67.3 | 65.5 | 61.5 | 63.5 | 64.4 |

## TABLE 6.3—Continued

### c. 1913 TO 1960, UNITED NATIONS AND DEWHURST DATA

| | 1913 (1) | 1928 (2) | 1937 (3) | 1950 (4) | 1958 (1960 for lines 1 and 2) (5) |
|---|---|---|---|---|---|
| 1. Index of volume of world exports, 1913 = 100 | 100 | 113 | 114 | 131 | 244 |
| 2. Rate of growth per decade, successive periods (%) | | 8.5 | 1.0 | 11.3 | 86.0 |
| *Shares of selected countries in world trade, current prices (%)* | | | | | |
| 3. United Kingdom and Ireland | 15.5 | 13.7 | 14.1 | | 9.3 |
| 4. France | 7.3 | 6.1 | 4.8 | | 5.0 |
| 5. Germany | 12.1 | 9.3 | 8.3 | | 7.5 |
| 6. Holland and Belgium | 6.7 | 5.4 | 6.0 | | 6.3 |
| 7. Switzerland | 1.5 | 1.4 | 1.3 | | 1.5 |
| 8. Scandinavia | 2.6 | 3.2 | 4.1 | | 4.2 |
| 9. Italy | 2.9 | 2.8 | 2.3 | | 2.6 |
| 10. Spain | 1.1 | 1.5 | 0.5 | | 0.6 |
| 11. Rest of Western Europe | 2.1 | 2.3 | 2.5 | | 2.1 |
| 12. Western Europe | 51.8 | 45.7 | 43.9 | | 39.1 |
| 13. North America | 12.9 | 17.3 | 16.0 | | 20.0 |
| 14. Oceania | 2.4 | 2.8 | 2.9 | | 2.5 |
| 15. Latin America | 7.5 | 8.6 | 8.4 | | 9.0 |
| 16. Africa | 3.6 | 4.4 | 5.4 | | 6.0 |
| 17. Asia, non-Communist | 9.0 | 12.8 | 15.9 | | 11.7 |
| 18. Communist bloc | 12.8 | 8.3 | 7.4 | | 11.7 |
| 19. Sum of lines 3–8, 13, and 14 | 61.0 | 59.2 | 57.5 | | 56.3 |

*Sources: Panel A*

The volumes in current prices, total and for the various countries, are from Michael G. Mulhall, *The Dictionary of Statistics* (London, 1892), "Commerce," p. 128. For lines 3–20 entries are averages of percentage shares calculated for each year shown in the column headings. The conversion to constant prices was by means of the Rousseaux indexes for 1820–89, extrapolated back to 1720, 1750, and 1780 by the Schumpeter-Gilboy indexes (within the latter the consumer goods index was weighted

0.8 and producer goods index 0.2). For these price indexes see Mitchell and Deane, *Abstract of British Historical Statistics*, pp. 468–69 and 471–73. The rates of growth in line 2 were calculated for the periods between midpoints of spans shown in column headings: the first period was 7.5 decades (from 1750 to 1825); the last was 0.95 decades (from 1875 to 1884 1/2); and all other periods were single decades.

*Panel B*

The source, except as indicated below, is League of Nations, *Industrialization and Foreign Trade* (Princeton, 1945), pp. 157–59 and 166–67. For a number of countries the total volume of trade (imports plus exports), not given directly in the basic source, was extrapolated for the missing quinquennia.

*Line 6:* For Holland, the estimate for 1881–85 was extrapolated from the total given for 1886–90 by the ratio of 1885 + 1890 to that of 1880 + 1885, as given in W. S. and E. S. Woytinsky, *World Commerce*, Table 21, pp. 50–51. For Belgium, the totals for years before 1901–05 were similarly extrapolated from data in the same source.

*Line 7:* The share for 1881–85 was assumed to be 2.0 per cent, similar to that in 1886–90.

*Line 8:* The data for Sweden are from the basic source. Those for Denmark for 1913 are from J. F. Dewhurst and associates, *Europe's Needs and Resources* (New York, 1961), App. 20–1, Tables A and B, pp. 1142–43 and were extrapolated back by the series in Kjeld Bjerke, "National Product of Denmark, 1870–1952," in Kuznets, ed., *Income and Wealth, Series V*, Table XII, p. 149. For Norway, the 1913 figure was also taken from Dewhurst and extrapolated back by the series in Woytinsky, *Welt in Zahlen, 5*, 181.

*Line 11:* Extrapolation back of 1901 is by the series in ibid., p. 180.

*Line 14:* Data are from Penelope Hartland, "Canadian Balance of Payments since 1868," in Parker, ed., *Trends in the American Economy in the Nineteenth Century*, Table 3, pp. 725–26 and Table A-2, p. 749. Comparison of these figures with those in Kenneth Buckley, *Capital Formation in Canada, 1896–1930* (Toronto, 1955), Table G, p. 134, which cover the period from 1901 to 1930, and of the latter with the League of Nation's estimates for the 1920s indicates that the Hartland totals are comparable with those of the League of Nations and can be used directly.

*Line 15:* Extrapolation back of 1906–10 is by the series in Butlin, *Australian Domestic Product*, Table 247, pp. 410–11; Table 248, pp. 413–14; Table 256, p. 436; Table 257, p. 437; Table 258, p. 438; and Table 262, p. 441.

*Panel C*

*Lines 1 and 2:* 1913 to 1950, from Ingvar Svennilson, *Growth and Stagnation in the European Economy* (Geneva, 1954), Table A.58, p. 292; 1950 to 1960, from U.N., *World Economic Survey, 1962: The Developing Countries in World Trade* (New York, 1963), Table 1-1, pp. 1–2.

*Lines 3–18:* From Dewhurst, *Europe's Needs*, App. 20–1, Tables A and B, pp. 1142–43. Other Western Europe (line 11) includes Austria, Finland, Iceland, Portugal, and Greece. The Communist bloc (line 18) includes Eastern Europe, U.S.S.R., Mainland China, Mongolia, North Korea, North Vietnam, and East Germany (the last only after 1937). The figures for 1913 are estimates for the interwar territory; figures for other years are for boundaries as of the date shown.

between 1881–85 and 1913 (Panel B, line 17); and it was only in the post-World War I period that the share of these countries (which excluded Japan) declined slightly but significantly (Panel C, line 19). Of course, the gross product of the few developed countries constituted a sizable proportion of total world output; but it may be plausibly inferred that their proportion of world trade was significantly higher, so that their propensity to engage in foreign trade has always been significantly greater than that of the less developed countries.

Obvious reasons can be adduced to suggest why developed countries would be more able and prone to engage in foreign trade than the less developed, but this inference is further supported by the finding, in Table 7.1 that the share in the total output of the world (GDP) assignable to the United States, Canada, Northwest Europe, Australia, and New Zealand, could be set in 1958 at roughly 51.5 per cent, whereas their share in world trade in 1958 was 56.3 per cent (Table 6.3, Panel C, line 19, column 5). Thus even in the late 1950s the share of the developed countries in world trade was a tenth higher than their share in world output —despite the inclusion of the United States, with its low foreign trade proportion (partly because of size) and with a product that alone was about 35 per cent of the world total. If this was the situation in the late 1950s, after a decline in the share of the developed countries in world trade and, more important, after decades of much faster aggregate growth in the developed countries than in the rest of the world, the greater foreign trade propensity of the developed countries, *relative* to their product, than of the rest of the world must have been even more marked in the past—and increasingly so as we move back toward the middle or second quarter of the nineteenth century.

In view of the importance of foreign trade in the functioning and growth of the developed countries in particular, it is of interest to consider the trends over time, at least in the foreign trade proportions. The combination of the high rate of growth of world foreign trade from the 1820s to

1913, thereafter dropping sharply, with the constant or rising share of developed countries in world trade suggests that the foreign trade proportions in these countries should have risen during the nineteenth and early twentieth centuries and declined after World War I. But broad comparisons of the growth rates of world trade, even when accompanied by shares of individual countries in current price volumes (as in Table 6.3) are not sufficient for a clear picture of the trends in the foreign trade proportions in individual developed countries. These can be shown only by detailed comparisons of foreign trade volumes with aggregate product for as many developed countries and over as long a period as data will permit.

Such comparisons are assembled in Appendix Table I of Paper X in the series "Quantitative Aspects of the Economic Growth of Nations," and a summary of the major results is given in Table 6.4. Our discussion will center on trends in the proportion of *commodity* foreign trade to aggregate product (different totals which, however, yield fairly similar results) in current prices, for which most data are available, and we shall refer to the proportion without any specifying adjective. At relevant points we shall comment on earlier periods not covered in Table 6.4, and on the proportions available for totals in constant prices or for trade including services.

1. For those older countries with records going back to periods before their economic modernization and industrialization, the foreign trade proportions in these early periods were much lower than those attained during the subsequent economic growth. Thus for Great Britain, according to Deane and Cole, Table 20, p. 80, and Table 13, p. 44, the rates of growth for the eighteenth century were about 9 per cent per decade for national income and about 16.5 per cent for foreign trade. It follows that if the foreign trade proportion at the beginning of the nineteenth century was about 25 per cent (it was 27.4 per cent for the United Kingdom in 1797–1805 and after some fluctuations rose to over 40 per cent by World War I), it would have been about

311

## TABLE 6.4

Proportions of Foreign Trade to National Product, Individual Developed Countries, Long Periods

| | Early Phases | | Pre-World War I | | 1920s | | 1950s | |
|---|---|---|---|---|---|---|---|---|
| | Date (1) | Proportion (%) (2) | Date (3) | Proportion (%) (4) | Date (5) | Proportion (%) (6) | Date (7) | Proportion (%) (8) |
| *A. Based on Volumes in Current Prices* | | | | | | | | |
| 1. *United Kingdom (GNP)* | | | | | | | | |
| a. Commodities | 1837–45 | 21.6 | 1909–13 | 43.5 | 1924–28 | 38.1 | 1957–63 | 30.4 |
| b. Commodities and services | 1837–45 | 26.0 | 1909–13 | 51.5 | | | | |
| 2. *France, Commodities* | | | | | | | | |
| a. Proportion to NNP | 1859 | 21.9 | 1908–10 | 35.2 | | | | |
| b. Proportion to physical product[a] | 1845–54 | 18.0 | 1905–13 | 53.7 | 1920–24 | 51.3 | 1957–63 | 41.2 |
| 3. *Germany, Commodities, proportion to net total uses*[b] | 1872–79 | 36.7 | 1910–13 | 38.3 | 1925–29 | 31.4 | 1955–59 | 35.1 |
| 4. *Italy (GNP)* | | | | | | | | |
| a. Commodities | 1861–70 | 20.6 | 1911–13 | 28.1 | 1925–29 | 26.3 | 1957–63 | 25.0 |
| b. Commodities and services | 1861–70 | 23.0 | 1911–13 | 33.8 | 1925–29 | 30.4 | | |
| 5. *Denmark (GDP), commodities* | 1870–79 | 45.6 | 1910–14 | 61.6 | 1921–29 | 57.3 | 1957–63 | 52.6 |
| 6. *Norway (GDP), commodities and services* | 1865–74 | 55.5 | 1905–14 | 69.2 | 1920–29 | 63.5 | 1947–56 | 77.4 |
| 7. *Sweden (GDP), commodities* | 1861–70 | 27.7 | 1911–13 | 40.4 | 1921–30 | 31.9 | 1957–63 | 36.5 |
| 8. *United States (GNP)* | | | | | | | | |
| a. Commodities | 1834–43 | 12.9 | 1904–13 | 11.0 | 1919–28 | 10.8 | 1954–63 | 7.9 |
| b. Commodities and services | 1834–43 | 14.5 | 1904–13 | 12.2 | 1919–28 | 12.4 | 1954–63 | 9.3 |

| | | | | | | | | |
|---|---|---|---|---|---|---|---|---|
| **9. Canada (GNP)** | | | | | | | | |
| a. Commodities | 1870–80 | 30.9 | 1911–13 | 32.2 | 1926–29 | 41.5 | 1956–60 | 31.2 |
| b. Commodities and services | | | 1911–13 | 35.9 | 1926–29 | 50.0 | 1956–60 | 36.8 |
| **10. Australia (GNP)** | | | | | | | | |
| a. Commodities | 1861–70 | 40.0 | 1911–13 | 38.9 | 1924/25–28/29 | 35.8 | 1956/57–62/63 | 27.7 |
| b. Commodities including gold and species | 1861–70 | 53.4 | 1911–13 | 41.9 | 1924/25–28/29 | 36.8 | 1956/57–62/63 | 27.9 |
| **11. Japan (GDP)** | | | | | | | | |
| a. Commodities | 1878–87 | 10.3 | 1908–13 | 29.5 | 1918–27 | 35.5 | 1950–56 | 18.8 |
| b. Commodities and services | 1878–87 | 13.1 | 1908–13 | 33.2 | 1918–27 | 41.0 | 1950–56 | 21.4 |

*B. Based on Volumes in Constant Prices[c]*

| | | | | | | | | |
|---|---|---|---|---|---|---|---|---|
| **12. United Kingdom** | | | | | | | | |
| a. 1880 prices | 1837–45 | 19.4 | 1909–13 | 46.4 | 1924–28 | 46.5 | 1957–63 | 60.3 |
| b. 1913 prices | | | 1909–13 | 44.1 | | | | |
| **13. France** | | | | | | | | |
| a. Proportion to NNP, 1901–10 prices | | | 1901–10, 1911 and 1913 | 28.2 | | | | |
| b. Proportion to NNP, 1938 prices | 1871–80 | 28.3 | 1911 and 1913 | 26.7 | | | | |
| c. Proportion to physical product, 1905–13 prices | 1875–84 | 48.2 | 1905–13 | 53.7 | 1925–29 | 62.2 | 1955–58 | 28.6 |
| **14. Germany, 1913 prices** | 1850–59 | 17.1 | 1910–13 | 38.7 | 1925–29 | 34.9 | 1955–58 | 64.6 |
| **15. Italy, 1913 prices** | 1872 | 13.2 | 1913 | 27.9 | 1925–29 | 32.2 | 1955–59 | 32.4 |
| **16. Denmark, 1912–13 prices** | 1875–76 | 53.6 | 1912–13 | 63.7 | 1923–24 and 1928–29 | 73.8 | 1957–63 / 1955–58 | 39.8 / 61.4 |
| **17. Norway, 1938 prices** | 1865–74 | 32.0 | 1905–14 | 49.3 | 1920–29 | 48.9 | 1947–58 | 48.8 |
| **18. Sweden, 1913 prices** | 1864 | 28.2 | 1911–13 | 40.1 | 1926–30 | 41.5 | 1957–63 | 38.4 |

TABLE 6.4—Continued

| | Early Phases | | Pre-World War I | | 1920s | | 1950s | |
|---|---|---|---|---|---|---|---|---|
| | Date (1) | Proportion (%) (2) | Date (3) | Proportion (%) (4) | Date (5) | Proportion (%) (6) | Date (7) | Proportion (%) (8) |
| 19. *United States*, 1913 prices | 1834–43 | 12.4 | 1904–13 | 10.9 | 1919–28 | 11.6 | 1954–63 | 10.9 |
| 20. *Canada* | | | | | | | | |
| a. 1900 prices | 1870–79 | 30.4 | 1910–14 | 38.0 | 1926–30 | 54.1 | | |
| b. 1949 prices | | | | | 1926–30 | 42.9 | 1956–60 | 36.6 |
| 21. *Japan*, 1934–36 prices | 1879–87 | 9.9 | 1908–13 | 30.8 | 1918–27 | 36.3 | | |

a.  Physical product, used for lines 2b and 13c, is the sum of value added in agriculture and manufacturing (including mining and handicrafts, and some construction).

b.  Net total uses, used for lines 3 and 14, is the sum of expenditures on private consumption, government consumption, and net domestic capital formation.

c.  Commodity trade only, except in Norway and Japan for which services are included.

*Source:* Based on Kuznets, "Quantitative Aspects: X," Appendix Table I. In several countries, particularly in Germany, territorial coverage differs for successive dates.

Initials in the stubs indicate the national product variant used (GNP—gross national product; GDP—gross domestic product; NNP—net national product).

half that in the early eighteenth century. For France, the trade proportion before the early 1850s, when modern growth can be assumed to have begun, and back to the 1820s averaged somewhat over 10 per cent, and it rose to above 20 per cent in the 1850s and climbed to 35 per cent in the period preceding World War I. For Germany, Michael G. Mulhall's estimates suggest a foreign trade proportion of about 13 per cent in 1840 (using the estimates in *The Dictionary of Statistics* for both income and commodity foreign trade), whereas the proportion based on the same set of estimates was 38 per cent in the 1870s and 35 per cent in the 1880s. For Italy, according to the Mulhall series, the foreign trade proportion was 10 per cent in 1830, 16 per cent in 1860, and 19.5 per cent in 1894 (the latter quite close to the modern estimates). In the case of Japan, which shifted from relative isolation to participation in world trade, the foreign trade proportion for the earliest decade available, 1878–87, was only 10 per cent.

While such relatively low foreign trade proportions prevailed before economic modernization in the older, eventually developed countries of Europe and elsewhere, two exceptions should be noted. First, the countries that began their development under the autarkic conditions of Communist regimes tended to show lower foreign trade proportions throughout the period of forced economic modernization and industrialization than in the earlier and freer periods. The proportion of exports to national income in Russia was estimated to be 10.4 per cent in 1913, whereas it was 3.5 per cent at its highest (in 1930) in the U.S.S.R. and ranged around 2 per cent in the 1950s.[15] The foreign trade proportion for Communist China is also probably lower than that for normal times in pre-Communist China. Second, for the offshoots of Europe overseas, which grew to be major and important members of the group of developed countries but began as small, essentially trade outposts of

15. See Franklyn D. Holzman, "Foreign Trade," in Bergson and Kuznets, eds., *Economic Trends in the Soviet Union*, Table VII-3, p. 290.

the European major powers, the early periods, before there was any substantial growth of domestic output, may have been characterized by high foreign trade proportions— possibly higher than those attained in later periods when the growth of domestic output far outpaced that of foreign trade. This observation also bears upon the long-term trends in foreign trade proportions in these young overseas countries in their process of growth as contrasted with corresponding trends in the older countries.

2. In all seven developed European countries and Japan in Panel A of Table 6.4, the foreign trade proportions (excluding or including services where available) rise from the earlier date to World War I: Germany is the one country in which this rise is slight, probably because the period is short; the proportions based on volumes in constant prices reaching back to 1850–59 more than double (compare lines 3 and 14). And the proportions based on volumes in constant prices rise too, except in France (line 13a) for which the period covered is also short. Finally, for Belgium and the Netherlands, we inferred trends in the foreign trade proportions indirectly. We found that the decade rate of growth of trade per capita, in constant prices, in Belgium was 36 per cent for 1870–1913 and in the Netherlands 40 per cent for 1850–80 and 31 per cent for 1880–1910; and product per capita most likely did not grow over these periods at such high rates. Indeed, using approximate growth rates for per capita product, we estimated that the foreign trade proportions (based on volumes in constant prices) either doubled or more than doubled in the two countries over the four or six decades preceding 1913.

In short, we have a firm basis for asserting that the trends in the trade proportions of the older developed countries in the period before World War I were generally and significantly upward, not downward.[16]

16. For a somewhat different view see Karl W. Deutsch and Alexander Eckstein, "National Industrialization and the Declining Share of the International Economic Sector, 1890–1959," *World Politics*, *13* (January 1961) and Kindleberger, *Foreign Trade*, pp. 179–83. The declining-share thesis seems puzzling in view of the evidence in the

3. The findings for the younger overseas countries are quite different. In the United States and Australia the foreign trade proportions decline slightly from the nineteenth century to World War I (lines 8a and 10a); as do the proportions including services for the former, and including gold and species for the latter (lines 8b and 10b), and the commodity trade proportion based on volumes in constant prices for the United States (line 19). In Canada the trade proportion rises slightly when based on volumes in current prices (line 9a) and somewhat more when based on volumes in constant prices (line 20a). The record is mixed, but it is clear that the proportions for these younger overseas countries do *not* show the consistent, significant upward trend from the nineteenth century to World War I that we found in the proportions for the developed countries of Europe and for Japan.

4. Attempts to establish long-term trends in the foreign trade proportions after 1913 run into difficulties caused by the two world wars and their immediate aftermaths and by the great depression of the 1930s. We therefore concentrate on the 1920s and late 1950s as the periods least affected, and then allow roughly for the effects of disturbances in other subperiods on the average levels.

Between the decade before World War I and the late 1920s, the foreign trade proportion declined in eight of the eleven countries in Panel A, with barely a drop in a ninth, the United States (line 8a), and it rose in only two: Canada (lines 9a and 9b) and Japan (lines 11a and 11b). But most of the declines were minor; and in the United Kingdom, France, and Denmark, the shift from current to constant prices converts the declines into rises (see lines 12a, 13b, 13c, and 16). One may thus conclude that, at least for the proportions based on volumes in current prices (for which we

---

text. It may be that these authors did not consider the longer span before World War I or draw any distinction between the older developed countries and the younger countries overseas. For a critical comment on the declining-share thesis see Robert E. Lipsey, *Price and Quantity Trends in the Foreign Trade of the United States* (National Bureau of Economic Research, 1963), pp. 36–40.

have the most evidence), the levels in the late 1920s were not much below those preceding World War I. This means, of course, that the *rises* in these proportions, characteristic of the older developed countries in the decades preceding World War I, had ceased.

When we shift to the late 1950s, the declines in foreign trade proportions, again largely in current prices, become more prominent in some major countries. This is true for the United Kingdom (line 1a), France (line 2b), Italy (line 4a), Denmark (line 5), the United States (lines 8a and 8b), Australia (line 10a), and Japan (lines 11a and 11b). And in all these countries the levels were lower in the late 1950s than in the pre-World War I period. In several countries in which the foreign trade proportion for volumes in current prices drops significantly in the late 1950s, the proportion based on volumes in constant prices does not: in the United Kingdom (line 12b), France (line 13c), and Italy (line 15). But since we should place more confidence in the proportions based on volumes in current prices, we may conclude that, with few exceptions, these proportions were significantly lower in the late 1950s than in the period just preceding World War I.

These findings of declines in foreign trade proportions after 1913, at least for totals in current prices (our evidence on constant price volumes is too limited so far)—moderate and not general between pre-World War I and the 1920s and more marked and general between pre-World War I or the 1920s and the late 1950s—would, of course, have been magnified if we had dealt with all five decades that have elapsed since 1913, rather than with the selected favorable periods of the late 1920s and the late 1950s. During the fifty years since 1913 a full decade was absorbed by the two world wars; another decade by the depression: and perhaps a third decade by the two immediate postwar recovery periods, and a quinquennium is only a moderate allowance for recovery, especially for countries that participated in the wars. This ratio of at least three disrupted decades—disrupted particularly with respect to foreign trade flows—

to a total of five, could hardly be matched in any five decades within the long period from the 1820s to 1913. Obviously, if with the selection of the more favorable periods in the late 1920s and late 1950s, we still find a general and substantial decline in the foreign trade proportions, particularly when we compare the pre-World War I decade with the late 1950s, this decline would be far more marked if the *full* period of the five decades following 1913 were included—wars, depression, and all.

The three broad conclusions suggested by the evidence above—the marked rise in the foreign trade proportions in the old developed countries before World War I, the absence of such a general rise in the proportions for the young overseas countries even before World War I, and the marked decline in the foreign trade proportions in the period since 1913—can be explained. But although the underlying factors can be identified, their relative and shifting weights do not admit of measurement and analysis.

The long-term changes in the foreign trade proportions in the course of economic growth may be viewed as the outcome of competition between the factors that induce growth of domestic output and those that induce growth of foreign trade flows. If then we ask why the proportions rose so markedly over the decades before World War I in the old developed countries, we must identify the factors that were more effective in inducing growth of foreign trade than of domestic output. First, the period was dominated by a great revolution in transportation, particularly of commodities, with the development of steam railroads and ocean transportation. Second, it witnessed a policy decision by the United Kingdom, the economic leader of the time, to foster international division of labor and freer trade and thus serve as the workshop of the world. Third, at least until the reversal in the last quarter of the nineteenth century there was a marked relaxation of trade barriers. Finally, with the new transportation facilities, there were the opening of the West in the United States and similar developments in Canada, Argentina, and Australia leading to European

specialization in industry; and there was a continuous absorption of previously closed areas into the network of world
trade (of which Japan was a conspicuous case, but not
unique). One could easily argue that these factors should
have made for rising trade proportions—particularly in the
older developed countries in Europe, where, because of
contiguous boundaries, even steam railroads made for a
marked expansion of foreign trade in addition to domestic
trade; where steam ocean transportation strengthened ties
with countries overseas; and where aggregate growth of
domestic output was kept down by losses of population and
labor force through emigration or a low rate of natural increase. The failure of these international trade-inducing factors to produce an upward trend in the foreign trade proportions of the young developed countries overseas may
have been due partly to the young countries' much higher
rates of domestic growth—bolstered by immigration and
high rates of natural increase—and partly to the fact that
the effect of the transport revolution may have been even
greater on the growth of domestic output than on foreign
trade. This probably was the case with the effect of steam
railroads on such continental mass countries as the United
States and Canada—and possibly even Australia, once it
ceased to be a trading outpost and entered a period of
rapid growth in immigration and population.

If the foreign trade proportions declined after 1913, while
the volumes of international trade continued to grow despite
wars and depression, the implication is that the aggregate
outputs of the developed countries were growing at rates
well above those of foreign trade. This finding, combined
with what we observed for the pre-1913 experience, indicates
that the retardation in the rate of growth of foreign trade
after 1913 was far more precipitous than that (if any) in the
rate of growth of aggregate output. And the further implication is that the major changes that characterized the post-
1913 period—world wars, the emergence of new autarkic
nations, and a widespread and prolonged world depression
—had a far more disturbing and retarding effect on foreign

trade than on national output. This, of course, is self-evident in the case of the Communist countries: their policies would affect the foreign trade flows of the former trade partners of Russia and China far more immediately and drastically than they would the domestic outputs of these partners. As for world wars, their disruption of foreign trade flows and ties is obviously far more profound than that of national output and the capacity to produce; and the recovery of such flows after a war to secularly higher levels is a more remote possibility than a similar recovery of domestic output. Even the effects of a prolonged depression are likely to be channeled, by policy design, into reduction of foreign trade volumes in order to sustain domestic output. It is hardly a surprise that the *international* dislocations that marked the post-1913 period depressed the *international* flows to a much greater extent than the *national* economic activity of the developed nations; and thus resulted in a marked lowering of the foreign trade proportions.

*International Flows of Capital*—The international flows of capital with which we are concerned here arise from the movements of merchandise, bullion and species, services (business and personal, such as tourism), immigrant remittances and funds, and factor incomes—excluding changes in international claims that may originate in war reparations or similar sources exogenous to normal economic intercourse among nations. And we are interested both in the time pattern of such international capital flows over the long period since the early nineteenth century and in their changing relative importance to the developed nations, both the main creditors and the main debtors among them.

Table 6.5 summarizes information relevant to the time pattern of international capital flows. Some of the data also bear upon the magnitude of these flows relative to trade and output, at least for the creditor nations.

Gross foreign investments outstanding are shown in lines 1–4 of Panel A for only three creditor nations. But these

## TABLE 6.5

### Foreign Capital Investments and the Shares of Major Countries, Long Periods

#### A. MOVEMENTS OF FOREIGN CAPITAL BEFORE WORLD WAR I, THREE MAJOR CREDITOR COUNTRIES
(ABSOLUTE FIGURES IN BILLIONS OF $)

| | Circa 1874 (1) | Circa 1880 (2) | Circa 1890 (3) | Circa 1900 (4) | Begin. 1914 (5) |
|---|---|---|---|---|---|
| *Gross foreign investment outstanding* | | | | | |
| 1. United Kingdom | 4.6 | 5.8 | 9.5 | 11.7 | 19.6 |
| 2. France | na | 3.0 | 4.0 | 5.6 | 9.0 |
| 3. Germany | na | 1.2 | 2.8 | 3.4 | 5.6 |
| 4. Total, lines 1–3 | 6.0 | 10.0 | 16.3 | 20.7 | 34.2 |
| 5. Successive differences in line 4 | | 4.0 | 6.3 | 4.4 | 13.5 |
| 6. Price index, U.K. exports, 1913 = 100 | | 109 | 92 | 84 | 92 |
| 7. Line 5, 1913 prices | | 3.7 | 6.8 | 5.2 | 14.7 |
| 8. Volume per year, 1913 prices | | 0.62 | 0.68 | 0.52 | 1.09 |
| 9. Total foreign investment, 1913 prices | 4.9 | 8.6 | 15.4 | 20.6 | 35.3 |
| *Shares of debtor areas in outstanding gross investment (%)* | | | | | |
| 10. Europe | | | | | 28 |
| 11. United States and Canada | | | | | 24 |
| 12. Oceania | | | | | 5 |
| 13. Latin America | | | | | 19 |
| 14. Asia and Africa | | | | | 24 |

#### B. ADDITIONS TO CUMULATED CAPITAL ABROAD, UNITED KINGDOM, 1821–1913 (MILLIONS OF £ PER YEAR)

| | Merchandise trade balance (1) | Business services balance (2) | Other current transactions balance (3) | Total current transactions (4) | Interest and dividend balance (5) | Total current balance (6) | Cumulated credit balance, beginning of period (7) |
|---|---|---|---|---|---|---|---|
| *Decades* | | | | | | | |
| 1. 1821–30 | −10.5 | +15.9 | −3.4 | +2.0 | +4.4 | +6.5 | 46.1 |
| 2. 1831–40 | −18.5 | +19.3 | −3.0 | −2.2 | +6.7 | +4.5 | 111 |

| | | | | | | | |
|---|---|---|---|---|---|---|---|
| 3. 1841–50 | −21.9 | +24.7 | −6.0 | −3.2 | +8.5 | +5.3 | 156 |
| 4. 1851–60 | −30.7 | +43.8 | −10.1 | +3.0 | +14.1 | +17.1 | 209 |
| 5. 1861–70 | −57.5 | +75.5 | −13.1 | +5.0 | +26.3 | +31.3 | 380 |
| 6. 1871–80 | −93.5 | +100.7 | −10.6 | −3.5 | +53.2 | +49.7 | 692 |
| 7. 1881–90 | −97.7 | +105.4 | −7.7 | +0.1 | +74.5 | +74.6 | 1,189 |
| 8. 1891–1900 | −145.4 | +105.8 | −11.2 | −50.9 | +97.1 | +46.2 | 1,935 |
| 9. 1901–10 | −158.3 | +140.8 | −17.3 | −34.7 | +132.2 | +97.4 | 2,397 |
| 10. 1911–13 | −134.3 | +180.0 | −27.5 | +18.2 | +187.9 | +206.1 | 3,371 |
| | | | | | | | (3,990) |
| *Longer periods* | | | | | | | |
| 11. 1821–50 | −17.0 | +20.0 | −4.1 | −1.1 | +6.5 | +5.4 | 46.1 |
| 12. 1851–80 | −60.6 | +73.3 | −11.3 | −1.5 | +31.2 | +32.7 | 209 |
| 13. 1881–1913 | −133.9 | +123.0 | −13.5 | −24.3 | +109.1 | +84.9 | 1,189 |
| | | | | | | | (3,990) |

C. FOREIGN CAPITAL INVESTMENTS AND FLOWS SINCE WORLD WAR I, SELECTED PERIODS, ALL COUNTRIES

(ABSOLUTE FIGURES IN MILLIONS OF $ PER YEAR)

| | 1921–29 (1) | 1930–38 (2) | 1921–38 (3) | 1951–55 (4) | 1956–61 (5) |
|---|---|---|---|---|---|
| 1. Total per year, flows from all creditor countries | 1,547 | −706 | 421 | 4,279 | 7,145 |
| 2. Price index, U.S. exports, 1913 = 100 | 145 | 97 | | 210 | 223 |
| 3. Price index, U.S. imports, 1913 = 100 | 131 | 74 | | 224 | 217 |
| 4. Flows adjusted for price changes (line 1 ÷ line 2) | 1,067 | −728 | 170 | 2,038 | 3,226 |
| 5. Flows adjusted for price changes (line 1 ÷ line 3) | 1,181 | −954 | 114 | 1,910 | 3,316 |
| *Shares of major creditors, flows in current prices (%)* | | | | | |
| 6. United Kingdom | 27.7 | 14.1 | 39.1 | 10.5 | 10.2 |
| 7. France | 21.8 | 1.3 | 38.9 | 2.5 | 6.2 |
| 8. Germany | | net debtor | | 2.2 | 9.2 |
| 9. United States | 43.0 | 78.1 | 13.6 | 78.4 | 67.4 |

TABLE 6.5—Continued

|  | 1921–29 (1) | 1930–38 (2) | 1921–38 (3) | 1951–55 (4) | 1956–61 (5) |
|---|---|---|---|---|---|
| *Shares of debtor groups* (%) | | | | | |
| 10a. Developed countries in total investment | 50.4 | 16.5 | 78.9 | 28.5 | 27.9 |
| b. Including Argentina | (56.2) | (12.2) | (93.1) | | |
| 11. Developed countries in private investment | | | | 56.9 | 62.2 |
| *Shares of types of source* (%) | | | | | |
| 12. Official donations | | | | 36.0 | 35.2 |
| 13. Official and international agency loans | | | | 21.1 | 18.8 |
| 14. Private | | | | 43.0 | 46.0 |

*Sources: Panel A*

Line 1: From Albert H. Imlah, *Economic Elements in the Pax Britannica* (Cambridge, Mass., 1958), Table 4, pp. 70–75.

Lines 2–3: From Herbert Feis, *Europe: The World's Banker, 1870–1914* (New Haven, 1930), pp. 47 and 71.

Line 4, col. 1: From U.N., *International Capital Movements During the Inter-War Period* (Lake Success, 1949), p. 1. Here and in lines 1–3 conversion to U.S. dollars is by official exchange rates.

Line 6: The price index in Imlah, Table 8, pp. 94–98, shifted directly from the 1880 base to 1913 (which is 96.9 on the 1880 base). The entries are unweighted arithmetic means of the price index for the years covered by the intervals between the successive columns (i.e. 6, 10, 10, and 13 years respectively, from 1874 to 1913 inclusive).

Line 9: For col. 1 the estimate of the foreign capital total of $6 billion (line 4) was deflated by the price index for the preceding 24 years, i.e. from 1850 through 1873, the accumulation during that period accounting for over three quarters of the 1874 total for the United Kingdom, and the latter accounting for over three quarters of the total shown in line 4. The entries in cols. 2–5 were derived by adding to the total in col. 1 the successive entries in line 7.

Lines 10–14, col. 5: Based on U.N., *International Capital Movements*, p. 2.

*Panel B*

The basic source is Imlah, Table 4, pp. 70–75. The entries in col. 2 are the sums of balances entitled: profits on foreign trade and services, insurance and brokerage, and net shipping credits—with the third of these three usually dominant, and the second smallest. The entries in col. 3 are the sums of balances from: movement of gold and silver bullion and species; sales of ships; emigrant funds; and ʰtourists, smuggling, and unrecorded imports. Of these four items, the last is dominant through most of the period.

Panel C

Cols. *1–3*: The major source is U.N., *International Capital Movements*, Table 1, pp. 10–14, underlying the summary in Simon Kuznets, "International Differences in Capital Formation and Financing," in Moses Abramovitz, ed., *Capital Formation and Economic Growth* (National Bureau of Economic Research, 1956), Table II-3, pp. 68–69. The developed countries exclude, however, Argentina, Czechoslovakia, and Latvia. The only adjustment made to derive the estimates in line 1 is to assume that the 1921 volume for the United Kingdom was equal to the average annual volume for 1922–29. The price indexes are from Lipsey, *Price and Quantity Trends*, Table A-1, pp. 142–43 and Table A-3, pp. 146–47. The entries are unweighted arithmetic means for the nine years covered in each of the first two columns. The entries in lines 4 and 5, col. 3, are equal to half the difference between (or algebraic sum of) cols. 1 and 2.

Cols. *4 and 5*: The basic sources for 1951–61 are U.N., *International Flow of Long-term Capital and Official Donations, 1951–59* (New York, 1961), Table 3, pp. 6–7; and U.N., *International Flow . . . 1959–61* (New York, 1963), Table 1, pp. 6–7. Because of the duplication in the first of these sources between credits to and from international lending agencies, the total flow is esti-mated by adding receipts of debtors (flows to non-Communist developed debtor countries, to Communist countries, and to underdeveloped countries). From the averages given in the two sources for 1951–55 and 1956–59, and annually for 1959–61, the entries in cols. 4 and 5 were derived. The same procedure was followed for the components or shares in lines 6–14. The price indexes in lines 2 and 3 are again from Lipsey, extrapolated from 1960 (the last year given) to 1961 by corresponding indexes in the *Economic Report of the President, January 1964*, Table C-6, pp. 214–15. The shares in lines 6–9 were taken to the total of all creditor countries, before correction for statistical errors (which are minor for 1951–59, and not available by coun-tries) and without regard to differences among countries in their contributions, directly or via the international lending agencies.

accounted in 1913–14 for as much as three quarters of the total gross outstanding; and if a shift could be made to net credit position, the share of these three would be even higher.[17] Although successive totals of accumulated credits may be affected by defaults, they provide a rough guide to the magnitude of flows that occurred in the time intervals covered by the stock figures.

The evidence in Panel A suggests that for the three major international creditor countries, capital outflows for the 1874–1914 period averaged between \$0.5 and \$1.1 billion per year, in 1913 prices. From Panel B of Table 6.3 we can approximate the annual volumes of foreign trade (commodities only, exports and imports combined), and these would range from over \$6 billion in 1881–85 to over \$13 billion in 1913, again in 1913 prices. If we allow about a fifth for the movement of services, the average outflow of foreign capital investment would amount to less than a tenth of the foreign trade volume, and in most periods much less. It would thus account for just a small percentage of national output of the major international creditors, a point to which we shall return later. Nor was there any marked rise in the volume of these flows, at least within the four decades covered in Panel A: the rise was much more moderate than those in national output and foreign trade flows. And yet the increase in the *cumulative* total of foreign capital invested was striking. The total in current values rose from \$6 billion in 1874 to \$34.2 billion in 1913–14, to more than 5 times; reduced to 1913 prices, it rose from \$4.9 to \$35.3 billion, a rate of growth per decade of

17. According to U.N., *International Capital Movements*, pp. 1–2, the United Kingdom, France, and Germany accounted for \$32.8 billion out of a total of \$44 billion (gross investment outstanding in 1913–14); but within the remainder, the United States was a creditor with \$3.5 billion outstanding, whereas its international debt was \$6.8 billion; and among "other countries" (with a total of \$2.2 billion outstanding) there were similar net debtors, such as Russia and Portugal. It is unlikely that a netting out would reduce the gross credits of the three major creditors as much proportionately as they would the gross credits of the other countries on the list.

64 per cent—significantly higher than the rates of growth of national output and foreign trade, whether of the creditor countries or of all debtor countries taken as a whole. Hence the proportion of the stock of foreign capital to the national output of either creditor or debtor nations—each group taken as a whole—must have risen significantly over the four decades preceding World War I.

This contrast between the moderate rate of growth in the foreign capital flows and the high rate of growth in the cumulative stock of foreign capital is due, if only in part, to the relatively small stock at the initial date; and this in turn results from the relative recency of sustained and cumulative foreign capital flows. Panel B of Table 6.5 provides a series back to 1821 for the United Kingdom—the largest international creditor by far—in which the initial total of accumulated foreign credits in 1821 amounted to only £46 million and by 1871 had increased to £692 million, or 15 times; whereas from 1871 to 1913 it increased to £3,990 million, or less than 6 times. This contrast would persist with adjustment for price changes and for the difference in length of the two periods. Furthermore, substantial foreign capital investments by France began only in the 1850s and were interrupted by the Franco-Prussian war; those by Germany began only in the 1870s;[18] and the credits outstanding for countries other than the United Kingdom in the 1820s, after the disrupting effects of the Napoleonic wars, should have been quite small. Therefore one may conclude that the rate of growth of cumulated foreign capital between the 1820s and the 1870s was probably even higher than that between the 1870s and World War I. It follows that over the century preceding 1913–14, there must have been a marked rise in the proportion of total (cumulated) foreign capital investment to national output, of either the creditor or the debtor countries, each group taken as a whole.

A substantial proportion of these capital flows went to developed countries. The easily available breakdowns re-

18. See Feis, *Europe: The World's Banker*, pp. 33 and 68.

late to 1913–14 alone; and, as lines 10–14 of Panel A suggest, at least half of foreign capital accumulated by that date was invested in the developed countries (the predominant part of the share of Europe, and the full shares of North America and Oceania); and with the addition of Argentina and Japan the proportion would probably rise to six tenths. But it may well be that with the passage of time the share of total capital flows going to the less developed parts of the world—both colonies and independent nations in Asia, Africa, and Europe—has increased; and the rate of growth of the foreign capital stock in the developed debtor countries, particularly after the 1870s, has increased at much lower rates than aggregate foreign capital investment. We can then ask whether foreign capital invested in these developed debtor countries after the 1870s has grown more slowly than their outputs—a question upon which the discussion of trends in foreign capital flow proportions to national product for various countries may shed some light.

Panel B shows that for the United Kingdom the positive balance on the international account of interest and dividends was about equal to the accumulation of capital credits abroad, for the long period from 1821 to 1913. Similarly, for the period 1874–1914 for the three major creditor countries combined, "the total of the estimated capital exports from the three countries practically equalled their aggregate income from the investments." [19] But this should not be taken to mean that there was no need for new international lending by parties other than those that received interest, dividends, or profits from abroad; or that the increase in foreign capital accumulation was somehow "automatic."

Panel C provides a summary of international capital flows for the period after 1913–14, excluding the years of the two world wars and of immediate postwar recovery. The interwar period, including the depression years, was marked by capital flows per year of $110–170 million in 1913 prices, a small fraction of the volume of about $1.1 billion for 1900–

19. See U.N., *International Capital Movements*, p. 1.

13. Moreover, Germany had become a net debtor and the United States had joined the ranks of major international lenders, although on net balance for the full period 1921–38, its capital investments abroad were still appreciably below those of the United Kingdom and France. And during the interwar period, even more than in the pre-1913 period, the developed countries absorbed most of the foreign capital flow—particularly if we take the full period into account.

The decade of the 1950s witnessed marked changes in international flows of funds. The average volume per year, in 1913 prices, was about $2 billion in 1951–55 and $3.3 billion in 1956–61, twice or three times as large as that in 1900–14. But over a third of this flow was in the form of official donations and another fifth in loans by governments (much of it in the later period by the U.S.S.R. and other Communist governments) or by international agencies where market considerations were tempered by political needs (although politics had considerable effect also on foreign capital flows in the interwar period and before World War I). Private capital flows accounted for only about 45 per cent of the total in the 1950s; and if one could approximate the strictly private component of foreign capital flows before World War I and limit comparison to private capital investment alone, much of the excess of the recent foreign fund flows over the pre-World War I flows would probably be eliminated. In the extreme case, if we compare private flows in 1951–61 with total foreign capital flows in 1900–14, the annual volume for the recent period would be about $1.2 billion compared with $1.1 billion in the pre-World War I period of about a decade and a half (in 1913 prices) —a very small rise and certainly much less than the rise in the national outputs of either creditors or debtors.

But the comparison understates the rise; and it is clear that the *total* flow of international funds in the 1950s, even when adjusted for price changes, was two or three times greater than that before World War I. The United States has obviously accounted for a lion's share of this increased flow, in contrast with its much more moderate share in the interwar period or before World War I. The share of the developed debtor countries in the total flow, less than three tenths in the 1950s, was much lower than in the earlier periods; but their share in the *private* flow of funds, about 60 per cent, was as high as before.

These findings—a much greater volume of international flows of capital funds in the 1950s and a much lower volume in the interwar period—must be combined with the effects of the war and immediate postwar periods if we are to compare the full post-1913 period with the century that preceded it. In general, the wars witnessed considerable repatriation of foreign capital investment by at least some of the major international creditors—a repatriation (and sometimes cancellation) not unlike that which occurred in the 1930s. It has been estimated that, compared with a gross foreign capital investment in 1913–14 of $44 billion, the total at the end of 1919 amounted to about $39–40 billion, rose to $47–48 billion by the end of 1938, and declined again to about $42 billion by the end of 1944.[20] While part of this stagnation and reduction in world foreign capital investment was due to repudiation (in particular of the Russian debts after the Communist revolution), much of it was due to repayment during the two wars and to the limitations imposed by war and depression, at least up to the second half of the 1940s, on outflows of foreign capital. Furthermore, the estimate of the present world total of foreign capital reflects a new development in international flows: the recent emergence of donations as a major source of financing, although not for developed debtor countries.

If we assume that in the decade and a half since the mid-1940s, the flow *to developed* countries was about $1 billion per year (in 1913 prices) and that this flow began after three decades during which net effective additions to foreign capital investments in developed countries were negligible, it is difficult to avoid the conclusion that the period since 1913 saw major disruptions of the international capital

20. See W. S. and E. S. Woytinsky, *World Commerce and Governments,* pp. 190, 200, 211, and 221.

flows *to developed* countries. As a result, the average flows during the last five decades and rates of growth in foreign capital stock between 1913 and the early 1960s were far lower than those in the pre-World War I past, and the proportion of these flows to the total outputs of the developed countries in the debtor group must also have been lower. The conclusion must be modified somewhat for the developed *creditor* countries, because the recent rise in outflow of funds from them, including donations and flows to nondeveloped countries, was more conspicuous; but nevertheless, for the period of five decades as a whole, it is reasonable to conclude that the volume of international capital investment and the stock of foreign capital investment expanded at a slower rate.

We may now ask what these movements of international capital funds, whose time pattern we tried to establish above, meant in terms of national output and capital formation for individual developed countries, whether creditors or debtors. The detailed comparisons needed to answer this question fully have been presented elsewhere.[21] Here we shall try only to summarize the major findings.

1. The proportion of the annual outflow of capital to national output varied between 1 and 4 per cent for the major creditor countries; at its highest, for relatively short periods, it was between 5 and somewhat over 7 per cent (for the United Kingdom, as a per cent of GDP in 1880–89 and 1905–14). It was, of course, more substantial as a share in the total national capital formation (gross) generated in the creditor countries, i.e. in total gross savings—amounting, in the United Kingdom, the creditor country for which our records are most continuous, to between a quarter and over four tenths of total national savings during the decades from the 1860s to 1913. In general, a proportion to national product of 1.5 to 3.5 per cent, as observed for Germany and France, meant a proportion to national savings (gross) of roughly between 7.5 and 18 per cent.

21. See Table 5.3 above; and for greater detail the appendix tables in Kuznets, "Quantitative Aspects: VI."

2. These international capital flows constituted small proportions of national product also for the large developed debtor countries, such as the United States. Over the long period from the beginning to the end of the nineteenth century, when the United States began to shift toward a creditor position and changes in the balance of payments turned in its favor, the foreign capital inflow in any decade amounted to little more than 1 per cent of national output (the highest was about 1.3 per cent in the 1830s); and in most decades it was well below 1 per cent. Since the gross domestic capital formation proportion averaged well over 20 per cent of GNP beginning with the 1870s and, exclusive of changes in inventories, ranged from 10 to 14 per cent of GNP in the decades from 1834 to 1858, foreign capital funds financed at best about a tenth of total capital investment within the country, and less in most decades. The record for Japan, the only other large developed debtor country for which we have data, is somewhat more ambiguous, being more discontinuous. In the period since 1887, the largest proportional inflow of foreign capital is observed for the decade 1897–1906, with a ratio to GNP of 4 per cent, and a share in gross domestic capital formation of about three tenths. But this inflow is preceded by a minor foreign capital inflow in 1887–96 (only 0.2 per cent of GNP); and followed by a capital outflow in 1907–16, and by an inflow in 1917–26 of less than 2 per cent of GNP and less than a tenth of domestic gross capital formation. Thus, at least quantitatively, foreign capital inflow did not loom large in Japan either, although there, as in the United States, it may have been significant in some temporary economic conjunctures.

3. In the case of the smaller developed debtor countries, foreign capital inflows were large in relation not only to domestic capital formation but even to total output. Taking again the period before World War I as the one in which the development of international capital flows was greatest, we find that in Canada in 1870, 1890, and 1900, and through 1910, the proportion of these inflows to GNP ranged up to 7.5 per cent, and their share in gross domestic capital forma-

tion was between three tenths and a half. In Australia the share in GNP between the 1860s and 1900 ranged from 3.5 to 10 per cent and in gross domestic capital formation from 21 to 52 per cent. In Norway in three decades, 1890–99, 1900–09, and 1920–29, capital imports amounted to more than 5 per cent of GNP and to between 30 and 40 per cent of gross domestic capital formation. In Denmark and Sweden there were two decades between the 1870s and World War I when the share of foreign financing in domestic capital formation was about 20 per cent or more. In the most striking case, Argentina, capital imports financed as much as 37 per cent of gross domestic capital formation in 1900–09 and 43 per cent in 1910–19, amounting in these two decades to 15.5 and 12.3 per cent of GNP respectively.

4. For the old major creditor nations, listed in Panel A of Table 6.5, the trends in the proportion of capital exports to national product follow the time patterns of total international flows discussed above. In the United Kingdom, there was a rise from the low percentages before the 1850s to higher proportions thereafter (the actual series are for Great Britain but come close to representing the United Kingdom), which reached a peak of 7.3 per cent in 1905–14. The proportion of capital exports to national product was far lower even in 1921–29, about 2.4 per cent, and in the 1950s it was down to between 1.1 and 1.5 per cent and may have been further offset by short-term flows of funds not fully reflected in the estimates, a point of particular bearing for many countries in the post-World War II years. In France, the highest proportion, about 3.7 per cent, was reached in the decade and a half before World War I; and the shares in the 1920s and the 1950s were distinctly lower, between 1 and 2 per cent. The record for Germany shows no rise in the capital export proportion before World War I, the share being roughly about 3 per cent in the 1880s and about 2 per cent in the decade before World War I; but after World War I there was a decline to a net debtor position in the interwar period and to proportions of less than 2 per cent even in 1956–61.

5. Among developed debtor countries, two rather distinct

trends are distinguishable. The United States and Japan shifted from a net debtor to net creditor position, the United States after World War I and Japan after World War II; but among the smaller developed countries for which we have continuous records, such a shift seems to have occurred only in Sweden and Denmark. On the other hand, in Norway, Canada, Australia, and, insofar as can be observed, Argentina, the net debtor status tends to persist. But even in these countries, the long records indicate a downward trend in the proportion of capital imports to national product and also to domestic capital formation. Thus in Canada the average share of capital imports in GNP was about 6 per cent in 1870, 1890, and 1900, about as high in 1901–20, but less than 1 per cent in 1921–30; it turned to capital *exports* in 1931–50, and was no more than 3 per cent even in 1956–61. In Australia, the proportion of capital imports to national product ranged between 1.5 and 2 per cent in the 1950s and between 1 and 4 per cent between 1910 and 1938; it was about 5.5 per cent between 1861 and 1900. There were similar declines in the proportion of capital imports to national product in Norway and Argentina.

This suggestion of reduction in proportional importance of capital exports for the countries that have been creditors through most of the period, and of capital imports for countries that have been debtors through most of the period, is, of course, consistent with the time pattern derived above —which indicates the marked retardation in the expansion of international capital flows in the five-decade period after 1913 as compared with the century that preceded World War I.

### INTERNATIONAL POLITICAL RELATIONS

The review above of trends in international flows of men, goods, and capital, clearly suggests that World War I constituted a divide: in the five decades after 1913 these international flows have grown at rates much lower than those over the century preceding 1913—and indeed some have declined markedly from the levels that prevailed in the decade to decade and a half before 1914. It is hardly necessary to note that this shift reflects the two major world wars and major changes in the world's political structure. But familiar as these changes in political aspects of international relations and structure since World War I are, it may be useful to comment briefly on one theme: the expansionist tendencies of the larger nations as they entered the process of modern economic growth and the changing consequences of these tendencies over the long period since the early nineteenth century.

The propensity to expand outward is suggested even by the greater volumes of foreign trade and the increasing spread of the international trade network to previously isolated areas, a trend reflected in part in the rapid growth of foreign trade proportions discussed above. Insofar as such growth was initiated by the more developed countries and was in a sense imposed on many parts of the world that had for various reasons been isolated previously, it contained an element of forceful expansion: the greater power of the developed nations imposed upon the reluctant partners the opportunities of international trade and division of labor. A clear case was the "opening" of Japan in the 1850s by Commodore Perry. The letter by President Fillmore addressed on that occasion to the Emperor of Japan contains the telltale sentence: "I have no other object in sending him [Commodore Perry] to Japan but to propose to your imperial majesty that the United States and Japan should live in friendship and *have commercial intercourse with each other*" (Italics supplied). This was followed by a revealing suggestion that while "the ancient laws of your imperial majesty's government do not allow of foreign trade, except with the Chinese and the Dutch . . . as the state of the world changes and new governments are formed, it seems to be wise, from time to time, to make new laws." [22]

22. See W. G. Beasley, *Selected Documents on Japanese Foreign Policy, 1853–1868* (London, 1955), p. 99.

Similar forceful actions directed at imposing trade ties and the corresponding institutions in formerly isolated areas of the world were numerous in the nineteenth and early twentieth centuries. Even when the resulting pressures did not eventuate in the imposition of colonial status, numerous restrictions such as extraterritoriality privileges of the resident citizens of Western developed nations and lack of tariff autonomy were imposed on the sovereignty of the native societies.

But the outward expansion accompanying the economic growth of some nations took on other and somewhat different forms. One was territorial expansion across contiguous borders, thus extending the land base of the original sovereignty. This type was particularly marked in the overseas offshoots of Europe where the European immigrants reached areas with sparse native populations and vast expanses beyond the first, narrowly circumscribed settlements on seashore borders close to the mother countries. In 1800, the territory of the United States amounted to less than 900 thousand square miles; by 1810, with the Louisiana Purchase, it grew to 1,716 thousand; by 1850, after the Mexican War, it was about 3,000 thousand;[23] and it has remained about the same since then, except for Alaska and Hawaii, which were admitted to statehood in the 1950s, and such territories as Puerto Rico and the Virgin Islands. More aggressive attempts at territorial expansion were made by some older large nations as they acquired the greater power inherent in modern economic growth: Germany engaged in a series of wars that began with those with Denmark (1864) and Austria (1866), extended to the Franco-Prussian War of 1870–71, and culminated in the two world wars; Japan waged successive wars with China, Russia, and eventually the United States and Great Britain; and the U.S.S.R. went to war against Finland and Poland.

Finally, there was the external expansion that imposed colonial status on many less developed areas, particularly in Asia and Africa but also to a lesser extent in the Carib-

23. See *Historical Statistics of the United States,* Series A 17, p. 8.

bean and in Polynesia. Such colonies should be sharply distinguished from those that constituted large settlements of Europeans. In the latter, the restrictions of political dependence were greatly tempered by the kinship of the dominant immigrant majority with the metropolitan countries, and the favorable relation of natural resources to population and the human capital represented by the latter permitted the highest levels of economic performance and the highest aggregate rates of growth in the world. In the native colonies there were vast differences—in historical heritage, institutional patterns of life, and even basic values—between the large indigenous population and the politically dominant minority, often limited to a handful of administrators, traders, other resident representatives of the developed economies, and missionaries.

The extent of this type of colonial expansion can easily be documented. In 1950, before the successful movement toward political independence of these native colonial areas began, the major colonies in Asia—India, Pakistan, Burma, Ceylon, Indonesia, Korea, Formosa, and the Philippines, all of which regained their formal political independence by the early 1950s—accounted for a population of about 584 million, or over 42 per cent of the total for all Asia (estimated to be 1,384 million in 1950).[24] The remaining colonies in Asia (largely in Indochina) accounted in 1950 for another 43.3 million; those in Africa, even in 1950, accounted for over 147 million, or over 70 per cent of a total population of 207 million; and those in Polynesia and the Americas for another 2.8 and 6.7 million, respectively.[25] Thus the total colonial population in 1950, including the recently freed countries, was about 785 million, or well over three tenths of world population. If we were to add

24. For the population of these Asian colonies see W. S. and E. S. Woytinsky, *World Commerce and Governments*, p. 653; for the population by continents in 1950, see U.N., *Demographic Yearbook, 1961,* Table 2, p. 120.

25. See Woytinsky, *World Commerce*, p. 665, for total colonial population in 1950.

the Chinese population—considering the restricted sovereignty and quasi-colonial status of China until well after World War I—the share would mount to over half of the world total.

It is not feasible here, nor is it within my competence, to deal effectively with these manifestations of outward expansion of the larger nations in the course of their economic growth. The variety of institutional changes imposed by the developed powers on diverse native societies throughout the world presents a particularly complex picture; and we are not in a position to evaluate the specific and varied consequences for the economic growth either of the developed countries or of the colonial and other areas that loom so large among the underdeveloped countries today. But although all the larger developed countries showed these tendencies either by expansion into empty contiguous territories or by the imposition of trade ties or colonial status on native societies in other parts of the world, we cannot conclude that such expansion was indispensable to their economic growth or constituted a major factor in it. Such may have been the case in one country or another and for certain types of expansion, but it probably was not for all. Thus, it is difficult to conceive of the growth of the United States without the extension of its economy across the North American continent. On the other hand, in view of the relatively limited trade ties between metropolitan countries and their colonies and the increasing substitutability of the products of modern technology for raw materials of the colonial areas, an assumed disappearance or re-isolation of the colonial areas of Africa and Asia should not have impeded to a significant degree the modern economic growth, in the dimensions and structure that it attained, of the larger and smaller countries of Europe. Indeed, in considering this question of indispensability, I should be inclined to stress the importance of territorial expansion to the young and "empty" countries that were the overseas offshoots of Europe, thus offering another argument for the distinction between these countries and the older developed nations whether in Europe or Japan (in addition to that of their reliance on immigration, already stressed in earlier discussion). But with respect to the significance for the larger developed nations, young or old, of their expansion to the native areas of Asia and Africa, it is difficult to make out a case for a great quantitative contribution to such economic growth of these developed nations as has in fact occurred, in view of the moderate share of trade with the native areas, or of capital investment in them, or of migration to them, relative to the aggregates of trade, capital investment, and migration among the developed countries themselves.

Indeed, one may argue that, ironically, the expansion toward the less developed, colonial, and quasi-colonial areas of the world aggravated international strains among the large developed countries more than it contributed to their economic growth and in the long run was more important to the economic growth of the nondeveloped areas themselves than to that of the metropolitan countries. In short, such expansion had a far greater effect on the international framework within which relations among the major developed nations and their changing identity were determined than on the growth of any one nation.

This is an obiter dictum answer to a large question, which has been rendered controversial by naturally partisan emotions and specific political interests, but it does at least indicate a judgment concerning the relevance of the processes under discussion to the analysis of modern economic growth as observed in the currently developed countries. In light of this answer, the analysis would stress the importance of territorial expansion for the young overseas offshoots of Europe and the role of outward expansion and the aggression that it generated in exacerbating relations among the developed countries and in inducing forced and rapid economic growth in previously lagging countries by fear of loss of sovereignty and freedom of action; but it would place little importance on the contribution to any developed countries of greater trade or greater capital exports to *underdeveloped* areas.

This of course is an evaluation, without documentation, of the process from the outside and in a long time perspective, and it may be quite different from the judgments of the active agents in these developed countries at the time, or from the evaluations of contemporaries who were influential in the social decisions leading to the type of outward expansion under discussion. It is impossible to offer here a documented and tested theory of the factors that made for such expansion as a corollary of the early phases of modern economic growth of so many large developed countries, but we can list some of them: (1) the increased power bestowed by the burgeoning economic growth of a large nation to use the rapidly extending means of transport and communication to penetrate into previously isolated or empty areas and thus secure greater supplies of raw materials and wider international division of labor; (2) the more rapid accumulation of resources by these growing nations that could be used to exercise their political power elsewhere; (3) the strengthening, in the initial phases of successful economic growth, of the sentiments of nationalism and national power and of the sincere belief that the institutional patterns, proved so successful at home, if imposed on other areas, would be beneficial to all; (4) the fear of the competition of other large developed nations and the acquisition of spheres of interest or colonial domination in the less developed countries as a preemptive action designed to forestall similarly exclusive actions by rivals; and (5) among some follower nations, which in their pre-growth past may have been victims (or considered themselves such), the desire to rectify past wrongs and recover past losses in sovereignty by the use of newly acquired means of power.

Obviously a wide variety of factors and motives can be offered to explain the tendencies toward outward aggression found in the larger nations in the course of their modern economic growth. Although these factors represent interpretations of the economic gains and contribution to *internal* growth to be derived from such expansion that are quite different from the judgment and evaluation suggested here, they are not necessarily inconsistent with it. Holding to this judgment should not be interpreted as a denial of the prevalence of views (or their possible weight) of contemporaries on the gains from colonies or colonial trade and investment—or from armed conflict for territorial acquisitions—in furthering the trends of expansion verging on aggression. This is not the first time in which judgments of gains from some policies at the time they were initiated or extended are at variance with those that can be assigned to them objectively, in retrospect, and with hindsight wisdom—assuming that one accepts the tentative view that has been suggested here.

However we may appraise the contribution to economic growth of the developed nations of the processes of outward expansion involving significant use of economic and political power, it is important to note the distinctive time pattern in these processes since the early nineteenth century. One aspect of this pattern is the high rate of territorial and colonial expansion in the nineteenth and early twentieth centuries, its abrupt break after World War I, and, in the case of colonial expansion, its sharp reversal after World War II. In all three forms—movement into relatively "empty" contiguous territory, the "opening up" of previously closed and isolated areas, and the extension of colonial domination—outward expansion proceeded at fairly high rates during most of the nineteenth and early twentieth centuries, although the rates may not have been constant within that long period and may have gone through phases with different timing for the different forms. The rates were certainly high for the peopling and territorial expansion of the United States, Canada, and the offshoots of Great Britain in Oceania. Furthermore, the greatly improved transportation and communication facilities and the growing economic power of the European countries and the United

States permitted penetration into previously isolated parts of the world and the opening up of previously closed areas —in the Far East by the middle of the nineteenth century and in Africa in the last quarter. As part of this extension of lines of transportation and communication, colonial domination spread, particularly into areas formerly protected by difficult terrain and the inadequate transport facilities at the disposal of the developed countries. It was hardly accidental that Japan was opened up by a squadron of steam warships—a relative innovation in the 1850s—and that Africa was partitioned only in the late nineteenth century, when its penetration by steam railroads became feasible and when the emergence of several major nations intensified international competition for spheres of interest.

The rate of such outward expansion slowed down after World War I. The absorption of the empty areas and the resulting limitations on further pioneer settlement were particularly clear in the case of the United States. The weakening of colonial domination, even when preserved, followed the defeat of several large developed colonial powers in World War I; the increasing realization of the limited economic gains from colonial domination and of the difficulties of assuring adequate and peaceful economic growth in the colonies so long as their growing elites lacked self-governing power; the appeals for national self-determination that were so forceful toward the end of World War I; and the establishment of the League of Nations, the first continuing international organization with some, admittedly feeble, supervisory and policing powers.

This fraying of colonial ties and the growing movement for political independence were greatly accelerated after World War II, when all the factors listed above assumed greater force and when the survival and strength of a rival political organization of economic development, represented by the U.S.S.R., added the danger of support of internal opposition by externally incited and organized subversion. In large part, the eventual political independence of the colonies was inherent in the Westernization of at least selected elites within the native populations. They, as well as the populations of the colonial powers themselves, became imbued with the Western outlook on freedom and equality, an inevitable accompaniment of long-lasting relations between the developed metropolitan countries and the native colonies. But the process was clearly accelerated by the two world wars, by the immediate political consequences thereof, and by some of the changes the wars produced in the views of the metropolitan countries themselves. One may also speculate on the extent to which the growing power of science-based technology to produce substitutes for natural raw materials led to a reevaluation, to a lower level, of the indispensability of colonies as sources of needed raw materials.

It would be an exaggeration to assert that the post-World War I decades saw complete disappearance of attempts to apply power to extend territory or widen colonial domination. The recently industrialized nations have exhibited expansionist tendencies similar to those observed in the more mature developed nations in the earlier phases of their economic growth. The U.S.S.R., for example, gained significantly after World War II both in territory and in spheres of contiguous influence. Communist China has already demonstrated its inclination in the same direction in the "rectification" attack on India; and if economic growth brings it greater economic power, it will probably continue to do so. Illustrations could easily be found even among countries still economically backward, such as Indonesia and Egypt, where only short periods of political independence have been sufficient to provide bases for outwardly aggressive policies. But if one compares the half century after 1913 with the preceding century, it is clear that the pace of expansion of colonial domination has been markedly reduced in the recent period and that there has been a sharp reversal, on net balance, with the rapid spread of political independence after World War II, despite the retention in many cases of close economic ties between the former metropolitan country and its former colonies.

The pre-1913 century contrasts sharply with the post-1913 half-century in another respect. The former was a period of uneasy peace punctuated by frequent but limited wars, whereas the latter was dominated by two world wars. The wars were not truly universal in the sense that *all* nations were engaged in armed conflict, but since most of the large developed nations were active participants, the wars were long, the magnitude of resources utilized was large, and the wars had significant effects not only on the combatants and participants but on almost all other nations in the world.

Some of these effects have already been considered in our attempt to establish long-term growth rates and secular changes in structure in the process of growth; those on international flows of men, goods, and capital have been touched upon in the preceding sections of this chapter, and others have been discussed elsewhere.[26] In the present connection only three brief comments, partly obvious and partly speculative, need be made.

The first is that the growing productive power of developed nations, derived from the science-oriented technology that played an increasing role in modern economic growth, has meant also greater power in armed conflict and greater capacity for protracted struggle—at least under conditions of war technology as it has been practiced in the recent past. The combination of the large amounts of resources devoted to war with the protracted duration of the conflict has become feasible only with modern technology: it permits a large increase in the numbers of people and a vast elaboration of means of transport and destruction used in the war for long periods without depleting supplies for the basic subsistence of the population of participating countries to a level at which further struggle would be impossible.

The second comment, based on Ralph G. Hawtrey's

26. See Kuznets, *Postwar Economic Growth*, Lecture 3, "The Aftermath of World War II," pp. 69–95.

views,[27] relates to wars as ultimate tests of changes in relative power among nations, tests to resolve disagreements as to whether such shifts have indeed occurred and whether the political adjustments pressed for are really warranted. We commented in Chapter 2 on the implication of the generally high rates of modern economic growth for the rapid emergence of significant shifts in relative economic power among nations. If wars are needed to confirm or deny such shifts, the rapidity and frequency with which shifts occur may be the reason for the frequent conflicts that serve as tests. Many of the wars of the nineteenth century can be viewed as such tests (e.g. the wars of Germany against Denmark, Austria, and France). But they were limited to only two or three contestants and, because of sufficiently sizable real imbalance, were terminated quickly.

This brings us to the third and most speculative question: Why did the limited wars of the nineteenth and early twentieth centuries "escalate," to use the modern term, into the two world wars? Possibly major wars are associated with the emergence in the course of modern economic growth of several large and developed nations. One could argue that in a war of "world" dimensions the participants on both sides must comprise large and economically developed countries supported by a variety of allies, countries with sufficient power to devote vast amounts of resources over a prolonged period to a major conflict. Hence, the bare century of uneasy peace in Europe that followed the Napoleonic wars may have been "peaceful" primarily because during much of that period there was only one large and economically advanced country in the part of the world that generated modern economic growth; the emergence of others, particularly Germany, after 1870 eventually led to World War I. In this sense it was a century of Pax Britannica that ended when the leading country could no longer lead and impose its peace on such a large part of the world. Admittedly there was the additional circumstance

27. See *The Economic Aspects of Sovereignty* (2d ed., London, 1952).

that this economically developed leader had the support of large and rapidly growing offshoots overseas that helped to maintain the long peace and participated in the conflicts, when they occurred, actively or decisively. Still, there are possible grounds for claiming that the existence of *several* large economically developed countries is a necessary, if not sufficient, condition for occurrence of "world" wars, if their relative magnitude is to approach those of World Wars I and II; and that if such a war should occur again, its changed magnitude in the future may also depend on the presence of several large and developed nations—with the scale of size and development of the participating countries even higher than those of the recent wars.

In addition to the differences in the rate of outward expansion and colonial domination and in the incidence of major wars, there is a further contrast between the post-1913 half century and the preceding century: in the post-World War I decades, political forms of organization of economic growth emerged that deviated markedly from those observed in the past, and their overt hostility to the previously existing social forms of economic growth has been dominant—even if it has varied in virulence from time to time and from country to country. We refer to the emergence in the post-World War I years of both Fascist and Communist authoritarian states; and the latter, represented by the major case of the U.S.S.R., expanded after World War II to include Mainland China and the Eastern European and Asiatic satellites of both. These developments contributed to a marked and lasting sharp fissure in the international structure of the world. One could argue that the spread of modern economic growth to countries further and further removed from the economic and social framework of Western Europe—the pioneer in the movement—had already produced such cleavages and that the U.S.S.R. was just a last item in an increasingly divergent series. Even in the case of Germany there were elements in the social framework after 1870 that made it rather distinctive, compared with Great Britain, France, or the rapidly growing offshoots of Western Europe overseas; and such differences were more striking in the case of Japan where, even more than in Germany, major hierarchical and traditional elements survived even as modern economic growth proceeded. But these and other follower countries that entered economic modernization before World War I were committed to international division of labor, despite the imposition of tariffs and other measures to encourage domestic industrialization, and to the market mechanism to assure adequate consumer sovereignty and increasingly wide participation of the population in the benefits of economic growth. Above all, there was no overt and proclaimed hostility to the social forms of economic growth existing in other countries.

The Communist countries, however, have shown the following characteristics: rejection of the "capitalist" forms of economic growth and the treatment of these other developed countries as the "enemy"; authoritarian management by a minority party of forced economic growth, with primary emphasis on producers' goods; sharp restriction of individual producers' and consumers' freedom and of the supply of consumer goods; and autarky that has erected iron curtains partly to foster the image of a fortress besieged by enemies and partly to isolate the population from free discussion and possibly unfavorable comparisons of their social and economic attainments with those under a more liberal type of social organization. In all these respects, the Communist countries represent a major and, unlike the Fascist countries, so far lasting deviation from the traditional social and institutional structures within which modern economic growth was accommodated.

The combination of overt and significant hostility to the already developed countries—which is still shared by many underdeveloped countries (particularly former native colonies)—with an authoritarian and ruthless management of forced industrialization, absent in the less developed countries, is distinctive of the Communist form of organization of economic growth. The question of its future evolution

347

is not one to which a clear answer can be given at present. It is particularly unclear whether further Communist economic development will be in the direction of greater openness and freedom—whether it will serve to expand the participation of the Communist countries in international division of labor and make them more akin to the free economic societies. But whatever the future, a retrospective view clearly suggests that the international framework within which economic growth was occurring changed radically after the early 1930s, when the main features of Communist economics became apparent in the U.S.S.R., and even more markedly after World War II, when this new form of organization spread to Mainland China and its basic features became better known.

One should add that the emergence of the Communist authoritarian type of organization for economic growth, like that of any new organizational form of a long-term, epochal process, may have had some beneficial effects also. Certainly other countries, both those that were already developed and those that were still to enter the economic modernization process, profited from its experience. For like any major innovation—and the Communist organization was a social innovation of major dimensions with a variety of aspects—some of its features could be adopted by others, so long as they did not contravene the basic and overriding criteria of the social and economic organization acceptable to these other societies. For example, it demonstrated that the management of a country's economy could be planned far more systematically and deliberately than was thought feasible in the pre-World War II years—even though many of the methods of making and enforcing such plans employed in the U.S.S.R. were not acceptable elsewhere, and even though the effectiveness of such plans is often by no means clear. It cannot be denied that, as a result, a significant change occurred in the climate of economic policy and economic growth in the rest of the world in post-World War II days.

348

# Trends in International Interdependence

The discussion of the trends in international relations relevant to economic growth—in the contribution to the growing transnational stock of knowledge and its utilization by an increasing number of developed nations; in the flows among nations, particularly the developed, of men in migration, goods in foreign trade, and capital in international movement; and in the political relations, particularly those with a significant element of power (outward expansion and war conflicts)—has been brief and selective, dealing far too sketchily with a wide and important field. But it has perhaps served to suggest the distinct aspects of international relations and the major changes observed in them. It may be useful here to bring the major findings together and to reflect on their bearing upon rates and structure of economic growth of developed countries.

We note first the trends in international relations that, despite possible variations in the rate of upward climb, show a fairly continuous advance from the early nineteenth century to date, with no evidence of any marked retardation or reversal after 1913. Their consequences do not differ greatly for developed nations, whether old or young, large or small. Such a relatively continuous advance can be observed in transport and communication facilities and in the stock of useful knowledge available for diffusion and application, partly by means of the ever-improving transport and communication channels but also largely through the spread of modern economic growth to an increasing number of developed countries—and even in the spread of some elements of such growth, of islands of modernity, within the still underdeveloped areas. These trends were important to all developed nations, large and small, old and young; and, as already indicated, they meant ever-increasing interdependence among nations because of the potential of closer contact and because of the sharing by an increasing number of nations of one and the same transnational stock of knowledge—including some of the ideological elements appropriate to it.

The other trends discussed in the preceding sections relate to the peaceful international flows of men, goods, and capital, and to outward expansion and conflict. And in both, the contrast between the pre- and post-1913 periods is marked. Between the early nineteenth century and 1913, international migration, at least between Europe and its offshoots overseas (or within Europe), grew at high rates, as did the volumes of international trade and the stock (although not the flows) of foreign capital investment. Outward expansion, either into contiguous empty territory in the overseas European-settled areas, in the opening up of previously closed areas, or in the extension of colonial domination, also proceeded at a high rate—all of this in a century of uneasy peace punctuated by frequent but limited wars. These partly peaceful, partly aggressive, processes slowed down or were reversed after 1913—with two major wars and the emergence of the Communist form of organization hostile to the developed countries that had dominated the scene. It is these trends that emphasize the importance of distinguishing in the analysis of economic growth between the older developed countries, largely in Europe, and the younger offshoots overseas, between large and small countries, and naturally also between the free market economies and the Communist authoritarian system. And they lead to the question whether the conditions for growth after 1913 were so different from those in the preceding century that effective comparisons of major aspects of economic growth between the two eras are not possible.

What are the combined effects on economic growth of developed countries of the two sets of trends suggested? And do the distinctions between old and young, large and small, developed countries dominate the major aspects of economic growth? An attempt to answer these questions in terms of the trends in the presently developed countries is feasible only for those countries that have experienced a long enough period of growth before 1913 to permit proper comparison—which immediately excludes all Communist countries, even if they are not to be excluded on other grounds. And the answers would obviously differ from one aspect of growth to another.

While a fully tested set of answers is beyond the scope of this monograph, Table 6.6 suggests a summary answer with respect to the aggregative aspects of growth. The comparison between the 43 years before 1914 and the 47 years from 1913 to 1960 is crude, but the aggregative measures should reveal any marked effect that the major wars and the disturbances in the international flows and structure had on the economic growth of the developed countries. The period back to 1870 covers a substantial portion of the total modern economic growth span of most countries; and while the pre-1913 periods for Switzerland and the Netherlands do not cover the full span, extension by the use of rough approximations only accentuates the results found for these two countries in the table, and the 1890–1913 period for Italy is used because the country entered modern economic growth only in the late nineteenth century.

Table 6.6 shows that in eight of the thirteen countries covered, the rate of growth of total product (columns 1 and 2) was lower in the post- than in the pre-1913 period. But with allowance for the generally prevalent retardation in the rate of growth of population (columns 3 and 4) and a shift to per capita product (columns 5 and 6), the rates of growth in the post-1913 period are higher in six of the thirteen countries; and in two of those that show declines, France and Germany, the declines are so small that another quinquennium of growth (and indeed only a few more recent years) at current rates would wipe them out, and a decade at current rates would convert the declines into rises. Finally, with a shift to product per man-hour (columns 7 and 8), the closest approach here to a measure of productivity, the rates of growth are higher in the post-1913 period in eight of twelve countries (and would probably be higher in Japan, were the man-hour data available); and

TABLE 6.6

Rates of Growth in Total Product, Population, Product per Capita, and Product per Man-hour, Developed Countries, Two Long Periods, 1870–1913 (I) and 1913–60 (II) (percentages per decade)

| | Total product | | Population | | Product per capita | | Product per man-hour | |
|---|---|---|---|---|---|---|---|---|
| | I (1) | II (2) | I (3) | II (4) | I (5) | II (6) | I (7) | II (8) |
| 1. United Kingdom | 24.4 | 20.7 | 9.2 | 4.5 | 13.9 | 15.5 | 16.3 | 19.5 (20.2) |
| 2. France | 16.9 | 15.7 | 1.8 | 1.9 | 14.9 | 13.6 | 19.6 | 23.0 (20.2) |
| 3. Germany, FR (1871) | 33.2 | 28.4 | 12.4 | 9.4 | 18.5 | 17.4 | 22.7 | 21.6 (20.4) |
| 4. Belgium | 30.5 | 15.1 | 10.0 | 3.8 | 18.7 | 10.8 | 22.3 | 18.0 (14.4) |
| 5. Switzerland (1890) | 26.7 | 29.8 | 11.8 | 7.2 | 13.4 | 21.1 | 16.7 | 26.7 (25.0) |
| 6. Netherlands (1900) | 24.8 | 30.1 | 15.0 | 14.2 | 8.5 | 13.9 | 11.4 | 18.2 (17.1) |
| 7. Denmark | 37.0 | 26.1 | 11.2 | 9.4 | 23.2 | 15.2 | 28.7 | 19.4 (18.7) |
| 8. Norway | 23.7 | 32.3 | 8.3 | 8.5 | 14.2 | 21.9 | 19.3 | 30.7 |
| 9. Sweden | 33.9 | 27.5 | 7.2 | 6.3 | 24.9 | 20.0 | 30.2 | 25.4 (24.5) |
| 10. Italy | 15.0 | 25.4 | 6.8 | 6.8 | 7.7 | 17.4 | 12.9 | 26.1 (22.1) |
| 10a. Italy (1890) | 22.6 | 25.4 | 6.9 | 6.8 | 14.7 | 17.4 | 20.4 | 26.1 (22.1) |

| | | | | | | | | | |
|---|---|---|---|---|---|---|---|---|---|
| 11. Japan (1880) | 37.8 | 45.0 | 10.9 | 13.3 | 24.3 | 27.9 | | | 26.8 |
| 12. United States (1871) | 52.7 | 34.5 | 23.0 | 14.0 | 24.1 | 18.0 | 26.5 | | (28.8) |
| 13. Canada | 45.1 | 34.9 | 19.1 | 18.6 | 21.8 | 13.7 | 22.7 | | 24.5 (24.3) |

*Sources:* The underlying series for all countries except Japan are from Angus Maddison, *Economic Growth in the West* (New York, 1964), Table A-2, pp. 201–02 for total product (gross domestic product in constant prices); Table B-1, pp. 205–06 for population (like product, adjusted to constant boundaries); Tables H-2 and H-3, pp. 232 and 233, for product per man-hour, presented in two somewhat different variants (of which the second is entered in parentheses in col. 8). For detailed notes on these series see the source. The entry in brackets in the stub is the initial date of the first period, if different from 1870. The output series for 1960, underlying column 2 were arithmetic means of 1959–61. Per capita product rates were derived from those for total product and population.

The series for Japan are from the most recent Hitotsubashi estimates used in the Ohkawa and Rosovsky study (see Kuznets, *Postwar Economic Growth*, Table 4, notes for Japan, p. 66).

the retardation in the growth of per man-hour product is substantial in only three of the four remaining countries.

Thus the rates of growth of per capita and per man-hour product for a variety of developed countries do not show uniform or marked deceleration in the post-1913 period, compared with the pre-1913 decades; and the result would be the same if for some countries we extended the pre-1913 period back to cover more fully the decades since their start in modern economic growth. While this is no proof that the complex of causal factors behind the rates of growth did not change markedly after 1913, at least the changes and ruptures in the international framework did not produce major breaks in secular aggregate growth rates. Of course, one may argue that (1) if not for the wars and the resulting disturbances, acceleration in the rates of growth of product per capita and per man-hour might have been more uniform—reflecting more clearly the increasing potential provided by the growing stock of useful knowledge and constantly improving channels for its transmission; and that (2) retardations were not more prevalent in the post-1913 period because the growth-retarding effects of major wars and international disruption were offset by the growth-accelerating effects of increase in the stock and transmissibility of useful knowledge. But this plausible conjecture cannot be tested with the present data; nor can it be supported by the argument that Sweden, one of the four countries with a decline even in the rate of growth of product per man-hour in the post-1913 period, was more affected by wars than other countries that showed an acceleration (e.g. Norway or the Netherlands); or that, of the three others—Denmark, Belgium, and Germany—only the last felt the impact of wars more sharply than most others (but perhaps not more than Japan in World War II). In short, in our present state of knowledge, it is safest to conclude that no matter what changes occurred in the post-1913 period, their effects on aggregate rates of growth of the developed economies were not so sharp as to force us to consider it a new era.

The effects may have been more marked on some structural aspects of economic growth. The world wars and their aftermaths (among which one might include even the Great Depression of the 1930s) were probably major factors underlying the rise in the share of government within the industrial structure of product and employment in countries that did not initiate their economic growth with a forcible economic intervention by government (as did Japan); but even so, this was only an acceleration in an upward trend that had already been manifested in many developed countries as a result of urbanization. We commented in Chapter 4 on the possible effects of wars on the share of property income, on the strengthening egalitarian tendencies, and on the size distribution of income. One may say, in general, that the modern welfare economy and state are a result of changes in social institutions and views to which wars and international disturbances, as well as the international competition for the allegiance of men, have contributed heavily. And, above all, there were the changes, noted in the preceding sections, in the international components of national structure—migration, foreign trade, and capital exports and imports—which were so sharp between the pre-1913 and post-1913 periods.

But while all these and possibly other effects of wars and international disruption on structural changes in the economic growth of developed countries may be admitted, other major structural trends—in industrial composition, in types of economic organization of the producing unit, in factor shares, in the allocation between consumption and capital formation, and even in the major trends of components within consumption and investment—do not seem to have been markedly affected by the shift from the pre- to the post-1913 period. In short, our discussion of the contrast between the bare century before World War I and the five decades that have passed since then suggests qualifications that must be kept in mind in any attempts to use both periods in the formulation and analysis of general characteristics and components of economic growth; but these are qualifications, not negation, and do not require that we treat the post-1913 period as a new era not comparable with the pre-1913 past.

Can we make a similar judgment concerning the distinctions between the large and small non-Communist developed countries or between the older countries of Europe and Japan, and the younger, immigrant countries overseas? The effects of size on the proportion of foreign trade to national product, and thus on dependence upon or relative gains from foreign trade, as well as on the possible contribution of capital imports to the financing of domestic capital formation, are, as indicated previously, quite large; and size may also have affected diversity of resources and of productive activities within the nation's boundaries and economies of scale in production, particularly when location within the boundaries is indispensable, no matter how far international specialization is pushed. Likewise, the marked differences between the younger developed countries overseas and the older developed countries revealed by the much higher rates of growth of population and aggregate product in the younger countries are obvious (and are illustrated in Table 6.6 and some of the tables in Chapter 2); and in further analysis an attempt should be made to appraise the specific contributions of immigration and of the relatively abundant natural resources of these young overseas countries. But are these effects of size and of what might be called "age" on the quantitative characteristics of aggregate economic growth and structural shifts so overriding that we must differentiate between large and small, old and young developed countries—to the point of separating them in comparative tables and formulating different theories of economic growth for each of these subgroups within the relatively small group of non-Communist developed countries?

The statistical comparisons and the discussion in the preceding chapters did not draw such distinctions. The implicit working assumption was that the developed countries—regardless of size or age—relying on one and the same source of modern economic growth and fitting economic growth within roughly similar social and institutional frameworks (with the market mechanism, with relative freedom for the population as producers, consumers, etc.) would reveal many common characteristics of such growth: in the rates of aggregate increase, in the structural shifts revealed by the industrial distribution of product and labor, in the distributions by factor shares and by size of income, or in the allocation of product among different uses. It seemed to us that in the present, rather undeveloped, state of tested knowledge concerning the quantitative characteristics of modern economic growth, comparison and analysis should extend over the full range of large and small, old and young nations, so long as there were similarities in the basic features of the social and institutional framework within which growth took place: the major role assigned to the market mechanism and the wide leeway permitted to the diversified economic and social drives of the population acting freely as producers, consumers, savers, and investors. This is not to deny the effects of size and age suggested above or to dispute the need to draw attention to differences in some of the features of modern economic growth associated with them. But in this necessarily summary treatment, the comparisons were, by design, as inclusive as the data permitted; and it is in future, more detailed and more penetrating analysis that an attempt could be made to gauge the full range of effects of size and age on various aspects of modern economic growth. In the present general review of the quantitative aspects of modern economic growth, the effects of size and age were not so dominant as to force us to treat—for all the aspects covered—large countries separately from small, and old countries separately from young.

We reached quite a different judgment on the distinction between non-Communist and Communist countries, even with the assumption that one or two of the latter are developed. We did cite some evidence for Communist countries in the preceding chapters but made no attempt to include them in any general comparison and summary. The suspect nature of much of the data for the Communist countries, the recency of their emergence, and the brevity of the period over which their patterns of growth could be studied, combined with the violent perturbations that have marked much of their short history and, above all, the radically different structure of their social and institutional framework from that for all the developed countries that entered modern economic growth well before the recent two or three decades, all bar us from including Communist developed countries with other developed countries and force us to treat them as a distinct group—even if the ultimate source on which their growth draws, exploitation of the transnational stock of useful knowledge, is the same. The references to them in this monograph are for the sake of complete coverage; no attempt is made to present the full record and to reach a better understanding of the mechanism of their economic growth through a study of the aggregates over time and of the interrelations of components in structural change.

# 7

## INTERNATIONAL INCOME DIFFERENCES—DEVELOPED AND UNDERDEVELOPED COUNTRIES

The discussion in Chapters 2–6 dealt with the quantitative characteristics of modern economic growth that could be derived from readily available data, and it emphasized some interrelations and ad hoc hypotheses for the presently developed countries. Yet, as noted in Chapter 2 (p. 37), modern economic growth in an adequate measure has spread to only a limited fraction of the world's population, and the effectively developed countries account today for a minority of world population. Hence it should be useful to devote the last substantive chapters of this monograph to a discussion of the international diversity in per capita product and in associated economic performance, with particular attention to the countries that are much less developed economically than those that were the focus of our discussion in the earlier chapters. We shall deal first with current differences in per capita product and their possible existence in the past (Chapter 7); second, with the economic structure of the underdeveloped countries and some political and social characteristics associated with low per capita product (Chapter 8); and finally, with some observations concerning the reasons for the limited spread of modern economic growth (Chapter 9).

### CURRENT DIFFERENCES IN PER CAPITA PRODUCT

The groupings in Table 7.1 are based upon two distinctions: that between Communist and non-Communist

TABLE 7.1

Gross Domestic Product, Population, and Product per Capita, World Total and Distribution among Developed, Communist, and Less Developed Countries, 1958 (product in U.S. dollars at factor cost)

| | GDP (billions) (1) | Population (millions) (2) | Product per capita ($) (3) | Share in world total (%) | | Relatives of world product per capita | |
|---|---|---|---|---|---|---|---|
| | | | | GDP (4) | Population (5) | Based on col. 3 (6) | GNP, 1957 (7) |
| *I. Non-Communist developed countries* | | | | | | | |
| 1. United States and Canada | 435.4 | 192.0 | 2,268 | 36.2 | 6.7 | 545 | 609 |
| a. United States | (406.5) | (174.9) | (2,324) | (33.8) | (6.1) | (559) | (622) |
| 2. Northern and Western Europe | 164.3 | 140.1 | 1,172 | 13.6 | 4.9 | 282 | 257 |
| 3. Other Europe | 106.8 | 115.8 | 992 | 8.9 | 4.0 | 222 | 184 |
| 4. Australia and New Zealand | 17.6 | 12.1 | 1,454 | 1.5 | 0.4 | 350 | 318 |
| 5. Total, lines 1–4, including Japan | 768.0 | 551.6 | 1,392 | 63.8 | 19.1 | 335 | 334 |
| *II. Communist countries* | | | | | | | |
| 6. U.S.S.R. | 144.8 | 206.8 | 700 | 12.0 | 7.2 | 168 | 145 |
| 7. Eastern Europe | 60.3 | 114.8 | 525 | 5.0 | 4.0 | 126 | 110 |
| 8. Mainland China | 55.0 | 657.0 | 84 | 4.6 | 22.8 | 20 | 18 |
| 9. Other Asia | 1.7 | 24.7 | 69 | 0.14 | 0.9 | 17 | 14 |
| 10. Total, lines 6–9 | 261.8 | 1,003.3 | 261 | 21.8 | 34.8 | 63 | 55 |
| *III. Non-Communist less developed countries* | | | | | | | |
| 11. Europe | 16.3 | 47.6 | 342 | 1.4 | 1.6 | 82 | 70 |
| 12. Latin America | 52.2 | 199.4 | 262 | 4.3 | 6.9 | 63 | 75 |
| 13. Middle East | 19.5 | 99.8 | 196 | 1.6 | 3.5 | 47 | 42 |
| 14. Asia[a] | 57.3 | 766.0 | 75 | 4.8 | 26.5 | 18 | 22 |
| a. India | (28.9) | (414.3) | (70) | (2.4) | (14.4) | (17) | (18) |

| | | | | | | | |
|---|---|---|---|---|---|---|---|
| 15. Africa[b] | 28.0 | 219.4 | 128 | 2.3 | 7.6 | 31 | 27 |
| 16. Total, lines 11–15 | 173.3 | 1,332.2 | 130 | 14.4 | 46.1 | 31 | 34 |
| 17. World total | 1,203.2 | 2,887.1 | 416 | 100.0 | 100.0 | 100 | 100 |

a. Excludes Middle East, Cyprus, and Japan; includes less developed Oceania.
b. Excludes Egypt.

*Sources: Non-Communist Countries:*

The basic source for cols. 1–6 is U.N., *Yearbook of National Accounts Statistics, 1963*, Tables 3A and 3B, pp. 321–31. These tables contain estimates of total and per capita gross domestic product expressed in U.S. dollars, Table 3A based on prevailing dollar exchange rates and Table 3B on "calculated parity rates." "In general, parity rates . . . were estimated by adjusting the official or free market exchange rates in 1938 for each country by the relative change in the level of prices from 1938 to the year in question, between the United States and the country concerned" (p. 330). Some adjustments for the exchange rates in 1938 were made when they were considered unrealistic (by shifting the base to 1929 or in other ways). The estimates used here are based on parity rate conversions; and when these were missing (for a few small countries), the adjustment was made by means of the estimates in Tables 3A and 3B for the residual for each continent. The population figures were derived by dividing total by per capita product.

The grouping of countries, when not self-evident, is as follows:

*Line 2:* Includes Belgium, Denmark, Finland, France, Iceland, Ireland, Luxembourg, the Netherlands, Norway, Sweden, the United Kingdom—all except Ireland with per capita income well above $700.

*Line 3:* Includes Austria, West Germany (and West Berlin), Switzerland, Italy, and the group labeled "Other" Europe in Table 3A, with per capita income in that table of $750 and only about 0.3 million of population.

*Line 5:* For Japan, not shown separately, in earlier uses of estimates similar to those in Table 3A we found that $400 would be a more reasonable level of per capita product than one below $300; and with the shift to parity conversion (applying the percentage adjustment derived from the basic source), it was set at $480. The total product was then calculated as the product of this per capita figure and total population.

*Line 11:* Includes Greece, Malta and Gozo, Cyprus (listed in the *Yearbook* under Asia), Portugal, and Spain.

*Line 12:* Includes all countries in the Western Hemisphere except the United States and Canada.

*Line 13:* Includes Egypt (listed in the *Yearbook* under Africa), Aden, Iran, Iraq, Israel, Jordan, Lebanon, Muscat and Oman, Saudi-Arabia, Syria, Turkey, Yemen, and "Other" Asia (in Table 3A), which appears to be dominated by Kuwait and Bahrain.

TABLE 7.1—*Continued*

*Line 14:* The total shown in the *Yearbook*, excluding Japan, Cyprus, and the Asian countries listed in the notes to line 13, plus the total shown for Oceania, excluding Australia and New Zealand (with 2.9 million of population).

*Line 15:* The total shown in the *Yearbook*, excluding Egypt.

### Communist Countries:

*Line 6:* According to Stanley Cohn, "The Gross National Product in the Soviet Union: Comparative Growth Rates," in *Dimensions of Soviet Economic Power*, Part II, Table 4, p. 76, gross national product in 1960 is $193.6 billion, on the basis of IMF conversion rates, compared with $504.4 billion for the United States—which, with 214.4 and 180.7 million respectively for population (according to U.N., *Demographic Yearbook, 1962*) yielded a ratio of the U.S.S.R. per capita to the U.S. per capita of 0.32. Allowing a higher rate of growth in per capita product in the U.S.S.R. than in the U.S. from 1958 to 1960, we set the ratio for 1958 roughly at 0.30; which, multiplied by the per capita of $2,324 for the U.S., yielded an estimate of $700 for the U.S.S.R. The estimate was thus based on official prevailing rates rather than parity rates. The latter could not be used because we have no "normal" past reference point within the history of the Soviet Union, for its relations to the rest of the economic world. However, Cohn, in the work cited, indicates that, with internal purchasing power conversion, the GNP of the U.S.S.R. in 1960 was $235.5 billion, i.e. about 20 per cent above the estimate used here. Since similar conversions were not applied to other countries (the parity calculations fall short of them), we did not use the higher figure. The population for the Soviet Union in 1958 was taken from James W. Brackett, "Demographic Trends and Population Policy in the Soviet Union," in *Dimensions of Soviet Economic Power*, Part II, Table A-1, p. 555.

*Line 7:* Includes Albania, Bulgaria, Czechoslovakia, East Germany (and East Berlin), Hungary, Poland, Rumania, and Yugoslavia. Population totals for 1958 were taken from the *Demographic Yearbook, 1962*, Table 4. Product per capita, for the group as a whole, was estimated by relating it to that for the U.S.S.R. According to Mikoto Usui and E. E. Hagen, *World Income, 1957* (Cambridge, Mass., 1959), the per capita GNP for these countries in 1957 was $456 compared with $600 for the U.S.S.R. We have, therefore, assumed a per capita product about 25 per cent lower than that for the U.S.S.R. and derived total product by multiplying population by the per capita product of $525.

*Line 8:* Gross domestic product was derived from T. C. Liu and K. C. Yeh, *The Economy of the Chinese Mainland: National Income and Economic Development, 1933–1959* (Princeton, 1965), Tables 8 and 10, pp. 66 and 68. On the basis of estimates for 1957 in 1933 prices, 1952 prices, and 1957 prices, and a preliminary estimate for 1958 in 1952 prices, the total for 1958 in each of the three sets of prices can be approximated. These were translated into the base year dollar values by the official conversion rates of yuan to the dollar, 3.839 in 1933, 2.343 in 1952, and 2.617 in 1957 (see Liu and Yeh, p. xvi) and shifted to 1958 prices by the price index implicit in the estimates of gross national product for the United States (see *Economic Report of the President, January 1963,* Table C-6, p. 178). Of the three estimates of gross domestic product for 1958—$31.2 billion (in 1933 prices), $55.0 billion (in 1952 prices), and $46.4 billion (in 1957 prices)—we used the highest in order to avoid the danger of underestimation. Population in 1957 is set at 637 million in Liu and Yeh, Table 24, p. 102, and at 643 million in U.N., *Economic Survey of Asia and the Far East, 1961,* Table 3–14, p. 91; we assumed 640 million for 1957 and 2.6 per cent growth from 1957 to 1958.

*Line 9:* Includes North Korea, North Vietnam, and Mongolia. Population was taken or estimated from *Demographic Yearbook, 1962,* Table 4; and the per capita product for the whole group was estimated by means of the ratio of per capita GNP to that given for Mainland China for 1957 in Usui and Hagen ($60 and $73 respectively).

*Col. 7:* Derived from ibid.

countries and that between developed and underdeveloped countries; and within the resulting three major divisions we distinguish further among large regions. The estimates refer to 1958, but the differences are representative of most of the 1950s and 1960s once we are beyond the immediate post-World War II recovery years. Before discussing the reliability of the estimates and the relevance of the conversions used to reduce them to a common denominator, we consider the estimates in Table 7.1 and the closely related tables that follow.

The developed countries, whose long-term growth was discussed in the preceding chapters, are all in Group I. Indeed, the group is somewhat too wide in that it includes some countries that may not be viewed as fully developed, e.g. Ireland and Italy. But even so, the non-Communist developed countries, as grouped here, represent less than a fifth of world population but account for almost two thirds of world product. Within this group, the subgroup of overseas descendants of Europe—in North America and Oceania —stands out with the highest product per capita, with about 7 per cent of world population and close to four tenths (38 per cent) of world product. At the other extreme is Japan, not shown separately, with a per capita product that is barely above the world average.

Within Group II, the Communist bloc, which accounts for over a third of world population and over a fifth of world product, there is a wide gap between the U.S.S.R. and the Eastern European countries, with per capita income well above the world average, and Communist China and its Asiatic satellites, with per capita income still among the world's lowest. As a result, the Communist countries of Asia, with twice the population of Communist Europe, have a total product that is only slightly over a quarter of the product of Communist Europe.

The less developed countries in Group III constitute the largest group of all, accounting for almost half (46 per cent) of world population, but for only about a seventh of world product. Within the group per capita income ranges widely:

from extremely low levels in non-Communist Asia (excluding Japan), to somewhat higher levels in Africa, to still higher levels in the Middle East, and to much higher levels in Latin America and in less developed Europe (Greece, Portugal, Spain).

The orders of magnitude suggested in columns 1–6 of Table 7.1 do not depend upon the judgment of the individual investigator: the relative per capita products for 1958 shown in column 6 (which reflect the various decisions described in the notes to the table) agree closely with those in column 7 which are analogous relatives for 1957 and are the result of work by other investigators. Further confirmation is found in a comparison of our results for 1958, regrouped for comparability of area, with the estimates for 1955 by still another group of investigators.[1] Of course, this is no proof of the reliability of the underlying estimates or of the relevance of the conversions used, but it does show that the results are relatively independent of the judgments of individual investigators and of the year chosen within the last decade.

While the summary in Table 7.1 deals with major, distinguishable regions, disregarding differences in per capita product among individual countries, in Table 7.2 the in-

---

1. See Thorkil Kristensen and associates, *The Economic World Balance* (Copenhagen, 1960), Table VII.2, p. 250. The comparison, again for per capita product, relative to the world average, is as follows:

|  | NDP, 1955 | GDP, 1958 (from Table 7.1, col. 6) |
|---|---|---|
| North America | 536 | 545 |
| Europe | 234 | 228 (except U.S.S.R. and Communist Eastern Europe) |
| Oceania | 273 | 350 (Australia and New Zealand) |
| U.S.S.R. | 157 | 168 |
| Eastern Europe | 130 | 126 |
| Latin America | 76 | 63 |
| Middle East | 46 | 47 |
| Asia | 21 | 28 (includes Japan) |
| Africa | 30 | 31 |
| World, $ | 350 | 416 |

dividual countries (over 150 in the underlying data) are grouped by per capita product for 1958. If we use per capita product as the sole criterion of economic development—an assumption subject to some qualifications discussed below but broadly tenable—and assume that the effectively developed countries are those with a per capita product of over $1,000, the developed group accounts for less than 14 per cent of world population but for more than 56 per cent of world product. If we reduce the lower limit to $575 per capita, the developed group accounts for less than a quarter of world population and for over 70 per cent of world product. At the other end of the scale, over half of the world's population resides in countries with a per capita product of less than $100, and over six tenths in countries with per capita product of less than $200. The latter underdeveloped group, with close to two thirds of world population, accounts for about an eighth of world product.

Panel B of Table 7.2 reveals the geographic concentration of the developed and underdeveloped countries, distinguished by per capita product. Of the broader developed group, with per capita product of $575 and over, about three tenths, in terms of population, are in Communist Europe (U.S.S.R.), somewhat less than four tenths in non-Communist developed Europe, and the remaining three tenths in the overseas offshoots of Europe in North America and Oceania. The dominance of the European people in the economically developed group is obvious. At the other end, almost all of the large population groups with per capita product of less than $100 or $200 are in Asia and Africa. The intermediate group, with per capita product between $200 and $575, is divided among Latin America (22 per cent), Communist Europe (28 per cent), Asia and Africa (15 per cent), and less developed Europe (12 per cent); and Japan accounts for over 22 per cent of the population in this group.

We may now ask what the wide contrasts in estimated per capita product in the world today, shown in Tables 7.1 and 7.2, really mean. And if we find that the differences have some significance, we may then ask whether they are of recent origin or have prevailed over a long period.

The first question, concerning the meaning of the estimates, can best be discussed under the following headings: (1) reliability, (2) scope, (3) comparative valuation, and (4) representativeness and generality.

*Reliability*—All data on economic processes are subject to error, and this is especially the case with estimates like national product that are attempts at measurement of a wide and variegated total of productive activities. Approximations to the magnitudes of errors in such synthetic estimates is largely a matter of judgment, although some components, to be sure, can be checked and tested by direct evidence. And if each term in a binary or multiple comparison is subject to some error, the possible errors in the differences are of particular interest here.

It might help us to see the possible effect more clearly if we use formal notation. Designate:

$P_d$: true value of per capita product, developed countries,

$P_u$: true value of per capita product, underdeveloped countries,

$p_d$: estimated value of per capita product, developed countries,

$p_u$: estimated value of per capita product, underdeveloped countries,

 e: proportional error in the estimate for developed countries,

 f: proportional error in the estimate for underdeveloped countries.

$$\text{Then } p_d = P_d(1 + e); \text{ and } p_u = P_u(1 + f).$$

If we are interested in the *true* ratio of per capita product of developed countries to per capita product of underdeveloped countries, i.e. in $R$ rather than in the observed ratio $r$, we can see that:

$$R = P_d/P_u = (p_d \div p_u) \times [(1 + f) \div (1 + e)].$$

TABLE 7.2

Distribution of Gross Domestic Product and Population among Countries Grouped by Product per Capita, 1958

A. DISTRIBUTION OF POPULATION AMONG PER CAPITA PRODUCT CLASSES

| | Less than $100 (1) | $101 to 200 (2) | $201 to 575 (3) | $576 to 1,000 (4) | $1,001 to 1,400 (5) | Over $1,400 (6) | Total (population— millions; GDP— billions of $) (7) | Per capita product ($) (8) |
|---|---|---|---|---|---|---|---|---|
| | | | *Shares in world totals (%)* | | | | | |
| 1. Population | 52.9 | 9.4 | 14.2 | 9.7 | 6.2 | 7.5 | 2,887.1 | 416 |
| 2. GDP | 9.6 | 3.2 | 14.4 | 16.3 | 17.3 | 39.2 | 1,203.2 | |
| | | | *Shares in population totals (%)* | | | | | |
| *Non-Communist developed countries* | | | | | | | | |
| 3. All | 0 | 0 | 17.1 | 11.0 | 32.5 | 39.3 | 551.6 | 1,392 |
| 4. Northern and Western Europe | 0 | 0 | 0 | 5.4 | 89.4 | 5.3 | 140.1 | 1,172 |
| 5. Other Europe | 0 | 0 | 0 | 48.6 | 46.9 | 4.5 | 115.8 | 922 |
| 6. North America, Australia, and New Zealand | 0 | 0 | 0 | 0 | 0 | 100.0 | 204.1 | 2,220 |
| *Communist countries* | | | | | | | | |
| 7. All | 68.0 | 0 | 11.4 | 20.6 | 0 | 0 | 1,003.3 | 261 |
| *Non-Communist less developed countries* | | | | | | | | |
| 8. Europe | 0 | 0 | 100.0 | 0 | 0 | 0 | 47.6 | 342 |
| 9. Latin America | 4.5 | 46.1 | 44.8 | 4.6 | 0 | 0 | 199.4 | 262 |
| 10. Middle East | 5.7 | 58.6 | 32.4 | 3.3 | 0 | 0 | 99.8 | 196 |
| 11. Other Asia | 90.5 | 9.0 | 0.5 | 0 | 0 | 0 | 766.0 | 75 |
| 12. Africa | 63.2 | 24.2 | 12.5 | 0 | 0 | 0 | 219.4 | 128 |
| *Other groupings* | | | | | | | | |
| 13. Asia | 89.3 | 8.2 | 2.3 | 0.2 | 0 | 0 | 1,547.5 | 86 |
| 14. Asia and Africa | 86.0 | 10.2 | 3.6 | 0.2 | 0 | 0 | 1,766.9 | 91 |

B. DISTRIBUTION OF POPULATION WITHIN MAJOR PER CAPITA PRODUCT CLASSES (%)

| | Less than $100 (1) | Less than $200 (2) | $201 to 575 (3) | Over $575 (4) | Total (5) |
|---|---|---|---|---|---|
| 1. Communist Asia | 44.6 | 37.9 | 0 | 0 | 23.7 |
| 2. Other Asia | 45.4 | 42.3 | 0.9 | 0 | 26.5 |
| 3. Middle East | 0.4 | 3.6 | 7.9 | 0.5 | 3.5 |
| 4. Total Asia (lines 1–3) | 90.3 | 83.7 | 8.9 | 0.5 | 53.7 |
| 5. Africa | 9.1 | 10.7 | 6.8 | 0 | 7.6 |
| 6. Asia and Africa (lines 4 and 5) | 99.4 | 94.4 | 15.6 | 0.5 | 61.3 |
| 7. Latin America | 0.6 | 5.6 | 21.9 | 1.4 | 6.9 |
| 8. Less developed Europe | 0 | 0 | 11.7 | 0 | 1.6 |
| 9. Communist Europe | 0 | 0 | 28.2 | 30.4 | 11.2 |
| 10. Non-Communist developed Europe | 0 | 0 | 0 | 37.7 | 8.9 |
| 11. North America, Australia, and New Zealand | 0 | 0 | 0 | 30.0 | 7.1 |
| 12. Total population, including Japan (millions) | 1,528.2 | 1,800.9 | 406.9 | 679.3 | 2,887.1 |

Sources: All underlying data are from sources cited in the notes to Table 7.1. The groupings of countries, other than those listed below, are identical with those in Table 7.1.
Panel A, line 13: Includes countries covered in lines 10 and 11 and Communist Asia.
Panel A, line 14: Includes countries in lines 12 and 13.

By substituting reasonably realistic values for $e$ and $f$ in the above equation and making various assumptions concerning the relation between these errors we can derive illustrative relations between the *observed* (estimated) and the *true* ratios of per capita product in developed countries to per capita product in underdeveloped countries.

*Fraction by Which the Estimated Ratio $(p_d/p_u)$ Must Be Multiplied to Approximate the True Ratio $(P_d/P_u)$*

| | I. Errors have same sign | | II. Errors have different signs | |
| --- | --- | --- | --- | --- |
| | Both are minus (1) | Both are plus (2) | e is plus (3) | f is plus (4) |
| 1. e = 5%; f = 10% | 0.95 | 1.05 | 0.86 | 1.16 |
| 2. e = 5%; f = 15% | 0.89 | 1.10 | 0.81 | 1.21 |
| 3. e = 7.5%; f = 15% | 0.92 | 1.07 | 0.79 | 1.24 |
| 4. e = 7.5%; f = 20% | 0.86 | 1.12 | 0.74 | 1.30 |

To illustrate, if the estimated ratio of per capita product in developed to that in underdeveloped countries is 10 to 1, and we assume that both are underestimates of true values (i.e. both $e$ and $f$ are negative) and that the underestimate is 5 per cent for developed and 10 per cent for underdeveloped countries, the estimated ratio should be multiplied by 0.95, and the true ratio will be 9.5 rather than 10.0.

Since the relation of the estimated to the true ratio is a function of the magnitudes of, signs of, and correlation between the errors in the two terms of the comparison, our judgment as to what the errors are likely to be should distinguish these aspects. And the errors with which we are concerned are those in estimates fully comparable in definition, i.e. as to scope and netness, and properly converted to a common unit. In other words, we deal here with errors of measurement or estimation, not with disparities resulting from incomparabilities in the definition or from the use of improper conversion bases.

While a defensible judgment requires knowledge of the details underlying a wide variety of estimates for a large number of countries, and is thus beyond my competence, some tentative propositions can be advanced to secure at least a preliminary result. I would argue that the errors in the estimates for both groups of countries are likely to be in the direction of understatement, in view of the difficulty of covering fully the wide scope underlying the standard definition of national product and the tendency toward underreporting of many economic activities. And such underestimation may be proportionately greater in the underdeveloped countries, because their statistical apparatus is weaker and a larger proportion of their activities lies outside the organized markets and is less susceptible of measurement.

If these tentative judgments are accepted, the ratios most relevant for our purposes are those in column 1 of the illustrative tabulation above. With errors in the estimates for developed countries reasonably assumed to be no greater than 7.5 per cent and in those for underdeveloped countries no greater than 20 per cent (which may be too large an allowance), the true ratio of the per capita products of the two groups of countries is likely to be between a tenth and a seventh lower than that actually estimated. The main value of the calculation is not the specific magnitudes derived, although they may be realistic, but its indication that ratios of the per capita products of developed to those of underdeveloped countries, derived from Table 7.1, are *overestimates* of a magnitude unlikely to be larger than a seventh.

*Scope*—The scope of national product is set by the line drawn between economic production and other activities classified as noneconomic even though they may yield goods. In standard national accounting, the line is drawn to include under economic production all market-oriented activities (as well as government) and all primary output whether marketed or for own consumption, but to exclude "all non-primary production performed by producers outside their own trades and consumed by themselves." [2] Thus

2. See U.N., *Studies in Methods*, p. 25.

the construction of barns by farmers, the spinning and weaving or clothmaking for own consumption by anyone not in the trade, and household services by family members are all excluded.

If we accept this definition for comparisons between developed and underdeveloped countries, no further questions or problems arise—except that of identifying a producer's "own trade." But if we consider the concept inappropriate for comparisons across a wide range of per capita product and structural differentials, a major question arises. It may be argued that for comparisons between economic societies with widely different shares of household versus market-oriented activities, the definition of economic production that excludes much household (or communal) activity will yield results biased in favor of the developed societies. The premise of this argument is that the proportion of output excluded by such a definition—production of nonprimary output for own consumption and services by family members within the household—to the economic output included is significantly greater in the underdeveloped than in the developed countries. And this argument can easily be supported by references to the commercialization and "marketization," in the process of modern economic growth, of a wide variety of consumer and producer goods that were turned out for own consumption within the household in earlier days—ranging from baking, canning, soapmaking, sewing, etc. to the household or communal work on house construction, tools, and other capital goods.

While the argument can be granted, the implied difference between outputs based on the wider and on the narrower national product concepts cannot be measured, except on the basis of a variety of intensive studies of economic activities within the household versus those that are market-oriented, for many countries at different levels of economic development. Few studies of this sort are available, and the task of distilling any reasonable approximations from them is not feasible here. But an illustrative suggestion can perhaps be derived from data on differences between developed and underdeveloped countries in the proportion of rural to total population, and in the shares of the agricultural sector in product and labor force—on the assumption that the greater proportion of excluded to included activities in the narrower, standard definition, is a positive function of the greater proportion of agriculture-dependent population in the underdeveloped countries. The average share of the agricultural sector in total product (in the early 1950s) was about 46 per cent in the underdeveloped countries and about 17 per cent in the developed; and its proportion in the labor force (excluding unpaid family labor) was about 58 per cent in the underdeveloped and 19 per cent in the developed countries (see Table 8.1). Likewise, rural population was about 70 per cent of total population in the underdeveloped and about 33 per cent in the developed countries (see Table 7.4).

In asking what these differences suggest concerning the greater proportions to be allowed for excluded, non-market-oriented activities in the underdeveloped than in the developed countries, we must remember that such activities are also found in the developed countries—both in the countryside and in the cities—and that perhaps for urban, nonagricultural population in the two sets of countries the difference in excluded proportions is not large. If then we make the fairly generous assumption that the net differences would be approximately one quarter of the total product of the agricultural sector of the underdeveloped countries (and zero in the developed countries), per capita product of the underdeveloped countries would be raised roughly a tenth; and the ratio of the per capita products of the two sets of countries would be reduced about the same fraction.

This estimate is only a reasonable guess; it could be raised or lowered—within narrow limits—without straining our sense of realism. The main point of the argument is that the proportion of the excluded activities is largely a function of the share of the agricultural sector, not of total product, and it is assumed to be some reasonable proper fraction of output already measured as the share of the A sector in total product. If the difference must be a proper fraction of agricultural output, and agricultural output is less than half of total product in underdeveloped countries, even maximum values of the proportion of excluded activities, consonant with these assumptions, would not result in a major scaling down of the ratios of the per capita products of developed to those of underdeveloped countries, as these ratios emerge from the current estimates.

*Comparative Valuation*—Assuming a reliable measure of an accepted concept of national product for the two groups of countries, we face the problem of conversion of the totals—each derived in domestic prices and currencies—to a common denominator. In Tables 7.1 and 7.2 the conversion is by 1938 currency exchange rates, sometimes linked to an earlier year for which the exchange rates were viewed as more realistic. But even when these rates reflect comparative prices of goods entering exchange between a country and its trading partners, they measure purchasing power only in terms of goods traded—which may not be the same as purchasing power in terms of *all* goods in the national products of the nations being compared, properly weighted by their shares in these aggregates (rather than by the shares of goods traded in international flows). Thus, even if we disregard the transitory effects of financial pressures and the more lasting effects of government intervention, exchange rates are likely to understate the true differences between prices in developed and less developed countries, because the prices of the goods in underdeveloped countries that are exported are likely to be higher in relation to prices of nonexportable goods than would be the case in developed countries.

A better basis for conversion of the national products of two countries to a common denominator would be the valuation of the two outputs at the same prices—a valuation that can be applied, of course, only to the goods that are identical or at least similar in the two countries. Such conversion is extremely helpful, even if it cannot extend to goods unique to only one of the countries and must deal arbitrarily with intricate problems of quality differentials. But even with this procedure, the best for the purpose, we must choose a single system of prices: use of the prices of the more developed country would affect the comparison differently from use of the prices of the less developed country. Resolution of the difference by taking a geometric mean of the ratios of the national products on the two bases is only mechanical; the analytical problem of the effect of base price weights on the comparison remains.

The discussion of the questions raised by the use of the exchange rates and alternative procedures is facilitated by reference to Table 7.3, which summarizes discrepancies between exchange rate and specific price conversions of national products for a limited number of countries and provides some supplementary relevant information. Although the data are largely for developed countries (in Panels A–C Italy has the lowest per capita product), the range in per capita product is substantial, and some basis is provided for reasonable approximations to what various types of specific price conversions are likely to yield.[3]

Several conclusions can be drawn from Table 7.3. First, in all cases use of the specific price indexes shows that the disparity in per capita product is exaggerated by currency exchange rate conversions, at least when the high per capita product of the United States is compared with the lower

3. Two related bodies of data could not be used here. One, for Latin America (see U.N., *A Measurement of Price Levels and the Purchasing Power of Currencies, 1960–62,* mimeographed document prepared for the Economic Commission for Latin America, 10th session, Mar de la Plata, May 1963), uses prices for capital cities alone; and we felt that these could not be taken to represent countrywide prices relevant to national product totals. The other, assembled by the Federal Statistical Office of West Germany (see *Preise, Löhne, Wirtschaftsrechnungen,* Series 10, *Internationaler Vergleich der Preise für die Lebenshaltung,* Stuttgart, 1963), presents price indexes of consumer goods weighted by German and other country quantity weights, but the adequacy of the coverage of the data for our purposes is uncertain.

## TABLE 7.3

Relation Between Conversions by Exchange Rates and by Specific Price Indexes, Selected Countries, 1955, 1950, and 1928–39

Individual countries
(in decreasing order of per capita GNP, exchange rate conversion)

| | Ratio to U.S. GNP per capita (100), exchange rate conversion (1) | Ratio to col. 1, specific price conversion | | | Three-country moving averages* | | | |
|---|---|---|---|---|---|---|---|---|
| | | U.S. prices (2) | Domestic prices (3) | Geometric mean of cols. 2 and 3 (4) | Col. 1 (5) | Col. 2 (6) | Col. 3 (7) | Col. 4 (8) |
| A. RATIOS OF SPECIFIC PRICE CONVERSIONS TO EXCHANGE RATE CONVERSIONS, 1955 | | | | | | | | |
| 1. France | 47 | 1.19 | 0.89 | 1.03 | | | | |
| 2. Belgium | 44 | 1.32 | 1.11 | 1.21 | 44 | 1.34 | 1.06 | 1.19 |
| 3. United Kingdom | 42 | 1.52 | 1.19 | 1.34 | 42 | 1.44 | 1.14 | 1.28 |
| 4. Norway | 41 | 1.49 | 1.12 | 1.29 | 40 | 1.51 | 1.17 | 1.33 |
| 5. Denmark | 37 | 1.51 | 1.19 | 1.34 | 38 | 1.55 | 1.17 | 1.34 |
| 6. Germany | 35 | 1.66 | 1.20 | 1.41 | 34 | 1.62 | 1.22 | 1.41 |
| 7. Netherlands | 31 | 1.71 | 1.26 | 1.47 | 27 | 1.74 | 1.17 | 1.42 |
| 8. Italy | 19 | 1.84 | 1.05 | 1.39 | | | | |
| B. RATIOS OF SPECIFIC PRICE CONVERSIONS TO EXCHANGE RATE CONVERSIONS, 1950 | | | | | | | | |
| 9. Belgium | 43 | 1.33 | 1.12 | 1.22 | | | | |
| 10. United Kingdom | 37 | 1.70 | 1.30 | 1.49 | 39 | 1.55 | 1.24 | 1.39 |
| 11. Denmark | 37 | 1.65 | 1.30 | 1.46 | 36 | 1.62 | 1.23 | 1.41 |
| 12. France | 35 | 1.51 | 1.11 | 1.29 | 35 | 1.63 | 1.23 | 1.42 |
| 13. Norway | 34 | 1.74 | 1.29 | 1.50 | 32 | 1.72 | 1.25 | 1.47 |

| | | | (9–11) | (10–12) | (11–13) | (12–14) | (13–15) | (14–16) |
|---|---|---|---|---|---|---|---|---|
| 14. Netherlands | 27 | 1.93 | 1.37 | 1.63 | 29 | 1.78 | 1.27 | 1.50 |
| 15. Germany | 26 | 1.69 | 1.15 | 1.39 | 22 | 1.83 | 1.21 | 1.49 |
| 16. Italy | 16 | 1.88 | 1.12 | 1.45 | | | | |

C. RATIOS OF U.S. PRICES TO DOMESTIC PRICES, GNP AND COMPONENTS, 1950, THREE-COUNTRY MOVING AVERAGES*

Groups of countries (using line numbers, Panel B)

| | (9–11) | (10–12) | (11–13) | (12–14) | (13–15) | (14–16) |
|---|---|---|---|---|---|---|
| | (1) | (2) | (3) | (4) | (5) | (6) |
| 17. Gross national product | 1.26 | 1.31 | 1.33 | 1.37 | 1.40 | 1.51 |
| 18. Household consumption | 1.21 | 1.29 | 1.29 | 1.31 | 1.32 | 1.45 |
| 19. Capital formation | 1.23 | 1.15 | 1.28 | 1.30 | 1.38 | 1.31 |
| 20. Consumption and capital formation | 1.21 | 1.26 | 1.29 | 1.31 | 1.33 | 1.42 |
| 21. Government consumption | 1.74 | 1.70 | 1.77 | 1.94 | 1.99 | 2.37 |
| *Components of household consumption* | | | | | | |
| 22. Food | 1.27 | 1.32 | 1.38 | 1.42 | 1.46 | 1.48 |
| 23. Alcoholic beverages and tobacco | 1.24 | 1.29 | 1.12 | 1.16 | 0.87 | 1.38 |
| 24. Clothing and footwear | 0.92 | 0.87 | 0.90 | 0.86 | 0.85 | 0.82 |
| 25. House: rent, light, fuel, water, household goods | 1.03 | 1.14 | 1.13 | 1.12 | 1.16 | 1.33 |
| 26. Household and personal services | 1.79 | 2.00 | 2.09 | 2.08 | 2.15 | 2.59 |
| 27. Transport and communication | 1.23 | 1.23 | 1.17 | 1.22 | 1.26 | 1.35 |
| 28. Recreation and amusement | 1.25 | 1.34 | 1.13 | 1.21 | 1.36 | 1.83 |
| 29. Education and health | 1.46 | 1.59 | 1.81 | 1.84 | 1.84 | 2.07 |

D. RATIOS OF COLIN CLARK'S I. U. CONVERSIONS TO EXCHANGE RATE CONVERSIONS, MOSTLY FOR 1928 OR 1929, COUNTRIES GROUPED IN DESCENDING ORDER OF PER CAPITA INCOME

| | (1) | (2) | (3) | (4) | (5) | (6) |
|---|---|---|---|---|---|---|
| 30. Number of countries | 5 | 5 | 5 | 5 | 4 | 4 |
| 31. Average ratio of per capita income to U.S. per capita (exchange rate conversion) | 0.74 | 0.47 | 0.30 | 0.20 | 0.13 | 0.07 |
| 32. Average ratio, I.U. to exchange rate conversion | 1.03 | 1.13 | 1.40 | 1.26 | 1.53 | 1.94 |

TABLE 7.3—*Continued*

* The three-country averages in cols. 5–8 of Panels A and B and in Panel C, as well as the averages in Panel D are unweighted geometric means of ratios for the individual countries.

*Sources: Panels A and B:* From Milton Gilbert and associates, *Comparative National Products and Price Levels* (Paris, 1958), Tables 2 and 4, pp. 23 and 28.

*Panel C:* The basic sources are the binary comparisons between the United States and each European country in ibid., Tables 38–41, pp. 99–106 and Milton Gilbert and Irving B. Kravis, *An International Comparison of National Products and the Purchasing Power of Currencies* (Paris, 1954), Tables 27–30, pp. 113–19.

*Panel D:* The source for 24 of the 28 countries is Clark, *Conditions of Economic Progress*, 3d ed., Chapter 3, pp. 75–218; and for four countries ibid., 2d ed., pp. 118, 120–23, 158–59. From these we calculated the ratios of purchasing power of currencies between a given country and the United States in I. U.'s (an international purchasing power unit calculated by Mr. Clark as the geometric mean of U.S. prices of a given country's output using U.S. quantity weights and the given country's weights); we then compared it with the exchange rate for 1928 in League of Nations, *The Network of World Trade* (Geneva, 1942) Annex IV, p. 172. Averages of the results are shown in line 31. The data underlying line 32, also from Clark, *Conditions*, 3d ed., are estimates of per capita income at market prices in the country's currency, converted to U.S. dollars by the 1928 exchange rate.

The following countries were included in the successive columns of Panel D: (1) Australia, New Zealand, Canada, Great Britain, Switzerland; (2) Denmark, Sweden, Norway, the Netherlands, Germany; (3) France, Belgium, Ireland, Austria, Spain; (4) Finland, Czechoslovakia, Italy, Hungary, Greece; (5) Yugoslavia, Estonia, Japan, Poland; (6) Bulgaria, Turkey, Brazil, British India (1931–32).

per capita products of other countries. Thus the ratios of
per capita product of these "other" countries to that of the
United States based on specific price conversion are invariably higher than those based on exchange rate conversion: the entries in columns 2–4 of Panels A and B (for 1955
and 1950 respectively) and in line 32 of Panel D (for 1928–
29) are, with one exception, all above 1. Even Colin Clark's
less elaborate calculations for 1928–29 confirm this finding.

Second, as we pass from the results of the exchange rate
to those of the specific price conversions, the upward adjustment of the ratios of per capita products in binary comparisons is markedly greater with the use of United States price
weights than when domestic price weights are used (compare columns 2 and 3 in Panels A and B). The implication
is that the negative association between quantity and price
ratios—if only for goods not entering international trade
and not affecting exchange rates—is distinctly stronger in
countries with lower per capita product. As a result, weighting by U.S. prices raises appreciably (relative to the exchange rates) the value of goods that are relatively cheap in
the lower product countries (e.g. labor-intensive goods) but
reduces much less the value of expensive goods (e.g. machinery) for which prices in the United States are relatively
low. The resulting upward adjustment is much lower if we
use the price weights of the lower per capita product country, which raise the values of some parts of the U.S. output
(e.g. machinery) but lower the values of others (e.g. labor-
intensive goods).

The result here is analogous with what we find in comparisons over time: when we use price weights for the *end*
of the period (a procedure that corresponds to the use of
the U.S. prices in the binary, cross-section comparisons), the
rate of growth (which corresponds to disparity between per
capita products in cross-section comparison) is distinctly
lower than when we use price weights for the *beginning* of
the period (a procedure that corresponds to the use of a
given country's prices in the binary, cross-section comparison). It is not without analytical significance that growth

379

seems so much larger when evaluated by the price system at the *beginning* of the growth period, looking *forward,* than when evaluated by the price weights at the *end* of the period, looking *backward*; and, also, that in cross-section comparisons, the disparity seems *greater* (with a smaller reduction from exchange conversion rates) when evaluated in terms of the price system of the country with *lower* per capita product than it does in terms of the price system of the country with *higher* per capita product. The results reflect a higher valuation of, and thus perhaps a greater incentive toward, economic growth when viewed from the vantage point of an early year or a less developed country rather than from that of a recent year or a developed country.

Third, Panel C reveals that the relatively higher price levels in the United States than in "other" countries are particularly marked for such labor-intensive categories as household and personal services, recreation and amusement, health and education, and government consumption; and much less marked in commodity production, transportation and communication, and capital investment. Indeed, for some consumer commodities (e.g. clothing and footwear), U.S. prices are relatively low. This finding is important in that it indicates the particular locus of the price weight differentials in the comparisons, and it has bearing upon extension of this analysis to the underdeveloped countries with much lower per capita products than those covered in Panels A–C of Table 7.3. Clearly, if the proportion of labor-intensive services in total product tends to decline as we move down the scale of per capita income, the effect on the specific price disparities will be damped and the adjustment ratio to be applied to per capita product relations derived from the use of exchange rate conversions will be lowered—a point to which we pass now.

Fourth, the extent to which the per capita product of a country, relative to the top product country (in this case the United States), is raised when we shift from exchange rates to specific price conversions, is *inversely* related to the country's per capita product—*if* we use the U.S. price weights as the common base. Thus, the ratios in column 2 of Panels A and B rise as we move down the array of per capita product relatives (based on exchange rates and shown in column 1); and this movement is also found in the "smoothed," three-country averages in columns 5 and 6. But this is not true of the adjustments based on the *given* country's price weights (column 3 of Panels A and B); the semblance of negative association for 1955 is due exclusively to the peculiar price structure for France and Belgium, other countries showing no systematic variation in their adjustment ratios.[4] Hence the inverse association of the geometric means in columns 4 and 8 with the relatives in columns 1 and 5 is due exclusively to the weight of the U.S. price-based comparisons in columns 2 and 6. We also find a negative association in lines 31–32, which are geometric means similar to those in column 8 of Panels A and B.

These findings, particularly the third and fourth, permit us to approximate roughly the effects of shifts from conversion by exchange rates to conversion by specific price weights, for the full range of per capita product differentials revealed in Table 7.1. In this calculation we assume that the ratio of specific price conversion to that by exchange rates is invariant to the relative position of the country, if the given country's price weights are used as the common set;

4. This result would be obtained if exchange rates reflected prices of goods entering trade, if prices of U.S. exports were not particularly representative of prices of aggregate product, and if prices of export goods in other countries were more representative of prices of total output. In that case, the source of the discrepancy between specific price and exchange rate conversions would lie primarily in the U.S. price structure—perhaps a not implausible assumption, since exports are a very small proportion of aggregate product in the United States. The discrepancy between specific price and exchange rate conversions, using United States prices, would, up to a point, be the wider, the lower a country's per capita product: the lower the per capita product, the higher the proportion of goods for which U.S. prices are high and the lower the proportion of goods for which U.S. prices are low—a condition not reflected in the exchange rates. But this is a conjecture requiring more formal definition and empirical evidence.

and we set this adjustment ratio at 1.20 for all countries
vis-à-vis the United States, as suggested in Table 7.3, Panels
A and B, column 7. Then, using the three-country averages
in columns 5 and 6, and observing their movements for both
1950 and 1955, we find that as we move down the array,
larger proportional declines in the product ratios in column
5 are accompanied by no larger proportional rises in the
adjustment ratios in column 6. We set the coefficient between these marginal declines in column 5 and marginal
rises in column 6 in the vicinity of the lowest per capita
product shown, at 0.25 (meaning that the proportional rise
in column 6 is a quarter of the proportional decline in
column 5), and assume the same coefficient for continuation
of the array down to lower relative per capita product
levels. We can then estimate the adjustment ratio (column
6) for the groups in Table 7.1 in Asia and Africa, with very
low per capita product (based on the exchange rate conversion). The results are shown in the following tabulation.

| Per capita product (U.S. $, 1958, conversion by exchange rates) | Derived adjust- ment ratio analogous to col. 6, panels A and B, Table 7.3 | Corre- sponding per capita product, U.S. $ | Adjust- ment ratio corre- sponding to col. 8, Table 7.3 | Corre- sponding per capita product, U.S. $ |
|---|---|---|---|---|
| 75 (Asia) | 2.96 | 222 | 1.88 | 141 |
| 130 (Africa) | 2.58 | 335 | 1.76 | 229 |
| 200 (Middle East) | 2.32 | 464 | 1.67 | 334 |
| 260 (Latin America) | 2.17 | 564 | 1.61 | 419 |
| 340 (Less developed Europe) | 2.03 | 690 | 1.56 | 530 |
| 1,060 (Developed Europe) | 1.53 | 1,622 | 1.35 | 1,431 |

These calculations, while realistic, are likely to err in the
direction of overcorrecting rather than undercorrecting disparities between specific price and exchange rate conversions, in particular because they assume that the trend
shown within the range of Panels A and B of Table 7.3—
for the rise in the upward adjustment ratio to diminish

rapidly as we move down the array of per capita product—
is not assumed operative. But accepting the calculation as
a maximum rather than average adjustment, we find that
whereas the range between the per capita products in the
United States and Asia on the exchange rate basis is 31 to 1
(i.e. $2,324 compared with $75), shifting both outputs to
U.S. prices cuts the range to 10.5 to 1; and using the geometric mean of U.S. and Asian price weight conversions
cuts it to 16.5 to 1.[5] The adjustment becomes proportionately narrower as we move up the array of per capita income; and one interesting effect is that expressing per capita
product of all lower product countries in U.S. prices reduces
not only the range of the disparity between them, on
the one hand, and the United States, on the other, but also
the disparity within the range. Thus, the relative difference

5. That these *may* represent an overcorrection in the adjustment for
price differentials is suggested by a recent study (which appeared after
this chapter was completed) by Wilfred Beckerman, entitled "International Comparisons of Real Incomes," *O.E.C.D. Development Center
Studies, No. 4, rev.* (Paris, September 1965, mimeo.). Following a review of the literature, Beckerman, by correlating selected measures of
physical volume of consumption per capita and real per capita income
for countries for which specific price conversions were available, estimates the real income for countries for which no specific price conversions could be made. The method obviously has merit, but the underlying data seem to have too narrow a range—both those for consumption items and those for countries at different levels of per capita
income. Consequently it is highly probable that extrapolations beyond
this range are subject to wide error, specifically to a bias toward under-
correction for price differentials. Beckerman's method yields relatives
for the truly underdeveloped countries (e.g. Ceylon, Ghana, and Thailand) that are extremely low—less than 5 compared with 100 for the
United States (for 1960, see Table 6, pp. 40–41). For the same countries,
the relatives of per capita GDP at factor costs in 1958, based on *exchange rate conversions,* given in U.N., *Yearbook of National Accounts
Statistics, 1964,* Table 6A, pp. 383 ff., are about 5 for Ceylon, about 7
for Ghana, and slightly over 3 for Thailand, with the United States
at 100.

J. P. Delahaut and E. S. Kirschen in "Les Revenus Nationaux du
Monde Non Communiste," *Cahiers Economiques de Bruxelles,* No. 10,
April 1961, present a coefficient of correction for price differentials
that yields results quite similar to ours.

between the per capita products of Asia and Africa, both converted to U.S. dollars by exchange rates, is between 130 and 75, or 1.7 to 1; when conversion is based on U.S. prices, the range drops to 335 to 222, or 1.5 to 1.[6]

6. As a matter of curiosity, but also for whatever substantive interest may be attached to it, one could make the same calculation for past comparisons, using the United States as one term and the most under-developed group as the other term. In another connection, we found that from 1840 to 1960 per capita product in the United States grew to 6.4 times its initial level in constant 1929 prices (see Kuznets, "Notes on the Pattern," Table 1, p. 377). This rate may have been exaggerated by the differential errors of estimate and changing scope discussed above; if we make allowance for such exaggeration, of about a tenth each, the multiplication factor would be reduced a fifth (i.e. to 6.4 divided by 1.21, derived by multiplying 1.1 by 1.1, or 5.3). Dividing the per capita product for the United States in 1958, $2,324, by 5.3 we get about $440 for per capita product in 1840 or so (more precisely 1838) in 1958 prices. Assume now that per capita product for Asia in 1838 was about the same as in 1958, not necessarily an unrealistic assumption for the aggregate excluding Japan. The 1838 ratio of U.S. to Asian product, using exchange conversion rates, is then 440 to 75, or almost 6 to 1.

We must now consider the adjustment required to shift the 1838 estimates from the exchange rate to the specific price conversion basis. If we assume that the growth rate for per capita product of the United States, which is based on volumes in 1929 prices, is already fully adjusted for the shift from initial to terminal price weights, and that the constancy of the per capita product assumed for Asia is likewise in the 1958 price structure, the conversion by specific U.S. 1958 prices can be derived indirectly by dividing 10.5, the range shown for 1958, by 5.3, the growth rate for the United States. The ratio of per capita product in the United States to that in Asia in 1838, both in U.S. 1958 prices, is then about 2. If, on the other hand, we assume that the growth rate is affected by shifts in price structure, and must take account of the lower level of United States per capita product in 1838, we can use the 1958 functional relation between income multiples and the adjustment. For a ratio of about 6 to 1, i.e. for a per capita product relative (to U.S. per capita) of about 17.0, the adjustment ratio, analogous to that in column 6 of Panels A and B of Table 7.3, would be about 1.95. On this basis, using U.S. prices as weights, the per capita product of Asia in 1838 would be about $145, or about a third of the United States per capita of $440. But this last calculation implies that the growth rate is to be reduced by the ratio of 2.96 to 1.95, or about a third.

*Representativeness and Generality*—If we accept the adjustments using the U.S. price weights derived above, the widest per capita product differential in Table 7.1, between the United States and Asia, of about 31 to 1 is reduced to 10.5 to 1. If we also allow for maximum errors of measurement and scope, about a tenth each, the differential is further reduced to 8.7 to 1. If we use the price weights of the less developed countries, the range is reduced to 25.8 to 1, and after allowance for differential errors of measurement and scope, to 21.3 to 1. If we use the geometric means as a resolution of the underlying problem, the range is reduced by the shift from exchange rate to

While the above calculations are crude, the results are not unreasonable, and they reveal some consistency between the growth rates over long periods and the cross-section disparities over a wide range in recent years. It should be noted that whether we assume that per capita income of the United States in 1838 is twice or three times as high as that of Asia, the bulk of the adjusted disparity shown for 1958 (of 10.5 to 1) is due to the higher rate of growth of the United States since 1838. A similar result would be derived with the specific price conversion based on the "given" country prices, in this case those of Asia—although it is more difficult to envisage the growth rate for the United States with U.S. outputs weighted by the price relatives for Asia. In this case the growth rate would be much higher, and the derived per capita product for the United States in 1838 much lower. But even if we used the growth rate as given and the constant adjustment coefficient of 1.2, the ratio of United States per capita product to that of Asia, based on the Asian price weights, would be 25.8 to 1 in 1958 and 5 to 1 in 1838.

Of the various assumptions used in these calculations, that of complete absence of rise in the per capita product of Asia is most subject to doubt. Per capita product of some underdeveloped countries may have risen—although at a much lower rate than that of the presently developed countries. If we were to assume that there was some rise, that per capita product in Asia was closer to $50 than $75 in 1838 (in U.S. prices), all the initial ratios of per capita product in the United States to that in Asia would be that much higher; and the proportional contribution of the initial difference, relative to that of the differential rate of growth over the period, that much greater.

All these calculations applied above to the extreme range could be repeated for less extreme current differences in per capita income, but they would require estimates of rates of growth over long periods for the two countries in the comparison.

specific price conversion from 31 to 1 to 16.4 to 1, and further after allowance for errors and bias to 13.5 to 1. In short, with rather generous allowances for the various errors and biases involved, the wide difference in per capita product in Table 7.1 of 31 to 1 is reduced to a range between 8.7 to 1 and about 21 to 1; and it cannot reasonably be brought lower than 8.7 to 1, and probably would not fall below 10 to 1 with more realistic assumptions. Downward adjustments to be applied to per capita product differences in Table 7.1 less extreme than the one between the United States and Asia would obviously not be as great.

The preceding calculations, perhaps too elaborate in combining limited data with numerous assumptions, were made in an attempt to judge whether, after realistic but generous allowances for error and bias in the basic estimates and their conversion to comparable units, much substance remained in the striking differentials in the per capita product summarized in Tables 7.1 and 7.2. Such an attempt is needed not only to warn against uncritical reliance on the estimates as they are usually shown but, perhaps even more, to counter their complete dismissal because of the serious errors and biases in them. It is not surprising that the difficulty of understanding a range in per capita product of 31 to 1 and the awareness of possible errors and biases would lead to complete dismissal of the results as too uncertain to merit attention.

It is in the light of this difficulty created by the defects of the estimates that the end result of our calculations is important. If, even with generous allowances for errors and bias, the range in per capita product between the United States and Asia is still 10 to 1 (it would probably be of the order of 5 or 6 to 1 between all non-Communist developed countries in Group I and all non-Communist underdeveloped countries in Group III in Table 7.1) the differences are no statistical illusion. They remain wide even when the U.S. price weights are used as base, and are all the more striking when the prices of the less developed countries are used.

If further support of what already may be obvious is needed, reference can be made to Table 7.4, which summarizes some easily available indexes of conditions of life in countries grouped by their per capita income. While the year of reference is sometimes earlier than that used in Tables 7.1 and 7.2, and the number of countries much smaller, the sample is recent and large enough to merit attention.

In comparing the underdeveloped countries with the developed, we find that in the former (columns 5 and 6) the lower per capita product is accompanied by higher mortality rates, particularly for infants (lines 6 and 7). The population adjusts to low income and product by devoting a larger proportion of its expenditures to prime necessities, such as food, leaving a smaller proportion of the absolutely low per capita expenditures for other goods (line 8); even so, per capita calorie consumption is distinctly lower (line 9), and a higher proportion of these calories is comprised of starchy staples rather than protein-rich, protective types of foods (line 10). Furthermore, in literacy and provision for education the underdeveloped countries lag far behind the developed (lines 12 and 13); and the low rate of energy consumption (line 11) suggests that much greater reliance must be placed on physical labor and human energy. All of these indicators, together with the much greater "rurality" of underdeveloped countries (lines 4 and 5), show that different levels of per capita product betoken major differences in conditions of life and work—that the divergences shown by the statistical estimates in Tables 7.1 and 7.2 are associated with great contrasts in productive performance and levels of living which, when related to per capita product as cause or effect, are overwhelming evidence of the significance of these estimates. This confirmation is strengthened further by consideration of the difference in economic structure of high and low per capita product countries, a topic to be covered in Chapter 8.

Yet it must be emphasized that we are dealing here with aggregates. This means that in the underdeveloped coun-

387

TABLE 7.4

Indicators of Living Conditions, Countries Grouped by National Income per Capita, Post-World War II Years

| | Groups of countries by per capita income | | | | | |
| --- | --- | --- | --- | --- | --- | --- |
| | $1,000 and over (1) | $575 to 1,000 (2) | $350 to 575 (3) | $200 to 350 (4) | $100 to 200 (5) | Under $100 (6) |
| *General* | | | | | | |
| 1. Number of countries, 1958 | 6 | 11 | 14 | 13 | 14 | 10 |
| 2. Population (millions) | 216.7 | 396.8 | 183.8 | 226.2 | 171.5 | 667.6 |
| 3. Per capita income, 1956–58 ($) | 1,366 | 760 | 431 | 269 | 161 | 72 |
| *Urbanization* | | | | | | |
| 4. Per cent of total population in urban areas (recent census) | 68.2 | 65.8 | 49.9 | 36.0 | 32.0 | 22.9 |
| 5. Per cent of population in communities of more than 100,000, about 1955 | 43 | 39 | 35 | 26 | 14 | 9 |
| *Mortality* | | | | | | |
| 6. Expectation of life at birth, 1955–58 (years) | 70.6 | 67.7 | 65.4 | 57.4 | 50.0 | 41.7 |
| 7. Infant mortality per 1,000, 1955–58 | 24.9 | 41.9 | 56.8 | 97.2 | 131.1 | 180.0 |
| *Food Consumption* | | | | | | |
| 8. Per cent of private consumption expenditures spent on food, 1960 or late 1950s (36 countries) | 26.2 | 30.5 | 36.1 | 37.6 | 45.8 | 55.0 |
| 9. Per capita calorie consumption, latest year (40 countries) | 3,153 | 2,944 | 2,920 | 2,510 | 2,240 | 2,070 |
| 10. Per cent of starchy staples in total calories, latest year (40 countries) | 45 | 53 | 60 | 74 | 70 | 77 |
| *Energy Consumption* | | | | | | |
| 11. Per capita kilos of coal equivalent, 1956–58 | 3,900 | 2,710 | 1,861 | 536 | 265 | 114 |

## Education

| | | | | | | |
|---|---|---|---|---|---|---|
| 12. Per cent of population, 15 years and over, illiterate, 1950 | 2 | 6 | 19 | 30 | 49 | 71 |
| 13. Per cent of school enrollment to four fifths of the 5–19 age group, latest year | 91 | 84 | 75 | 60 | 48 | 37 |

*Sources:* All lines except 2, 4, and 8 are from U.N., *Report on the World Social Situation* (New York, 1961), Chap. 3, Table 1, p. 41 and Table 5, pp. 47–49. Entries in lines 3–13 are unweighted arithmetic means of figures for individual countries.

*Lines 1 and 2:* Number of countries and population for which per capita national income is given. Unless otherwise indicated in the stub, the country coverage for other indexes is close to that in line 1.

Population is from the sources given for Table 7.1. Of world population of 2.89 billion in 1958, 1.86 billion are covered here. The chief omissions are Mainland China (0.66 billion), most of the Middle East, and most of Africa.

*Line 3:* Conversion from domestic currency to U.S. dollars is by money exchange rates.

*Line 4:* Underlying data are from U.N., *Demographic Yearbook, 1963,* Table 5, and *1960,* Table 9. The usual limits are communities of 2,500 and over, or otherwise of distinctively urban character.

*Line 8:* Underlying data are from U.N., *Compendium of Social Statistics: 1963,* Statistical Papers, Series K, No. 2 (New York, 1963), Table 103, pp. 572–73. Five of the countries, not covered in *Report on the World Social Situation,* are entered in the groups in which GDP per capita in 1958 falls (for these see the source notes to Table 7.1).

*Line 11:* Includes coal, coke, lignite, petroleum and products, natural and manufactured gas and energy.

*Line 13:* Excludes preprimary and higher education.

389

tries there may be islands of modernity, where advanced technology is used and per worker productivity is high; that at least some consumers in these countries can obtain the products of recent advances in science and technology; and that there may be a curious combination of the most traditional low productivity sectors, on the one hand, with the most modern and advanced, on the other. With the availability of modern products and methods through international trade and through adaptation of the existing transnational stock of useful knowledge, it is thus possible, for example, for Communist China to produce an atomic bomb and for India to develop a system of airlines, even though per capita product in both countries is less than $100. And although this per capita product for underdeveloped countries today may be lower than that in Western Europe or the United States over a century ago, the range of feasible production and consumption choices available to these underdeveloped countries today is much wider than it was for the richest countries over a century ago. The low product estimates mean only that the relative weight of the modern segments, in economic terms, is so small and that of the traditional low product per worker sectors is so large that the average is dominated by the latter and only slightly affected by the former.

### TRENDS IN DIFFERENCES IN PER CAPITA PRODUCT

We may now turn to the question whether the wide differentials in per capita product in the world today are of recent origin or have prevailed over a long period. A detailed answer to this question would require estimates of per capita product for all or most countries in the world, including those presently underdeveloped, over a period at least as far back as the late eighteenth century (and for many interesting aspects even further back). Such data are available only for some of the presently developed countries, and even for some of these for too short a period. Past records are particularly scanty for the presently underdeveloped countries. The few that are at hand suggest that over long periods, the per capita product was either constant or rose moderately.

Thus for India (present territory) a careful evaluation of past estimates and of some relevant long-term data by Moni Mukherjee, of the Indian Statistical Institute, indicates that per capita income (in 1948–49 prices) rose from about 170 rupees in the early 1860s to about 260 rupees in the late 1930s, about 53 per cent in eight decades or about 5 per cent per decade.[7] For Jamaica, a study by Gisela Eisner reveals that per capita gross domestic product (in 1910 prices) declined from £15.6 in 1830 to about £11.8 in 1870, and then rose to £15.8 in 1930, showing no rise over the century, while population grew from about 0.37 to 1.01 million; per capita consumption expenditures rose, however, from £11.2 in 1830 to £13.5 in 1930, but mostly after 1890.[8] For Mexico, a comparison by Henry G. Aubrey of a crude estimate for 1803 with one for 1934 shows "a national income of 150 to 180 of 1934 pesos per capita in 1803, only slightly below the per capita income of 1934, according to the estimates of the General Bureau of Statistics"; and, despite the reservations, Aubrey considers the result "not entirely unlikely." [9] We could add some estimates for Egypt which show only rough stability of per capita income between the beginning of the century and World War II. But the sample is far too small to be of much value in the present connection; and what is more important, it is obviously biased in the selection of both countries and periods. Among the countries in the underdeveloped group in Table 7.1, a number must have shown a marked rise in per capita product, at least as large as and perhaps larger than that in per capita product of developed countries—if only for recent

7. See *The National Income of India: Trends and Structure,* in preparation, Chap. 2.

8. See *Jamaica, 1830–1930* (Manchester, 1961), Tables 8.II, 8.VI, and LXIV, pp. 119, 123, and 319.

9. See "National Income of Mexico," *Estadistica, 8* (July 1950), 188–89.

and shorter periods. Thus in Latin America the rate of growth in per capita product since the late 1920s was no lower than that for most older developed countries.[10] And if in 1958 the per capita product of Ghana was $170, of the Federation of Malaya $186, and of Jamaica as high as $398, it is not unlikely that about half a century ago the per capita product of all three was not much greater than that of India today ($70); and if so, the growth over the last five decades, ranging from 140 to over 450 per cent, was probably higher than that of the developed countries taken as a group.[11] In short, without a fairly comprehensive set of long-term records for most countries, one cannot secure a defensible answer; and the use of scattered small samples may easily lead to the wrong conclusions.

Yet the question can be answered fairly acceptably if we draw carefully the line of division between low and high per capita product countries, or between the developed and underdeveloped. This is not a matter of semantics but of clarity in the nature of the comparisons in whose long-term trend aspects we are interested.

We may start with those underdeveloped countries whose present per capita product is low, say below $100 as shown in Tables 7.1 and 7.2. With their present average per capita product about $75, the rate of increase over the past century could hardly have been marked—since it would have implied very low initial levels, insufficient to sustain life under the prevailing conditions. If we allow a maximum rise of about 50 per cent of the initial level, we then must ask what the initial per capita product and its rate of growth were in the rest of the world. With the group of low income countries accounting today for well over half of the population of the world and excluding all countries, particularly the presently developed, that show high per capita product and many that show high rates of past growth, it is reasonable to conclude that: (1) about a cen-

10. See Kuznets, *Postwar Economic Growth*, Table 8, pp. 139–42.
11. All the figures are from U.N., *Yearbook of National Accounts Statistics, 1963*, Table 3B.

tury ago the per capita product of these other countries must have been *no lower,* and was possibly higher, than that of the presently underdeveloped countries; and (2) the rate of growth for the aggregate of these countries, other than those with per capita product below $100 today, must have been appreciably higher than the maximum allowed for the latter (i.e. higher than 50 per cent in a century), since the presently developed countries grew at rates of about 15 per cent per decade (or quadrupled in a century) and their population was an increasing proportion of the world total. Consequently, the disparity between the per capita product of the presently low underdeveloped countries and that of the rest of the world must have increased over the last century and perhaps further back; and in this sense, the currently wide disparities are recent.

Instead of starting with the present underdeveloped countries with low per capita product, keeping their identity over the projection a century or so back and distinguishing them from a changing residual population (including that of the developed countries), we can start with the presently developed countries, those in Group I of Table 7.1. Their weighted average per capita product is well over $1,000, and the rate of growth in their per capita product over the past century was high, about 15 per cent per decade. Has the disparity between this group of countries and the rest of the world widened? The answer is probably "yes" if we assume that the initial per capita product in these countries was already distinctly higher than that of the rest of the world a century ago (the one exception among presently developed countries is Japan) and assume further that the rate of growth in their per capita product, in the aggregate, must have been appreciably higher than the rate for the rest of the world, which included the populous presently underdeveloped countries. But if the disparity widened, and appreciably, over the century, the present wide per capita product differentials are, in this sense too, recent.

Finally, we can answer the question even more definitively by comparing the two extreme groups: the presently underdeveloped countries with less than $100 per capita product and the presently developed countries in Group I of Table 7.1. If we assume that the rate of growth of per capita product of the presently developed countries was 15 per cent per decade so that it quadrupled in a century, while that for the presently low underdeveloped countries was 50 per cent over the century at the maximum, the range a century ago in per capita product in 1958 prices should have been between $1,392/4 and $75/1.5, or about 7 to 1, instead of 18.5 to 1. Thus almost six tenths of the present differential is due to the assumed difference in the rates of growth of per capita product over the last century.

Obviously, if we deal with *presently* developed and underdeveloped countries, keep their identity unchanged in projecting into the past, and recognize that it is the high rate of sustained growth that places countries in the developed group and the absence of such growth in the underdeveloped group, the difference in the dichotomy distinguished *must* increase automatically over the period. This follows *by definition,* provided that the initial levels of per capita product are in favor of the presently developed countries; and, historically, this has been the case, with the single exception of Japan. No other answer would be possible unless we classified countries not by *present* levels of development but by some *earlier* ones.

The implications of this observation may be followed more easily by reference to Table 7.5, which is purely illustrative but attempts to employ reasonably realistic growth and relative income level parameters. The table deals in time units intended to represent about a decade and a half each, so that the span of twelve units covers 18 decades. We assume throughout that the "normal" rate of growth in per capita product is 23.3 per cent per time unit, corresponding to 15 per cent per decade; that the population growth rates are the same for all country groups; that the countries eventually becoming developed, i.e. entering the process by the end of the 12th unit, account for half of world population, while the truly and consistently underdeveloped countries that show no growth in their per capita product account for the remaining half; and that of the eventually developed countries, the earlier group starts with a per capita product about twice as high and the later group with a per capita product one and a half times as high as that of the underdeveloped half of world population.

With these assumptions common to both cases, the two differ significantly in the connection between time of entry and the initial rates of growth. In Case 1, simpler but less realistic than Case 2, each follower country enters development one time unit behind the preceding one, but regardless of the time of entry, the growth in per capita product is always the same—at the "normal" 23.3 per cent per time unit. Thus no late entrant can catch up with the developed countries ahead of it in the process (assuming that its initial per capita product is not materially higher). Hence there is a widening gap between all truly underdeveloped countries, on the one hand, and all eventually developed countries, on the other; and also a continuous and widening (up to a limit) gap within and among Groups I and II, the developed countries themselves, which varies with time of entry. The proportional differences among leaders and laggers, whether the latter eventually become developed countries or remain underdeveloped, will widen or be constant at best; they will never diminish. And to the extent that Case 1 is applicable, the wide differences in per capita product between developed and underdeveloped countries and among the developed countries themselves are largely the result of recent growth.

Case 2 is somewhat more realistic. Here we assume that the latecomer can accelerate the rate of growth of its per capita product sufficiently to catch up with the leader in five time units, except that the initial proportional disparity in per capita product between Groups I and II is maintained (if the catching up of Group II were more complete, the conclusions would be reinforced). We assume further that after the latecomer has caught up within

TABLE 7.5

Illustrative Calculation of Disparities in Product per Capita Between Developed and Underdeveloped Countries, Long Periods

| | | | Per capita product at end of time units: | | | | | |
|---|---|---|---|---|---|---|---|---|
| Groups of countries (population of each developed country equals 5% of world total) | Pregrowth (1) | 1st (2) | 2nd (3) | 4th (4) | 6th (5) | 8th (6) | 10th (7) | 12th (8) |
| CASE 1. GROWTH RATE THE SAME REGARDLESS OF TIME OF ENTRY | | | | | | | | |
| *Group I. Early developed countries* | | | | | | | | |
| 1. Pioneer | 200 | 247 | 304 | 463 | 704 | 1,070 | 1,628 | 2,476 |
| 2. 1st follower | 200 | 200 | 247 | 375 | 571 | 868 | 1,320 | 2,007 |
| 3. 2nd follower | 200 | 200 | 200 | 304 | 463 | 704 | 1,070 | 1,628 |
| 4. 3rd follower | 200 | 200 | 200 | 247 | 375 | 571 | 868 | 1,320 |
| 5. 4th follower | 200 | 200 | 200 | 200 | 304 | 463 | 704 | 1,070 |
| 6. Average for lines 1–5 | 200 | 209 | 230 | 318 | 483 | 735 | 1,118 | 1,700 |
| *Group II. Late followers* | | | | | | | | |
| 7. 5th follower | 150 | 150 | 150 | 150 | 185 | 281 | 428 | 651 |
| 8. 6th follower | 150 | 150 | 150 | 150 | 150 | 228 | 347 | 528 |
| 9. 7th follower | 150 | 150 | 150 | 150 | 150 | 185 | 281 | 428 |
| 10. 8th follower | 150 | 150 | 150 | 150 | 150 | 150 | 228 | 347 |
| 11. 9th follower | 150 | 150 | 150 | 150 | 150 | 150 | 185 | 281 |
| 12. Average for lines 7–11 | 150 | 150 | 150 | 150 | 157 | 199 | 294 | 447 |
| *Group III. Underdeveloped throughout (50% of world population)* | | | | | | | | |
| 13. Average | 100 | 100 | 100 | 100 | 100 | 100 | 100 | 100 |
| 14. World average | 137.5 | 139.9 | 145.1 | 167.0 | 210.1 | 283.5 | 403.0 | 586.8 |
| *Comparative rates of growth (% per time unit)* | | | | | | | | |
| 15. Group I (line 6) | | 4.7 | 9.9 | 17.5 | 23.3 | 23.3 | 23.3 | 23.3 |
| 16. Group II (line 12) | | 0 | 0 | 0 | 4.7 | 12.5 | 21.6 | 23.3 |
| 17. World (line 14) | | 1.7 | 3.7 | 7.3 | 12.2 | 16.2 | 19.2 | 20.7 |

CASE 2. GROWTH RATE ACCELERATES TO CATCH UP WITH PIONEER IN 5 TIME UNITS
(PRESERVING RELATIVE DISPARITY BETWEEN GROUPS I AND II)

| | | | | | | | | |
|---|---|---|---|---|---|---|---|---|
| *Group I. Early developed countries* | | | | | | | | |
| 18. Pioneer | 200 | 247 | 304 | 463 | 704 | 1,070 | 1,628 | 2,476 |
| 19. 1st follower | 200 | 200 | 257 | 426 | 704 | 1,070 | 1,628 | 2,476 |
| 20. 2nd follower | 200 | 200 | 200 | 360 | 647 | 1,070 | 1,628 | 2,476 |
| 21. 3rd follower | 200 | 200 | 200 | 280 | 547 | 1,070 | 1,628 | 2,476 |
| 22. 4th follower | 200 | 200 | 200 | 200 | 425 | 905 | 1,628 | 2,476 |
| 23. Average for lines 18–22 | 200 | 209 | 232 | 346 | 605 | 1,037 | 1,628 | 2,476 |
| *Group II. Late followers* | | | | | | | | |
| 24. 5th follower | 150 | 150 | 150 | 150 | 228 | 528 | 1,221 | 1,857 |
| 25. 6th follower | 150 | 150 | 150 | 150 | 150 | 377 | 949 | 1,857 |
| 26. 7th follower | 150 | 150 | 150 | 150 | 150 | 248 | 679 | 1,857 |
| 27. 8th follower | 150 | 150 | 150 | 150 | 150 | 150 | 446 | 1,328 |
| 28. 9th follower | 150 | 150 | 150 | 150 | 150 | 150 | 270 | 873 |
| 29. Average for lines 24–28 | 150 | 150 | 150 | 150 | 166 | 291 | 713 | 1,554 |
| *Group III. Underdeveloped throughout* | | | | | | | | |
| 30. Average | 100 | 100 | 100 | 100 | 100 | 100 | 100 | 100 |
| 31. World average | 137.5 | 139.9 | 145.6 | 174.0 | 242.8 | 381.9 | 635.2 | 1,057.6 |
| *Comparative rates of growth (% per time unit)* | | | | | | | | |
| 32. Group I (line 23) | | 4.7 | 10.7 | 22.1 | 32.2 | 30.9 | 25.3 | 23.3 |
| 33. Group II (line 29) | | 0 | 0 | 0 | 5.2 | 32.4 | 56.5 | 47.0 |
| 34. World (line 31) | | 1.7 | 4.1 | 9.3 | 18.1 | 25.4 | 29.0 | 29.0 |

the allotted span, its rate of growth drops back to "normal," i.e. to 23.3 per cent per time unit. One important implication of the assumption is that the later the entry, the higher the rate of growth in the initial period of catching up, i.e. in the first five time units after initiation of growth. The form assigned to the catching up process is oversimplified, but modifications for the sake of greater realism are not likely to change the major results significantly.

Here again the disparity in per capita product between the truly and persistently underdeveloped countries in Group III and those in Groups I and II widen. But among the eventually developed countries (Group I), the earlier entrants, whose per capita product grows through time unit 8 at significantly higher rates than those for the world and whose share in world product is therefore continuously increasing up to that time, sustain a decline in their aggregate growth thereafter, and their rate of growth slips below that for the world (see lines 32 and 34). Thus, if we were to define Group I as the developed countries and Groups II and III as the underdeveloped, the differentials in per capita product between the former and the latter would widen through time unit 8 but would contract significantly between time units 8 and 12. In that sense, the current per capita product differentials in the world, if time unit 12 is considered current, would go back 60 years at least, and would not be the result of recent disparities in growth rates.

Case 2 demonstrates what should perhaps be obvious otherwise: the per capita products of developed and underdeveloped countries will converge *only* if a few of the latter enter the growth process with accelerated rates; and such convergence will be eliminated and divergence will prevail if the high growth rate countries are automatically shifted into the developed group. In terms of the original question, the answer is obvious. If we draw the line to include among the developed countries all or the preponderant proportion of those that have already entered the growth process in a significant fashion, the current contrast will necessarily be the cumulative result of disparities in rates of growth over the long period preceding the present. In such a distinction, widening divergence would automatically result from the way the line is drawn and would be neither surprising nor significant. If, however, the line were drawn to limit the developed countries to the pioneers and early followers, and include the late followers among the underdeveloped countries, the recent decades *might* show convergence of the per capita products of the two groups; and with this line of distinction, widening divergence between developed and underdeveloped countries in the course of modern economic growth does not follow automatically.

# 8 ECONOMIC AND SOCIAL STRUCTURE OF UNDERDEVELOPED COUNTRIES

While many aspects of the economic structure of underdeveloped countries are familiar, a brief examination here may indicate the specific components that reflect the failure to exploit the wide potential of modern growth, or contribute to that failure. Such an examination, supplemented by a review of some noneconomic characteristics (in the next section), may help to explain why modern economic growth has been attained by only a few countries that comprise a limited proportion of world population.

The data in Table 8.1 are largely from United Nations sources, and most of them have been organized and discussed in the series of papers, "Quantitative Aspects of the Economic Growth of Nations," published in *Economic Development and Cultural Change.* The grouping of countries by per capita product in 1958 is similar to that followed in Table 7.4, but with two significant changes. First, all Communist countries are omitted because their authoritarian character and the orientation of economic processes to plans formulated by a dictatorial minority result in peculiarities of economic structure that make these economies incomparable in many respects with those in which freedom of economic activity and consumer sovereignty prevail. Second, since per capita product is a misleading guide to the level of economic development in Japan, Israel, and Venezuela, we include Japan with countries having

400

incomes of $575–999, which, with countries with incomes of $1,000 or more, make up the developed group; and we combine Venezuela and Israel with countries with incomes of $350–574 and identify this group and countries with incomes of $200–374 as intermediate, between the developed and the underdeveloped group. The unweighted arithmetic means and the comparisons in Table 8.1 were only slightly affected by these shifts; but the adjustment seemed desirable, and would have been extended to other similarly marked cases (e.g. the countries in the Middle East that derive high per capita income from their oil, without having much other economic activity) if they had entered the sample.

Lines 2–4 indicate that the proportions of economically active to total population do not differ significantly between the developed and underdeveloped countries. The lower ratio of male labor force to total male population in the underdeveloped countries is partially offset by the higher proportions in these countries of males in total population (for columns 1 and 2, males are 49 per cent of total population; for columns 5 and 6 they are 50 and 53 per cent). Since the differences are slight, disparities between developed and underdeveloped countries in product per *worker,* or per member of the economically active population, are as wide as those observed in per *capita* product; and the distinctive features of the economic structure of underdeveloped countries would bear not only upon the implications of the low per capita income but also on the sources of the low per worker product.

These features of the economic structure of underdeveloped countries, suggested by the data in Table 8.1 and by related materials that cannot be as easily tabulated, are (1) industrial origin of product and attachment of labor force; (2) type of enterprise and distribution of labor force by status; (3) distribution of product by factor shares and by size of income; (4) allocation of product between consumption and capital investment, and the structure of the former component; (5) degree of participation in foreign

## TABLE 8.1

### Economic Structure, Countries Grouped by 1958 Product per Capita, Post-World War II Years*

| | Groups of countries by per capita GDP, 1958 | | | | | |
|---|---|---|---|---|---|---|
| | $1,000 and over (1) | $575-999 (2) | $350-574 (3) | $200-349 (4) | $100-199 (5) | Under $100 (6) |
| *Economically active as % of total population, last census* | | | | | | |
| 1. Number of countries | 14 | 6 | 11 | 17 | 24 | 12 |
| 2. Total | 42.7 | 49.3 | 36.8 | 38.7 | 39.2 | 43.7 |
| 3. Male | 62.4 | 67.0 | 56.6 | 56.8 | 58.7 | 58.3 |
| 4. Female | 23.6 | 32.3 | 17.0 | 20.6 | 19.6 | 27.4 |
| 5. Female labor force as % of total labor force | 28.1 | 33.4 | 23.1 | 26.6 | 25.0 | 30.0 |
| *Major sectors, product and labor force, early 1950s* | | | | | | |
| 6. Number of countries | | 16 | | 5 | 12 | |
| *Share in product (%)* | | | | | | |
| 7. Agriculture and related industries (A sector) | | 17.4 | | 20.5 | 46.0 | |
| 8. Mining, manufacturing, construction, utilities, transport and communication (M+ sector) | | 47.7 | | 34.0 | 21.5 | |
| 9. Services (S sector) | | 34.9 | | 45.5 | 32.6 | |
| *Share in labor force, excluding unpaid family labor (%)* | | | | | | |
| 10. A sector | | 19.3 | | 37.9 | 57.6 | |
| 11. M+ sector | | 46.2 | | 29.8 | 19.5 | |
| 12. S sector | | 34.5 | | 32.3 | 22.9 | |
| *Relative sectoral product per worker* | | | | | | |
| 13. A sector to countrywide | | 0.90 | | 0.54 | 0.80 | |
| 14. M+ sector to countrywide | | 1.03 | | 1.14 | 1.10 | |
| 15. S sector to countrywide | | 1.01 | | 1.41 | 1.42 | |
| 16. M+ and S sectors to A sector | | 1.13 | | 2.37 | 1.60 | |
| 17. S sector to M+ sector | | 0.98 | | 1.24 | 1.29 | |
| 18. Index of intersectoral inequality | | 3.8 | | 34.8 | 23.3 | |

*Distribution of GDP, more detailed structure, 1950s*

| | | | | | | |
|---|---|---|---|---|---|---|
| 19. Number of countries | 16 | 16 | 10 | 7 | 16 | 10 |
| *Share in GNP (%)* | | | | | | |
| 20. A sector | 14.0 | 15.1 | | 33.7 | 32.7 | 49.8 |
| 21. M+ sector | 50.9 | 39.4 | | 29.0 | 28.6 | 22.8 |
|   a. Mining | 2.4 | 10.6 | | 1.7 | 4.6 | 1.5 |
|   b. Manufacturing | 31.2 | 15.9 | | 15.3 | 11.2 | 9.5 |
|   c. Construction | 6.7 | 5.4 | | 4.7 | 4.8 | 4.0 |
|   d. Electric, gas, and water | 2.1 | 1.8 | | 1.3 | 1.1 | 0.8 |
|   e. Transport and communication | 8.7 | 5.8 | | 5.9 | 6.9 | 7.0 |
| 22. S sector | 35.0 | 45.5 | | 37.3 | 38.7 | 27.4 |

*Manufacturing, 1953*

| | | | | | |
|---|---|---|---|---|---|
| 23. Engaged as % of total labor force (assumed to be 0.42 of population) | 26.0 | 32.3 | 13.9 | 4.1 | |
| 24. Value added per engaged, 1948 $ | 5,707 | 2,262 | 1,389 | 567 | |

*Structure of manufacturing, late 1950s*

| | | | | | |
|---|---|---|---|---|---|
| 25. Number of countries | 16 | 8 | 6 | 17 | 9 |
| *Share in value added (%)* | | | | | |
| 26. Food, beverages, and tobacco | 16.7 | 34.8 | 34.3 | 38.2 | 34.8 |
| 27. Textiles | 6.3 | 6.4 | 20.2 | 10.8 | 17.6 |
| 28. Clothing and footwear | 5.0 | 10.1 | 4.3 | 5.4 | 2.5 |
| 29. Wood products | 5.3 | 5.8 | 4.0 | 7.2 | 5.3 |
| 30. Paper, printing, and publishing | 9.9 | 5.8 | 4.4 | 4.4 | 5.0 |
| 31. Leather and rubber | 2.0 | 1.7 | 3.3 | 2.2 | 3.5 |
| 32. Chemicals | 9.1 | 9.1 | 9.4 | 10.1 | 12.8 |
| 33. Nonmetallic minerals | 4.5 | 7.1 | 5.5 | 6.4 | 4.5 |
| 34. Basic metals | 10.6 | 3.2 | 4.4 | 1.9 | 1.9 |
| 35. Metal products | 28.0 | 13.4 | 9.0 | 10.6 | 9.5 |
| 36. All other | 2.5 | 2.7 | 1.2 | 2.8 | 2.6 |
| *Value added per engaged as relative of value added per engaged in all manufacturing* | | | | | |
| 37. Food, beverages, and tobacco | 1.27 | 1.15 | 1.16 | 1.34 | 1.15 |
| 38. Textiles | 0.72 | 0.86 | 0.91 | 0.72 | 0.80 |

TABLE 8.1—*Continued*

Groups of countries by per capita GDP, 1958

| | $1,000 and over (1) | $575–999 (2) | $350–574 (3) | $200–349 (4) | $100–199 (5) | Under $100 (6) |
|---|---|---|---|---|---|---|
| 39. Clothing and footwear | | 0.56 | 0.60 | 0.53 | 0.56 | 0.56 |
| 40. Wood products | | 0.74 | 0.69 | 0.69 | 0.67 | 0.54 |
| 41. Paper, printing, and publishing | | 1.16 | 1.14 | 1.05 | 1.86 | 1.35 |
| 42. Leather and rubber | | 0.95 | 1.13 | 1.06 | 1.00 | 1.67 |
| 43. Chemicals | | 1.72 | 2.03 | 1.59 | 1.80 | 1.71 |
| 44. Nonmetallic minerals | | 0.96 | 1.08 | 0.85 | 1.00 | 1.00 |
| 45. Basic metals | | 1.19 | 1.60 | 1.69 | 1.36 | 1.46 |
| 46. Metal products | | 0.95 | 0.93 | 0.87 | 0.81 | 0.86 |
| 47. All others | | 0.83 | 0.84 | 0.80 | 1.33 | 0.81 |
| *Structure of labor force by status, early 1950s* | | | | | | |
| 48. Total number of countries | 18 | | 15 | | 16 | |
| 49. Number showing employers and own-account workers separately | 8 | | 11 | | 10 | |
| *Share in total labor force (%)* | | | | | | |
| 50. Employers and own-account workers | 22 | | 30 | | 53 | |
| 51. Employers | 5 | | 5 | | 7 | |
| 52. Own-account workers | 18 | | 27 | | 43 | |
| *A Sector* | | | | | | |
| 53. Share in total labor force | 19 | | 42 | | 60 | |
| 54. Share of employers plus own-account workers in A labor force | 61 | | 41 | | 66 | |
| 55. Share of employers in A labor force | 12 | | 7 | | 9 | |
| 56. Share of own-account workers in A labor force | 51 | | 39 | | 53 | |
| *M + Sector* | | | | | | |
| 57. Share in total labor force | 48 | | 28 | | 20 | |

| | | | |
|---|---|---|---|
| 58. Share of employers plus own-account workers in M+ labor force | 11 | 21 | 31 |
| 59. Share of employers in M+ labor force | 3 | 3 | 4 |
| 60. Share of own-account workers in M+ labor force | 6 | 21 | 26 |
| *S Sector* | | | |
| 61. Share in total labor force | 33 | 30 | 20 |
| 62. Share of employers plus own-account workers in S labor force | 17 | 25 | 35 |
| 63. Share of employers in S labor force | 5 | 4 | 5 |
| 64. Share of own-account workers in S labor force | 10 | 20 | 32 |
| *Factor shares in national income, late 1950s* | | | |
| 65. Number of countries | 13 | 9 | 8 |
| *Share in national income (%)* | | | |
| 66. Compensation of employees | 60.4 | 55.4 | 47.2 |
| 67. Income of unincorporated entrepreneurs | 21.2 | 26.6 | 32.2 |
| 68. Income from assets | 18.4 | 18.0 | 20.6 |
| 69. Household property income | 8.4 | 9.4 | 11.2 |
| 70. Corporate savings and taxes | 7.7 | 7.7 | 7.5 |
| 71. Government income from property and enterprise | 2.3 | 0.9 | 1.9 |
| *Relative participation income per worker* | | | |
| 72. Share of compensation of employees in participation income, % (line 66 + line 67) | 74 | 68 | 59 |
| 73. Share of entrepreneurial income in participation income | 26 | 32 | 41 |
| 74. Relative participation income per employee [line 72 ÷ (100 − line 50)] | 0.95 | 0.97 | 1.26 |
| 75. Relative participation income per entrepreneur (line 73 ÷ line 50) | 1.18 | 1.07 | 0.77 |
| 76. Index of inequality | 8 | 4 | 24 |

TABLE 8.1—Continued

| | Groups of countries by per capita GDP, 1958 | | | | | |
|---|---|---|---|---|---|---|
| | $1,000 and over (1) | $575–999 (2) | $350–574 (3) | $200–349 (4) | $100–199 (5) | Under $100 (6) |
| *Distribution of GNP by type of use, 1950s* | | | | | | |
| 77. Number of countries | 13 | 5 | 8 | 9 | 16 | 5 |
| *Share in GNP (%)* | | | | | | |
| 78. Private consumption expenditures | 64.2 | 65.9 | 73.3 | 75.6 | 73.2 | 74.7 |
| 79. Government consumption expenditures | 13.8 | 12.2 | 12.9 | 11.7 | 11.9 | 11.2 |
| 80. Gross domestic capital formation | 22.0 | 22.7 | 20.9 | 16.9 | 16.4 | 15.2 |
| 81. Net change in foreign claims | 0.1 | −0.7 | −7.1 | −4.2 | −1.5 | −1.2 |
| 82. Gross national capital formation (line 80 + line 81) | 22.1 | 22.0 | 13.8 | 12.7 | 14.9 | 14.0 |
| *Transition from GNP to private consumption expenditures, 1950s* | | | | | | |
| 83. Number of countries | 13 | 13 | 7 | 7 | 12 | |
| *Share in GNP (%)* | | | | | | |
| 84. Indirect taxes less subsidies | 10.5 | | | 7.5 | 8.7 | |
| 85. Capital consumption | 8.0 | | | 7.2 | 6.6 | |
| 86. National income (100 − lines 84 and 85) | 81.5 | | | 85.3 | 84.7 | |
| 87. Corporate savings and taxes | 6.3 | | | 4.5 | 5.2 | |
| 88. Other items (government income from entrepreneurship and property minus interest on public debt) | −0.4 | | | 0.3 | 1.1 | |
| 89. Household income from factor shares (line 86 − lines 87 and 88) | 75.6 | | | 80.5 | 78.4 | |
| 90. Net transfers to households | 7.2 | | | 1.9 | 1.0 | |
| 91. Personal income (line 89 + line 90) | 82.8 | | | 82.4 | 79.4 | |
| 92. Direct taxes on households | 10.9 | | | 3.7 | 2.1 | |
| 93. Disposable income (line 91 − line 92) | 71.9 | | | 78.7 | 77.3 | |
| 94. Personal savings | 6.2 | | | 2.3 | 3.4 | |
| 95. Private consumption expenditures (line 93 − line 94) | 65.7 | | | 76.4 | 73.9 | |

*Structure of private consumption expenditures, 1950s*

| | 14 | 4 | 9 |
|---|---|---|---|
| 96. Number of countries | | | |
| *Share in PCE (%)* | | | |
| 97. Food, beverages, and tobacco | 42.9 | 43.6 | 55.5 |
| 98. Clothing | 12.7 | 12.3 | 10.5 |
| 99. Rent, water, light, and fuel | 11.8 | 10.5 | 10.7 |
| 100. Furniture and furnishings | 6.4 | 5.5 | 3.9 |
| 101. Household operation | 3.6 | 4.5 | 4.1 |
| 102. Personal care and health | 4.5 | 4.7 | 4.1 |
| 103. Transport and communication | 7.7 | 10.7 | 5.1 |
| 104. Recreation and amusement | 6.3 | 5.6 | 2.5 |
| 105. Other services | 4.1 | 2.6 | 3.6 |
| *Government expenditures for education and health, late 1950s* | | | |
| 106. Number of countries | 11 | 7 | 15 |
| *Share in GNP (%)* | | | |
| 107. Education | 3.1 | 2.0 | 2.7 |
| 108. Health | 1.5 | 1.2 | 1.0 |
| 109. Total (line 107 + line 108) | 4.6 | 3.2 | 3.7 |
| 110. Share in private consumption expenditures (line 109 ÷ line 95) | 7 | 4 | 5 |
| *Proportion of foreign trade to GNP, late 1950s* | | | |
| 111. Number of countries | 20 | 20 | 22 |
| *Percentage deviations of actual proportion from the theoretical estimate based on relation to size of GNP, unweighted geometric means* | | | |
| 112. Total trade proportion (commodities and services) | +25 | +5 | −22 |
| 113. Commodity trade proportion | +23 | +3 | −19 |

TABLE 8.1—*Continued*

• Countries are grouped by per capita gross domestic product in 1958 (as derived for Table 7.1) except that Japan, with a per capita product of $480, is included in col. 2 and Israel and Venezuela, with per capita products of $905 and $650, respectively, are included in col. 3. The purpose of these shifts is to maintain comparability with the classification in Table 7.1 into developed and less developed countries.

In several instances when the component shown in the stub was not given separately rough approximations were made.

*Sources: Lines 1–4:* Data are from U.N., *Compendium of Social Statistics: 1963*, Table 66, pp. 365 ff. except for three countries, for which data are from the *Demographic Yearbook, 1960*, Table 12, pp. 450 ff.

*Line 5:* Derived from lines 2–4. The proportions of female population to total population are: col. 1 – 50.8; col. 2 – 51.0; col. 3 – 50.0; col. 4 – 50.0; col. 5 – 49.9; and col. 6 – 47.2 per cent.

*Lines 6–18:* Data are from Kuznets, "Quantitative Aspects: II," App. Tables 1 and 3, pp. 62-67 and 75–81. The measure of intersectoral inequality in line 18 is the sum of differences between the percentage shares in product and labor force, signs disregarded (for discussion see ibid., p. 45).

*Lines 19–22:* Data are from U.N., *The Growth of World Industry, 1938–1961: National Tables* (New York, 1963), usually the average for 1950–60. For a few countries the data are for net domestic product and for a few others, for product in constant prices.

*Lines 23–24:* Data are from U.N., *Patterns of Industrial Growth*, Table 9, pp. 104 ff. We classified Northern North America and Oceania of Industrialization Class I under col. 1; European countries of Industrialization Class I under col. 2; Industrialization Classes II and III under cols. 3 and 4; and Industrialization Class IV under cols. 5 and 6.

*Lines 25–47:* Data are from *Growth of World Industry*, and in most cases for 1958.

*Lines 48–64:* Unpaid family labor and unclassified labor force are excluded. Data are from the *Demographic Yearbook, 1955*, Table 16 and from International Labour Office, *Yearbook of Labour Statistics, 1963* (Geneva, 1963), Table 4.

*Lines 65–77:* Data are from U.N., *Yearbook of National Accounts Statistics, 1963*, country tables, and Kuznets, "Quantitative Aspects: IV," App. Table 6, pp. 78 ff. In most cases the figures are for 1958–62 and interest on public debt, etc. is included.

*Line 76:* The derivation of the index is described in the notes to lines 6–18.

*Lines 77–82:* Data are from "Quantitative Aspects: VII," App. Table 1, pp. 62–63.

*Lines 83–95:* Data are from ibid., App. Table 2, pp. 64–67.

*Lines 96–105:* Data are from ibid., App. Table 5, pp. 76–79. Expenditures on tourism, etc., are excluded.

*Lines 106–109:* Data are from U.N., *Report on the World Social Situation*, Chap. 4, Table 3, p. 71.

*Lines 111–13:* Data are from "Quantitative Aspects: IX," App. Table 3, pp. 84–85.

trade. The order follows that of our discussion of the economic growth of the developed countries, in Chapters 2-6, although with some omissions; and the summary that follows is a recapitulation of our earlier discussion, but inverted in a sense, stressing the structural aspects of *absence* rather than *presence* of modern economic growth.

*Industrial Structure*—Four features of the industrial structure of product and labor force in the underdeveloped countries merit explicit attention: (1) the relatively high share of agriculture and related branches (forestry, hunting, and fishing)—the A sector; and the relatively low share of the extended industry sector (mining, manufacturing, construction, water, energy, and transport and communication) —the M+ sector; (2) the structure of manufacturing, the central branch of the M+ sector; (3) the share of the services group, comprising trade, finance, and real estate, personal, business, and professional services, and government— the S sector; (4) the relatively wide inequality in sectoral product per worker.

1. The share of the A sector in total product in the underdeveloped countries is well over 40 per cent—about 46 per cent (line 7, columns 5 and 6) and 50 per cent (line 20, column 6) compared with only 14 to 17 per cent in the developed countries. Conversely, the share of the M+ sector in total product is less than a quarter in underdeveloped countries, compared with about 50 per cent in developed countries (lines 8 and 21). The finding is not surprising if two considerations are taken into account. First, since per capita income in the underdeveloped countries is low, most of the output goes into household consumption and most of the latter has to be allocated to foods and other prime necessities that are the direct product of the A sector. Hence in a low per capita income country with a closed economy, where domestic output is the only source of supply for domestic needs, the share of the A sector in total product must be large and that of the M+ sector must be small. Second, any significant modification of this conclusion to allow for effects of foreign trade would imply that an

underdeveloped country imports a substantial proportion of its food needs, paying for them by exports of products of the non-A sectors. In view of the primitive state of transportation and trade organization in underdeveloped countries, this possibility is remote, except in those small underdeveloped units possessing easily accessible mineral resources that command world markets and are organized by means of foreign capital and management.[1]

The share of the A sector in the labor force is higher than that in total product in underdeveloped countries; and the contrast between underdeveloped and developed countries is wider in the share of the A sector in the labor force than in its share in total product. Thus, for product, the range in line 7 is from 46 per cent for underdeveloped countries to 17.4 per cent for developed, or 2.6 to 1; for labor force, the range in line 10 is from 57.6 to 19.3 per cent, or 3.0 to 1. Likewise, the range in the share of the M+ sector in product in line 8 is from 21.5 to 47.7 per cent, or 1 to 2.2; in labor force in line 11 from 19.5 to 46.2 per cent, or 1 to 2.4. This means that the per worker product in the A sector is lower, relative to countrywide product per worker, in the underdeveloped countries than in the developed countries. It follows that the lag in productivity, the backwardness of the underdeveloped countries, is more conspicuous in the A sector, in agriculture, than it is in the nonagricultural sectors. This too is not surprising since the non-A sectors of even underdeveloped countries contain some modern branches with high per worker product—in mining, manufacturing, transport and

1. Such sources of comparative advantage in international trade would significantly affect the economic and industrial structure of small units only. In this connection one may note that if the means in Table 8.1 had been weighted by population (or some other relevant measure of magnitude), the share of the A sector would have been even higher and that of the M + sector even lower. Thus for the three largest underdeveloped countries—India, Pakistan, and Indonesia—the shares of the A sector in total product were 50, 60, and 56 per cent respectively, all above the average shown (see Kuznets, "Quantitative Aspects: II," App. Table 1, pp. 62–67).

communication, professional and some government services —to a proportional extent that could hardly be duplicated in the huge A sector.

The low per worker product in the A sector of underdeveloped countries, low both absolutely and relative to their countrywide per worker product, may be due to an unfavorable land–man ratio, requiring greater inputs of labor per unit of output. According to Colin Clark, who converted agricultural land to standard farm land, the supply of land per male engaged in agriculture in a post-World War II year is only 0.057 square kilometers in Asia (excluding Japan), compared with 1.61 for the overseas offshoots of Europe (the United States, Canada, Australia, and New Zealand) and 0.069 for developed non-Communist Europe.[2] But the figure for Africa is 0.3, for Latin America, 0.7; and although it is lower for Japan (0.042) than for the rest of Asia, agricultural output per worker in Japan is higher than in most of Asia. Land availability and climate are surely important factors affecting productivity of agriculture; but no summary measures are available to test their general bearing vis-à-vis other factors in a country's economic structure.

One major implication of the relatively low per worker product in agriculture in the underdeveloped countries is that a large proportion of the population is attached to a sector with low productivity operating under conditions of rural life and isolation that cannot easily be penetrated by modern economic methods. If the share of the A sector in the labor force is 60 per cent or more in the populous underdeveloped countries, and if the sector is dominated by low productivity agriculture which, in the nature of the case, follows traditional procedures, the overwhelming proportion of the population lives under conditions, and is affected by long-standing traditional patterns of organization, that inhibit the process of modernization.

2. While the extended industry sector accounts for more

2. See *Conditions of Economic Progress* (3d ed.), Table XXXIII, facing p. 309.

than a fifth of the total product in the underdeveloped countries, less than 10 per cent is allocable to manufacturing proper; and even in countries with per capita incomes of $100—199 the share of manufacturing is still only a ninth (line 21, columns 5 and 6). In considering the structure of manufacturing, we deal with a branch of the economy that, however important as a locus of modernization, accounts for a small proportion of the product in underdeveloped countries and for even a smaller proportion of their labor force. Furthermore, in many countries, small-scale firms and handicrafts are included in manufacturing.

The major manufactures in underdeveloped countries are foods and textiles, which together account for over half of total value added; the next two in importance are chemicals and metal manufactures, which together account for over a fifth (lines 26, 27, 32, and 35, column 6). The structure is distinctly different from that of manufactures in developed countries, where metal products alone account for over a quarter (line 35, columns 1 and 2). Indeed, the branches within manufactures whose shares are significantly smaller in the underdeveloped countries than in the developed countries are metal products (less than 10 per cent compared with 28 per cent); basic metals (less than 2 per cent compared with over 10 per cent); and paper, printing, and publishing (5 per cent compared with about 10 per cent). But it is significant that for such capital-intensive industries as chemicals (mostly petroleum), the share in manufactures of underdeveloped countries is as high as, or higher than, that in the developed countries (line 32); that, at the other end, in the developed countries, food, beverages, and tobacco are the second largest branch of manufactures (line 26, columns 1 and 2); and that, as already indicated in Chapter 3, consumer goods are predominant even in the manufactures of developed countries—for the products of almost all branches listed in Table 8.1 are primarily consumer goods, with the exception of parts of basic metals, metal products, and nonmetallic minerals.

The indexes of value added per worker in the different

branches of manufacturing, relative to all-manufacturing value added per worker, are fairly similar for developed and underdeveloped countries (lines 37–47). The differences among the branches reflect differences in capital equipment per worker and in the character of the labor force—the former explaining the high indexes in food and related products, in chemicals, and in basic metals; the latter explaining the low ratios in textiles and clothing and footwear, where a high proportion of employment, in all countries, consists of lower paid female wage-earners. It is significant that metal products, the branch that is probably the most representative of the production of producer goods, is characterized by per worker value added that is, in all groups of countries, *below* the average for all manufacturing. In fact, these producers of producer goods are in branches that, unlike many of those turning out consumer goods (such as textiles, many foods and tobacco, paper, etc.), have smaller scale units with less capital equipment per worker.

The differences in structure of manufacturing indicated in Table 8.1 are often viewed as indications of the inability of underdeveloped countries to produce their own producer goods, particularly capital equipment. But one may legitimately ask whether this inability is more important than the inability to produce other manufactured goods—since the exceedingly small share of *total* manufacturing in the aggregate product of underdeveloped countries combined with the low level of aggregate product, total or per capita, would usually mean a small absolute volume of manufacturing production; and this would not permit a scale of operation adequate for satisfactory efficiency requirements, except for one or two branches. If the economy is capable of only a small volume of manufacturing, it may be economically more rational to concentrate on branches in which the comparative advantage is high, or at least in which the comparative disadvantage is not too grave, rather than attempt complete coverage of all branches for the sake of a domestic supply of producer goods. Indeed, it is interesting that, as one would expect, branch concentration is greater in the underdeveloped than in the developed countries; the two largest of the 11 branches account for over 52 per cent of total value added in the underdeveloped and for 44.7 per cent in the developed. But such measures depend upon the detail of the classification, and the topic cannot be pursued further here.

3. If we exclude from services those closely related to production of commodities (transportation, communication, and water, gas, and electricity), the share in total product is not much lower in the underdeveloped than in developed countries—33 per cent and 35 per cent respectively (line 9), or 27.4 per cent in the lowest income group and 38.7 per cent in the next lowest group, compared with 35 per cent in the two highest groups (line 22). Since the S sector includes returns from finance and real estate, it may have a greater proportion of property income than the A and M+ sectors, but this difference is probably small. Contrasted with this rather negligible shortfall of the share in the S sector in the total product of the underdeveloped compared with developed countries, is the much more significant difference in its share in the labor force (excluding unpaid family labor). The share of the S sector is only 23 per cent in the underdeveloped countries, compared with 34.5 per cent in the developed countries (line 12). Per worker product in the S sector, relative to countrywide product per worker, is therefore distinctly *higher* in the underdeveloped than in the developed countries: the relatives are 1.42 and 1.01 respectively (line 15). Moreover, the relative product per worker for the S sector is distinctly higher than that for the M+ sector in the underdeveloped but *not* in the developed countries (line 17).

The S sector is much more heterogeneous than the other two major sectors distinguished in Table 8.1; and without a detailed examination of both product and labor force in sub-branches, no fully tested explanation of the high relative per worker product in the underdeveloped countries is possible. The inclusion of a larger proportion of property incomes could have only a limited effect. Participation incomes (wages and salaries, and entrepreneurial income) however differ widely within the sector. The low per worker product in some branches in underdeveloped countries would tend to bring the relative per worker product for the sector below the countrywide average (e.g. domestic service, and services that are clearly a form of disguised unemployment, such as peddling). But this tendency is probably far outweighed by that in other branches. Professional and government services, for example, which require extensive education or experience, demand a minimum standard of living that is a large multiple of the countrywide per worker product, and their incomes may also reflect a scarcity of education and requisite talent. Still other services, such as those of the traders and moneylenders, may derive a per capita income that is a large multiple of the countrywide average because of the high returns on scarce capital and the monopoly position of these groups vis-à-vis their customers or debtors. The factors that make for a high relative per capita product in the professional and high skill service branches and in those that control liquid capital, are obviously much less dominant in the developed countries. Thus the high relative product per worker in the S sector in the less developed countries may be due partly to the scarcity and monopoly elements in the supply of certain types of capital and services, and partly to the minimum income requirements (for adequate performance of functions) of some highly educated and responsible service groups which necessarily constitute a larger multiple of the countrywide per worker product in the underdeveloped than in the developed countries.

4. With relative product per worker in the A sector distinctly below, and that in the S sector distinctly above, the countrywide product per worker in the underdeveloped countries, intersectoral differences in product per worker are wider in the underdeveloped than in the developed countries. A simple measure of this inequality is the sum of differences, signs disregarded, between the percentage

shares of the sectors in product and in labor force—which reflect the deviations of sectoral per worker product from countrywide per worker product, the former weighted by the shares of the sectors in total labor force.[3]

This measure of intersectoral inequality in product per worker (line 18) is much wider for underdeveloped countries (23.3) than for developed countries (3.8). That the index is even larger for the intermediate group is not necessarily significant. Both the level and the range of the measure depend upon the classification of sectors (we distinguish only three here) and the countries included. In a more detailed classification for a sample of 38 countries, distinguishing eight sectors—with the data for labor force and product better adjusted for time coverage—we found that the measure of intersectoral inequality ranged from about 17 for 9 developed countries, to about 25 for 14 intermediate countries, and to over 44 for 15 underdeveloped countries.[4] Thus the evidence of wider intersectoral inequality in product per worker in the underdeveloped countries is confirmed, and the negative association with countrywide per worker product more clearly perceived.

If intersectoral differences in product per worker approximate or suggest differences in *income* per worker received by distinct groups within the labor force (excluding unpaid family labor, as our calculations do), one possible implication follows. It may be assumed that the ratio of population to labor force is higher for the A sector than for the non-A sectors in both developed and underdeveloped countries; and that there may be some inverse correlation between number of dependents and product per worker among various labor force groups within the population. Hence intersectoral inequality in product (and income) per worker means even wider inequality in income per capita of population groups attached to and dependent upon the various sectors. But the interesting questions in the present connection are whether this inverse association between

3. See Kuznets, "Quantitative Aspects: II," p. 45.
4. See "Quantitative Aspects: VIII," Table 5, Panel B, p. 20.

per worker product and number of dependents is greater in the underdeveloped than in the developed countries; and whether the range in the intersectoral inequality in product (and income) *per capita* between the underdeveloped and the developed countries is even wider than that in the intersectoral inequality in product *per worker*. No data are at hand to provide an answer to these questions.

*Type of Enterprise and Status Structure of Labor Force*—The relevant classification of enterprises or economic producing units here is by size and degree of dependence upon individual proprietorship and management—with the range from small, individually owned and operated units, with little or no hired labor, to huge corporate and other impersonal entities, with large numbers of employees and a bureaucratic organization, whether under private or public auspices.

Direct statistical evidence is available on the distribution of either product or labor force by type and scale of enterprise for only a few countries, but the industrial structure, reviewed above, and the employment status of labor force, to be noted below, both clearly suggest that the share of small, individually owned productive units and firms, in either product or labor force, is far larger in the underdeveloped than in the developed countries. Agriculture, except for the limited plantation sector, is dominated by such units even in most developed countries, let alone the underdeveloped; and handicrafts, cottage industries, traditional transport, and the like are, by definition, small units. The share of all these branches combined, in total product and particularly in total labor force, is much greater in underdeveloped than in developed countries. Even the share of the government sector, a distinctive type of non-personal enterprise different from individual proprietorship and management, tends to be lower in the underdeveloped than in developed countries, as suggested by the share of government consumption expenditures in gross national product in line 79.

This greater dominance of small, individually owned

417

and managed producing units in the underdeveloped countries is reflected in the data on employment status of the
labor force in lines 50–64. These data distinguish employees
(wage-earners and salaried people) from employers of hired
labor (but also including in some countries directors and
managers), and own-account workers (farmers and other individual proprietors employing no hired labor). This distribution by employment status is shown not only for total
labor force but also for the three major industrial sectors.

The proportion of total labor force accounted for by
employers plus own-account workers is far larger and that
accounted for by employees is far smaller in the underdeveloped countries than in the developed: 53 and 47 per cent
respectively for the underdeveloped countries and 22 and 78
per cent for the developed countries (line 50). The difference is not due to the share of employers, which averages
between 5 and 7 per cent of total labor force in all groups
of countries (line 51) but to the share of own-account workers, which is 43 per cent of total labor force in the underdeveloped and only 18 per cent in the developed countries
(line 52).

In addition to this distinctively high share of own-account
workers in the total labor force of underdeveloped countries, there are interesting differences within the three major
sectors distinguished. The labor force attached to the A
sector is characterized by high shares of employers plus own-
account workers in *all* groups of countries—between 41 and
66 per cent (line 54). But the proportion of employers is
slightly lower and that of own-account workers slightly
higher in the underdeveloped than in the developed countries—9 and 53 per cent for the former countries and 12 and
51 per cent for the latter (lines 55 and 56).

The share of employers plus own-account workers is distinctly lower in the labor force attached to the M+ and S
sectors than in the labor force in the A sector. But here the
contrast between the underdeveloped and developed countries in the higher share in the former of own-account work-

418

ers and lower share of employees is much more marked than in the structure of the A sector.

Clearly, the greater share of own-account workers in the total labor force of underdeveloped countries, reflecting the greater dominance of small scale, personal productive units, is due partly to the distinctive industrial structure (i.e. the greater share of the A sector), and partly to *intra*sectoral differences in scale that favor own-account enterprises. Indeed, with the data in lines 50–64 it is possible to calculate the effect of each. Thus, if we assume that the industrial structure of the labor force in the underdeveloped countries is the same as that for labor force in the developed countries, the share of own-account workers for the former would be 33.1 rather than 43 per cent; and this means that *intra*sectoral differences contribute 33.1 − 18.0, or 15.1 percentage points to the total difference of 43 − 18, or 25 percentage points in line 52. Conversely, if we accept the industrial structure of the underdeveloped countries, but assume that the intrasectoral structure of labor force by employment status was the same as in the developed countries, the share of own-account workers in the total labor force of the underdeveloped countries would be 33.8 per cent; and the contribution of the *inter*sectoral differences in weight would be 33.8 − 18.0, or 15.8 percentage points. Thus the differences in weights of the three major industry sectors and the intrasectoral differences in structure by employment status contributed about equally to the total spread between the underdeveloped and the developed countries in the share of own-account workers in labor force.

For another sample of countries, in lines 65–71, we have shares in national income of compensation of employees and of income of individual entrepreneurs (i.e. employers and own-account workers), the two forming the participation income of the total labor force. By comparing the distribution of participation income between employees and entrepreneurs with that of the labor force between the two groups we can derive participation income per entrepreneur and per employee as relatives of the countrywide participation income per worker (lines 72–76). In the underdeveloped countries the per worker income of employees is distinctly higher than that of entrepreneurs, and this may be due largely to the greater weight among the latter of farmers and low-income handicraft workers; whereas in the developed countries the per worker income of entrepreneurs is distinctly higher than that of employees. The weighted inequality between the two groups of workers is wider in the developed and underdeveloped countries than in the intermediate group, but much wider in the underdeveloped than in the developed countries.[5]

*Factor Shares and Size Distribution of Income*—The first distinctive feature of the allocation of income by factor shares is that the share of income from assets is no lower for underdeveloped countries than for the developed countries (line 68). The income measured here is the return on material assets excluding the equity of individual, noncorporate entrepreneurs. Such income received by households constitutes a somewhat greater share of national income in the underdeveloped than in the developed countries (line 69); but despite the somewhat lower shares in the former countries of corporate savings (before taxes) and of government income from property and enterprise the share of total income from assets does not drop below the level in the developed countries.

The share of income from material assets equals the ratio of these assets to national income multiplied by a yield rate. Income-yielding material assets, including land and reproducible capital, are probably no greater multiple of national product in underdeveloped countries than in developed: the possibly lower reproducible capital–output ratio for underdeveloped countries would be compensated

5. These results, based on a larger sample and more recent data, are more consistent and credible than those in Kuznets, "Quantitative Aspects: IV," Table 3, lines 13–15, pp. 30–31.

in the total capital–output ratio by the inclusion of land, whose weight in total capital would be larger. But the income from assets, shown separately here and in national accounts, represents returns only on those assets that are outside the equity of individual, noncorporate enterprises. If we assume, realistically, that the proportion of the equity of individual entrepreneurs (employers and own-account workers) is about a quarter of the total capital stock (net of accumulated depreciation) in the developed countries, and that the ratio of total capital to national income is about 4, the yield rate in developed countries would be 18.4 (see line 68), divided by (4 x 0.75), or 6.1 per cent.[6] But in underdeveloped countries the equity of individual, noncorporate enterprises must be a much larger proportion of total capital. If we set it at 0.6 (compared with 0.25 for developed countries) and assume the same total capital–national income ratio of 4, the yield on capital other than entrepreneurial equity in underdeveloped countries would be 20.6 divided by (4 x 0.4), or almost 13 per cent. Since interest rates and rates of return on capital, particularly liquid funds or capital organized in sizable corporate enterprises, are indeed much higher in the underdeveloped than in the developed countries, the finding that the share of income from assets in national income is no lower in underdeveloped than in developed countries becomes comprehensible.

Two consequences follow. First, the returns on equity in the hands of individual entrepreneurs would presumably be proportionately much greater in the underdeveloped than in the developed countries—so long as the rate of return on entrepreneurial equity is assumed to be no lower in the former countries than in the latter. As a result, the share of returns on *all* material capital in total national income would be significantly larger in the underdeveloped than in the developed countries. In that sense, it is in the underdeveloped rather than in the developed countries that

6. For a discussion of the coefficients in this paragraph see ibid., pp. 15–23.

income from material capital accounts for a large share of the product and dominates income from labor—primarily because the rate of return on capital is high.

But, second, we face a problem in calculating the returns on capital represented by the equity of entrepreneurs, particularly own-account workers, in the underdeveloped countries. If we assume that such returns are at the rate of yield for material assets outside entrepreneurial equity (i.e. those in line 68) and use the ratios employed above, the property income component of the total income of noncorporate entrepreneurs would be 1.5 (i.e. 60/40) times 20.6, the share of income from assets shown separately, or 30.9 per cent of national income. Since the total income of noncorporate entrepreneurs in underdeveloped countries is 32.2 per cent of national income, we are left with only 1.3 per cent of national income as the labor compensation of individual entrepreneurs and own-account workers who account for more than half of total labor force (53 per cent)—while the employees' share is 47.2 per cent of national income. Even if we cut the returns on the equity of entrepreneurs to a third of the yield-rate of capital outside of entrepreneurial equity, the property income component in total income of entrepreneurs would still be (20.6 × 1.5 ÷ 3), or 10.3 per cent of national income, leaving only 21.9 per cent for the labor component and implying a labor income per entrepreneur and own-account worker that is less than half of the per worker income of employees.

Obviously, either the labor income per worker or the property income yields, or both, must be lower for individual entrepreneurs and own-account workers than the labor income and capital returns for other groups in underdeveloped countries. This is due only in part to the industry mix, i.e. to the larger share of agriculture as the source of incomes of individual entrepreneurs than as the source of compensation of employees or of income from assets outside the equity of individual entrepreneurs. It also reflects the curious mixture of capital and labor involved in the activities of small-scale, individual enterprises—particularly of own-account workers—where the income derived from a combination of labor and capital, no matter how low, may still be higher than the income the same labor and capital could yield if used separately, at least in the short run foreseeable and manageable by the individuals concerned. Under such conditions it is not the distinction between capital and labor that is important but the distinction within capital and within labor between components that can move independently in the markets and those that must be joined together. Consequently, three rather than two factor categories—labor, capital, and the joint labor–capital–management complex—are important in an economy with a large sector of individual small-scale enterprises. It should be emphasized that in the underdeveloped countries these small and primarily own-account enterprises account for over half of total labor force and perhaps also for half of total material assets. Thus the Classical and Marxian classifications of productive factors (and hence of factor shares) fit this situation as poorly as they do the one in developed countries where the large investment in human capital appears to be embodied in the labor compensation of employees.

In turning now to the size distribution of income in the underdeveloped countries, we face a scarcity of data that prevents the derivation of reliable averages like those used for other structural aspects in Table 8.1; and we must, therefore, place greater reliance on detailed analysis presented elsewhere.[7] The conclusions may be summarized as follows.

First, for the distributions among families or consuming units of personal income before taxes and excluding income in kind provided by governments, the shares of the top ordinal groups are distinctly higher in the underdeveloped than in the developed countries. Thus, the share of the top 5 per cent ranges from 30 to 40 per cent of total income for underdeveloped, and between 20 and 25 per cent for developed, countries.

7. See Kuznets, "Quantitative Aspects: VIII."

Second, the income shares of the larger, low ordinal groups do not show such significant differences between the two groups of countries. Thus, in the distributions referred to in the paragraph above, the share of the lowest 60 per cent of family units is about 30 per cent of total income in both the underdeveloped and the developed countries.

Third, the intermediate groups, between the lowest 60 and the top 5 or 10 per cent, account for distinctly lower shares of total income in the underdeveloped than in the developed countries. Thus in the underdeveloped countries the share of the group between the low 60 and the top 10 per cent varies from 20 to 30 per cent; whereas in the developed countries the share of the similar group (between the low 60 and the top 10 per cent) ranges somewhat below 40 per cent. This finding is a crude reflection of the relative absence in the underdeveloped countries of "middle" classes —and it will be pointed up when we consider below the *absolute* levels of per capita or per family income in the underdeveloped countries.

Fourth, these findings for a distribution of personal income among families, before adjustments for scope of income or size of family unit, are modified in various ways when these adjustments are attempted. The allowances for direct taxes and income in kind provided by governments only accentuate the wider inequality of the size distribution in underdeveloped compared with developed countries— because such taxes are not only larger relative to personal income but also more progressive, and the weight of services in kind provided by government, largely to the lower income groups, is greater in developed than in underdeveloped countries (see Table 8.1, lines 92 and 109). On the other hand, the adjustment for size of family units, in numbers of their members, is likely to reduce income inequality more in the underdeveloped countries, because larger family units are a larger share in the upper brackets of the distribution than in the developed countries. The adjustment in the shift from distribution of personal income to distribution of consumer expenditures would also

424

reduce inequality more in the underdeveloped countries because of the greater concentration of savings in the upper income brackets. Yet, after all these adjustments—on the basis of exceedingly meager data and crude allowances—the size distribution of income remains more unequal in the underdeveloped countries than in developed: the income shares of the very top ordinal groups are higher, though the shares for the much larger low ordinal groups are not significantly lower.

These conclusions are not surprising in view of the wider intersectoral differences in product per worker revealed in the earlier discussion of the industrial structure of product and labor force in the underdeveloped countries. And, indeed, further analysis suggests that the higher share of top income groups in the underdeveloped countries is due partly to the wider intersectoral differences, particularly between the agricultural and nonagricultural sectors of the economy, the latter concentrated in urban areas, and partly to the probably wider inequality in the income distribution of the urban population in underdeveloped countries than in that of the urban population in developed countries.

All the measures discussed above are relatives of the country's average income and must be related to the wide contrast in absolute per capita income between underdeveloped and developed countries. If per capita income in underdeveloped countries is, in terms of comparable purchasing power, between a sixth and a tenth of per capita income in developed, the top 5 per cent group in underdeveloped countries, which receives from 30 to 40 per cent of total income and thus has an average income from 6 to 8 times higher than the countrywide average, has an income per capita that is barely up to the *average* income per capita of the developed countries. Hence, evidence on the size distribution of income within the underdeveloped countries not only reveals the cleavage between the low incomes of the lower 90 or 95 per cent and the *relatively* high income of the top 10 or 5 per cent, but also indicates that only a small group in the underdeveloped countries commands an

425

income and can afford a standard of living equal to that of the vast majority of the population in the developed countries. If such income or standard of living is in some way indispensable for the productive performance required by modern economic growth, the smallness of the group in underdeveloped countries with such an income minimum poses grave difficulties. *If* these high income groups function so as to maximize the country's economic growth, the observed inequality *may* be a more efficient distribution system than a more egalitarian alternative. But the "if" is important; and the contribution of the top groups in the income pyramid must be weighed against the potential increase in the contribution of the groups below the top that might result from narrower inequality in the income distribution.

*Patterns of Income Use*—Some of the distinctive aspects of consumption (the main use of income in all countries) in the underdeveloped countries have already been touched upon in connection with data on conditions of life in Table 7.4. Here we summarize briefly these and other familiar aspects.

In the major use-structure of gross national product in the present standard national accounts (lines 78–82), the underdeveloped countries differ from developed countries in several respects: a larger share for private consumption (73 to 75 per cent compared with 64 to 66 per cent for developed countries); a slightly lower share for government consumption (11 to 12 per cent, compared with 12 to 14 per cent); a distinctly lower share for gross domestic capital formation (15 to 16 per cent, compared with 22 to 23 per cent); and an even lower share of gross *national* capital formation (14 to 15 per cent, compared with 22 percent). If we replace government consumption by the truly final component in it—direct services in education and health (lines 107–09), the share of total ultimate consumption in the purer and less duplicated gross national product is about 84 per cent for the underdeveloped countries, leaving 16 per cent for gross national capital formation; whereas the corresponding shares for the developed countries are 76 and 24 per cent respectively. If we assume that capital consumption is roughly 0.4 of gross capital formation, the shares in net national product are 90 per cent for ultimate consumption and 10 per cent for net national capital formation in underdeveloped countries; and 84 and 16 per cent respectively in developed countries.

It is hardly surprising that with the much lower per capita product in the underdeveloped countries, their gross or net capital formation proportions—which represent gross or net national savings rates—are distinctly lower than those of the developed countries. Rather it is surprising that these national savings and investment proportions are no smaller relative to those in developed countries. And, indeed, since the data cover the 1950s and early 1960s, capital formation shares in underdeveloped countries may well be much higher than they were over a long-term past. But even if we allow for wider differences, not much spread is possible—given the limited gross capital formation proportions even in the developed countries. If for underdeveloped countries we assume that a gross capital formation proportion of about 7 per cent is needed to replace capital consumed and that enough capital must be provided to permit GNP to grow 1 per cent per year while the reproducible capital–output ratio remains 3 to 1, the minimum proportion is 10 per cent, compared with 24 per cent in the developed countries—in a period of generally high capital formation proportions. A shift of a few percentage points in the distribution of gross national product would remove or greatly reduce the difference. These observations indicate that the minor shifts involved in bringing the capital formation proportions in the underdeveloped countries closer to those in the developed countries may not be too difficult to attain. We may then ask whether the capital formation proportions are crucial, or whether even more depends upon the level and structure of the much larger component of total product, ultimate consumption by households.

427

Within total consumption expenditures, the share devoted to food and related products is, as already indicated,
significantly larger in underdeveloped countries (line 97).
But the difference shown greatly understates the difference
in the share of food proper, at farm values and excluding
the cost of transportation, distribution, and additional processing involved in moving food from the farms to the ultimate consumers. The share of foods excluding beverages
and tobacco is about 9 percentage points lower in the developed countries and about 8 percentage points lower in
the underdeveloped countries.[8] The proportion of transportation, distribution, and extra processing in the total
cost of food to consumers is much lower in underdeveloped
than in developed countries, perhaps about a fifth in the
former and at least a half in the latter.[9] This means that
the share of food proper is 47.5 per cent in underdeveloped
countries, compared with 34 per cent in developed countries; and in terms of farm values, the shares are 38 and 17
per cent respectively, a range of over 2.2 to 1, instead of
1.3 to 1 as shown in line 97. Indeed, with more groups distinguished, especially at the underdeveloped end of the
classification, the range in the share of food at farm values
in total expenditures might widen to 1 to 5, as suggested
in Kuznets, "Quantitative Aspects: VII," p. 48.

The shares in total consumer expenditures of food and
household operation, the latter dominated by domestic
service, are the only two that are distinctly higher in the
underdeveloped than in the developed countries. The
shares of all other categories are lower, the most marked
relative shortages being in durable consumer goods—furniture and furnishings (line 100) and transport and communications, dominated by passenger cars (line 103)—and recreation and amusement services (line 104). Finally, if we add
to the private consumer expenditures the education and
health services provided by governments directly, and usually at low or no cost to the users (lines 107–109), the shares

8. See Kuznets, "Quantitative Aspects: VII," Table 10, p. 24.
9. See ibid., pp. 42–47.

of these items in *total* ultimate consumption would also be significantly smaller in the underdeveloped than in the developed countries.

Here again, since we deal with shares of totals, the differences in absolute level of per capita consumption expenditures must be kept in mind. For all the broad categories shown in lines 97–109, the absolute per capita expenditures, in comparable prices, are appreciably lower in the underdeveloped than in the developed countries—even for food at farm values, excluding additional transportation, distribution, and processing services. Such contrast in absolute levels is all the greater for those expenditure components with shares in the total that are lower in the underdeveloped countries. Thus if we assume, on the basis of data discussed above, that the range in per capita consumption expenditures, in comparable prices, between underdeveloped and developed countries is from 1 to between 5 and 9, the per capita expenditures in the former countries on such items as furniture and furnishings, or transport and communications, would be between an eighth and a fourteenth of those in the developed countries.

In general, the shortages in the consumption levels in the underdeveloped countries—even for food, let alone other goods—serve not only to suggest how populations "adjust" their consumption to a low level of income and command over resources, but also to explain the low level of per capita product. Obviously, above the minimum consumption needed to keep body and soul together and permit *some* work, other consumption items—ranging from extra protective food to extra clothing, housing, education, and transport—are indispensable for *higher* productivity of labor than is possible at the minimum of consumption. The implication of this observation is that the low level of consumption may be as important in explaining the low productivity in the underdeveloped countries as the low level of material capital stock or of material capital formation.

*Foreign Trade Proportions*—We come now to the last aspect of the economic structure of underdeveloped countries to be explicitly discussed here: the extent to which they participate in foreign trade. The obvious measure—the proportion of foreign trade to total output (say gross national product)—cannot be used directly for, unlike other aspects of economic structure, it is affected in the first instance by the size of a country. As already observed in Chapter 6, even for developed countries the larger the gross national product, the smaller the foreign trade proportion tends to be; and the underlying relation can be demonstrated by simple but realistic models.[10] Indeed the size factor is so dominant that it dwarfs other determinants of foreign trade proportions, even the degree of economic development reflected in per capita product; and the effects of such development can be seen only after the effects of size have been measured and eliminated.

It is for this reason that the entries in lines 112 and 113 are not geometric means of *actual* proportions, but of relative *deviations* of actual foreign trade proportions (in the late 1950s) from those estimated on the basis of a function connecting these proportions with the size of country as measured by GNP. Once this adjustment is made, it becomes clear that the extent of participation in foreign trade by underdeveloped countries is distinctly lower than that of developed countries. Thus, if the average foreign trade proportion *expected* on the basis of size were the same for the two groups of countries (say 25 per cent for total trade, in commodities and services), the entries in line 112 show that the average actual trade proportion for underdeveloped countries would be less than 20 per cent and that for the developed countries would be more than 31 per cent. This finding is contrary to the general impression that underdeveloped countries depend excessively on foreign trade, in the sense that their proportions of exports and imports to domestic product are too high. It is not underdevelopment but size that is the factor underlying these high proportions.

10. For a detailed discussion of the model, as well as of the application from which entries in Table 8.1 are derived, see Kuznets, "Quantitative Aspects: IX," pp. 7–25.

Indeed, underdevelopment, in and of itself, cannot induce high rates of exports and imports to domestic product, for the implicit backwardness of transportation, trade organization, and technological knowledge in general would make large volumes of foreign trade impossible, barring such exceptional cases as the concentration of mineral resources easily accessible to developed country users. It is the *small size* of many underdeveloped countries—in comparison with the large, developed partners with which they trade— that is the basis for the high proportions of foreign trade, combined often with a concentration of exports of one or a few commodities to one or a few large developed country importers.

Underdevelopment affects foreign trade proportions, and thus relative dependence upon or gains from foreign trade, in two opposite ways. Since it limits the size of *aggregate* product (because of low per capita productivity), other conditions being equal, underdevelopment tends to *raise* foreign trade proportions. On the other hand, since it reflects backward technology and thus relative inaccessibility to world markets, other conditions being equal, underdevelopment tends to *lower* foreign trade proportions. The distinction between these two variables—size and level of development—that affect foreign trade proportions seems to me important, because of their implications for policy measures and because size, in particular, also affects commodity and geographic concentration of exports.

*Relation of Cross-section Comparisons to Growth Trends in Economic Structure*—The summary discussion above of the economic structure of underdeveloped countries was intended to deal with the major aspects that are both causes and consequences of the low per capita or per worker product, aspects in the economy that were conspicuous either as sources of its low productivity or as the loci of its most immediate impact. That many of the structural aspects, e.g. the structure of ultimate consumption and the limited engagement in foreign trade (relative to size), could be viewed as both consequences and causes was only to be expected.

The review was necessarily summary and, more important, did not emphasize sufficiently the variety of levels and structure within the wide group referred to as underdeveloped countries. Although we have restricted the use of the term "underdeveloped" to countries with per capita product below $200 (in 1958 prices), it should be noted that within this category there is much diversity—with respect to size, supply of natural resources, proximity to world markets, and even level of development itself. But an effective analysis of the variety in level and structure within the large group of underdeveloped countries would require a separate monograph.

One aspect of the comparisons presented in Table 8.1 may bear, however, on the analysis of long-term trends in the economic structure of developed countries and deserves explicit discussion here. The table reveals a clear association between many aspects of economic structure and per capita product: a negative correlation between per capita product and the shares of the A sector in total product and labor force; a negative association between per capita product and the range in intersectoral inequality in product per worker; and also fairly pronounced associations, positive or negative, with other aspects of economic structure—distribution by factor shares, inequality in size distribution, structure by use, and foreign trade proportions. To be sure, the broad classifications used in the table are a crude way of studying association, which could be analyzed more incisively by the application of elaborate statistical methods to the data for the individual countries. And, in fact, elaborate cross-section regressions have been used by other scholars to specify more carefully the nature of the associations between level of economic growth, usually as measured by per capita product, and various components of the economic structure of the countries or other area units in their samples.[11]

11. See, for example, Hollis B. Chenery, "Patterns of Industrial Growth," *American Economic Review*, 50 (September 1960).

The question arises whether these cross-section associations provide a reliable base for inferring past long-term trends in economic structure associated with growth over time in product per capita (or any similar index of economic growth)—on the implicit assumption that the economic structure of presently developed countries was in their pre-development past like that of the less developed countries today. If cross-section analysis could be used toward this end, it would have enormous value, in view of the wealth of economic data available for many countries for recent years compared with the paucity of long-term records on national product and other important aspects of economic performance, even for the developed countries.

In attempting to answer this question, let us assume that cross-section analysis is adequate in its coverage of countries with a full range of per capita product levels and other characteristics that influence economic structure; that, for the period covered, the data represent an approximation to secular levels and do not contain too large a component of short-term change; and that the pattern of the regression function is correct, so that, for example, linear functions are not used when the true long-term experience deviates significantly from linearity. These criteria of adequacy of cross-section analysis as a basis for inferring long-term trends are more demanding than they seem at first glance. Judging the adequacy of the samples of countries and particularly of the variables covered by the data implies some knowledge of the factors, other than those represented by per capita product, that may affect the aspects of economic structure that are being studied.[12] Judging the adequacy of the period implies accounting for the possible effects not only of business cycles and similar short-term

12. Indeed, the discussion below emphasizes the omission, in usual cross-section analysis, of a complex of innovational factors associated with economic growth that is not reflected in per capita product or in the customarily available data on economic structure. In that sense, we are not assuming full knowledge of the variables as a criterion of adequacy of cross-section analysis; for by definition, full knowledge would exclude any errors in inference.

disturbances but also of the long swings, which may affect the rates of aggregate growth and structural changes. Finally, if the true trends in structure are nonlinear, as in the case of the size distribution of income where we suspect that the inequality first widens and then contracts in the process of economic growth, the cross-section regression that covers the full range must also be nonlinear—with all the complications that this entails for multiple regression analysis and all the difficulties of discerning the true patterns with a limited number of countries in the sample.

But even if cross-section analysis satisfies these requirements (subject to the qualification suggested in note 12), it may still be a faulty basis for inferring past trends in economic structure, at least as such analysis is usually made. Because of the difficulties of measurement on the basis of data for a single point in time, the usual analysis does not take account of technological innovations and changes in consumer tastes; and these innovations and changes may have an impact opposite to that of the general effects of per capita product differentials. The point can be illustrated by reference to the relation between per capita income and the shares of expenditures on various groups of goods within total consumer expenditures. In line 98 of Table 8.1, the share of consumer expenditures on clothing rises from 10.5 per cent for underdeveloped countries, to 12.3 per cent for the intermediate groups, to 12.7 per cent for developed countries. On the basis of this cross-section finding one would infer that, with a rise in per capita product over time, the share of consumer expenditures on clothing has risen. In fact, it has declined in several developed countries.[13] Of course, the crude comparison in Table 8.1 may conceal a more complicated association, and more careful analysis might reveal another pattern of regression. But the difference between the trends and the cross-section association more likely reflects changes in consumer preferences

13. See Chap. 5 and Kuznets, "Quantitative Aspects: VII," p. 16. This paper contains a more detailed discussion of and illustrations relevant to the problem discussed here.

—away from clothing and toward other, newer goods (e.g. passenger cars). The prevalence of changes in technology and tastes that run counter to cross-section income or expenditure elasticities of demand is easily seen in the case of many new food products and other products with low unit cost and mass demand. For example, the cross-section income or expenditure elasticity of demand in the United States for ice cream and frozen orange juice is probably below 1; yet the shares of these foods in total consumer expenditures or in national output have risen in recent decades. By contrast, the cross-section elasticity of demand for furniture is probably well over 1, but its share in total consumer expenditures or in national output has probably declined. And if cross-section associations and trends are found to diverge for consumer goods, they may also follow different patterns for other finished goods; and such divergence may even apply to related aspects of structure, such as industrial shares in total employment.

In the preceding paragraph, the inadequacy of cross-section analysis for the study of trends was considered only with respect to sign, i.e. direction of expected association. In the illustrations given, changes in technology and taste were pushing the structural change in one direction, whereas cross-section association with per capita product suggested structural change in the opposite direction; and the dominant effect of changes in technology and taste overshadowed and denied the association expected from cross-section analysis. But even if the effects of technological and taste innovations and the cross-section effects of per capita product differentials agree in direction, they may differ in magnitude. As a result, coefficients derived from cross-section associations, which relate a given absolute or proportional change in structure with a given absolute or proportional differential in per capita product, may prove to be erroneous as inferences regarding coefficients over the long period. For example, a cross-section coefficient indicating that for every addition of 5 per cent to per capita product (in constant prices) 3 per cent is added to the share of manufacturing in total product (or 5 per cent to the share of metal-working value added in total manufacturing value added) may be either too high or too low a measure of what happened on the average in the long-term past when per capita product rose 5 per cent.

This conflict between inferences from cross-section analysis and the actual patterns of long-term trends in economic structure could perhaps be resolved by introducing a specific allowance into cross-section analysis for the missing complex of variables—an allowance that distinguishes between old and new products, old and new industries, and thus old and new technology and tastes. Whether meaningful quantities can be assigned to this additional complex of variables—which might be designated innovational—is a moot question. How do we identify old and new, and at what point or phase does new become old? The main trouble, however, is that the capacity to identify new and old and to specify the dates and phases implies an already given knowledge of the past, of trends and structure; and if such knowledge is available, there is no need to infer it from cross-section analysis. It is the great advantage of such analysis, at least in the present connection, that it is supposed to help us to infer the past without direct, and often unprocurable, data on it. But if in order to render it a reliable base for such inferences we must possess direct knowledge of the past anyway, the advantage of cross-section analysis disappears and it becomes superfluous.

The value of such analysis for generating some preliminary hunches is not to be denied. But unless innovational changes can somehow be taken into account in the use of the cross-section data proper, use of its results may lead to erroneous inferences concerning past changes in structure in the process of growth. And the same applies, pari passu, to applications of cross-section analysis to projections into the future. For its use in such projections is justified because it is supposed to reveal past patterns of movements, which, with the help of additional assumptions (modifying past trends or keeping them unchanged), are then projected into the future. But if cross-section analysis is a faulty guide to past trends, it cannot provide an adequate base for tenable projections into the future; and consequently it can hardly provide a useful guide to consideration of *long-term* policy questions, which usually involve choices among alternative projected trends in growth rates and structures.

### NONECONOMIC CHARACTERISTICS OF UNDERDEVELOPED COUNTRIES

In addition to their economic structure, the societies of underdeveloped countries display distinctive noneconomic characteristics. Undoubtedly some of these have a direct bearing upon the economic structure and the low per capita product, either as important consequences or as major determining factors, or both. Without a theoretical framework that would establish the connections between economic and noneconomic aspects of social structure, we cannot specify them; and we have no such framework at hand. But I shall proceed on the assumption that the economic and many noneconomic characteristics of social structure are interrelated as both causes and effects, and present selected illustrations of the observable association between level of economic development and some noneconomic aspects of various societies. The illustrations may be useful, if only in calling attention to this association and in helping to place the purely economic analysis of economic growth in a broader perspective.

The easily available data that illustrate some of the noneconomic characteristics associated with differences in economic development and structure between underdeveloped and developed countries bear upon: (1) demographic patterns, (2) political structure, and (3) cultural aspects.

*Demographic Patterns*—Lines 1–4 of Table 8.2 indicate that in recent years the birth rates in underdeveloped countries have been more than double those in the developed countries: 43 and 20 per 1,000, respectively. While

437

TABLE 8.2

Selected Demographic Patterns, Countries Grouped by 1958 Product per Capita, Mostly Post-World War II Years*

| | 1958 per capita GDP groups | | |
| --- | --- | --- | --- |
| | $575 and over (1) | $200 to 575 (2) | Less than $200 (3) |
| *Birth and death rates (per 1,000), 1957–59* | | | |
| 1. Number of countries | 20 | 26 | 40 |
| 2. Crude birth rate | 19.8 | 35.0 | 42.8 |
| 3. Crude death rate | 9.8 | 9.6 | 17.6 |
| 4. Crude rate of natural increase | 10.0 | 25.4 | 25.2 |
| *Birth and death rates (per 1,000), countries with records back to 1911–13* | | | |
| 5. Number of countries | 19 | 12 | 6 |
| *Averages for 1957–61* | | | |
| 6. Crude birth rate | 19.4 | 32.7 | 38.0 |
| 7. Crude death rate | 9.9 | 9.0 | 12.1 |
| 8. Crude rate of natural increase | 9.5 | 23.7 | 25.9 |
| *Averages for 1911–13* | | | |
| 9. Crude birth rate | 26.0 | 35.1 | 39.6 |
| 10. Crude death rate | 15.2 | 22.6 | 27.9 |
| 11. Crude rate of natural increase | 10.8 | 12.5 | 11.7 |
| *Age composition of population around 1960 (%)* | | | |
| 12. Number of countries | 19 | 22 | 34 |
| 13. Under 15 years of age | 27.4 | 39.8 | 43.3 |
| 14. 15 to 59 years of age | 58.2 | 52.6 | 51.3 |
| 15. 60 and over | 14.4 | 7.6 | 5.4 |
| 16. Ratio of young to 15–59 (lines 13 and 14) | 0.47 | 0.76 | 0.84 |
| 17. Ratio of old to 15–59 (lines 15 and 14) | 0.25 | 0.14 | 0.11 |
| 18. Ratio of young and old to 15–59 (line 16 + line 17) | 0.72 | 0.90 | 0.95 |
| *Size of private households, late 1950s and early 1960s* | | | |
| 19. Number of countries | 10 | 11 | 9 |
| 20. Average CBR | 19.7 | 36.9 | 38.8 |
| 21. Average number of persons per household | 3.4 | 4.6 | 5.0 |
| *Share of household population (%) in households of:* | | | |
| 22. 1 through 6 | 84.3 | 58.3 | 55.6 |
| 23. 7 and 8 | 10.7 | 20.7 | 24.6 |
| 24. 9 and over | 5.0 | 21.0 | 19.8 |
| *Birth parity structure, late 1950s* | | | |
| 25. Number of countries | 17 | 10 | 5 |
| 26. Average CBR | 19.9 | 37.1 | 44.2 |

TABLE 8.2—*Continued*

| | 1958 per capita GDP groups | | |
|---|---|---|---|
| | $575 and over (1) | $200 to 575 (2) | Less than $200 (3) |
| *Births of successive order, as % of total live births* | | | |
| 27. 1st and 2nd | 60.6 | 42.6 | 37.8 |
| 28. 3rd and 4th | 26.5 | 25.9 | 29.2 |
| 29. 5th and 6th | 8.4 | 15.4 | 17.5 |
| 30. 7th and higher | 4.5 | 16.1 | 15.5 |
| *Partition ages of parents in cumulated array of births by increasing age of each parent, late 1950s* | | | |
| 31. Number of countries | 14 | 13 | 9 |
| 32. Average CBR | 19.6 | 32.5 | 39.1 |
| *1st quartile:* | | | |
| 33. Age of mother | 23.7 | 22.5 | 22.2 |
| 34. Age of father | 26.6 | 26.8 | 26.4 |
| *Median:* | | | |
| 35. Age of mother | 27.7 | 26.7 | 26.5 |
| 36. Age of father | 30.7 | 31.8 | 31.5 |
| *3rd quartile:* | | | |
| 37. Age of mother | 32.4 | 32.0 | 31.9 |
| 38. Age of father | 35.7 | 37.9 | 38.2 |
| *Birth rates for older married men, post-World War II years* | | | |
| 39. Number of countries | 14 | 14 | 13 |
| 40. Average CBR | 19.6 | 32.2 | 43.6 |
| 41. Upper quartile CBR | 4.9 | 8.0 | 10.9 |
| 42. Married men, 35.0+, as % of total population | 16.7 | 12.3 | 10.8 |
| 43. Married men, 40.0+, as % of total population | 13.9 | 9.8 | 8.2 |
| 44. Married men, above partition age in line 38, as % of total population | 16.3 | 10.9 | 9.1 |
| 45. Upper quartile of births per 1,000 married men (line 41 ÷ line 44 × 100) | 30 | 73 | 120 |

* The grouping of countries is identical with that in Table 8.1. All entries are unweighted arithmetic means of figures calculated for individual countries.
*Sources:* All data are from U.N., *Demographic Yearbook.*
Lines 1–4: *1962*, Tables 14 and 18.
Lines 5–11: *1951*, Tables 5 and 12, and *1963*, Tables 19 and 23.
Lines 12–18: *1963*, Table 5.
Lines 19–24: Data on households from *1962*, Table 12, and *1963*, Table 33. For a few countries for which population in households of 10 or over was not given, we assumed the average per household was 12,

439

TABLE 8.2—*Continued*

and completed the series accordingly. Birth rates, for the same years, are from *1963*, Table 19.

*Lines 25–30:* Data on birth order are from *1959*, Table 15. For some countries, mostly developed, the distribution applies to legitimate rather than total births. Birth rates, for the same years, are from *1962*, Table 14.

*Lines 31–38:* Data on ages of parents are from *1959*, Tables 11 and 13. For each country the births shown by age of mother and those shown by age of father were cumulated, each in increasing order of age of parent, and partition lines were drawn at the three quartiles. Birth rates, again for the same years, are from *1962*, Table 14.

*Lines 39–45:* Data on married men by age (lines 42 and 43) are from *1962*, Table 13; *1954*, Table 4; and *1949–50*, Table 5. Line 44 was interpolated arithmetically on the basis of lines 38, 42, and 43. Data on birth rates, for the same years, are from *1962*, Table 14; *1954*, Table 9; and *1949–50*, Table 16. Entries in line 41 are one fourth of those in line 40.

the death rates were also higher, almost double those in the developed countries—18 compared with 10 per 1,000— the level and particularly the absolute discrepancy, some 8 points, were distinctly lower than the level and the absolute discrepancy of the birth rates, some 23 points. As a result, the rate of natural increase in the underdeveloped countries was more than double than that in the developed countries—25.2 compared with 10.0 per 1,000. Thus, since international migration was of some importance in only a few countries, the population in the underdeveloped areas has been growing in recent years at an overall rate of some 2.5 per cent per year, compared with growth in developed countries of only about 1 per cent per year.

This higher rate of population growth in underdeveloped than in developed countries is a relatively recent trend— associated with the substantial decline in the death rates, which, in relevant terms, was much greater in the under-developed than in the developed countries. The shifts are suggested in lines 5–11, which present the vital rates for the much smaller number of countries with continuous records back to 1911–13. The average birth rates declined between 1911–13 and the 1950s in all three groups of countries but insignificantly in the underdeveloped group. The declines in the death rates were far more substantial—ranging from a third of the 1911–13 level for the developed countries to more than a half for the underdeveloped countries; and what is more important, they were, in absolute terms, only 5.3 per 1,000 for the developed and 15.8 per 1,000 for the underdeveloped countries. It is largely this substantial decline in death rates in the underdeveloped countries, combined with maintenance of high birth rates, that explains the shift over the period in the disparity in rates of natural increase: while in 1911–13 these average rates of natural increase for developed and underdeveloped countries differed little (10.8 and 11.7), by the 1950s the disparity between them rose to 16.4 (between 9.5 and 25.9)—primarily because the rate of natural increase more than doubled in the underdeveloped countries.

If we could extend the comparisons back in time, we would find that rates of natural increase and of population growth in the developed countries in the nineteenth and early twentieth centuries exceeded those in the underdeveloped areas. A comparison of the rates of population growth in the area of European settlement, excluding Latin America (the results would only be strengthened if we included Latin America)—which represents the locus of economic development dominated by developed countries —with those in the rest of the world, dominated by underdeveloped countries, shows that from 1750 through 1920, the former exceeded the latter by a substantial margin.[14] While the birth rates in underdeveloped countries may have been higher over long periods in the past, particularly when compared with the older developed countries (as distinct

14. See also Chap. 2. The area of European settlement as defined in the text includes Europe, Asiatic U.S.S.R., North America, and Oceania. The percentage rates of population growth per decade for this area and the rest of the world were respectively: 1750–1800—6.4 and 4.0; 1800–50—8.6 and 4.2; 1850–1900—11.0 and 4.8; 1900–20— 9.6 and 4.4. Then a reversal occurred: 1920–30—10.4 and 11.8; 1930–40 —7.8 and 13.5; 1940–50—3.6 and 15.4; 1950–60—13.3 and 22.9.

These rates are based on the Carr-Saunders estimates for 1750–1900 in U.N., *Determinants and Consequences of Population Trends*, Table 2, p. 11; and on the estimates for 1920–60 in U.N., *Demographic Yearbook, 1963*, Table 2.

from the "young" countries overseas), the higher rate of natural increase in underdeveloped countries has emerged clearly and significantly only since the 1930s.

Some demographic implications of these higher rates of population growth, associated with high birth rates, in the underdeveloped countries are suggested in the remaining sections of Table 8.2. The effects on the age composition of population, making for large shares of groups under 15 years of age and for small shares of the adult groups, are indicated in lines 12–18. If we take the groups between 15 and 59 years of age to represent the working component of population, and those under 15 and over 60 to represent dependents—a rough approximation—the higher shares of groups under 15 years of age in the underdeveloped countries, only partly offset by the lower shares of groups over 59 years old, indicate high ratios of dependents to population in the working ages.

Of possibly greater significance are the effects of the higher birth rates on size of family and household, average number of children per family, and the distribution of births by approximate age of parents (lines 19–45). The grouping of countries throughout is by per capita product but the latter is clearly and inversely associated in the 1950s with crude birth rates, and the findings based on countries grouped by birth rates are similar.[15] We are thus in effect tracing the differential impact of birth rates on family structure in the less developed and the more developed countries.

Private households (covered in lines 19–24), according to the definition recommended by the United Nations (but defined differently in some countries), consists of "the persons who jointly occupy the whole or part of a housing unit, usually share the principal meals and have common

15. See Simon Kuznets, "Demographic Aspects of Modern Economic Growth," a paper submitted to the World Population Conference, organized by the United Nations, in Belgrade, September 1965.

provisions for basic living needs; a person living alone or occupying a separate room in a part of a housing unit, but who does not join with any of the other occupants of the housing unit to form part of a multi-person household, is considered to constitute a separate household." [16] The average number of persons in private households in the underdeveloped countries is almost one and a half times as large as that in the developed countries (line 21); and the proportion of population belonging to large households (7 members or more) is close to half of the total population of the less developed countries, compared with less than a sixth in the developed countries (lines 23 and 24). These differences are clearly associated with, although not necessarily entirely due to, the higher birth rates in the less developed countries and the larger number of children per household.

In turn, these higher birth rates are largely due to a greater propensity of the population in the less developed countries to have many children. Birth parity refers to the order of birth of the child; the first, second, and third child born may be defined as low parity births and higher order births as high parity. The proportions of births of first and second order are far greater in the developed than in the less developed countries; and conversely the proportions of high parity births are far greater in the less than in the more developed countries (lines 25–30). This means that much of the difference in crude birth rates between developed and less developed countries is due to the greater incidence in the latter of high parity births. Thus, if births were limited to first and second order (line 27), the resulting crude birth rate for the developed countries would be $19.9 \times 0.606$, or roughly 12 per thousand; and that for the underdeveloped countries in column 3 would be $44.2 \times 0.378$, or roughly 16.7 per thousand. The disparity would be less than 5 per thousand, or less than half the lower rate —instead of over 24 per thousand, or more than the actual

16. See U.N., *Demographic Yearbook, 1962*, p. 36.

lower rate. It is the differences in the high order births that are the primary reason for the higher birth rates and larger average households in the less developed countries.

But higher order births ordinarily occur to older parents; and if this association is assumed, some important consequences follow. We arrayed total births by increasing age of mother and father (separately) within each country, estimated the partition ages at the first, second, and third quartiles of births in each array, and found that the *minimum* age of fathers for the upper quartile of births is 38.2 years in the underdeveloped countries—distinctly higher than that in the developed countries, 35.7 years (line 38). We also estimated the proportion of married fathers of this minimum age and above to total population (line 44). This proportion is an underestimate because in many underdeveloped countries consensual, not legally registered, marriages, although prevalent, are not covered by the data. The true proportion for *all* married men, including partners in consensual unions, would be larger.[17] But even a generous allowance for such understatement would not raise the proportion in line 44, column 3 more than a fifth, while leaving the proportion in column 1 practically unchanged. With this adjustment, the number of births per 1,000 of married men 38.2 years old or more is close to 100 in the less developed countries, while that per 1,000 of married men 35.7 years old or more is only 30 in the more developed countries.

The economic significance of this finding becomes clear when we link it with the association between age of parents and parity of births. This association means that most of the births to parents of advanced ages, particularly in the underdeveloped countries, are likely to be of high parity. The finding therefore implies that in the less developed countries one in ten families with a father over 38.2 years old and presumably with several children already, perhaps four or five, will have more children. Also clearly implied

17. For a more detailed discussion of this problem, affecting marriage rates and proportions of married men, see Kuznets, "Demographic Aspects."

is the continued presence of dependent children in a large proportion of households until the father reaches, on the average, the late 50s or mid-60s.

A similar analysis could be made of the continued child-bearing by mothers of advanced ages, more prevalent in the less than in the more developed countries, to study its effects on the propensity of married women to participate in the labor force, particularly in jobs away from home. But the data in Table 8.2 and the brief comments above are sufficient to indicate the importance of the distinctive demographic patterns that have characterized the underdeveloped countries in the last decade or two. The higher birth rates and rates of natural increase mean greater demands for investment to equip the rapidly growing population, and they indicate greater pressures upon already limited resources. They also affect the size of the household, the working (and savings) life spans of the family units and of their individual members, and the capacity of families and individuals to respond to the differential economic opportunities that may arise.

*Political Structure*—In shifting now to the differential aspects of political structure, we enter a field for which, with rare exceptions like the date of formal political independence, quantitative observations based on well-established data cannot be made easily. Unlike analysis of demographic movements in which we can count numbers and measure such clearly defined magnitudes as births, deaths, age, etc., and of economic processes in which the market provides an invaluable yardstick, the study of political processes and structure must rely upon the qualitative judgments of experts in the field; and only by means of such judgments can we group countries into different categories. Evaluation of such judgments is beyond the competence of an economist, and they are accepted here as given. Although the findings for such groups are based on a consensus of judgments and not on clearly testable quantitative data, their associations with economic performance and growth must still be viewed as significant, for they do suggest the

445

interdependence between economic and political aspects of society that renders the process of economic growth so complex.

Table 8.3 summarizes these judgments concerning various aspects of political structure for countries grouped largely by per capita product in recent years—modified somewhat by other evidence on economic growth and performance. The distinctly underdeveloped countries are represented by Group C; while the developed, defined somewhat more inclusively than in preceding tables, are represented by Group A. It was impossible to eliminate the Communist countries from the sample covered in the table, but there are only 12 in a total of 113, and they have little effect on the crude proportions. Thus, of the 19 countries in Group A, only three are Communist; and the distinctive political structure of these countries explains why so many shares in column 3 are 84 (i.e. 16 ÷ 19) rather than 100 per cent. Group C, which includes 57 countries, also contains only three Communist countries, and these cannot have much effect on the proportions in column 5. The same can be said for Group B, with 94 countries of which only 9 are Communist. The findings in Table 8.3 can thus be viewed as applicable to the grouping of non-Communist countries; and with emphasis on the comparison of Groups A and C, these findings can now be briefly summarized.

1. A large proportion of underdeveloped countries has only recently attained political independence (line 3)—a fact that has been prominent in newspaper headlines in recent years—with the most rapid increase in politically independent units in Africa. To put it differently, political dependency was prevalent among the underdeveloped countries until relatively recent years. Since even among the politically independent underdeveloped countries (e.g. China in the nineteenth and early twentieth centuries) limitations on sovereignty were imposed by Western powers, the evidence on the recency of fully independent political status among presently underdeveloped countries is striking.

2. Because of relative inexperience with political inde-

TABLE 8.3

Selected Political and Cultural Characteristics of Countries Grouped by
Economic Development, Post-World War II Years*

| | Number of countries (19 in Group A unless otherwise indicated) | | Proportion of countries showing specific characteristics (%) | | |
| --- | --- | --- | --- | --- | --- |
| | Group B (1) | Group C (2) | Group A (3) | Group B (4) | Group C (5) |
| *Product per capita* | | | | | |
| 1. GNP per capita very high or high ($600 and over) | 94 | nd | 100 | 3 | nd |
| 2. GNP per capita very low (less than $150) | 94 | 57 | 0 | 54 | 81 |
| *Political characteristics* | | | | | |
| *Recency, stability, effectiveness* | | | | | |
| 3. Political independence before 1914 | 92 | 55 | 88(17) | 39 | 29 |
| 4. Political modernization advanced (full agreement among political elite on desirability of modernization) | 93 | 57 | 100 | 42 | 21 |
| 5. General government stability dating at least from interwar or beginning of postwar period | 65 | 33 | 100 | 46 | 33 |
| 6. Party system stable | 59 | 31 | 89 | 41 | 26 |
| 7. Interest articulation by anomic groups (riots, demonstrations, etc.) infrequent or very infrequent | 81 | 50 | 88(17) | 23 | 14 |
| 8. Legislature fully effective | 79 | 48 | 79 | 15 | 0 |
| 9. Executive strong | 71 | 41 | 78(18) | 32 | 17 |
| 10. Bureaucracy modern | 55 | 22 | 84 | 7 | 0 |
| *Representativeness* | | | | | |
| 11. Regime on a broadly representative system | 77 | 45 | 84 | 30 | 18 |
| 12. Electoral system competitive | 69 | 42 | 84 | 36 | 19 |
| 13. Autonomous groups fully tolerated in politics | 90 | 54 | 84 | 31 | 15 |
| 14. Interest aggregation by legislature significant, moderate, or limited (rather than negligible) | 76 | 48 | 84 | 39 | 21 |

447

TABLE 8.3—*Continued*

| | Number of countries (19 in Group A unless otherwise indicated) | | Proportion of countries showing specific characteristics (%) | | |
|---|---|---|---|---|---|
| | Group B (1) | Group C (2) | Group A (3) | Group B (4) | Group C (5) |
| 15. Interest aggregation by executive moderate, limited, or negligible (rather than significant) | 84 | 53 | 89 | 31 | 42 |
| 16. Interest articulation of associational groups (trade unions, business assns., and similar groups) significant or moderate (rather than limited or negligible) | 90 | 56 | 84 | 16 | 0 |
| 17. Interest articulation of political parties significant or moderate (rather than limited or negligible) | 72 | 44 | 74 | 44 | 36 |
| 18. Interest articulation of non-associational groups (kinship, lineage, ethnic, religious, status groups) limited or negligible | 94 | 57 | 79 | 17 | 5 |
| *Political leadership* | | | | | |
| 19. Status or regime constitutional (rather than authoritarian or totalitarian) | 71 | 38 | 84 | 46 | 32 |
| 20. Horizontal power distribution (legislative, executive, judicial) significant | 85 | 52 | 79 | 21 | 2 |
| 21. Political leadership nonelitist | 76 | nd | 74 | 45 | nd |
| 22. Personalismo (tendency to follow or to oppose a leader, for personal, individual, or family reasons) negligible | 75 | 44 | 95 | 48 | 36 |
| 23. Regime's leadership's charisma (belief in its extraordinary quality) negligible | 79 | 45 | 94(18) | 42 | 44 |
| 24. Role of police not politically significant | 80 | 49 | 84 | 23 | 12 |
| *Other characteristics* | | | | | |
| 25. Historically western (associated with Europe, including Greece but not Turkey) | 93 | 57 | 95 | 9 | 0 |

TABLE 8.3—*Continued*

| | Number of countries (19 in Group A unless otherwise indicated) | | Proportion of countries showing specific characteristics (%) | | |
|---|---|---|---|---|---|
| | Group B (1) | Group C (2) | Group A (3) | Group B (4) | Group C (5) |
| 26. Racially homogeneous (90% or more of one race) | 88 | nd | 95 | 31 | nd |
| 27. Linguistically homogeneous (majority language 85% or more; no significant single minority) | 93 | 57 | 68 | 41 | 32 |
| 28. Literacy, 50% or more of total population | 88 | 53 | 100 | 39 | 17 |

* Groups A, B, and C are distinguished by their economic development, judged by per capita product and capacity for sustained growth.

Group A includes 19 countries characterized as developed, 16 non-Communist (Australia, Belgium, Canada, Denmark, Finland, France, Germany FR, Italy, Luxembourg, the Netherlands, New Zealand, Norway, Sweden, Switzerland, the United Kingdom, and the United States) and 3 Communist (Czechoslovakia, East Germany, U.S.S.R.). When coverage of Group A is not complete, the number is given in parentheses in col. 3.

Group B includes 94 other countries classified by economic development: 12 in Europe (5 Communist); 21 in Latin America (1, Cuba, Communist); 28 in Asia (3 Communist); and 33 in Africa.

Group C includes 57 of the 94 countries that are characterized as "very underdeveloped," i.e. having low per capita product and "little or no prospect of attaining sustained growth within the foreseeable future" (p. 65). Of these three are Communist (Albania, North Vietnam, and North Korea), and the distribution by continents is 1 in Europe, 9 in Latin America, 16 in Asia, and 31 in Africa.

For more details on the identity of countries, their characteristics, and the distinctions by degree(e.g. frequent, infrequent, significant, moderate, etc.) see the basic source.

*Source:* Data are from Arthur S. Banks and Robert B. Textor, *A Cross-Polity Survey* (Cambridge, Mass., 1963).

pendence, or for other reasons, underdeveloped countries are characterized by instability of government and party system (lines 5 and 6), relatively ineffective and premodern government (lines 8–10), frequent acts of disruptive groups (line 7), and lack of agreement among the political elite on the desirability of modernization (line 4). These and many other characteristics discussed below can at best be recognized only on the basis of broad judgments, and the range of the degree to which they apply to individual underdeveloped countries can be fairly wide. But the contrast with respect to these characteristics between the underdeveloped countries in Group C and the developed countries in Group A is sharp; and unless the known differences in economic performance have in themselves biased the judgments concerning political structure, the association cannot be dismissed as insignificant.

3. Two aspects of the representativeness of political regimes can be usefully distinguished. One is the extent to which the regime is truly representative, providing political mechanisms by which the interests of various groups can secure a hearing, and thus tolerating dissident groups. Here again there is a marked contrast between underdeveloped and developed countries. The prevalence of representative regimes, with strong, elected legislatures and with effective tolerance of autonomous political groups, is much lower among the underdeveloped countries (lines 11–15). The second aspect concerns the nature of articulated interest groups. Here the distinction is between political parties and groups with economic interests—regardless of such considerations as kinship, creed, or ethnic affiliation —on the one hand, and groups bound largely by familial, language, religious, and similar noneconomic ties, on the other. As one might have expected, we find that the latter groups are far more important, with respect to formulation of their interest, in the underdeveloped than in the developed countries (line 18) while political parties and economic association groups are far less important (lines 16 and 17).

4. The distinctive characteristics of political leadership in the underdeveloped countries flow largely from the lack of representativeness of their political regimes and from the dominance of kinship, ethnic, and religious groups. Under such conditions, one could hardly expect an equita-

ble distribution of power among the various branches of government (legislative, judicial, executive, line 20), or a non-elitist political leadership (line 21). Rather one would expect that political leadership would have a strong tinge of personal and charismatic appeal (lines 22 and 23) and that in enforcing the power of such leadership, the police would play a conspicuous role (line 24)—unless the kinship, ethnic, and religious groups agree on the identity of the leadership and the political system is sufficiently representative to permit orderly and peaceful contests for leadership, neither of which is likely.

The association just summarized between economic performance and growth and political structure is unmistakable, and it suggests that, at least until the present, modern economic growth was achieved in countries which now have a political structure quite different from that prevailing in most underdeveloped countries. But it sheds only an oblique light on what might be called the political requirements of modern economic growth or on the specific aspects of political structure that constitute obstacles to, or inducements for, economic growth.

The *minimum* requirements can, perhaps, be formulated, if only in general terms. First, clearly some minimum political stability is necessary if the members of the economic society are to plan ahead and be assured of a relatively stable relation between their contribution to economic activity and their rewards. One could hardly expect much economic growth under conditions of political turmoil, riots, and unpredictable changes in regimes. Second, since a country's sovereign government must resolve the conflicts of interest that inevitably arise in the course of economic change and growth, it must be able to recognize these conflicts in good time and minimize their constraining effects on further economic growth. Finally, since these conflicts are among various groups in society, and these groups must have some means of expression so that their interests can be considered by the government when its broad decisions are made, some minimum representativeness is required.

451

But assuming agreement on these obvious political requirements—stability, flexibility, and representativeness—
we still cannot specify their minimum levels. As with many
other social processes, the requirements are a matter of
degree; absolute magnitudes cannot be assigned to them.
Too much stability of political structure, which usually
results in inflexibility or unresponsiveness, may be as inimical to modern economic growth as too little stability; too
much flexibility—response to economic change without
careful consideration of costs to those affected by it—may
be as destructive of economic growth as too little flexibility;
and unselective representativeness—greater concern with
short-term interests of some groups than the longer-term
future—may constrain economic growth as much as too
little representativeness. Nor can we specify the extent to
which economic growth, once initiated, will, in and of itself, modify political structure in the desirable directions
or establish a firm basis for deciding whether, or to what
extent, the requirements are met in the presently underdeveloped countries.

Yet the absence of a cogent, and quantitatively testable,
theory of interrelations between political structure and
modern economic growth is no ground for dismissing two
obvious implications of the associations in Table 8.3. First,
unlike almost all presently developed countries, most of
the underdeveloped countries today face problems of economic growth after a long period of political dependence—
usually imposed by the Western economically advanced
countries. The consequences are obvious: an association
still persists between important elements of modern economic growth and the dominant and disliked Western
power; native leadership, which has concentrated for a long
period on attaining political independence, has shown slight
interest in and had little experience with domestic economic problems; and the generally acute shortage of politically and administratively experienced personnel after independence has created grave difficulties.

Second, however tentative the judgments of the characteristics of political structure in Table 8.3, and however little we know of the political conditions of economic growth, it seems warranted to argue that the structures suggested must generate formidable obstacles to economic growth in many underdeveloped countries. Political instability and nonrepresentativeness of the regimes, combined with an authoritarian structure dominated by personalist leaders and backed by familial and ethnic ties and the police, are hardly favorable conditions for economic growth—even in the early phases of the transition from the traditional, premodern economic society. Whether these aspects of political structure result from the recency of political independence (thus partly overlapping the first implication) or whether they are present in underdeveloped countries that have long been politically independent, and whether these features of political structure in underdeveloped countries are an inevitable concomitant of poor economic performance and technology, the fact of the association remains, and one must accept the strong suggestion of interrelations that it provides. Indeed, if political structure provides a framework within which economic activity takes place and there is some connection between the two, and if this framework in underdeveloped countries reflects past patterns of social and economic life within which, *by definition,* modern economic growth was effectively absent, at least some of the elements of political structure must be inconsistent with modern economic growth and will constitute obstacles to it as long as they exist.[18]

18. Comparison of the present political structure of the underdeveloped countries with that of the now developed countries immediately before their entry into modern economic growth would also be illuminating—provided that one could adjust for the effects of changes in worldwide political climate on the acceptability of various political arrangements. This topic is clearly beyond my competence. I can only suggest that whatever the early political structure of the developed countries, the current structure, revealed in Table 8.3, indicates that modern economic growth necessitates some minimum political requirements.

This argument applies to other noneconomic aspects of social structure discussed in the next section.

*Other Aspects*—Demographic movements, political structure, and even economic patterns describe the behavior of individuals in society acting as economic, political, and family units; but these units must also be affected by other elements in social structure and institutions, and reflect scales of values and priorities. And, of course, these other institutions and sets of values are, in turn, partly determined by the demographic, political, and economic structures. Without attempting to deal at length with these other institutions and scales of values, it seems useful to discuss them briefly under two headings: integration and orientation.

*Integration.* By integration I mean the extent to which institutional and spiritual conditions of life within underdeveloped countries, either in the immediate past or at present, foster unity, cooperation, and coherence among the various groups, regions, etc. within the country. It affects economic structure directly and indirectly: directly, in its bearing on the division of labor and market relations; indirectly, in its bearing on political organization, the body responsible for policy decisions on issues often crucial for a country's economic growth.

If then one asks whether integration is as widespread in underdeveloped countries as in the developed, the likely answer is negative. This statement is supported by data on greater prevalence of racial and linguistic heterogeneity in underdeveloped countries in Table 8.3 (lines 26 and 27). Indeed, transportation and communication facilities have been technologically weak in underdeveloped countries, even those that have been politically independent and unified for centuries (such as China); the boundaries of many, until recently politically dependent, may be artificial in the sense of enclosing many different tribes and communities; and over long periods of political dependence or unstable native political structure, the extended family unit or clan or tribe has been relied on for protection. It is, therefore, hardly surprising to find that in many underdeveloped countries today integration, countrywide community of feeling, is far weaker and linguistic, religious, and racial ties are far stronger than in the developed countries (not that the latter are entirely free of such divisive tendencies).

Although the basic units of integration within the traditional social structure in many underdeveloped countries are different from those prevailing in the more nationalistic —and more fully integrated—developed countries, not all their aspects are necessarily inimical to economic growth. The extended family or clan can provide a favorable environment for the development of entrepreneurship with a long time horizon, which a small, nuclear family could not do under similar conditions; and linguistic or ethnic heterogeneity to some degree fosters economic specialization—specific caste or ethnic minorities concentrate on specialized functions and develop skills otherwise unattainable. But if one must admit that the underdeveloped countries often contain diverse loci of economic specialization and that family, clan, ethnic, and religious ties may be a positive factor in such specialization, the fact remains that the specialization is limited to essentially indivisible, noneconomic groups, that the weak national ties impede the selection of individuals for the most efficient division of labor, and that the weak feelings of community of kind as a basis for central direction by a strong and efficient government are inimical to economic growth. And if the frictions among the various groups are intensive, the absence of a stable political and social framework may be damaging indeed.

One aspect of this problem of integration deserves explicit note. In the past some premodern societies achieved political and even some economic integration by special innovations and devices that overcame the divisive effects of weak transport and communication facilities and of associated linguistic or other heterogeneity. The great empires of the past—the Inca in Latin America, and the Chinese and Indian in Asia—managed by major social innovations to organize large population masses into unified and long-lasting political and social units. In China the reliance on

455

a single, nonphonetic written language that supplemented the various spoken dialects, on an imperial bureaucracy using that language, on a system of canals, and on one of tribute, represented such innovations that lasted for centuries. In India the spread of the caste system, and of a unified religion that organized economic and related activities in articulated order, emphasized division of labor but at the same time established rigid hierarchical relations among the various social functions, while the spread of one religion provided a degree of unity for the country, despite numerous invasions and much political instability.

Some such elaborate social and political structures, which organized large population groups into what at the time were fairly advanced social units, were shattered by the direct invasion of European powers. Thus affected, for example, were the empires of Latin America and the Ottoman Empire in the Middle East. In several instances the large native population groups that had previously been governed from the center no longer had such contacts and became relatively isolated, because the invading minority and its immediate descendants did not integrate the country in a widely pervasive process of economic growth, a failure common among Latin American countries with large Indian or other non-European populations.[19] But in

19. Wendell C. Gordon provides data in *The Economy of Latin America* (New York, 1950), Table 2, p. 352, for the 1940s on the racial structure of population in 20 countries of Latin America, distinguishing white (76 to 100 per cent Caucasian), Mestizo (Indian–white with no more than 75 per cent of either white or Indian blood), Indian (76 to 100 per cent Amerindian), and Negroid (individuals with high proportions of Negro blood). Table 5, p. 355 presents national income or national product, again for the 1940s for the same 20 countries. The Spearman coefficient of rank correlation between per capita income and the proportion of whites, for all 20 countries, is +0.6; for 15 countries, excluding those with large Negroid proportions, it is close to +0.7. The coefficients of rank correlation between per capita income and the proportion of Indian plus Negroid population are −0.7 for all 20 countries, and −0.8 for the 15 countries. Obviously per capita income is inversely associated with the proportion of the native Indian population.

many populous countries in Asia, and in some in Africa—China and India being the most prominent because they are the largest—these past innovations survived: China still uses a nonphonetic written language in addition to a variety of spoken dialects; and linguistic, caste, and regional diversity in India is still marked. All these great innovations of the past are, however, major obstacles today—for clearly a simple phonetic written language in China and linguistic unity and effective abolition of caste barriers in India would greatly facilitate the adoption of patterns of modern economic growth. If we had greater knowledge of the institutional heritage of other presently underdeveloped countries, we could probably demonstrate that many social innovations that served as a basis for premodern economic growth have persisted beyond their usefulness and are now obstacles to the change needed for economic growth under the vastly different conditions of today.

*Orientation.* By orientation we mean the views shared by the major groups in the population with respect to human fate and fortune in this world, and the scale of values generated by such views. As suggested in Chapter 1, in the discussion of the concept of an economic epoch in general and of the modern economic epoch in particular, these views may be of crucial importance in influencing individual and social activity. While subject to change as economic and social conditions change, they have their own pattern of life; and if they tend to persist beyond the conditions to which they have been a response, they must be considered as partly autonomous.

Such views and the basic orientation are determined in part by education, by the institutions that govern the relations between successive generations, and by exposure of the population in a given country to outside influences. This is hardly the place for extended discussion of this subject, but we might mention the difficulty of establishing such views by means of hard data—which would provide testable ex ante evidence—and the resultant reliance on weak inferences from actions of individuals and groups (in which, all too often, actions are "explained" by views and motives that are, by circular reasoning, imputed to the actions). Orientation is mentioned explicitly to call attention to two relevant observations, both purely factual, but again requiring prolonged exploration not possible here.

The first, suggested by line 25 of Table 8.3 is that practically none of the low income underdeveloped countries of today can be characterized as historically Western, i.e. as a member of the concert of European nations or their direct descendants (in North America and Oceania); while the developed countries, with the single and conspicuous exception of Japan, are European by membership or descent. If the term "European civilization" denotes a set of views and a scale of values of distinctive orientation, evolved in the course of a commonly shared long history, a common set of religions, and much continuous internal intercourse, then it may be argued that the spiritual framework within which most of modern economic growth has occurred is distinctly European in cast and orientation. And, by the same token, we may argue that for centuries almost all underdeveloped countries of today were outside the orbit of, and had no contact with, European history and civilization, inheriting a tradition and orientation that, having evolved separately, may have something in common with, but is also very different from, European civilization—the locus of origin and development of the modern economic system.

The differences may range from relatively specific aspects, such as the disparagement of manual labor and material experimentation and adulation of literary scholarship and exegesis in traditional China compared with the shift from medieval scholasticism to modern science in Western Europe, to broader contrasts suggested by comparison of the eternal cycle of the transmigration of souls in the traditional religion of India with the emergence in eighteenth-century Europe of the emphasis on human reason, dignity, and welfare in the present world. Adequate coverage of even the major differences would require extensive knowledge of both the content of the European framework of modern economic growth and the views and scales of values that characterize various underdeveloped countries, today and in the immediate past; and it is neither feasible nor perhaps necessary to attempt such coverage here.

The major point—the difference in the systems of views and scales of values—is, we hope, obvious. The real question is as to its significance. Can we assume that because modern economic growth emerged within the framework of Western civilization there was a reciprocal process of enrichment between the economic processes and the intellectual and spiritual framework? Or should we assume that the presently underdeveloped countries, despite their isolation from European civilization, have also evolved a system of views and scale of values that are easily adaptable to the requirements of modern economic growth—but that a failure to take advantage of the growth potentials of modern technology has resulted from the aggressive and constraining policies of the economically developed West? Whatever importance we attach to this latter question suggesting a kind of devil theory of economic backwardness (and it is of some importance) we find it difficult to avoid the judgment that the orientation of the underdeveloped countries of today, their systems of views and scales of values—which we call traditional and which are more properly described as results of adjustment to a long history quite different from that of the European countries and their descendants—must contain many elements that are inconsistent with, hence obstacles to, modern economic growth.

The second observation is, we hope, also obvious: that most underdeveloped countries have been affected by the expansion of the developed countries and the penetration of modern economic growth and of its values to almost all parts of the world, if in differing degrees. Most of them contain groups, however small, that have had close contact with European civilization, have gone through its educational system, or have otherwise learned from its intellectual and spiritual heritage. Some of these contacts have been under adverse circumstances, others under favorable.

Whatever the circumstances, there was a selective penetration of European views and scales of values into the underdeveloped countries, which, because they contrasted with many of the traditional views and values, often produced much strain and ferment. Consequently we cannot contrast the spiritual framework of underdeveloped countries, in its pristine, purely traditional form, with the European framework of modern economic growth because contacts with the West have already disturbed the traditional framework, both materially and spiritually. A key aspect of the situation may be the fact that some elements of modernization (e.g. those limited to a small elite) could be adopted much more easily than others (e.g. those that had to have widespread impact, affecting large groups in the population). Moreover, the demonstration effects may have been greater with respect to some activities (e.g. consumption) than others (e.g. production). And if we recognize that these selective impacts of the nonmaterial framework of modern economic growth have occurred while most of the distinctive aspects of the native traditional views and values have been retained, we can more readily appreciate the combination of drives and resistance, of inducements for and obstacles to, modern economic growth in many underdeveloped countries today.

# 9 THE SPREAD OF MODERN ECONOMIC GROWTH

The summary description in the preceding chapter of the distinctive economic, demographic, and political structures and other aspects of the underdeveloped countries should not lead to the conclusion that a combination of them all means that economic growth in these countries is impossible. The coexistence of economically backward with economically developed nations provides both an inducement and an opportunity for growth in the areas that lag behind; and, given a minimum of political stability and limited constraint by institutions and views inimical to modernization, the opportunities for substantial rates of growth over a relatively short period are wide. Indeed, the estimates for the recent decade indicate substantial increases in total and per capita product for most underdeveloped countries.[1] The weight of the evidence above bears not so much upon the impossibility of economic growth in the underdeveloped countries, but upon the consequences of past failure to modernize and grow, and upon the major structural changes that must be made in order for the process of growth to continue on a sustained and adequately cumulative basis. In particular, it suggests some of the reasons why modern economic growth has spread to such a limited proportion of total world population. It is to a brief discussion of this point that we turn now.

1. See U.N., *Yearbook of National Accounts Statistics, 1963,* Table 2A, pp. 318–19, for growth rates per year in GDP and GDP per capita for 1953–61.

461

The statement is made designedly in terms of population, rather than countries or political units: the latter are too diverse in size to provide meaningful measures. If then we concentrate on proportions of world population, we find that by the late 1950s the non-Communist developed countries, as given in Table 7.1, accounted for less than a fifth. If per capita product is our criterion and we set the minimum level at $575 for a developed country (Table 7.2), the proportion of world population in developed countries rises to somewhat less than a fourth. If we set the 1780s as the date of the Industrial Revolution, which ushered in modern economic growth, one and three quarter centuries have elapsed; and in that period an epochal innovation has spread to only a quarter of the world population. Is this rate of spread low, and if so, why?

Obviously, some elements of modern economic growth have penetrated to almost all corners of the earth and have thus affected to some degree almost all of the world population. But we are dealing here with a spread effective enough to raise a country's economic performance in the aggregate, not merely to produce islands of modernity. And the answer to our question depends, of course, upon the definition of spread of modern economic growth as a thorough transformation of a country's economic and social framework. With this introduction, we may approach the question by considering (1) the restricted locus of the pioneering impact of modern economic growth; (2) the length of the transition period and the slowness of the process of spread; and (3) the increasing difficulties associated with the widening gap between the developed countries and those still to be developed.

### RESTRICTED LOCUS

As to the restricted locus, England and Wales, which pioneered in the introduction of modern economic growth, had at the time (circa 1781) a population of some 7.5 million; and the addition of Scotland would not raise the total

462

above 9 million. In 1751, the figure for Great Britain was about 7.4 million; in 1801, about 10.8 million. World population was estimated to be 728 million in 1750 and 906 million in 1800.[2] Thus in the 1780s Great Britain accounted for only slightly over 1 per cent of world population. At the time several countries in the world had far larger populations, the most conspicuous case being China, with a population probably well over 200 million.[3] And some countries in Europe were also substantially larger, even if we disregarded what eventually became unified Germany and Italy: in 1800, the population of France was estimated to be 27.3 million, and that of Russia (present territory of the U.S.S.R.) 37.0 million.[4] Why did the Industrial Revolution occur in a small country like Great Britain rather than in a larger unit that had already organized and controlled large masses of population? And, if it did originate in a relatively small country, why didn't it also occur simultaneously in the other countries within the European framework rather than be confined for some decades, as it was, to Great Britain?

These are clearly questions to which only speculative answers can be given, and although we do not intend to answer them, they are relevant in the present connection because they point the direction in which the answers must be sought. If we ask why the Industrial Revolution did not occur in China, for example, we are implicitly asking why modern science failed to develop there, despite the fact that in earlier centuries Medieval Europe borrowed both science and technology from the advanced Far East (and the

2. The population totals for Great Britain are from Deane and Cole, *British Economic Growth*, Table 2, p. 16. The estimates of world population (Carr-Saunders) are from U.N., *Determinants and Consequences of Population Trends*, Table 2, p. 11.

3. According to Bennett, *The World's Food*, p. 9, the population of Greater China (China proper, with the addition of Manchuria, Korea, Outer Mongolia, Chinese Turkestan, and Formosa) was 270 million in 1750 and 345 million in 1800.

4. See W. S. and E. S. Woytinsky, *World Population and Production*, Table 17, p. 44.

Middle East): the three major technological innovations of the Middle Ages—the compass, gunpowder, and printing—had their origin in Chinese technology. Further pursuit of this question would lead us to examine the institutional and ideological framework that made the earlier technological advances possible and the integration of great population masses into a single, large political unit feasible; and we would be led to search for the ways in which this framework might have impeded the emergence of experimental science and its application to technological problems incident to the limited efficiency of labor that lacked both the tested knowledge of natural processes and the drive to material accomplishments that might benefit human welfare.

This statement is closely allied to our earlier observations that the *survival* of the institutional and spiritual framework, which at one time permitted integration of large population groups into viable political units, may constitute obstacles to modern economic growth in many populous underdeveloped countries today. It may seem paradoxical that the small population of Western Europe—whose size (excluding Russia) amounted in 1750 to less than a fifth of that of the population of Asia—as an inheritor of the Greco-Roman and Judaic civilizations, should have completed a long process of learning from the more advanced countries; and having gone through an intellectual, political, and geographical revolution, should have provided the basis for the Industrial Revolution that ushered in modern economic growth, which then proceeded to sweep outward. One important factor was the distinctive historical heritage; another may have been the small numbers; and a third may have been the political diversity that provided many loci for experimentation with social and material technology.

Another direction in which an answer might be sought is suggested if we ask why, among the European countries themselves, the Industrial Revolution occurred in Great Britain rather than in the much larger France or Russia.

It may well be that given the continental location of these countries, the means by which their political unification was attained produced a political and social framework that was unfavorable to vigorous entrepreneurial drives aimed at technological and economic innovations. Great Britain, on the other hand, was separated by the Channel and well past its period of laying claims to territory on the continent, had had a history of continuous participation in Western European economic civilization, and had enjoyed substantial gains from the immediately preceding period of geographical expansion. Consequently, when it was faced with shortages and bottlenecks of the old technology (e.g. an inadequate supply of wood for fuel and as a general industrial material and the need to find a new source of industrial power) and with the increasing pressures on labor by new growth industries (e.g. spinning in the cotton textiles) Great Britain could solve the problem more easily than the other relatively developed countries of Europe, and in so doing lay the basis for a new technology with a potential so much larger than the old as to constitute what eventually proved to be an Industrial Revolution. It is reasonable to contend that in this combination of noninvolvement in ambitious European politics of size, in the accumulation of long experience with the older economic civilization of Europe, and in the access to the fruits of the preceding geographic expansion, Great Britain was a unique case, unmatched by any other European country of the day. If the situation was as indicated above, the Industrial Revolution could not have occurred concurrently in other countries in Europe, let alone in the rest of the world.

Whether restrictive locus of pioneering impact is an inherent characteristic of all revolutionary breakthroughs to a new economic epoch is an intriguing question that merits some investigation. It may be argued that such breakthroughs originated in response either to major bottlenecks within the economic technology of the current epoch or to new opportunities of sufficient magnitude so that their exploitation proved to constitute a new epoch—or to both

465

the bottlenecks and then, after a while, the opportunities that initial solutions of the bottlenecks provide. If this combination of events is the case, it may then be argued that the constraints imposed by the old economic technology are more acute in the old countries that have a long history of that technology and may have reached its limits than in those that are newcomers to it or those that have an exceptional supply for its essential needs. To illustrate the response to bottlenecks in the old technology: eighteenth-century Great Britain, with its scanty forests and deep mines, was under pressure to find a source of fuel and power, whereas Sweden, with its abundance of woods, and for that matter the Netherlands, which had no wood, coal, or iron ore, faced no such problem.

As for epochal opportunities, they are not likely to be equally available to all countries equipped to exploit them if they are a matter of natural resources, or geographical location, or other unequally distributed endowments. Thus, only the countries with easy access to the Atlantic Ocean could take advantage of the geographical expansion of Europe beginning in the fifteenth century, which initiated the epoch of merchant capitalism, whereas the Italian cities, many of the German states, and many of the countries in Central and Eastern Europe, were less favorably situated. And, of course, Great Britain had an enormous advantage in its coal and iron ore, the sinews of the early phases of modern economic growth. These arguments suggest that in any breakthrough to a new epoch, only a few countries can satisfy the requirements of successful pioneering: sustained experience with the older economic technology that would lead both to an appreciation of its bottlenecks and to the development of methods for dealing with them; a favorable position with reference to new opportunities, particularly if such opportunities are, as it were, exogenous; and a social and ideological framework that permits the concentration of sufficient energy on overcoming the major bottlenecks, or on exploiting the new opportunities as is eventually and necessarily the case, or on both.

466

We still must face the question of size. Are the one or two pioneer countries large or small? It may be argued that since there are only one or two pioneers, size is relatively unimportant; the locus of pioneering impact is self-limiting and most of the world population is beyond its influence, at least in the early phase of a new economic epoch. But two additional arguments can be adduced that favor the smaller countries as candidates for pioneers. The first, purely formal, is that there are many more small countries than large —given the usual skewness in the distribution of politically independent units by size—and hence, other conditions being equal, there is a greater chance that the pioneer will be small rather than large. Second, if in the existing state of population and technology in the world, a political unit is large by the standards of the time, it may well be too large to be optimal. In other words, if the formation and maintenance of a large political unit require development of political and social innovations, integration in the economic realm may be lagging. In fact, the political framework that is evolved may not favor a sustained drive toward economic innovations—an observation that is applicable to many old large empires, ranging from the Persian to the Roman to the Chinese.

The above suggestions that pioneer beginnings of new economic epochs are likely to have an exceedingly narrow locus are purely speculative and would require marshaling of more evidence than is possible here. But they have some value because they bear upon an important aspect of the mechanism of spread of an economic epoch. If such an epoch is defined, as it was in Chapter 1, as a long historical period in which the economic growth of a fairly *large number* of separately organized human societies stems from a common source constituted by the epochal innovation, we can now add that these epochal innovations begin by a breakthrough in one or two probably small pioneer countries and then spread, with some delay, to other countries. And, clearly, the arguments adduced above to explain why only one or two countries are likely to be the pioneers apply also to followers, suggesting differences in preparedness for the exploitation of the new epochal innovations, in experience with the old economic technology, in natural resource endowments for the new technology, and even in capacity to learn from the pioneers and to resist their possibly inimical policies (once they have become strong and aggressive). The model of spread of an economic epoch thus suggested inevitably produces differential rates of growth among the pioneers, early followers, and late followers—with whatever consequences for international relations and internal growth that may be implied by such differences in initial position, timing of the growth process, and rates of growth. This feature has certainly been prominent in the spread of modern economic growth, and it would not be surprising to find that it characterized the earlier economic epochs also.

### LENGTH OF TRANSITION PERIOD

If modern economic growth began in a country that accounted for slightly over 1 per cent of world population, and in a century and three quarters spread and transformed the economies of countries accounting for between a fifth and a quarter of world population, has the rate of spread been low or high? We have no criteria by which to judge such a rate. If, as was noted in Chapter 6, the modern economic epoch is the *first* in history with universal scope, i.e. with the capacity to reach and affect every corner of the earth, there is no historical precedent by which to judge the rate of spread in terms of world population.

Indeed, one could easily wax eloquent in support of both sides of the proposition. One could marvel that within the short period of less than two centuries, an exceedingly brief tag-end to thousands of years of human history, as much as a fifth to a quarter of mankind managed to attain overall levels of economic performance and per capita standards of living that are far higher than the highest enjoyed by even the most advanced people in the past; and one could argue that the rate of spread has been striking indeed, since its continuation for another four or five centuries would raise all of mankind to truly millennial levels of economic and material attainment. Or one could stress that, despite the enormous gains in science- and invention-based power of man to command vast resources and bend enormous natural forces to human ends, between three quarters and four fifths of mankind still suffer from low economic performance, and a large proportion of these from truly inadequate standards of living; and that, despite almost two centuries of spread, modern economic growth has failed to improve substantially the material lot of most of mankind—even if it has permitted a larger number to survive longer—so that they have fallen increasingly behind the small fraction of world population in the economically advanced countries.

These two positions are not inconsistent, since they reflect two aspects of one process; but they can hardly advance our understanding of some of the testable characteristics of that process. Abandoning evaluations implicit in terms like "quite fast" and "too slow," we turn to some observable characteristics of the process—in particular, the length of time involved in the spread of new technology even within the pioneering country to a point where it begins to exercise a widely transforming effect on the economy and in the adoption of the new technology and the associated institutions by the follower countries.

Before the pioneering breakthrough to modern economic growth can exercise an impact elsewhere, not only must the major desirable effects be evident within the country of origin, but means must be available by which the knowledge and resources can be transferred to other countries with endowments and institutions that make it possible for them to follow in the wake of the pioneer. With reference to the first point, it may be argued that while the major inventions associated with the Industrial Revolution in Great Britain had all been introduced and proved feasible by the 1780s, their cumulative effect on the economy, shifting it

469

from an agricultural to an industrial country, was not to become evident until several decades later. In 1770, agriculture accounted for about 45 per cent of the national income of England and Wales; for Great Britain, the share of agriculture in 1801 and 1811 was still between 33 and 36 per cent, compared with 21 to 24 per cent for manufacturing, mining, and construction;[5] and the pace of industrialization accelerated markedly only after 1811. More important, the spread of iron (later steel) as the basic industrial material and of steam as a source of industrial power took a number of decades, requiring the development of machines for processing metals, as well as several major innovations to extend the use of steam from stationary purposes to its application in transportation, first in inland waters, then on land, and finally, in the mid-nineteenth century, to the oceans.

It is impossible to pinpoint the date at which the outlines of the revolutionary transformation of technology, and the associated changes in economy and society became apparent —when the transformation thus became available, as it were, for study, imitation, and spread. But even if we set the date at the end of the 1820s, the earliest reasonable date after the Napoleonic wars, the period since the Industrial Revolution (i.e. the total period over which the *spread* of modern economic growth could occur) is thus shortened by at least three decades. And one could argue, with some justification, that the new economic epoch became evident only after steam railroads with their far-reaching effects on size of markets and industrial technology had proven themselves. In that case the transition period from revolutionary beginnings to the realization of the potentials of the new epochal innovation by other countries is at least five decades; and the period over which modern economic growth could have spread is reduced from a century and three quarters to a century and a quarter. While the historical record is complicated by the Napoleonic wars, it is hardly an accident that the transition to modern industriali-

5. See Deane and Cole, Tables 35 and 37, pp. 156 and 166.

zation in the first group of follower countries cannot be dated before the late 1830s.

If the above observation has general validity, specific dates of major inventions and innovations should perhaps be viewed as points on a continuum that stretches from the earliest search for these innovations to their first successful applications demonstrating feasibility (at which the dates are usually set), then to the cumulative unfolding of their effects to a level sufficiently high in the pioneer country to induce increased recognition, imitation, and participation by other countries. In other words, the results of application of an epochal innovation must reach some minimum *threshold* before the process of spread may be expected to begin.[6] And clearly the length of the transition period from the revolutionary breakthrough to the time that the threshold is reached depends partly upon the nature of the epochal innovation, partly upon the capacity of the pioneer country or countries to exploit the new opportunities at a high and sustained rate, and partly upon the extent of communication and shared antecedents between the pioneer and other, would-be follower, countries.

Having considered the time span between the beginnings of modern economic growth and the date at which the process of spread may reasonably be expected to begin, we turn to the process of spread itself. Several observations can be made as we distinguish the groups of would-be follower countries by their distance, geographical and historical, from the pioneer country. If we begin with Western European countries, which shared with Great Britain a long stretch of common history, a number of similar institutions, and a not too dissimilar heritage of views and values, we

6. This comment implies that individual inventions, smaller elements in the complex of epochal innovation, have far less impact than a large subcomplex, consisting of interrelated inventions (as in the case of steam and iron) and carried to a minimum of development where its wide ramifications can be seen. This implication would be particularly true of impact on, and response by, the larger groups in other countries, particularly the governments (as distinct from individual entrepreneurs).

471

find that even there several major institutional and political changes had to be made either before or during the transition to modern economic growth. If the political unification of Germany and Italy was a necessary antecedent or concomitant of successful modern industrialization, many steps had to be taken in the conversion from the political Balkanization of these countries at the end of the Napoleonic wars to the unified political structure, at the end of the second or third quarter of the nineteenth century. Equally crucial changes were required in the separation of the Netherlands from Belgium in 1830, in the political structure of France after the restoration of the Bourbons, and in the political framework of the Austro-Hungarian Empire. Major internal legislation, often subject to group conflicts, was needed with respect to property rights, control over land, freedom of labor, structure of industry, control of railroads, and the like. And, as we move eastward, it becomes clear that modern industrialization within Russia had to await a shift of internal forces that would permit the abolition of serfdom and adoption by a central government of a policy that would foster and encourage industry.

Such major structural changes can hardly proceed at high speed without threatening the unity of a country; and while some modern economic growth can occur without them, a sustained cumulation of the growth may require such changes and may be retarded by delay in making them. This comment is made to indicate that even among the European countries nearest and most closely allied historically to pioneering Great Britain, entry into modern economic growth may have been delayed, awaiting major required political and institutional changes. Furthermore, once modern economic growth began, a substantial period would have been required to observe whether the process was successfully cumulative and had not run into some serious obstacles—so that a country could be said to have joined the ranks of developed nations only after several decades beyond the transition period had elapsed. Thus, the rate of spread, in terms of the established extension of modern economic growth to the first group of European followers, assuming that growth began in this group in the late 1830s, could not be fully ascertained until the late 1860s or the 1870s.

Similar comments can be made concerning the societies of descendants of Western European countries overseas, when these settled in relatively empty areas and thus constituted overwhelming majorities. Even when political independence was attained early, as in the United States, some decades had to elapse during which the new political framework was developed and the capacity of the new country for sustained life and growth established; and, to the extent that the impressive growth depended on large and continuous immigration, until means of transport from and conditions in Europe provided the flow. The distinctive transition to modern industrialization did not begin in the United States until the later 1830s, which also witnessed the beginning of a large immigration flow that was to add significantly to its high rate of aggregate growth. Despite this, the adjustment of the social and economic structure to modern economic growth was not smooth or unhalting thereafter, as shown by the Civil War. In other countries, the delay in the formation of an adequate political structure, while due partly to lack of pressure from internal growth, meant in turn a delay in possible participation in modern economic growth. In Australia, convict shipments were discontinued in 1840 and self-governing power was granted to Victoria and other states in 1850 (their constitutions were introduced in the 1850s), but the Federal Commonwealth was not established until the end of the century. In New Zealand, a parliamentary system and representative government were established in 1856. In Canada, a proper political framework was provided by the North America Act of 1867. The timing is significant, even if we assume that the delay was partly due to absence of internal growth, in turn possibly due to meager immigration flows—for it is clear evidence that despite presumably favorable resource supplies, the conditions for effective participation in modern economic growth were not present until well into the second half of the nineteenth century. And the delay in establishing a viable political framework was even longer in the case of Argentina (a country with a population overwhelmingly of European stock), despite attainment of political independence early in the nineteenth century.

The conditions in other areas with populations that were overwhelmingly native, inheritors of long distinctive histories, and isolated from Europe, were more pregnant of difficulties and delays—even when these areas were colonies of an advanced European country or, as in the case of many Latin American countries, were managed by a domestic elite that consisted largely of descendants of the original Iberian colonizers. Domination by a distant metropolitan power had some positive effects: it provided stability, some infrastructure, development of exports, and opportunities of contact that eventually led to the emergence of a native elite trained in European civilization and ready to serve as carriers of modernization. But the formation of these native nuclei of modernization was a slow process; and it took decades before the strengthening of native cadres, combined with the changing views of metropolitan powers on the value of colonial possessions, could result in political independence, and only then could attention shift to issues of long-term economic growth under native auspices.

In Africa and some parts of Asia, many of the native societies were not reached by the expansionary drives of the advanced Western powers until late in the nineteenth century—partly for technological, partly for political reasons. Thus, if colonization made any contribution to the eventual economic modernization of former colonial areas, it was slow and often late; and it is hardly surprising that the effective spread of modern economic growth to these areas is only now beginning. In the politically independent countries in Latin America and Africa with large, still traditionally oriented majorities, the task of integrating these majorities in a widespread and effective process of economic growth was delayed by a political and institutional framework that, at least until recent decades, permitted the small elites to profit from the economic advantages of their position, without embodying strong incentives and pressures for change that would spread the benefits and lay the foundition for greater modernization of the economic and social structure.

The large states in Asia that remained politically independent, particularly China and Japan, are especially interesting. Aggressive expansion by the developed Western countries in this direction was probably delayed in part by technological deficiencies of transportation, which may explain why significant use of force was not made until the first Opium War with China in 1842 and the "opening" of Japan in the 1850s. These dates are three quarters of a century after the initiation of modern economic growth in Great Britain; and it would be interesting if idle speculation to ask whether, if these aggressive contacts with the Far East had been made half a century earlier, the entry of Japan and China into modern economic growth would also have occurred that much earlier. But the differences between Japan and China in response to these exogenous shocks pose a major analytical problem in the study of the spread of modern economic growth. Japan responded rather promptly by reshaping its institutions, and entered the process in the 1870s, while China was continuously beset with difficulties in attempts to make the needed structural changes, and consequently its entry into modern economic growth was delayed at least a hundred years. But pursuit of this line of thought is beyond our present interest. All we need to note are the delay in the reaching out by the advanced European units to these areas, and the problems facing China—which then, as now, accounted for a quarter of world population—in adjusting the political and social framework to the requirements of relatively successfully exploitation of the modern growth potential.

These are scattered and casual comments on a broad theme. But inadequate and episodic as they are, they point unmistakably to an obvious aspect of the spread of modern economic growth. The one and three quarter centuries that have elapsed since the Industrial Revolution may seem, at first, to be a long period within which such spread could have occurred. But the period seems all too short if we allow for the time required (1) to bring the revolutionary beginnings to fruition as a new epochal transformation; (2) to adjust the inherited political and social framework, even in European countries and among European descendants in the "empty" countries overseas, at least to permit sustained economic growth; (3) to improve the technology of transport and communication that permits the adequate flow of people to the empty countries overseas, as well as the expansion by the advanced countries, primarily European, to the previously isolated and economically underdeveloped countries in Asia and Africa; and (4) to bring about a change from the prolonged colonial status of many of these countries (and, despite political independence, of the dominant native population in many Latin American countries), with native elites permitted to develop only very slowly and the hold of the metropolitan countries (or domestic, ethnically different, elites) only slightly weakened. The distribution of world population, *even in 1800*, was overwhelmingly dominated by the non-European countries with their long history distinct from that of the countries that were the locus of the early phases of modern economic growth; (in that year, population in the area of European settlement, including Latin America, was less than a quarter of world population, while that of Asia and Africa was more than three quarters). And since Africa and Asia still accounted for more than six tenths of world population in 1950, it is hardly surprising that modern economic growth, defined in terms of an adequate transformation of a country's aggregate economic performance and the associated social structure, has spread to only a fifth or a quarter of world population.

# Spread of Modern Economic Growth

One other aspect of the spread of modern economic growth calls for explicit discussion: the dependence of its measurement upon the line drawn between the developed and other countries, upon the criteria by which a country is recognized as developed. The common procedure, which we have followed, is to set a minimum per capita or per worker product as the dividing line and modify it if that per unit product or a higher one is due to a fortuitously rich endowment with a valuable natural resource (e.g. oil), or if a per unit product that is below the minimum is nevertheless accompanied by a marked degree of industrialization and other features of modern economic development. But we must still explain how the minimum per unit product is established, as well as the general purpose of this operational definition. It is important to bring to the surface what is implicit in such a definition, for this may shed light not only upon evaluation but even upon the analysis of economic growth.

We begin by suggesting that in distinguishing developed countries, we are trying to identify the units that exploited the growth potential of modern material and social technology with some minimum degree of adequacy. Although we do not know and cannot measure this potential, we do know that some countries show much higher rates of economic performance than others and have an economic structure with a greater share of industries and processes identifiable with more recent technology, and we conclude that these have tapped the growth potential more successfully than others. Then we array the per capita or per worker product and draw a line at what we conceive as a minimum adequacy level.

In drawing *one* minimum line for all countries we are making a crucial assumption concerning the growth potential for each. We are assuming that if we could estimate this specific potential for each country, taking account of its natural and other endowments beyond social control, it would differ from country to country but its range would not exceed the spread between the minimum per capita or per worker product and the highest attained. In fact, the growth potential afforded by the existing stock of technology and related knowledge is quite different for different countries, either because of some relatively transient factors or because of more lasting specific conditions. We recognize this for the countries that have high per unit product merely because they happen to possess quantities of oil or gold, and whose growth potential as measured is far too high, compared with other countries, and we therefore exclude these units, in which conditions unrelated to *social* capacity lift the growth potentials and attainment. By the same logic, we include countries in which per capita or per worker product is below the minimum because of conditions beyond the control of society—so that despite a *percentage* utilization of their growth potentials greater than in other countries, their per capita products are much lower; Japan is perhaps in this category. But while we include Japan, we would hesitate to include an Eskimo nation (assuming there is one) whose growth potential in the Arctic ice wastes is, under present and past conditions, exceedingly low, but whose per unit product may be quite high as a percentage of the potential.

For obvious reasons, we wish to limit diversity in growth potentials that reflect diverse natural conditions and concentrate on the differences in economic growth among countries in which natural conditions *beyond the control of man and society* are not too extreme. In classifying societies as developed or underdeveloped and in interpreting these terms as differences in attainment *possible* with varying degrees of individual and social ingenuity, we are implicitly assuming that the latter rather than conditions beyond the control of man are crucial. For our interest in the economic growth process is in the capacities of man and society, not in differential conditions beyond human control. And by using the term "underdeveloped" we imply that these countries are less developed than they could be, that they have a much greater potential than they utilize.

This is probably an acceptable working assumption for the broad review of a wide field in which we have been engaged and particularly for drawing some rough minimum line between $500 and $600 (in 1958 prices) per capita. For we are saying that the diversity in natural, uncontrollable conditions (including genetic capacities of people) is no wider than the one reflected in the range between the highest and lowest per capita or per worker product within the group of developed countries themselves; and that none or very few of the countries below the lower limit, including those at the bottom of the array, are incapable, because of socially uncontrollable natural conditions, of reaching this level of per unit product.

But for a more detailed analysis, particularly of international differences in per capita or per worker income throughout the array, the assumption would have to be carefully scrutinized and the relation between the growth potential and natural endowments of individual countries specified. For example, in an attempt to explain the extremely high per worker income of the United States, one would have to weigh the contribution of successful adjustment of social institutions to requirements of modern economic growth against that of an unusually rich natural endowment which cannot be duplicated in most other countries. And one would have to follow a similar approach in exploring the growth potentials of countries in the tropical zones in terms of their resource endowment and the current and immediately foreseeable stock of technology and other relevant knowledge. The broad assumption concerning limits in the differences in growth potentials imposed by diverse natural conditions and in their effect on growth differentials over a long period has permitted us to ignore such problems. But they would have to be faced in a closer analysis of differential conditions for economic growth in diverse individual countries.

The assumption of limited diversity of conditions un-

479

controllable by man in the course of modern economic growth bears upon our measure of the spread of modern economic growth. Two questions are immediately suggested: Has the minimum level of the per unit product of a developed country risen over the period simultaneously with the growth potential provided by modern technology? If so, how much has this rise exceeded the rise in per capita or per worker product of the underdeveloped countries and thus widened the gap between this product and the "minimum" line of development?

The first question can be answered affirmatively: the vast expansion of the worldwide stock of material and social technology has raised the absolute per worker product that could be expected in a developed country, even one with a relatively poor natural resource endowment and in the initial phase of modern economic growth (this is in essence the definition of a "minimum" line of development). But the second question causes difficulties, for modern economic growth has spread and its geographical scope and variance have widened, but we have not yet specified the criteria by which we set the minimum per capita or, for the present purposes more relevant, per worker line.

The difficulties can be pointed up by means of a statistical illustration. In 1840, Great Britain—the leading country and the only one that reflected modern economic growth—probably had a per capita product of between $400 and $500 (GDP at factor cost, 1958 prices)—a rough figure based on available current estimates and long-term series. If we set the value at $450 per capita, use $575 as the dividing line today (as we did in Table 7.2), and translate these two per capitas into about $1,100 and $1,400 per worker, it does not mean that the rise in the minimum line was only from $1,100 in 1840 to $1,400 in the late 1950s. While $575 per capita and $1,400 per worker are *minimum* levels in 1958, with a fairly wide range above them (the top per capita in 1958, for the United States, was $2,324, or well over four times the minimum), $1,100 per worker in 1840 in Great Britain must have been far above the minimum. But what was the "minimum" per worker development line in 1840? We have no answer; and we certainly cannot apply the range indicated in 1958, when the minimum was less than a fourth of the top value, to the 1840 level for Great Britain. The result, a per worker minimum product of less than $300, would clearly be too low since, with the growth capacity of the time, most countries could exceed this level after a limited initial period of modern economic growth.

The upshot of this discussion is that the rise in per worker product that would indicate a minimum degree of successful exploitation of the potential of modern economic growth cannot be assumed to be as great as the rise in the per worker product of the developed country at the *top* of the array—which, as the statistical illustration suggests, would be between five and sixfold between 1840 and the late 1950s. But the rise did occur; and whether it was appreciably greater than that in per worker product of the less developed countries, is a matter of judgment. A plausible judgment is, however, possible if we deal with underdeveloped countries at the bottom of the array at the present time, say those with per capita product below $100 (in 1958 prices)—a group that still accounts for well over a half of world population (see Table 7.2, line 2). If for this group, with an average per capita product of about $75 and a per worker product of about $185 (i.e. per capita divided by 0.4), we assume a growth since 1840 of 50 per cent, its per worker product in 1840 would be $120 at the lowest. If then we assume that the minimum per worker product in developed countries has at least doubled since 1840, for 1840 it would be about $700 (i.e. $1,400, the minimum per worker product in 1958, divided by 2).[7] The range in 1840 between per worker product of the underdeveloped countries and the "minimum

7. This minimum is over 60 per cent of the per worker product shown for Great Britain in 1840 and may well be too high. To be sure it was exceeded at the time by the per worker product in the United States, which had not yet entered its industrialization process; but since the United States was exceptionally endowed with natural resources, this showing may not be significant.

line" of development is then from $120 to $700, or about 1 to 5.8; in 1958, it is from $185 to $1,400, or 1 to 7.6. The gap between the per worker performance of the large group of underdeveloped countries at the bottom of the array and the "minimum level" at which a country can be characterized as developed has thus widened appreciably, despite assumptions that tend to underestimate this aspect. This means that, other conditions remaining equal, it has become increasingly difficult for the less developed countries to reach the "minimum line," to participate in the spread of modern economic growth. But conditions have not remained equal: a great many changes in political organization and international relations have operated to make it easier for less developed countries to reach the "minimum level."

Our discussion so far has stressed modern economic growth as some minimum exploitation of the growth potential provided by modern technology, but it has disregarded the questions of exploitation "for what" and "how." These interrelated questions shift our attention from supply to demand; and serve to remind us that the primary purpose of economic performance and economic growth is to satisfy some positive end-goals of society, not to utilize production potentials merely because they are at hand. We should therefore ask whether the spread of modern economic growth, as measured by the attainment of some minimum per capita product, reflects the spread of some minimum realized capacity to satisfy the wants and needs consonant with the increased productive power of man.

The answer would involve an examination of the uses of national product and of the conditions under which members of society produce it and receive claims to it, and an attempt to relate these uses and claims to some accepted end-goals. The substitution of household consumption for national product would not be proper since some government consumption satisfies obvious communal needs, and some capital formation is indispensable for future ultimate wants. All the specific categories of use, as well as the con-

482

ditions imposed upon members of society in the production and distribution processes, must be examined. Such examination, some lines of which were suggested in our discussion of the national product definitions in Chapter 1 and of the factors affecting the level and structure of consumption in Chapter 5, is beyond our capacity and scope here.

Per capita product thus is only a crude measure of the realized capacity to satisfy an accepted set of end-goals of economic activity, but it is at present one of the few measures available and, in fact, is the only comprehensive one. The measure is therefore generally taken to indicate the extent to which the growing potential of modern technology has been exploited for useful ends, without hopelessly compromising these ends. And if we were to draw some minimum levels of realized capacity to satisfy these end-goals—which could conceivably be lower than the minimum per capita product (since the latter contains sizable components that do not contribute directly to such end-goals)—we might find that the spread of modern economic growth, in terms of the satisfaction of demand, was different from the spread in terms of utilization of the growing production potential.

If we use a modified minimum per capita product to reflect realized capacity to satisfy some accepted goals for all countries, we are again assuming limited diversity—in this case, in the end-goals and in the methods of attaining them that are accepted in the various countries—just as in our earlier discussion we assumed implicitly a limited diversity in conditions of growth uncontrollable by man and society. Thus, it would make little sense to use per capita product, household consumption, or any other aggregate as a common minimum of realized capacity to satisfy accepted end-goals for a group of countries comprising some with a large proportion of slaves and others with free populations; or some that impose rigid controls on the freedom of individuals to choose their jobs or the goods that they consume, and others that do not. And since economic activity is part of life in general, there is always the possibility that the diverse methods by which economic output is produced and distributed may cause different impacts on the rest of life and its costs and satisfactions that are not reflected in economic aggregates or its components. Thus in using the per capita product as a common yardstick for all countries in measuring their realized capacity to satisfy some end-goals of economic activity we are implicitly assuming that the diversity of the uses of product and the ways by which it is turned out are limited, and that the noneconomic costs and returns do not outweigh the measured economic results. Needless to say, this is a broad assumption even if applied to non-Communist countries only; a more penetrating analysis of uses of product and conditions of production might mean a change in the composition of the group of developed countries; and a change in the accepted end-goals might yield not only different groupings, but also different trends in the spread of modern economic growth.

This leads to one final observation in the consideration of the demand side of economic growth. The way in which we measure the spread of economic growth viewed as the *realized* capacity to satisfy some minimum wants and needs depends upon our definitions of the end-goals of economic activity. Yet, however defined, there is little question that it has spread significantly, since many countries with prevailing institutions that permit a variety of choices and a relatively free selection among ends and means evince such growth. In discussing the spread of modern economic growth as the capacity to satisfy some end-goals that can be attained by successful exploitation of the potential provided by modern technology, we must distinguish between aspiration and realization. The former has spread much more rapidly than the latter, if only because of the tremendous advance in transportation and communication and the influence of demonstration effects. Of course, aspiration may have always outpaced realization in all countries, developed and underdeveloped. But the recent increased exposure of the underdeveloped countries to the more ad-

vanced countries and their closer contact have probably produced a wider gap between aspiration and realization than
existed in the presently developed countries in earlier times.
We have no evidence to support this conjecture, but it is
plausible, and it warrants examination as a possible factor
in the currently strained relations between underdeveloped
and developed countries and in the attempts of the underdeveloped to force the pace of their growth.

The brief comments in this subsection merely illustrate
the obvious proposition that the measure of the spread of
modern economic growth depends upon the definition of
growth and upon the minimal levels at which we would
say that such growth has been attained. What is perhaps
less apparent at first glance is that if we define modern economic growth as the utilization of a potential provided by
modern technology—the epochal innovation of the modern
economic epoch—we must be able not only to distinguish
that potential for individual countries, despite a variety of
conditions within them that are not controllable by modern
material or social technology, but also to recognize its exploitation for some positive end-goals. That recognition
depends upon our ability to analyze the uses of economic
output and the conditions under which it is produced—and
thus evaluate them in reference to the accepted range of
end-goals. Such analysis of differentials in growth potentials
and in the acceptable end-goals and institutions that serve
them is prohibitively difficult and, in any case, not feasible
here. We have therefore adopted the simple procedure of
using quantitative criteria (such as per worker or per capita
product) as common to all countries—thus assuming a
limited diversity of underlying conditions with respect to
both the growth potentials and the relations between aggregate product and end-goals, and excluding the more obvious
exceptions to that assumption from the universe of our
comparisons. Although it is important to recognize the assumption of this procedure, we need not be so overwhelmed
by its limitations as to discard an admittedly crude, yet

most valuable, set of comparisons. These comparisons at
least limit and check what might otherwise be an uncontrollable propensity to take extreme positions based on
partial impressions.

# 10 A POSTSCRIPT

## DESIGN OF THE STUDY

The study summarized in the preceding chapters was designed on one guiding assumption: modern economic growth, once identified, would prove to be a significant, orderly, and distinctive body of long-term economic experience. It would be significant in having dominated long-term economic change in a number of societies and in having affected most of mankind. It would be orderly in that several of its observable and revealing characteristics would be common to the nation-states identified as developed; in that these common characteristics would be interrelated, in terms of analytically plausible associations among various aspects of economic and social behavior; and in that its spread internationally would display some reasonable sequence. It would be distinctive in that the combination of common characteristics, and perhaps the sequence of spread would differ significantly from previous experience—so that modern economic growth could be studied as distinct and separate from that in premodern times. The implication that a common source of growth, a common group of typical factors, determined such significantly widespread, systematically related, and distinctive growth trends, led to the concepts of the economic epoch and the epochal innovation, and to the use of the term "modern economic growth" to describe the current epoch of spreading application of science to processes of production and social organization

487

—the topics with which we began the discussion in Chapter 1.

In order to specify the scope of our empirical observations, we identified as modern economic growth the secular trends in "developed" countries over a sufficiently long period (say five decades) and as far back as possible to the date at which the shift from premodern trends began (the earliest, in England, in the late eighteenth century). Furthermore, "developed" countries, with some exceptions, were identified as politically independent nations having the highest per capita products and, in fact, accounting for between a seventh and a quarter of world population. The underlying rationale is that such levels of per capita product could have been attained only through decades of the high growth rates that typify modern economic growth, and that, consequently, the high per capita product countries must have managed to engage in that growth process. By identifying modern economic growth with sustained high rates of increase in per capita product we have implicitly stated that such high rates are a common characteristic of modern economic growth. The circularity of this sequence—evident in the definitional steps of any inquiry—would be empty only if we had found that the high rate of growth of per capita product was the *single* common characteristic—for then we would find only what we put in. In fact, and this is the substance of much of the discussion in the preceding chapters, we find a variety of associated characteristics which suggest not only the important consequences of the high rate of growth of per capita product but also the mechanism by which this rate was realized, sustained, or impeded.

But before turning to these associated characteristics, we should note the three kinds of countries—with high per capita product—that were excluded from the group of "developed" countries as defined above; exceptions that limit the scope of the empirical observations. The first was any nation below a minimum size (usually less than a million population). Such nations were excluded on the ground that although they are politically sovereign, they may be too much within the orbit of larger countries to manifest independent economic growth. The second was any nation, usually small, whose high per capita product was due to some exceptional natural resource endowment, such as oil. Such nations were excluded on the ground that the high per capita product had little to do with antecedent growth rates that transform an economy and society over a long period. Finally, we excluded, except for casual references, the Communist countries, on the ground that the whole cast of their economic and social institutions has been too different and their beginnings too recent to warrant inclusion for the purpose of testing for common and associated characteristics of modern economic growth.

Each of these exclusions reflects problems in generalization and analysis that go beyond the specific criteria employed: the economic growth of a politically independent nation with a much larger population than a million, and indeed of any size, may not be independent; natural resource endowments may substantially affect modern economic growth anywhere, favorably by raising per capita product or adversely by keeping it low (as may have been the case in Japan); and we can point to several non-Communist developed countries whose social and political institutions were rather distinctive and different in the past. But if we were to limit the universe of developed countries to those most similar in size, natural resource endowment, and social institutions, we might be reduced to studying one country; and even if there were several units from which to derive general characteristics, the generalizations might be of little value precisely because the diversity in significant conditions had been reduced too much.

For the resulting group of developed countries—mostly in western, northern, and central Europe; the European offshoots overseas such as the United States, Canada, and Australia; and Japan—we emphasized quantitative characteristics of economic growth. This emphasis has limited our analysis for two reasons. First, for some of these countries (e.g. the Netherlands, Switzerland, Belgium, and even France) long-term economic records are relatively poor; and second, some important aspects of modern growth, e.g. the accumulation of useful knowledge and the rate of technological change, do not lend themselves to quantitative measurement—at least at present. Nevertheless, it seemed important to stress testable, quantitative data on major aspects of what is essentially a process of quantitative change—even though the quantities are, as always, attached to qualitatively different, and significantly distinct, aspects of economic activity and categories of its results.

In listing the common characteristics of modern economic growth revealed by the long-term records for the developed countries, we shall be selective rather than complete. Rather than present a complete summary of what is already a summary discussion, in the preceding chapters, of more detailed evidence presented elsewhere, we felt that it would be more useful to select a few major characteristics, particularly those that seem to have widest general implications. They are listed below in the general order followed in Chapters 2–9, from the aggregative aspects of modern economic growth, to the structural, and then the international.

### CHARACTERISTICS OF MODERN ECONOMIC GROWTH

1. The high rates of increase in per capita product (ranging from less than 15 to about 30 per cent per decade) characteristic of modern economic growth have been accompanied, in most developed countries, by substantial rates of population growth—ranging about 10 per cent per decade and much higher than in the premodern centuries. This has meant rates of increase in aggregate product ranging from over 20 to close to 50 per cent per decade, an enormous rise in total output within the developed countries, and a multiplicity of consequences of substantial population growth, ranging from pressures on natural resources to relative size of successive generations, and to wide differentials in rates of natural increase among various economic and

490

social groups. The findings on the rate, structure, and mechanism of modern economic growth, derived from past records, are primarily for countries with a substantial rate of increase in population; and the relation of the latter to these findings must be recognized and hopefully distinguished—if the conclusions are to be applied to other countries where the pattern of population growth may be quite different.

2. A rate of 15 per cent per decade (which means quadrupling in a century) produced a rise in per capita product that was too high to be explained, except in small part, by rises in inputs per head. Input of man-hours per head could have increased only slightly, if at all, since the working day and week typical of the presently developed countries before their modernization were long, and the proportion of total labor force to total population was subject to age–sex limitations. Input of capital per head of total population could and did rise much more than man-hours per head, but its contribution to the rise of output was limited by the moderate weight of incomes from capital in total income. The scanty available data suggest that increase in inputs per head of man-hours and material capital combined accounted for less than a fifth of the secular rise in production per capita, and for a decreasing fraction in recent decades. Modern economic growth is distinguished by the fact that the rate of rise in per capita product was due primarily to improvements in *quality,* not quantity of inputs—essentially to greater efficiency or output per simple unit of input, traceable to increases in useful knowledge and better institutional arrangements for its utilization.

3. The high rate of growth of efficiency, referred to under point 2, has been pervasive, characterizing all major production sectors of the developed economies. If the rise in output per unit of input in agriculture was lower than that in industry, it was still so large compared with premodern levels that one can speak of an agricultural as well as of an industrial revolution. The rise in the capacity and efficiency of transportation and communication has been even more

striking. And if our measures suggest that product per unit in the services proper (trade, personal, government) have risen less than that in commodity production and transportation, this may be a reflection in part of the difficulty of measuring output in such services and the possible understatement in these measures. The pervasive effect of technological and organizational changes on efficiency in all sectors is significant because it implies that all components of the economy and society were affected and under pressure to alter their institutional arrangements, and because, in combination with other factors to be noted below, these trends in efficiency serve to explain the rapid shift in the structure not only of product but also of productive factors, particularly labor.

4. Trends in the sectoral origin of aggregate output, which generally accompanied modern economic growth, include the following: a decline in the share of agriculture and related industries; rises in the shares of manufacturing and public utilities; shifts within manufacturing from less to more durable products, and to a limited extent from consumer to producer goods; increases in the shares of some service groups (personal, professional, government) and declines in the shares of others (domestic service). These are all well known, and their main feature is recognized in the term "industrialization," often used as a synonym for modern economic growth; but it is the effect of the combination of these shifts in industrial origin of aggregate output with the trends in efficiency within the various sectors, noted under point 3, that must be stressed here. This combination produced marked shifts in the sectoral allocation of the labor force: a somewhat greater decline in the share of agriculture and related industries, a somewhat lesser rise in the share of industry, and a distinct rise in the share of services (whose share in output showed rather mixed trends). These shifts in the industrial attachment of labor (there were also shifts in the allocation of capital among industries, but we know less about them) are important for they mean changes in conditions of life and work of the population, affecting

the use of income and other links in the mechanism of economic growth.

5. The trends in the industrial distribution of aggregate output, noted above, reflect changes in the structure of final demand, which in turn may be due either to the rise in per capita product (with different income elasticities of demand) or to technological changes which do not affect all categories of final goods at the same rate. Furthermore, the trends for individual countries also reflect changes in export and import opportunities, in turn due to shifts in transportation costs, inclusion of new countries in the network of world trade, differential impacts of technological change on comparative advantages, and so on. The important point to be noted here is that a high rate of growth in per capita product implies a rapid shift in the structure of final demand—whether due to persistent income elasticities or to technological changes; and that the factors that induce a high rate of growth of per capita product usually make for a greater rate of expansion of foreign trade and of changes in the international division of labor (except, of course, under Communist autarky). Thus modern economic growth is characterized by rapid shifts in the industrial structure of product, and consequently by rapid shifts in shares of labor attached to various sectors in the country—much more rapid shifts than appear to be true of the premodern centuries.

6. A similarly rapid shift occurred in the distribution of aggregate product and allocation of the labor force (and probably capital) among economic units classified by size and type—ranging from the small own-account individual firms to the large impersonal corporations and government. The movement away from agriculture—the sector that dominated premodern economies—meant a marked reduction in the share of small own-account enterprises in aggregate output and of individual entrepreneurs and own-account workers in the labor force. And these intersectoral shifts were accompanied by growth in the scale of firms and changes in the type of organization within sectors such as

manufacturing or trade—from the small unincorporated firm to the large corporate unit. With the rapid shifts in industrial structure and rapid change in technology there were also rapid shifts in allocation of product among types and sizes of producing firms, and consequently in the allocation of the labor force—by the size of the enterprises to which it was attached, by status as between entrepreneur-own-account and employee—with a marked rise in the share attached to larger enterprises and in the share of employees in the labor force. In general, such rapid shifts occurred in most allocations directly related to and connected with industrial structure—e.g. among employees, from blue- to white-collar jobs, or from less to more skilled occupations. Obviously high interindustry, interstatus, and interoccupational mobility of the labor force is a characteristic of modern economic growth.

7. The marked and rapid changes in the structure of product and particularly in the industry, status, and occupation structures of the labor force are important aspects of modern economic growth because they call for and imply a capacity for rapid institutional adjustments and for inter- and intragenerational mobility of the population (and of capital). The differential impacts of technological changes and higher per capita product on structure of final demand and on the international division of labor set up a chain reaction in which the responses of the population as members of the labor force became important links in the changes of institutional patterns of life that in turn affected economic growth. The rates of structural shift involved were too high to be accommodated by differences in rates of natural increase among various groups in the population and labor force—just as the rate of growth of per capita product was too high to be accounted for by increases in inputs per capita.

Furthermore, the demographic growth differentials were not necessarily associated positively with differentials in economic growth opportunities revealed by the shifts referred to above. Nonagricultural population did not have a

494

higher rate of natural increase than agricultural; nor did employees compared with own-account workers, or white-collar workers compared with blue-collar; the association was, if anything, inverse. Consequently considerable migration in space and occupational shift within or between generations were required to adjust the labor supply to the changing demands of shifting industrial and type of firm structure; and this extensive mobility, of which urbanization was one important facet, affected conditions of life and consumption, the mechanism of fitting people into their roles in the economy, and the institutions of transmission of skill from one generation to the next, and even influenced the views that people were likely to have of their roles and obligations in the economy and society. To the extent that rapid shifts in the economic position of various population and labor force groups may have been productive of friction, government played a greater role, and a national consensus that would limit such friction and preserve political unity assumed increasing importance.

8. While a rapid shift characterized the industrial and type of firm structure of national product and the closely related allocations of labor force and population, in some aspects of economic structure the trends associated with modern economic growth were far less pronounced. This seems particularly true of what might be called the distributional aspects. If we could establish an unequivocal distribution of income by factor shares between capital and labor (which calls for allocation of such a "mixed" category as entrepreneurial income) it would probably indicate trends that were fairly limited—which, given the higher rate of growth of material capital than of labor, would mean a marked decline in the rate of return on capital compared with the return on labor (without allowance for greater investment in the latter). The trends in the size distribution of income were not marked either, at least relative to the order of change observed in industrial distributions of product and inputs. To be sure, in the more recent decades, the size distributions of income in the developed

countries have tended toward a narrowing of inequality—toward smaller shares of upper income groups and larger shares of the lower groups. But these shifts have been relatively moderate; and it is rather significant that despite the impressive and sustained increase in per capita product that has characterized modern economic growth, the "poor" are still with us—although the standard by which this category is measured has also been rising in absolute terms.

Yet in one respect this impression of limited long-term changes in the size distribution of income may be misleading—at least in comparing modern economic growth with premodern times. The rate of intergroup mobility, of shifts in identity of the population units in the upper and lower groups of the size distribution of income, may have been far higher in the modern economic growth epoch than in the earlier centuries. With the rapid interindustry and interoccupational shifts, and with the new industries and occupations representing the major sources of higher incomes, the entrepreneurial innovators connected with these industries and occupations were not likely to be those attached to the older established ones.

9. Another aspect of economic structure in which the trend has been moderate is the allocation of product by use, particularly between capital formation and consumption. To be sure, the gross capital formation proportions (to national domestic product) rose from about 10 to about 20 per cent and the net probably from 5 per cent or less to between 10 and 15 per cent. But despite the enormous rise in reproducible capital stock per capita or per worker, consumption still accounted for the overwhelming proportion of gross and net national product. And while there were marked trends within capital formation (from inventories and construction to producers' equipment) and within consumption (with an increase in the share of government consumption and shifts within household consumption from foods and clothing to consumers' durables and personal, recreation, health, and education services), the needs of modern economic growth for material capital were mod-

erate, accounting for a relatively modest fraction of total output, which rose only a few percentage points over the long period. This slight change is consistent and connected with other trends characterizing modern economic growth, specifically the high rate of growth in efficiency and the rapid shifts in industrial and occupational structure. Because of these shifts in structure, the proportion of consumption to total output remained high—an effect partly of urbanization, partly of technological changes creating demand for new consumer goods, and partly of greater need for quasi-capital types of consumer expenditures (education, health, etc.). And because of the modest capital formation proportions, combined with a high rate of technological change, the proportion of growth in capital input per capita to growth in product per capita remained low.

10. The international aspects of economic growth are characterized by three prominent trends. First, the technological revolution in transportation and communication facilitated contact among various parts of the world, particularly between the developed countries and others—in terms of effective ease, for the first time in the history of human societies; beginning in the late nineteenth century conditions were thus radically different from those in the premodern centuries. Second, modern economic growth spread sequentially from its pioneer beginnings in eighteenth-century England to various follower countries, with the timing of entry continuing into the recent decades of the twentieth century and presumably into the future. Third, until the entry of Japan in the late nineteenth century, followed by the U.S.S.R. in the 1930s, modern economic growth was concentrated in European countries and their offshoots overseas, whose per capita incomes were well above average, even before industrialization, and certainly much higher than the incomes of the countries in Asia and Africa. These three features of economic modernization, added to the high rates of aggregate growth and the shifts in the internal economic structure already referred to above, led to a variety of associated trends in the international aspects of

the modern growth process observed among the developed countries and in their relation to the underdeveloped parts of the world.

11. The international flows of men, goods, and capital were at high rates from the second quarter of the nineteenth century to World War I. The migration streams were particularly important for the overseas offshoots of Europe—in North America, Oceania, and several Latin American countries (such as Argentina and Uruguay)—however useful they may have been to the countries of origin as a safety valve in the periods of population pressure on land and early transition to industrialization. These differences between countries of origin and destination of international migration—in relatively free response to economic push and pull—resulted in much higher rates of aggregate growth in the young and "empty" countries overseas as well as other differences in characteristics of economic growth between the old and young countries.

12. Because of the rapid growth of the volume of goods in foreign trade between the 1820s and World War I, the proportions of foreign trade to aggregate product rose significantly during this scant century—both in the older developed countries and in the steadily increasing number of underdeveloped countries drawn into the network of world trade. The only group that did not show marked rises in foreign trade proportions was the young countries overseas—Canada, Australia, the United States (and possibly others)—although even in these the declines date from the time when they were probably small trading outposts of their European mother country, with relatively high proportions. Thus, up to 1913 a law of an "increasing" rather than a "declining" share of foreign trade in aggregate product seemed to operate.

13. Paralleling the expansion of foreign trade and reflecting the spreading ties of the older developed countries with their offshoots and colonial areas overseas and the use of capital loans for political purposes, foreign capital investment flows also grew rapidly from the second quarter of the

nineteenth century to World War I. Quantitatively the volumes were limited, and as proportions of total domestic capital formation they were substantial only in the smaller developed countries that were closely related to some one major developed world creditor country (e.g. Canada and Argentina in relation to Great Britain). But granted the limited volumes and the political element in their channeling, the international flows of capital funds grew proportionately and were at their peak on the eve of World War I.

14. With World War I came a radical change in international flows of men, goods, and capital—an effect not evident in aggregate rates of growth or in trends in internal structure of developed economies. The two world wars, the major worldwide depression of the 1930s (which reflected the failure to adjust to the aftermath of World War I), and the emergence of Communist regimes hostile to the economically developed countries could not but cause this adverse change in the international flows. The effect on international migration was particularly marked, and it has never recovered to levels at all approaching the pre-World War I proportions. Almost as striking was the effect on economically oriented international flows of capital funds, excluding politically motivated grants and donations. And, despite continued major improvements in transportation and communication, even proportions of foreign trade to aggregate output are barely back to the levels attained on the eve of World War I; and they certainly do not show rises similar to the upward trend in the nineteenth and early twentieth centuries.

15. The expansion in the volumes and proportions of international flows of men, goods, and capital before World War I was presumably due to the same factors and forces that were responsible for the high rates of aggregate growth and the rapid shifts in internal structure characteristic of modern economic growth; and in that sense all these aspects of economic growth are interconnected. But it is a moot, if highly intriguing, question whether the world wars of the twentieth century and the deep world fissure resulting

from the emergence of Communist states are also consequences of the same forces and are thus highly likely, if not inevitable, consequences of modern economic growth. However the question is answered, the relevant trends in modern economic growth are clearly the results of its sequential spread, the high level of aggregate growth, and the rapid shifts in internal structure. The sequential spread, rather than simultaneous emergence, meant inequalities in the rate of aggregate growth even among the countries that eventually became developed, let alone between all of these and the underdeveloped areas of the world. The high rates of aggregate growth meant that the absolute differences in growth rates even among developed countries were wide, and therefore cumulated rapidly into marked shifts in relative economic and political power among nations—a situation usually provocative of international strain and conflict. The rapid shift within developed countries among population groups in their roles and shares in the economy may have been productive of internal strains; and in combination with the weakening of family, religious, and local ties, may have led to increasingly vigorous nationalism as the basis for the necessary consensus, and may thus have produced a climate favorable to international conflict. In all these respects, the spread of modern economic growth to a number of large developed countries constituted a necessary, if not sufficient, condition for world wars and for the increasing strain of backwardness which forced the powerful central governments to take a more active part in the initiation of economic modernization.

The summary statements above stress the characteristics of modern economic growth that were common to the developed countries as defined here for purposes of measurement and analysis; the relations, largely among these countries but also between them and others, in the spread of modern economic growth; and the connections among the common characteristics and between them and the international aspects of spread.

500

# A Postscript

That we found several common characteristics is not surprising, since the permissive source of modern economic growth was the major additions to the world stock of useful knowledge—a source potentially available to all countries —and its usefulness is with reference to material means to satisfy human wants that are common to much of mankind. The material achievements of modern technology underlying economic growth in the current epoch are, after all, relevant to human wants that, broadly conceived, date back for centuries. The dreams of our forebears, whether of the effortless abundance in a long-lost Eden or of greater power suggested by the Icarus legend, are akin to ours; and the specific ways of realizing such dreams are revealed to us by modern technology, whose products—whether an abundance of food, motor cars, or television sets—appeal to most people who come into contact with them.

Nor are the associations among these common characteristics of modern economic growth unexpected. For if some of them relate to production and others to consumption, it is man who is both the producer and the consumer; and the conditions under which he functions in one capacity will determine in large part his function in the other. Furthermore, greater basic knowledge and technological capacity will not only produce more goods at lower cost but also reduce mortality—so that until the birth rates decline, a rise in product per capita and a higher rate of population growth will go hand in hand. And there may be an obvious connection between increased productive power and greater diversification of demand. Thus, the common characteristics are interrelated because they stem from a common cause, because they reflect different aspects of activity and response of the same group of people, or because, given some persistent structure of human wants, aggregate levels and structures of components are causally connected.

The association between the aggregative and internal structure characteristics of modern economic growth, on the one hand, and the character of its spread and the effects on international relations on the other, again stems from a common source. The increased power of technology applies to international transport and communication; it carries across national boundaries the consequences of the rapid shifts in internal structure of developed nations; it contributes to the sequential spread because the institutional changes required to provide the proper auspices for economic modernization are so radical that simultaneous emergence in many countries is difficult. Even if one rejects the validity of a fixed set of economic development prerequisites, one may still argue that conditions for the shift from preindustrial to modern economic growth were not so minor as to be common to many nations at any given time —especially if one considers the historical distance of most of the world from the small European subcontinent in which economic modernization emerged and from its overseas offshoots to which this process spread first.

One can thus find a good deal of "order," of community and association among the aggregative, structural, and international characteristics of modern economic growth. However, since the statements above may seem to claim too much, it is only appropriate, in concluding this summary postscript, to discuss the qualifications and the questions that they raise.

### QUALIFICATIONS AND QUESTIONS

We may grant the possibly wide errors in many of the long-term estimates used in this survey and the absence of even approximate estimates for some of the developed countries in our group, but it would serve no useful purpose to discuss the related qualifications. They do not lend themselves to general treatment and require detailed examination of the estimates and careful scrutiny of the associations used in explanations. All one can say is that an effort has been made to present the findings in a form that seems justified by the underlying data, given the rough magnitudes of possible error.

It is of greater interest to deal briefly with three broad

qualifications of the findings. The first stems from the dependence of our measures and of the very meaning of economic growth on a system of values operative in a vaguely defined and yet distinctive framework of social institutions. The second is suggested by the variability and diversity in the parameters of economic growth, even for the limited sample on which most of the discussion has been based. The third is indicated by a recognition that we are attempting to gauge the major trends of the modern epoch of economic growth before the epoch is ended—with the attendant difficulties in understanding some of the more recent manifestations and in evaluating the significance of past trends for current prospects and policies.

1. The dependence of the basic definitions of economic activity, aggregative and structural, and of the measures of performance, on a broad scheme of views reflecting the operating social institutions, has already been indicated and illustrated in Chapter 1. Clearly, our very finding of high rates of growth of per capita product is contingent upon a scheme of values that recognizes economic products over and above some bare minimum needed to hold body and soul together as something positive—a view not fully acceptable to religious ascetics, however commonly it is held today or has been held in many societies. More important, our definitions and measures imply some major assumptions concerning *acceptable* institutional methods for securing economic goods—barring slavery and concentration camps, for example, as acceptable ways of increasing supplies of economic goods.

We mention these rather obvious aspects of our measures of economic activity and growth not to deny or minimize their validity: they do reflect, if only broadly, the value system of the current economic epoch and contain a number of elements that are common to this and other epochs in human history. The point is rather to emphasize the *quality* aspects of economic growth, in terms of costs and returns based on broader criteria of human welfare than are reflected in the market place, even if modified by government intervention or other noneconomic influences. Our broad assumption, which limits the group of developed countries to those with an institutional framework having a modicum of consumer sovereignty and political freedom, formulates the criterion of quality in only a minimal and vague fashion. Hence, the same rates and structure of economic growth as measured in our substantive chapters may conceal considerable differences in human costs and gains not reflected in our measures of output and input. Such quality differences, either among countries or within one country over time, can be easily envisaged; but it would be difficult to translate them into quantitative equivalents that could somehow be combined with the commonly used grosser measures of output and input, income and costs.

2. The variability over time and diversity in space in the empirical coefficients of modern economic growth have been demonstrated in Chapters 2–6 and need no further elaboration. It will have been noted that while in the preceding section we referred to growth rates in aggregate or per capita product as high, i.e. above a substantial minimum, reference was not to single values but to fairly wide ranges. And, indeed, average rates of growth in per capita product, even over long periods approaching a century, were as low as 15 and as high as 30 per cent per decade; and the relative spread in long-term rates of growth of population and of aggregate product was even wider. Likewise, while all countries showed fairly similar trends in the share of agriculture versus that of the industry sectors, the trends were not of the same magnitude; and even currently there are fairly notable diversities among the developed countries in the sectoral structure of output, not closely related to the level of economic development, at least as measured by per capita income. And if the differences and changes in long-term incremental capital–output ratios, revealed in Chapter 5, can be attributed to the neglect of other productive factors, the more intensive production–function studies for one or two countries also reveal significant changes in the coefficients from one long period to the next.

Of course, such variability and diversity in the growth parameters, which introduce an element of disorder into the "order" summarized in the preceding section, may be explained; and in many cases the explanation, i.e. the establishment of association with other factors not considered in the previous discussion, contributes to the understanding of the process. But in the nature of the case the explanation must be ad hoc and incomplete, not so much because of insufficient data, but essentially because we are dealing with experimentally uncontrolled situations in which the variety of possible causative factors cannot be exhaustively tested. Thus, having found some significant differences, we usually try to find relevant factors to account for them. But given the limitations of our data and established knowledge, it is often too easy to suggest some explanatory factors without considering others whose effects would run in the opposite direction and whose failure to have a visible effect is still to be explained.

The necessarily tentative character of the explanations by which we reduce variability and diversity to some order, as a possible base for more specific application of past trends, must be particularly emphasized because of two presently inescapable limitations on our data. The first is the fact that modern economic growth can be observed for only a few countries over a period long enough to reduce confusion between underlying trends, long swings, and more transient changes—if we exclude, as we should, countries smaller than a low minimum, natural resource pools, and, for the time being at least, the Communist countries. We are left with ten countries in Europe (if we include Italy in addition to the United Kingdom, France, Germany, the Netherlands, Belgium, Switzerland, and the three Scandinavian countries), four or five overseas offshoots of Europe (the United States, Canada, Australia, New Zealand, and possibly the Union of South Africa), and Japan—a grand total of fifteen or sixteen countries. We could add one or two Latin American countries, but the point is clear without piling up detail: there are far too few units for which, even with complete coverage of data, modern economic growth can be observed, given the variety of factors affecting growth parameters (size, natural resources, changes in technology, location with respect to centers of international trade, historical and cultural heritage, political structure, etc.). To use statistical terminology: the sample is small and the number of relevant variables fairly large—which leads to a few degrees of freedom with which to test any hypothesis in which the parameters are calculated from the empirical observations (rather than derived from purely imaginative constructs, *independent* of the observations). And this means that only the grossest differentials and similarities can be given any weight.

This limited number of countries that can yield a long-term record of modern economic growth remains a serious constraint because of the second limitation: the danger of drawing inferences from cross-section comparisons to apply to long-term growth processes. In the substantive chapters a number of disagreements were found between the expectations based on cross-section analysis and the actual growth trends revealed by the time series, sometimes only of direction and sometimes also of magnitude; and the major reasons for such disagreements were suggested in Chapter 8. Obviously, the many units that could be used for cross-section analysis cannot be substituted for the few units with long-term time series directly reflecting modern economic growth, because many of the inferences might yield coefficients quite different in sign or size from the true growth parameters. The relevance of this observation to the current wide use of cross-section studies to derive parameters for projections over time needs no elaboration.

3. While the limited sample of developed countries available for study is partly the result of the limited spread of modern economic growth, and the limited spread in turn suggests that the modern economic epoch has still not run its course, it would be presumptuous to claim that we know where we stand today within the full span of the modern epoch. Yet, if we disregard the possibility of an abrupt end

# A Postscript

by an atomic holocaust in the near future, we can reasonably assume that modern economic growth still has a fairly long course to run even in those countries where economic modernization began over a century ago, let alone those countries, including the Communist, in which entry into the process of economic modernization was more recent—and especially the other countries which have so far remained underdeveloped and to which modern economic growth may still spread. By making this assumption we remove from consideration an abrupt end either by destruction or by some major breakthrough in the field of useful knowledge with a potential that would justify recognizing the initiation of a new epoch.

If the above argument holds, our sample for the study of modern economic growth is quite small, and each unit in the sample presents an incomplete record; consequently whatever trends exist in the characteristics of modern economic growth and in the sequence of its spread can only be conjectured, on the basis of this small segment. The point can be clarified by an opposite assumption: assume that in country X, which has belonged to the developed group for a long time, modern economic growth has run its full course —so that its aggregative and structural characteristics, which would remain unchanged until the new epoch begins at some future time and perhaps in another place, indicate the terminal stage of modern economic growth. On this assumption we could evaluate how far other units that have not completed their current epochal growth have to go; and in particular we could also infer convergence of any deviant unit toward the completed pattern suggested by country X. But it is difficult to argue that any observable country is at present like the assumed country X in that it portrays the full typical potential of modern economic growth. To be sure, we could construct some hypothetical model of country X, similar to those propounded in Classical and Marxian economics, and in this way try to extrapolate what we have learned from the long-term past into the long-term future. But the point here is that such speculative projections are needed precisely because the process of epochal change that we are studying has not yet been completed and the little that we really know about it is subject to qualification.

If any illustration is required, it is conspicuously provided by the difficulties in analyzing the Communist economies, or even in extrapolating some trends in some of the developed countries in our sample. Differences in institutional and political structure between the Communist countries and those in our sample were so large that the former had to be excluded from a comparative analysis aimed at the common characteristics of modern economic growth. But if within three to five decades the Communist countries that entered the industrialization process first have progressed to the point where their basic capital framework is completed, and peaceful coexistence continues, the desires of their populations for greater freedom and the drive toward greater economic efficiency may bring about a dissolution of minority dictatorship, a broadening of the political framework, recovery of consumer sovereignty, and a sufficient minimum of individual freedom. At that stage—of a typical welfare state with a broad democratic framework—it might become necessary to include the Communist states in our sample of developed countries, and view them as another group of units in modern economic growth, differing in the character of their transition phases but converging toward the others as they mature.

The suggestion is clearly speculative and may well be unrealistic in assuming the effective disappearance of the heritage of the distinctive transition years in the history of the Communist countries; but it is useful in suggesting that because we are dealing with an incomplete unfolding of the modern growth epoch—excluding from the present sample countries which, in the longer run, may clearly belong to it—our findings must be qualified. But there are other questions that suggest the opposite qualification. How far can the rise in per capita product, decline in the share of agriculture and rise in the shares of other sectors, decline in man-hours, or reduction in the working span of life by late entry and earlier retirement—all trends clearly observed so far—be carried forward into the future? The question suggests possible limits to these trends, limits that may be due more to lack of imagination than to any more serious foundation of relevant knowledge. But if we admit the question at all, it suggests that at some future time some of the trends observed so far will cease to be operative and will no longer characterize modern economic growth. In that sense, what we consider important in the present sample may cease to be important at a later stage of modern economic growth, and our true records are too short to provide safe guidance to *changes* in trends.

The comments above on the three major qualifications of our findings may be put simply by saying that our measures fail to reflect important differences in quality of economic growth even within the small sample of non-Communist developed countries; that there is much variability and diversity in our findings that cannot be reduced to fully testable order; and that the trends observable so far are too incomplete to provide a truly safe guide to current problems—which, as always, must be handled with reference to a proximate future, not merely the passing present. These qualifications place the findings in this study in their proper perspective, a perspective that reveals them as necessarily partial contributions to a wide theme.

# LIST OF REFERENCES

This list is not meant to be a comprehensive bibliography on economic growth. It is a brief alphabetical list of books and articles specifically referred to in this monograph and is designed as an aid to the reader who may want a particular reference.

Abramovitz, Moses, "Resource and Output Trends in the United States since 1870," National Bureau of Economic Research, *Occasional Paper 52,* New York, 1956.

Aubrey, Henry G., "National Income of Mexico," *Estadistica, 8* (July 1950).

Aukrust, Odd, "Trends and Cycles in Norwegian Income Shares," in Milton Gilbert and Richard Stone, eds., *Income and Wealth, Series VI,* London, Bowes and Bowes, 1957.

―――― and Juul Bjerke, "Real Capital and Economic Growth in Norway, 1900–56," in Raymond Goldsmith and Christopher Saunders, eds., *Income and Wealth, Series VIII,* London, Bowes and Bowes, 1959.

Australia, Bureau of Census and Statistics, *Year Book of the Commonwealth of Australia, 1951,* Canberra, 1951.

Banks, Arthur S. and Robert B. Textor, *A Cross-Polity Survey,* Cambridge, Mass., Massachusetts Institute of Technology Press, 1963.

Beasley, W. G., *Selected Documents on Japanese Foreign Policy, 1853–1868,* London, Oxford University Press, 1955.

Beckerman, Wilfred, "International Comparisons of Real Incomes," *O.E.C.D. Development Center Studies, no. 4* (revised), Paris, September 1965, mimeo.

Bennett, Merrill K., *The World's Food,* New York, Harper, 1954.

Bergson, Abram, "National Income," in Abram Bergson and Simon Kuznets, eds., *Economic Trends in the Soviet Union,* Cambridge, Mass., Harvard University Press, 1963.

――――, Hans Heymann, Jr., and Oleg Hoeffding, *Soviet National Income and Product, 1928–48: Revised Data,* Rand RM-2544, November 15, 1960.

Bjerke, Juul, "Some Aspects of Long-Term Economic Growth of

Norway," a paper presented at the 1959 Conference of the International Association for Research in Income and Wealth held at Portoroz, mimeo.

Bjerke, Kjeld, "The National Product of Denmark, 1870–1952," in Simon Kuznets, ed., *Income and Wealth, Series V*, London, Bowes and Bowes, 1955.

―――― and Niels Ussing, *Danmarks Nationalprodukt, 1870–1950*, Copenhagen, Gads, 1958.

Brackett, James W., "Demographic Trends and Population Policy in the Soviet Union," in *Dimensions of Soviet Economic Power*, Joint Economic Committee Hearings, December 10–11, 1962, Washington, D.C., 1962, Part II.

Brownlee, John, "The History of the Birth and Death Rates in England and Wales Taken as a Whole, From 1570 to the Present Time," *Public Health, 29* (July 1916).

Buckley, Kenneth, *Capital Formation in Canada, 1896–1930*, Toronto, University of Toronto Press, 1955.

Burns, Arthur F., *Production Trends in the United States since 1870*, New York, National Bureau of Economic Research, 1934.

Butlin, N. G., *Australian Domestic Product, Investment and Foreign Borrowing, 1861–1938/39*, Cambridge, Cambridge University Press, 1962.

―――― , "Colonial Socialism in Australia, 1860–1900," in Hugh G. J. Aitken, ed., *The State and Economic Growth*, New York, Social Science Research Council, 1959.

Canada, Dominion Bureau of Statistics, *National Accounts, Income and Expenditures*, various issues.

―――― , *Seventh Census of Canada, 1931, Occupations and Industries*, Vol. VII, Ottawa, 1934.

Chenery, Hollis B. "Patterns of Industrial Growth," *American Economic Review, 50* (September 1960).

Clark, Colin, *Conditions of Economic Progress*, 2d ed., London, Macmillan, 1951.

―――― , *Conditions of Economic Progress*, 3d ed., London, Macmillan, 1957.

Cohn, Stanley, "The Gross National Product in the Soviet Union: Comparative Growth Rates," in *Dimensions of Soviet Economic Power*, Joint Economic Committee Hearings, December 10–11, 1962, Washington, D.C., 1962, Part II.

Creamer, Daniel, Sergei P. Dobrovolsky, and Israel Borenstein, *Capital in Manufacturing and Mining: Its Formation and Financing*, National Bureau of Economic Research, 1960.

David, Paul H., "The Deflation of Value Added," *Review of Economics and Statistics, 44* (May 1962).

# List of References

Davis, Kingsley and Judith Blake, "Social Structure and Fertility: An Analytic Framework," *Economic Development and Cultural Change, 4* (April 1956).

Deane, Phyllis and W. A. Cole, *British Economic Growth, 1688–1959,* Cambridge, Cambridge University Press, 1962.

Delahaut, J. P. and E. S. Kirschen, "Les Revenus Nationaux du Monde Non Communiste," *Cahiers Economiques de Bruxelles,* no. 10 (April 1961).

Denison, Edward F., "The Sources of Economic Growth in the United States and the Alternatives Before Us," Committee for Economic Development, *Supplementary Paper No. 13,* New York, 1962.

Deutsch, Karl W. and Alexander Eckstein, "National Industrialization and the Declining Share of the International Economic Sector, 1890–1959," *World Politics, 13* (January 1961).

Dewhurst, J. F. and associates, *Europe's Needs and Resources,* New York, Twentieth Century Fund, 1961.

Edding, Friedrich, "Internationale Tendenzen in der Entwicklung des Ausgaben für Schulen und Hochschulen," *Kieler Studien, No. 47,* Kiel, 1958.

Eisner, Gisela, *Jamaica, 1830–1930,* Manchester, Manchester University Press, 1961.

Feis, Herbert, *Europe: The World's Banker, 1870–1914,* New Haven, Yale University Press, 1930.

Firestone, O. J., *Canada's Economic Development, 1867–1953, Income and Wealth, Series VII,* London, Bowes and Bowes, 1958.

Friedman, Milton, *A Theory of the Consumption Function,* National Bureau of Economic Research, 1957.

Fuchs, Victor R., "The Growing Importance of the Service Industries," *Journal of Business of the University of Chicago, 38* (October 1965).

————, "Productivity Trends in the Goods and Services Sectors, 1929–61: A Preliminary Survey," National Bureau of Economic Research, *Occasional Paper 89,* New York, 1964.

Gallman, Robert E., "Commodity Output, 1839–1899," in William N. Parker, ed., *Trends in the American Economy in the Nineteenth Century, Studies in Income and Wealth,* Vol. 24, National Bureau of Economic Research, 1960.

Garland, J. M. and R. W. Goldsmith, "The National Wealth of Australia," in Raymond W. Goldsmith and Christopher Saunders, eds., *Income and Wealth, Series VIII,* London, Bowes and Bowes, 1959.

Germany, Statistisches Bundesamt, *Preise, Löhne, Wirtschaftsrech-*

*nungen*, Series 10, *Internationaler Vergleich der Preise für die Lebenshaltung*, Stuttgart, 1963.

Gerschenkron, Alexander, *Economic Backwardness in Historical Perspective*, Cambridge, Mass., Harvard University Press, 1962.

Gilbert, Milton and Irving B. Kravis, *An International Comparison of National Products and the Purchasing Power of Currencies*, Paris, Organisation of European Economic Cooperation, 1954.

────── and associates, *Comparative National Products and Price Levels*, Paris, Organisation of European Economic Cooperation, 1958.

Gille, H., "The Demographic History of the Northern European Countries in the Eighteenth Century," *Population Studies, 3* (June 1949).

Gini, Corrado and Stefano Somagyi, *Proceedings of the International Congress for the Study of Population*, Vol. VII, Rome, Istituto Poligrafico dello Stato, 1934.

Goldsmith, Raymond W., "The Growth of Reproducible Wealth of the United States of America from 1805 to 1950," in Simon Kuznets, ed., *Income and Wealth, Series II*, Cambridge, Bowes and Bowes, 1952.

──────, *The National Wealth of the United States in the Postwar Period*, National Bureau of Economic Research, 1962.

────── and Christopher Saunders, eds., *Income and Wealth, Series VIII*, London, Bowes and Bowes, 1959.

────── and others, *A Study of Saving in the United States*, Vol. III, Princeton, Princeton University Press, 1956.

Gordon, R. A., "Differential Changes in the Prices of Consumers' and Capital Goods," *American Economic Review, 51* (December 1961).

Gordon, Wendell C., *The Economy of Latin America*, New York, Columbia University Press, 1950.

Gottschalk, Louis, ed., *Generalization in the Writing of History*, Chicago, University of Chicago Press, 1963.

Grabill, W. H., C. V. Kiser, and P. K. Whelpton, *The Fertility of American Women*, New York, Wiley, 1958.

Habbakuk, H. J., "English Population in the Eighteenth Century," *Economic History Review, 6* (December 1953).

Hansen, W. Lee, "A Note on the Cost of Children's Mortality," *Journal of Political Economy, 65* (June 1957).

Hartland, Penelope, "Canadian Balance of Payments since 1868," in William N. Parker, ed., *Trends in the American Economy in the Nineteenth Century, Studies in Income and Wealth*, Vol. 24, National Bureau of Economic Research, 1960.

# List of References

Hawtrey, Ralph G., *The Economic Aspects of Sovereignty,* 2d ed. London, Longmans, Green, 1952.

Hoffmann, W. G., *The Growth of Industrial Economies,* Manchester, Manchester University Press, 1958.

Holzman, Franklyn D., "Foreign Trade," in Abram Bergson and Simon Kuznets, eds., *Economic Trends in the Soviet Union,* Cambridge, Mass., Harvard University Press, 1963.

Hood, William C. and Anthony Scott, *Output, Labor and Capital in the Canadian Economy,* Ottawa, Royal Commission on Canada's Economic Prospects, 1957.

Hoselitz, Bert F., *Sociological Aspects of Economic Growth,* Glencoe, Free Press, 1960.

Houthakker, H. S., "An International Comparison of Household Expenditure Patterns, Commemorating the Centenary of Engel's Law," *Econometrica,* 25 (October 1957).

Imlah, Albert H., *Economic Elements in the Pax Britannica,* Cambridge, Mass., Harvard University Press, 1958.

International Labour Office, *Yearbook of Labour Statistics, 1963,* Geneva, 1963.

Italy, Istituto Centrale di Statistica, *Indagine Statistica sullo Sviluppo del Reddito Nazionale dell' Italia dal 1861 al 1956,* Rome, 1957.

Italy, Istituto Centrale di Statistica, *Sommario di Statistiche Storiche Italiane, 1861–1955,* Rome, 1958.

Johansson, Osten, "Economic Growth and Structure in Sweden, 1861–1953," a paper presented at the 1959 Conference of the International Association for Research in Income and Wealth held at Portoroz, mimeo.

Jostock, Paul, "The Long-Term Growth of National Income in Germany," in Simon Kuznets, ed., *Income and Wealth, Series V,* London, Bowes and Bowes, 1955.

Kendrick, John W., *Productivity Trends in the United States,* Princeton, Princeton University Press, 1961.

Kindleberger, Charles P., *Foreign Trade and the National Economy,* New Haven, Yale University Press, 1962.

Kirk, Dudley, *Europe's Population in the Interwar Years,* Princeton, League of Nations, 1946.

———, "Major Migrations since World War II," in Milbank Memorial Fund, *Selected Studies of Migration since World War II,* New York, 1958.

Kiser, Clyde V., "Differential Fertility in the United States," in Universities-National Bureau of Economic Research Committee, *Demographic and Economic Change in Developed Countries,* Princeton, Princeton University Press, 1960.

Koffsky, Nathan, "Farm and Urban Purchasing Power," in National Bureau of Economic Research, *Studies in Income and Wealth*, Vol. 11, New York, 1949.

Krause, John T., "Changes in English Fertility and Mortality, 1781–1850," *Economic History Review, 11* (August 1958).

Kristensen, Thorkil and associates, *The Economic World Balance*, Copenhagen, Munksgaard, 1960.

Kuczynski, Robert R., *The Measurement of Population Growth*, London, Sidgwick and Jackson, 1935.

Kuznets, Simon, *Capital in the American Economy*, Princeton, Princeton University Press, 1961.

——, "A Comparative Appraisal," in Abram Bergson and Simon Kuznets, eds., *Economic Trends in the Soviet Union*, Cambridge, Mass., Harvard University Press, 1963.

——, "Demographic Aspects of Modern Economic Growth," a paper submitted to the World Population Conference, organized by the United Nations, in Belgrade, September 1965, mimeo.

——, *Economic Change*, New York, W. W. Norton, 1953.

——, "Economic Growth and the Contribution of Agriculture: Notes on Measurement," in *Proceedings of the Eleventh International Conference of Agricultural Economists*, London, Oxford University Press, 1963.

——, "International Differences in Capital Formation and Financing," in Moses Abramovitz, ed., *Capital Formation and Economic Growth*, National Bureau of Economic Research, 1956.

——, "Introduction," in Hope T. Eldridge and Dorothy Swaine Thomas, *Demographic Analyses and Interrelations*, Vol. III of *Population Redistribution and Economic Growth, United States, 1870–1950*, American Philosophical Society Memoirs, Vol. 61, Philadelphia, 1964.

——, "Long Swings in the Growth of Population and in Related Economic Variables," *Proceedings of the American Philosophical Society, 102*, No. 1 (February 1958).

——, "Long-Term Changes in the National Income of the United States of America since 1870," in Simon Kuznets, ed., *Income and Wealth, Series II*, Cambridge, Bowes and Bowes, 1952.

——, "National Income: A New Version," *Review of Economics and Statistics, 30* (August 1948).

——, *National Income and Its Composition, 1919–1938*, New York, National Bureau of Economic Research, 1941.

——, "Notes on the Pattern of U.S. Economic Growth," in Edgar O. Edwards, ed., *The Nation's Economic Objectives*, Chicago, University of Chicago Press, 1964.

# List of References

———, "Population Change and Aggregate Output," in Universities-National Bureau of Economic Research Committee, *Demographic and Economic Change in Developed Countries,* Princeton, Princeton University Press, 1960.

———, *Postwar Economic Growth: Four Lectures,* Cambridge, Mass., Harvard University Press, 1964.

———, "Quantitative Aspects of the Economic Growth of Nations: I. Levels and Variability of Rates of Growth," *Economic Development and Cultural Change,* 5 (October 1956).

———, "Quantitative Aspects of the Economic Growth of Nations: II. Industrial Distribution of National Product and Labor Force," *Economic Development and Cultural Change,* 5 (July 1957 Supplement).

———, "Quantitative Aspects of the Economic Growth of Nations: IV. Distribution of National Income by Factor Shares," *Economic Development and Cultural Change,* 7 (April 1959, Part II).

———, "Quantitative Aspects of the Economic Growth of Nations: V. Capital Formation Proportions: International Comparisons for Recent Years," *Economic Development and Cultural Change,* 8 (July 1960, Part II).

———, "Quantitative Aspects of the Economic Growth of Nations: VI. Long-Term Trends in Capital Formation Proportions," *Economic Development and Cultural Change,* 9 (July 1961, Part II).

———, "Quantitative Aspects of the Economic Growth of Nations: VII. The Share and Structure of Consumption," *Economic Development and Cultural Change,* 10 (January 1962, Part II).

———, "Quantitative Aspects of the Economic Growth of Nations: VIII. Distribution of Income by Size," *Economic Development and Cultural Change,* 11 (January 1963, Part II).

———, "Quantitative Aspects of the Economic Growth of Nations: IX. Level and Structure of Foreign Trade: Comparisons for Recent Years," *Economic Development and Cultural Change,* 8 (October 1964, Part II).

———, "Quantitative Aspects of the Economic Growth of Nations: X. Level and Structure of Foreign Trade: Long-Term Trends," in press.

———, *Secular Movements in Production and Prices,* Boston, Houghton Mifflin, 1930.

———, *Shares of Upper Income Groups in Income and Savings,* National Bureau of Economic Research, 1953.

———, *Six Lectures on Economic Growth,* Glencoe, Free Press, 1959.

————, "The State as a Unit in Study of Economic Growth," *Journal of Economic History*, *11* (Winter 1951).

———— and Ernest Rubin, "Immigration and the Foreign Born," National Bureau of Economic Research, *Occasional Paper 46*, New York, 1954.

League of Nations, *Industrialization and Foreign Trade*, Princeton, 1945.

————, *The Network of World Trade*, Geneva, 1942.

Lindahl, Erik, Einar Dahlgren, and Karin Kock, *National Income of Sweden, 1861–1930*, London, P. S. King and Son, 1937.

Lipsey, Robert E., *Price and Quantity Trends in the Foreign Trade of the United States*, National Bureau of Economic Research, 1963.

Liu, T. C. and K. C. Yeh, *The Economy of the Chinese Mainland: National Income and Economic Development, 1933–1959*, Princeton, Princeton University Press, 1965.

Logan, W. P. D., "Mortality in England and Wales from 1848 to 1947," *Population Studies, 4* (September 1950).

Long, Clarence D., *The Labor Force under Changing Income and Employment*, National Bureau of Economic Research, 1958.

Maddison, Angus, *Economic Growth in the West*, New York, Twentieth Century Fund, 1964.

Mitchell, B. R. and Phyllis Deane, *Abstract of British Historical Statistics*, Cambridge, Cambridge University Press, 1962.

Mukherjee, Moni, *The National Income of India: Trends and Structure*, in preparation.

Mulhall, Michael G., *The Dictionary of Statistics*, London, George Routledge and Sons, 1892.

Nimitz, Nancy, *Soviet National Income and Product, 1956–58*, Rand RM-3112, Prel., June 1962.

Ohkawa, Kazushi and Henry Rosovsky, "The Role of Agriculture in Modern Japanese Economic Development," *Economic Development and Cultural Change, 9* (October 1960, Part II).

———— and others, *The Growth Rate of the Japanese Economy since 1878*, Tokyo, Kinokuniya Bookstore Co., 1957.

Ohlin, P. G., "The Positive and Preventive Check: A Study of the Rate of Growth of Pre-industrial Population," Ph.D. dissertation, Harvard University, 1956.

Perroux, François, "Prise de Vues sur la Croissance de l'Economie Française, 1780–1950," in Simon Kuznets, ed., *Income and Wealth, Series V*, London, Bowes and Bowes, 1955.

Rosovsky, Henry, *Capital Formation in Japan, 1868–1940*, New York, Free Press of Glencoe, 1961.

Schmookler, Jacob, *Invention and Economic Growth*, Cambridge, Mass., Harvard University Press, 1966.

518

# List of References

Schultz, T. W., "Capital Formation by Education," *Journal of Political Economy, 68* (December 1960).

———, "Reflections on Investment in Man," *Journal of Political Economy, 70,* Part 2, October 1962, Supplement.

Shaw, William H., *Value of Commodity Output since 1869,* National Bureau of Economic Research, 1947.

Shionoya, Yichi, "Patterns of Industrial Growth in the United States and Sweden: A Critique of Hoffmann's Hypothesis," *Hitotsubashi Journal of Economics, 5* (June 1964).

Social Science Research Council, *Bulletin No. 54,* New York, 1946.

———, *Bulletin No. 64,* New York, 1954.

Solow, Robert M., "Technical Change and the Aggregate Production Function," *Review of Economics and Statistics, 39* (August 1957).

Stolnitz, George J., "A Century of International Mortality Trends," *Population Studies, 9* (July 1955) and *10* (July 1956).

Sundbärg, Gustav, *Aperçus Statistiques Internationaux,* Vol. 11, Stockholm, 1908.

Svennilson, Ingvar, *Growth and Stagnation in the European Economy,* Geneva, United Nations, 1954.

Thomas, Dorothy Swaine, "Age and Economic Differentials in Interstate Migration," *Population Index, 24* (October 1958).

Umemura, Mataji, "An Analysis of the Employment Structure in Japan," *Hitotsubashi Journal of Economics, 2* (March 1962).

United Nations, *Compendium of Social Statistics: 1963,* Statistical Papers, Series K, No. 2, New York, 1963.

———, *Demographic Yearbook,* various issues

———, *The Determinants and Consequences of Population Trends,* New York, 1953.

———, *Economic Survey of Asia and the Far East, 1961,* Bangkok, 1962.

———, *Economic Survey of Europe in 1956,* Geneva, 1957.

———, *The Growth of World Industry, 1938–1961: National Tables,* New York, 1963.

———, *International Capital Movements During the Inter-War Period,* Lake Success, 1949.

———, *International Flow of Long-term Capital and Official Donations, 1951–59,* New York, 1961.

———, *International Flow of Long-term Capital and Official Donations, 1959–61,* New York, 1963.

———, *A Measurement of Price Levels and the Purchasing Power of Currencies, 1960–62,* document prepared for the Economic Commission for Latin America, 10th session, Mar de la Plata, May 1963, mimeo.

———, *Patterns of Industrial Growth, 1938–1958,* New York, 1960.

———, *Report on the World Social Situation,* New York, 1961.

———, *Studies in Methods, Series F, No. 2, Rev. 1,* New York, 1960.

———, *World Economic Survey, 1962: The Developing Countries in World Trade,* New York, 1963.

———, *Yearbook of International Trade Statistics, 1960,* New York, 1962.

———, *Yearbook of National Accounts Statistics,* various issues.

United Nations Educational, Scientific and Cultural Organization, "Progress of Literacy in Various Countries," *Monographs on Fundamental Education, VI,* Paris, UNESCO, 1953.

United States, Bureau of the Census, *Census of Manufactures, 1947,* Vol. I, Washington, D.C., 1950.

———, *Historical Statistics of the United States, Colonial Times to 1957,* Washington, D.C., 1961.

———, *Statistical Abstract of the United States,* various issues.

———, *12th Census of the United States, Vol. VII, Manufactures, Part I,* Washington, D.C., 1902.

United States, Department of Commerce, *National Income, 1954 Edition,* Washington, D.C., 1954.

———, *Survey of Current Business,* various issues.

———, *U.S. Income and Output,* Washington, D.C., 1958.

United States President, *Economic Report of the President,* various issues.

Urlanis, B. Ts., *Growth of Population in Europe* (in Russian), Moscow, Gozpolitizdat, 1941.

Usui, Mikoto and E. E. Hagen, *World Income, 1957,* Cambridge, Mass., Massachusetts Institute of Technology Press, 1959.

Willcox, Walter F., ed., *International Migrations. II. Interpretations,* New York, National Bureau of Economic Research, 1931.

Woytinsky, W. S., *Die Welt in Zahlen,* Vol. I, 1925; Vol. V, 1927; Vol. VII, 1928; all Berlin, Rudolf Mosse Verlag.

——— and E. S. Woytinsky, *World Commerce and Governments,* New York, Twentieth Century Fund, 1955.

———, *World Population and Production,* New York, Twentieth Century Fund, 1953.

Yasuba, Yasukichi, *Birth Rates of the White Population in the United States, 1800–1860,* Baltimore, Johns Hopkins University Studies in History and Political Science, 1961.

# INDEX

# Index

growth, *64, 352,* urban, 272; product: growth, *64, 352,* industrial structure, *89,* use structure, *237*

Developed countries: coverage, 488–89; debtor, 327–28; distinction between underdeveloped and, 392–94, 477–86; foreign trade proportion, 316; as a group, 30; increase in number, 37; initial growth, 291–92; labor force, 401; large vs. small, 356; living conditions, 387, *388–89;* old vs. young, 356; population, 19, *362, 364, 368–69,* 373, 462; product, 310, *362, 364, 368,* 372; territorial expansion, 336, 339–42, 459, 475

Dividends. *See* Income from assets

Domestic service, 143, 428

Dwellings: capital invested in, 145; construction, 227; share in capital formation, *252–56,* 257, 258; share in household expenditures, 268–69; share in services sector, 144

Economic activity: coverage, 371–74; definition, 503; international diversity, 31; means and ends of, 21, 22; in modern epoch, 24; qualitative aspects, 490, 503

Economic growth: definition, 1; and epochal innovation, 8; and internal patterns, 7; international aspects, 1; unit of study, 16–19; and structural shifts, 6 MODERN: basis for, 15; characteristics, 28–29, 63, 487, 490–500, 501–02; in China, 475; of Communist countries, 347–48; compared with premodern, 67–70; a condition for war, 500; and

cross-section analysis, 431–37; diversity of, 71, 504–05; and education, 287–89; effect of war, 70; and entrepreneurial activity, 58; epochal innovation, 8–16; follower nations, 471–72; and goals of society, 482–84; and international relations, 285, 349–58; in Japan, 475; locus, 462–68, 497; and migration, 55; measures of, 25, 400; and natural resources, 479; order in, 505; period of, 66; pioneer nation, 8, 462–68; and political structure, 451–53, 456, 465, 472–76; and population, 36, 39, 56–62; potential, 466, 477–78, 481, 482; and productivity, 29, 81; quality features of, 503; and size of nation, 467; and social structure, 456; spread, 31, 468–69, 472, 473, 484–86, 497, 500, 506; and stock of knowledge, 6, 30, 57, 58, 82, 84, 155, 286–94, 349, 480; steadiness of, 77; and technology, 2, 10–12, 81, 286–87, 476; and territorial expansion, 338; timing, 15, 24, 68, 290, 291, 292, 471–72, 497; transition to, 468–77; in underdeveloped countries, 461

Economies of scale, 84, 103, 158, 188, 303, 356

Education, 387, *389,* 497; and economic growth, 82, 287–89; and employees' compensation, 190, 218; government expenditures on, *407,* 426, 428; investment in, 82, 185, 228–29; and per capita product, 152; and quality of labor, 183–85; and structure of labor force, 194

Efficiency. *See* Productivity

Egalitarianism, 12, 13–14, 15, 22, 215, 355

523

# Index

# Index

# Index